New Hampshire

AN EXPLORER'S GUIDE

The Old Man of the Mountain, the symbol of the Granite State

New Hampshire

AN EXPLORER'S GUIDE

CHRISTINA TREE & PETER RANDALL

Second Edition

The Countryman Press
Woodstock, Vermont

Dedications

To Martha Rudneski Tree, my mother
— C.T.

To the memory of my mother,
Virginia Chase Randall
— P.E.R.

Library of Congress Cataloging-in-Publication Data
Tree, Christina.
New Hampshire: an explorer's guide / Christina Tree & Peter Randall.—2nd ed.
p. cm.
Includes indexes.
ISBN 0-88150-283-9
1. New Hampshire—Guidebooks.
I. Randall, Peter. II. Title.
F32.3.T74 1994
917.4204'43—dc20
94–13631
CIP

Maps by Alex Wallach, except map on page 6 by Mapping Specialists, Ltd., Madison, WI

Book design by Glenn Suokko

Cover photograph of New Castle, NH by David Brownell

Back cover photograph of Christina Tree by Walter Chapin; photograph of Peter Randall by Holly Perrault

Published by The Countryman Press, Inc. P.O. Box 175 Woodstock, Vermont 05091

Printed in the United States of America by Edwards Brothers

10 9 8 7 6 5 4 3 2 1

Explore With Us!

Welcome to the most widely used and comprehensive travel guide to the Granite State. As we have expanded our guide in response to the increase in places to lodge, dine, and visit in New Hampshire, we have also been increasingly selective, making recommendations based on years of conscientious research. All inclusions—attractions, inns and restaurants—are chosen on the basis of personal experience, not paid advertising.

Our Explorer's Guides to the northern New England states were the first on the market since the Depression Era WPA series, and they remain the most knowledgeable guides available. We want anyone who buys this guide to feel confident to venture beyond the tourist towns, along roads less traveled, and to places of special hospitality and charm.

We hope you'll find our new design attractive and easy to read. Although we've kept the organization simple, the following points will help to get you started on your way.

WHAT'S WHERE

In the beginning of the book you'll find an alphabetical listing of special highlights and important information that you may want to reference quickly. You'll find advice on everything from where to buy the best local cheeses to where to write or call for camping reservations and park information.

LODGING

Prices: Please don't hold us or the respective innkeepers responsible for the rates listed as of press time in 1994. Some changes are inevitable. The state rooms and meals tax is 8 percent as of this writing, but that also may change.

RESTAURANTS

In most sections, please note a distinction between Dining Out and Eating Out. In the Dining Out section, menu prices, with the exception of *prix fixe*, are not listed. The costs of à la carte entrées are as follows:

Moderate: $12–18 · Expensive: $18–25 · Very Expensive: over $25

By their nature, restaurants in the Eating Out group are generally inexpensive.

KEY TO SYMBOLS

☞ The special value symbol appears next to lodging and restaurants that combine quality and moderate prices.

✐ The kids alert symbol appears next to lodging, restaurants, activities, and shops of special appeal to youngsters.

We would appreciate your comments and corrections about places you visit or know well in the state. Please address your correspondence to Explorer's Guide Editor, The Countryman Press, PO Box 175, Woodstock, Vermont 05091-0175.

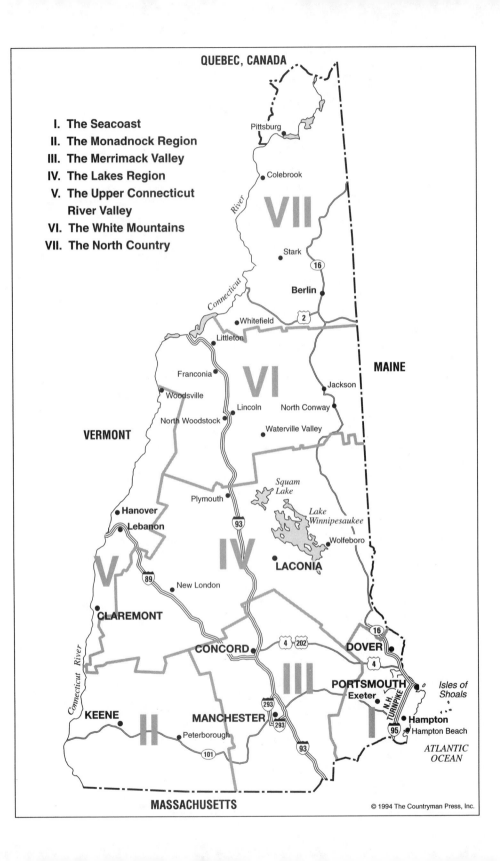

Contents

Introduction

Within the past decade the number of visitors who can be accommodated in New Hampshire on any one night has more than doubled. Many of these new "beds" (a travel-industry buzzword) are in the condominium complexes that have sprouted around ski areas and lakes. Some are in large new hotels that have appeared in old tourist towns like North Conway. Others are in the hundreds of new inns, bed & breakfasts, and lodgings that have opened off the beaten path in recent years.

For the tourist, as well as the native, finding those places has not been easy; thus, *New Hampshire: An Explorer's Guide* is a book intended for New Hampshire residents and visitors. No other portrait of the state gathers so much practical information between two covers. All listings in this book are free; there is no paid advertising.

The book's chapters are organized into areas that coincide with those covered by local chambers of commerce. Each section begins with a "verbal snapshot" of the landscape and historic background. Sources of information, how to get around, and descriptions of everything to see and do from winter sports to places to swim and picnic follow. Then come capsule descriptions of places to stay. Our focus is on inns and bed & breakfasts because we feel that the Mobil and AAA guides do a fine job with motels. We have personally visited more than 90 percent of the lodgings included (that other 10 percent has been highly recommended, and we have contacted them by phone). We include prices for lodging, because categories like "moderate" and "expensive" can be misleading, depending on what they include. Please allow for inflation and add the state room and meals tax. Some inns also add a service charge; be sure to inquire.

After lodging come critiques of local upscale restaurants (*Dining Out*) and of the everyday options (*Eating Out*). We also describe shops worth seeking out and the special events of that area.

New Hampshire had more lodgings for visitors back in the 1800s, when it was the most-touristed state in New England, than it did for most of the twentieth century. From the seacoast through the lakes region to the White Mountains, hundreds of wooden hotels were built during the last half of the nineteenth century for summer visitors who came to enjoy dramatic scenery, cool breezes, and genteel hospitality. Most tourists came by train and stayed at one hotel for a week, a month, or for the entire summer season.

The automobile changed this vacation pattern because it gave the traveler more mobility. Most of the big, wooden hotels were destroyed by fire, while others were closed and razed, unable to compete with the more economical cabin colonies and, later, motels. For New Hampshire there was a real decline in the number of accommodations available for visitors.

This situation changed dramatically during the 1980s, however, when the state experienced an explosion of new lodgings. The proliferation of inviting places to stay—all around the state, not just along tried and true tourist routes—inspired the authors to present an accurate picture of attractions and facilities *throughout* the state.

Lodging options have widened considerably along New Hampshire's seacoast, inviting visitors to linger long enough in and around historic Portsmouth to sample the region's many fine restaurants, theater, museums, boat excursions, and sandy beaches.

Ten years ago the Monadnock Region was a place to go day hiking or to a concert or play. Now, almost every picturesque town offers an inn or B&B and sources of information about swimming, hiking, and biking.

Lake Winnipesaukee, the state's largest lake, has been a popular tourist destination since the turn of the century. Less developed than the western side of Lake Winnipesaukee are the northern and eastern sections of the lakes region—perfect places for those who enjoy country drives, roadside vegetable stands, and just poking around in antiques shops. Center Sandwich, Tamworth, Eaton, and Wakefield, for example, are less visited; yet they have comfortable inns and plenty to explore.

In the area we've called the Western Lakes (because it harbors so many lakes, not just Sunapee), myriad, widely scattered lodging places offer access to swimming, sailing, summer theater, fine dining, and hiking up the mountains of Sunapee, Kearsarge, and Cardigan.

In the Upper Valley Region you can take in a concert and some fine art at Dartmouth's Hood Museum, then canoe the Connecticut River from inn to inn.

Only in the past decade have the state's largest ski resorts, Loon Mountain and Waterville Valley, become full-fledged, year-round resorts. They are part of the Western Whites, a rugged part of the White Mountains that is relatively untouristed beyond the spectacular natural sites in Franconia Notch.

North Conway and the Mount Washington Valley Region have always been popular with skiers (there are six downhill ski areas within 20 miles of North Conway), and with outdoor lovers wanting spectacular scenery and some of the most challenging hiking in the East. Now, an enormous variety of factory outlet stores has become another popular reason to travel to North Conway.

The least-touristed section of the state is the North Country, the vast forested area north of the White Mountains. Fast-running rivers are perfect for fishing or canoeing. You can camp on picturesque wilderness lakes and fall asleep to the calls of loons, watch moose grazing beside the road, or ride to Canada on your snowmobile.

The urban communities of the Merrimack Valley, the state's industrial heartland, also have long been ignored by visitors; yet here are several of the best museums, two of the largest state parks, and a growing number of fine restaurants.

One author of this book is a "visitor" and the other, a "native." Chris Tree has explored the Granite State for more than 20 years as a travel writer whose New England stories appear regularly in the *Boston Globe* Sunday travel section. She is the author of *How New England Happened* (a historical guide to the region); co-author of *Best Places to Stay in New England* and the Explorer's Guides to Maine and Vermont. She is also the contributing editorial consultant for *New England: The Berlitz Travelers Guide*.

Peter Randall was born in New Hampshire and lives in the same seacoast town where his first American ancestor arrived in 1640. Educated at the University of New Hampshire, Peter is a former editor of *New Hampshire Profiles* magazine and worked for several daily and weekly newspapers before starting a small publishing company in 1976. Concentrating on local and town histories, his company has published more than 200 titles. An accomplished photographer, he has authored nine other books, including guides, works of history, and collections of photographs.

The authors wish to thank the staffs of the New Hampshire Office of Vacation Travel, especially Ann Kennard and Betty Lund, and the local chambers of commerce who helped provide and check information for the book, especially Nancy Gorr of the Monadnock Region and Kathy Trudeau of the Lake Sunapee Business Association. Others to whom Chris owes special thanks include Freda Haupt, Lois Ford, Debbie Albee, Steve Smith, Kathe Dillmann, Kay Shumway, John Day, and Ann Keefe. We would also like to thank our editors, Christopher Lloyd and Helen Whybrow, for their support and patience.

Christina Tree
Peter E. Randall

What's Where in New Hampshire

AGRICULTURAL FAIRS

New Hampshire boasts a baker's dozen summer and fall country fairs. Part of the social fabric of the nineteenth century, and still popular today, the country fair is the place where farm families meet their friends and exhibit their best home-canned and fresh vegetables, livestock, and handwork such as quilts, baked goods, and needlework. Horse and cattle pulling, 4-H competitions, horse shows, and woodsmen's competitions are joined by midways, food stalls, and exhibits of farm implements, home furnishings, and a host of other items. The "New Hampshire's Rural Heritage" pamphlet from the **New Hampshire Department of Agriculture** (271-3551), Box 2042, Concord 03302-2042, lists the dates and locations of all fairs. These events are also mentioned in the *Special Events* sections of this book. The largest fair is Deerfield, held annually at the end of September, but other popular fairs include Hopkinton and Lancaster, both held on Labor Day weekend; Cheshire Fair in Swanzey, held in early August; and Sandwich on Columbus Day weekend. Additionally, many local towns and organizations hold annual one-day fairs. Check with local chambers of commerce for exact dates.

AIR SERVICE

Manchester Airport, which inaugurated a spacious new terminal in 1994, is the state's major airport, served by United Airlines, USAir, Northwest Airlink, and Continental with nonstop flights to Washington, New York, Chicago, Philadelphia, Pittsburgh, and Boston. The **Lebanon Regional Airport** is linked to New York and Boston via Northwest Airlink and by Business Express. In addition, the state offers 20 airfields without scheduled service. Flying schools are located at Lebanon, Keene, Manchester, Laconia, Rochester, and Claremont. For details contact the New Hampshire Division of Aeronautics (271-2251), 65 Airport Road, Concord 03301.

ANTIQUARIAN BOOKSHOPS

It's hard to resist a good old book, and New Hampshire has enough dealers in used, rare, and antiquarian books to keep any bibliophile busy just looking for bargains, to say nothing of actually sitting down and reading newly found treasures. Among the specialty dealers are shops selling first editions and books related to espionage, gardening, the White Mountains, hot-air ballooning, and women's studies. One shop has only 750 volumes while several others approach 100,000 titles to search. For a list of dealers, write the New Hampshire Antiquarian Booksellers Association, c/o The Portsmouth Bookshop, 110 State Street, Portsmouth 03801. The association sponsors an annual mid-September book show and fair in Concord. This event attracts some 85 dealers from 10 states.

MIKE ROUNDS

ANTIQUES

The New Hampshire Antiques Dealers Association (RFD 1, Box 305 C, Tilton 03276), lists some 170 dealers and nearly 20 group shops in this state, more than enough to keep the antiques buff happy. From the seacoast to the mountains and from the lakes region to Monadnock there are dealers in nearly every community, and the diversity of items offered equals any to be found in New England. Perhaps the largest concentration of shops is along Route 4 in Northwood and Epsom, but nearby Concord, Hopkinton, and Contoocook have nearly as many shops. Meredith, Centre Harbor, and Center Sandwich also have many shops as does Hillsboro, Peterborough, Fitzwilliam, and Route 1 in the seacoast area. The association's annual show is held in early August in Manchester, but several other annual shows are listed elsewhere in this book.

APPALACHIAN MOUNTAIN CLUB

Founded in 1876 to blaze and map hiking trails through the White Mountains, the AMC was a crucial lobbying group for the passage of the Weeks Act. Today it continues to support environmental causes and cater to hikers, maintaining hundreds of miles of trails and feeding and sheltering hikers in a chain of eight "high huts" (see *High Huts of the White Mountains* and *Hiking*) in the Presidential Range, each a day's hike apart. Pinkham Notch Camp, a comfortable complex at the eastern base of Mount Washington, serves as headquarters for the high huts and as a year-round center for a wide variety of workshops in subjects ranging from nature drawing to North Country literature as well as camping and cross-country skiing. The AMC also maintains a hostel-like camping and lodging facility at Cardigan, runs shuttle buses for hikers around Mount Washington, and much more. Their guidebooks (see *Canoeing* and *Hiking*) remain the best of their kind.

APPLE AND FRUIT PICKING

New Hampshire has many orchards and farms where you can pick your own apples, pears, peaches, and berries and press cider. The vegetable- and fruit-picking season begins in the early summer, while apples and other tree fruits ripen as fall begins. Many orchards have weekend festivals with fresh-baked apple pies, donuts and cider, pumpkins, tractor-pulled wagon rides, music, and other activities aimed at making a perfect family outing. Don't forget to visit the orchards in the spring when the trees are blossoming. From the **New Hampshire Department of Agriculture** (271-3551), Box 2042, Concord 03302-2042, request the "New Hampshire's Rural Heritage," "Harvest New Hampshire," and the "Apple Growers Association" brochures.

AREA CODE

603 covers all of New Hampshire.

ART MUSEUMS AND GALLERIES

New Hampshire's two major art museums are the **Currier Gallery of Art** in Manchester and the **Hood Museum of Art** at Dartmouth College. The Currier's collection includes some outstanding nineteenth- and twentieth-century European and

American works and is departure point for tours to the Zimmerman House, designed by Frank Lloyd Wright. The Hood Museum's permanent collection ranges from some outstanding ancient Assyrian bas-reliefs to a huge abstract piece by Frank Stella. Both museums stage changing exhibits. (See "The Manchester Area" and "Upper Valley Towns" for descriptions of each museum.) "The New Hampshire Visual Arts Map," published by the League of New Hampshire Craftsmen Foundation (see *Crafts*), includes a descriptive listing of more than a dozen galleries scattered around the state. Another important source of cultural information is the New Hampshire State Council on the Arts (271-2789), 40 North Main Street, Concord 03301.

AUTOMATIC TELLER MACHINES

The official New Hampshire Highway lists locations of the following ATMs: Mac, Pocketbank, Cirrus, and American Express. For more information call 1-800-523-4175.

BANDS

Town bands are still popular in New Hampshire, and many hold summer concerts in outdoor bandstands. Schedules change yearly, so check with local chambers of commerce. Conway, North Conway, Alton, Wolfeboro, Exeter, and Hampton Beach are among the places with regular band concerts. The Temple Band claims to be the oldest town band in the country.

BED & BREAKFASTS

B&Bs appear under their own listing within the *Lodging* section of each chapter. We don't list everyone, but we checked out every B&B we could find. Our selection ranges from working farms to historic mansions and from two-guest-room, private homes to larger places with a score or more of rooms.

B&B rates in this book are for two persons (unless otherwise specified); single rates are somewhat less.

BICYCLING

The Monadnock Region is the state's liveliest bicycling scene. **Monadnock Bicycle Touring** offers self-guided inn-to-inn tours. *Peterborough Bike Tours* by Ann Harrison of the Peterborough hostel describes 10 local one-day tours. **Spokes & Slopes** in Peterborough rents mountain and touring bikes and **The Pedl'ing Fool** in Hillsboro assists self-guided tours and offers guided tours. The **New England Bicycling Center** in Danbury offers bikes, maps, room, and board. In the Waterville Valley area **Ski Fanatics** of Campton offers mapped routes, mountain-bike rentals, and 10-mile group rides; **Mountain Valley Bikes** in Town Square also rents mountain bikes. The **Loon Mountain Bike Center** in Lincoln (see "The Western Whites") rents mountain bikes for use on local cross-country and selected alpine ski trails (bikes may be hooked

ADOLPHE BERNOTAS

to the gondola); from Loon buses also shuttle bicyclists to Echo Lake for guided (slightly downhill) tours the 6 miles back. The **Biking Expedition** in Henniker (see *Bicycling* in "The Concord Area") offers guided biking tours geared to seventh- through twelfth-graders throughout New England and in other parts of the country, in Canada, and in Europe. The **Granite State Wheelmen,** for resident bicycling enthusiasts, schedules frequent rides throughout the state. Contact K. Lachairte, 83 Londonderry Road, Windham 03087. The guide to the state's best bike routes is *30 Bicycle Tours in New Hampshire* by Adophe Bernotas (Backcountry Publications).

BIRDING

New Hampshire is not a bird-watcher's paradise like the Everglades, but there are several places that should be visited. **Coastal Route 1A from Seabrook to New Castle** provides numerous ocean, harbor, and salt-marsh vantage points for observing shorebirds and sea fowl of all types, as well as various ducks and larger wading birds, especially in the summer when snowy egrets, great and little blue heron, glossy ibis, and black-crowned night heron are common. **Lake Umbagog,** described in "Berlin and Route 16 North," has nesting eagles and osprey, loons, and other freshwater birds. In the course of the book we have described many of the 31 sanctuaries maintained by the **New Hampshire Audubon Society** (224-9909). You might want to visit or contact Audubon House, the society's headquarters at 3 Silk Farm Road (Box 528), Concord 03302-0516, for more birding information. Regional Audubon chapters offer bird walks throughout the year. See a full listing in "The Concord Area" for more information.

BOATING

New Hampshire law requires all boats used in fresh water to be registered, a formality that most marinas can provide. Or contact the **New Hampshire Department of Safety, Motor Vehicle Division** (271-2251), Hazen Drive, Concord 03301, or the **Division of Safety Services** (271-3336). In the Lake Winnipesaukee area, contact the **Safety Services Marine Division** (293-2037), Route 11, Glendale. Boats used in tidal waters must be registered with the United States Coast Guard. Contact the **USCG Portsmouth Harbor Station** (436-0171), New Castle 03854; the **New Hampshire Port Authority** (436-8500), Box 506, 555 Market Street, Portsmouth 03802; or the **New Hampshire Department of Safety, Marine Services Division** (431-1170), Portsmouth State Fish Pier, Box 1355, Portsmouth 03802. Also contact the **New Hampshire Marine Dealers Association** (228-3599), Box 218, Concord 03301. (Also see *Canoeing.*)

BOOKS

Many New Hampshire books are mentioned throughout this guide. For a general history of the state, try *New Hampshire* by Elting and Elizabeth Morison (Norton). A good general history is Jere Daniell's *Colonial New Hampshire: A History* (Kraus International), while another favorite is Ralph Nading Hill's *Yankee Kingdom: Vermont and New Hampshire* (Countryman). William Schaller's *New Hampshire Backroads* (American Geographic Society) is a collection of photographs and text. The latter publisher has also released *New Hampshire: Portrait of the Land and its People. The New Hampshire Atlas & Gazetteer* (DeLorme Publishing) has maps of all major communities in the state. Check with independent bookstores, most of which have strong local book sections and should be checked for titles that might not be available elsewhere.

BUS SERVICE

New Hampshire enjoys better bus service than any other New England state. **Concord Trailways** (1-800-639-3317) serves Manchester and Concord; Laconia, Meredith, and Centre Harbor in the Lake Winnipesaukee Region; Franconia, North Conway, and Jackson in the White Mountains. **Greyhound Bus Lines** (1-800-231-2222) stops daily in Portsmouth's Market Square, connecting the seacoast with nationwide bus service. **C&J Trailways** (431-2424; 742-2990) provides many bus trips daily, connecting Logan Airport and downtown Boston with Dover, Durham, and Portsmouth, New Hampshire; Newburyport, Massachusetts; and Portland, Maine. **Vermont Transit** (802-864-6811 or Greyhound, 1-800-231-2222) stops in Nashua, Manchester, Concord, New London, and Hanover en route from White River Junction (VT) to Boston. It also stops in Keene and Fitzwilliam en route from Brattleboro (VT) to Boston; another route includes stops in Charlestown and Walpole. See "The Merrimack Valley" for service connecting with Boston's Logan Airport.

CAMPGROUNDS

New Hampshire camping opportunities range from primitive sites with few amenities to full-service areas with water and sewer hookups, electricity, TV, stores, recreation buildings, playgrounds, swimming pools, and boat launching. The most complete information is available from the **New Hampshire Campground Owners' Association** (846-5511), Box 320, Twin Mountain 03595. Their free directory lists 171 private, state, and White Mountain National Forest (WMNF) campgrounds. State and WMNF campgrounds are also listed in this book. Most private areas take reservations and some are completely booked by the end of one summer for the next. The state-owned campgrounds operate on a first-come, first-served basis only and offer few amenities, but many are on lakes with sandy beaches. Most **WMNF sites** are also on a first-come, first-served basis, however, a toll-free reservation system (1-800-280-2267) operates for some sites in the following campgrounds: White Ledge (Conway); Covered Bridge (Kancamagus); Sugarloaf I and II (Twin Mountain); Basin, Cold River, and Hastings (Evans Notch); Dolly Copp (Pinkham Notch); and Campton, Russell Pond, and Waterville (near I-93). The reservation service operates March through September (Monday to Friday 12–9, weekends 12–5). Reservations may be made 120 days before arrival, but 10 days before arrival is the minimum time.

CANOEING

New Hampshire offers many miles of flat-water and white-water canoeing opportunities. The Androscoggin, Connecticut, Saco, and Merrimack rivers are perhaps the most popular waters for canoeing, but there are many other smaller rivers as well. Many folks also like to paddle the numerous lakes and ponds of New Hampshire. Since spring runoffs have an impact on the degree of paddling difficulty to be found on a river, make sure you know what your river offers before heading downstream. The best source of information is the *AMC River Guide: New Hampshire and Vermont*, published by the Appalachian Mountain Club,

5 Joy Street, Boston, MA 02108. Also see *Canoe Camping Vermont and New Hampshire Rivers* (Backcountry Publications). Also contact the **Merrimack River Watershed Council** (224-8322) in Concord for information on the Merrimack River. The **Connecticut River Watershed Council** (675-2518) in Cornish publishes *The Complete Boating Guide to the Connecticut River* and sponsors occasional guided trips. The **Ledyard Canoe Club** (646-2753) in Hanover and **North Star Canoes** (542-5802) in Cornish both rent canoes; inquire about self-guided inn-to-inn tours (802-333-9124) on the Connecticut. **Saco Bound** (447-2177) in Center Conway offers rentals and a variety of programs as well as general information about the Saco and Androscoggin rivers.

CHILDREN, ESPECIALLY FOR

Children's museums are described in the Portsmouth, Peterborough, Manchester, and Concord chapters. While it is technically a science museum in Vermont (just across the bridge from Hanover, New Hampshire), the **Montshire Museum** in Norwich gets our vote for the most stimulating museum in this category, both inside and out. The **White Mountain Attractions** add up to the state's single largest family-geared magnet. With members ranging from the excursion vessel M/S *Mount Washington* on Lake Winnipesaukee to the gondola at Wildcat Mountain, from natural phenomena like Lost River (in North Woodstock) to theme parks like Story Land (in Glen) and Six Gun City and Santa's Village (both in Jefferson), this is a highly organized promotional association with a helpful visitors center just off Exit 32, I-93, in North Woodstock. Phone 745-8720 or 1-800-FIND-MTS, or write Box 10, North Woodstock 03262.

Other attractions with child appeal range from **Friendly Farm** in Dublin to New England's biggest video center in Weirs Beach. All are described as they appear, region by region.

CHILDREN'S SUMMER CAMPS

More than 100 summer camps are located in New Hampshire. For a free brochure contact the **New Hampshire Camp Director's Association** (437-2121), Box 427, Londonderry 03053.

CHRISTMAS TREES

Plantation-grown New Hampshire Christmas trees are the perfect accent for the holidays. These trees have been planted specifically to be harvested at about 10 years of age. Some growers allow you to come early in the season to tag your own tree, which you can cut at a later time for the holidays; others allow choose-and-cut only in December. Contact the **New Hampshire Department of Agriculture** (271-3551), Box 2042, Concord 03302-2042, and ask for the "Harvest New Hampshire" brochure.

COLLEGES AND UNIVERSITIES

Higher education opportunities range from two-year schools to the highly regarded University of New Hampshire and Dartmouth College. A descriptive brochure of 13 accredited, 4-year institutions is available from the **New Hampshire College and University Council** (669-3432), 2321 Elm Street, Manchester 03104.

CONSERVATION GROUPS

See the *Appalachian Mountain Club*, the Audubon Society of New Hampshire (under *Birding*) and the *Society for the Protection of New Hampshire Forests* (SPNHF).

JON-PIERRE LASSEIGNE

CRUISES

Few summer activities are as relaxing as a boat ride, and New Hampshire has many trips available from the ocean to the lakes. The two most popular cruises are the M/V *Thomas Laighton* (Isles of Shoals Steamship Company), which sails several times daily from Portsmouth to the off-shore Isles of Shoals, and the M/S *Mount Washington* on Lake Winnipesaukee. Squam Lake has two small boat cruises, and Lake Sunapee has several also. For details see *Boat Excursions* in the relevant chapters.

COVERED BRIDGES

New Hampshire harbors some 60 covered bridges. These are marked on the official state highway map, and we have tried to describe them within each chapter. The country's longest covered bridge, rebuilt in 1990, connects Cornish with Windsor, Vermont (technically the New Hampshire line runs to the Vermont shore, so it's all in New Hampshire). The state's oldest authenticated covered bridge (1827) links Haverhill and Bath. The Swanzey area near Keene (see "Peterborough, Keene, and Surrounding Villages") boasts the state's greatest concentration of covered bridges: five within little more than a dozen miles.

CRAFTS

The **League of New Hampshire Craftsmen** (224-3375), with headquarters at 205 North Main Street, Concord 03301, is one of the country's oldest, most effective statewide crafts groups. It maintains a half dozen shops displaying work by members, sponsors the outstanding annual Craftsmen's Fair in early August at Mount Sunapee State Park in Newbury, and publishes the **New Hampshire Visual Arts Map,** an extremely useful free pamphlet that is a guide to museums, galleries, and studios throughout the state.

EMERGENCIES

New Hampshire's telephone books have full listings of local emergency numbers inside the front cover. The **New Hampshire Poison Center** number is 1-800-562-8236. Hospital and ambulance numbers are also included at the beginning of each chapter in this book.

EVENTS

The *Official New Hampshire Guidebook* (see *Information*) lists current events, and in each chapter we have listed special events that occur year after year (see *Special Events*). April through August phone 1-800-258-3608 for a recording of upcoming events.

FACTORY OUTLETS

Several areas of New Hampshire have become tourist destinations just because of their shopping opportunities. The best-known region is **North Conway,** where some 200 shops, discount stores, and factory outlets have given the term "shopping trip" a new meaning. If you can't find what you want to buy there, you probably don't need it. North Hampton also has a large outlet shopping complex, but seacoast shoppers often drive across the Piscataqua River to Kittery, Maine, where outlets are nearly as numerous as in North Conway. Remember, Maine has a sales tax, New Hampshire does not.

FARMERS' MARKETS

Many farms used to have roadside stands where they sold their produce, and many still operate in New Hampshire, but the current trend is to sell through farmers' markets—once-a-week gatherings of many farmers. Open mainly from late June through Columbus Day, markets operate in Concord, Conway, Dover, Exeter, Hampton, Portsmouth, Laconia, Manchester, Milford, and Warner. Fresh fruits and vegetables, baked goods, honey, and crafts are among the items for sale. Many of the state's organic farmers sell their produce at these markets. "New Hampshire's Rural Heritage" lists farmers' markets locations and hours and is available from the **New Hampshire Department of Agriculture** (271-3551), Box 2042, Concord 03302-2042. Also see listings in this book.

FISHING

Freshwater fishing requires a license for anyone age 12 and older. Some 450 sporting goods and country stores sell licenses, or contact the **New Hampshire Fish and Game Department** (271-3421), 2 Hazen Drive, Concord 03301. The White Mountain National Forest issues a special brochure on trout fishing in the forest. No license is required for saltwater fishing. Party boats leave several times daily from April until October from docks at Rye, Hampton, and Seabrook harbors. Most of these boats have full tackle for rent.

FOLIAGE

Color first appears on hillsides in the North Country in mid-September, and by the end of that month Crawford and Pinkham notches are usually spectacular. The colors spread south and through lower elevations during the first two weeks in October. Columbus Day weekend is traditionally the time New England residents come "leaf peeping," and it's the period we suggest you avoid, if possible. At least avoid the traditional foliage routes—the Kancamagus Highway, Route 3 through Franconia Notch, and Route 16 to North Conway on those three days. Come a week earlier instead and try to get off the road entirely. This is prime hiking weather (no bugs). The state maintains a **Fall Foliage Hotline** (1-800-258-3608) with "conditions" updated regularly. The wise traveler will make reservations for overnight accommodations well in advance for the foliage season, since even such areas as Lincoln or North Conway, with hundreds of rooms, are fully booked on key weekends.

GOLF

We describe golf courses as they appear region by region. They are also listed in the *Official New Hampshire Guidebook* (see *Information*).

HIGH HUTS OF THE WHITE MOUNTAINS

The most unusual lodging opportunities in the state are found in the White Mountains, where the Appalachian Mountain Club operates eight full-service high mountain huts. Generally the huts are open from June through Labor Day, but several welcome hikers through September and two are open on a caretaker-basis all year. Guests hike to the huts, most of which are located a day's walk apart so that you can walk for several days and stay in a different hut each night. You sleep in co-ed bunk rooms equipped with mattresses and blankets. Meals are huge and varied. Reservations are required.

A shuttle service allows you to park at the trailhead for one hut, then ride back to your vehicle after your hike. Contact the **Appalachian Mountain Club Pinkham Notch Camp** (466-2727, for overnight or workshop reservations), Route 16, Box 298, Gorham 03518.

HIKING

New Hampshire offers the most diverse hiking in New England. The **White Mountain National Forest** alone has some 1,200 miles of hiking trails, and there are additional miles in state parks. A long, difficult section of the **Appalachian Trail** cuts through New Hampshire, entering the state near Hanover, crossing the highest peaks, including Mount Washington, and exiting along the rugged Mahoosuc Range on the Maine border. The White Mountains is the most popular hiking area, and the many trails offer easy to challenging routes. The most spectacular climbs are on the Franconia Ridge and over the Presidential Range, which includes **Mount Washington**, at 6,288 feet the highest peak in the northeast. Although relatively low compared to the Rockies, for example, Mount Washington

ROBERT J. KOZLOW

records the worst weather for any surface station outside of the polar regions. Hikers are urged to use caution and to consult weather forecasts before venturing onto the exposed areas above tree line. Over 110 people have died on Mount Washington; some of them in the summer when caught unprepared by extreme changes in weather conditions. White Mountain hiking information is available from the Appalachian Mountain Club Pinkham Notch Camp (466-2725 for weather, trail, or general information; 466-2727 for overnight or workshop reservations), Route 16, Box 298, Gorham 03518, or from the White Mountain National Forest. (For details, see "Mount Washington's Valleys.") There is plenty of hiking elsewhere in New Hampshire as well. **Mount Monadnock** in southern New Hampshire is one of the most climbed peaks in the world, and **Kearsarge** in central New Hampshire offers a relatively easy walk to its summit and nice views. Several lower mountains in the Lake Winnipesaukee region are easily climbed. **Mount Major,** in particular, is easy and has a fine view across the lake. These hikes are described elsewhere in this book, but for more details one of the following books is recommended. *The AMC White Mountain Guide* has the most comprehensive trail information available for hiking anywhere in New Hampshire, but also see *50 Hikes in the White Mountains, 50 Hikes in New Hampshire, Waterfalls of the White Mountains, Ponds and Lakes of the White Mountains,* and *Walks & Rambles in the Upper Connecticut River Valley* (all Backcountry Publications), the *Monadnock Guide* (Society for the Protection of New Hampshire Forests, Concord), and the guidebook of the Squam Lakes Association of Holderness. An exciting hiking project now under way is the creation of the **Heritage Trail,** which will run the length of the state following the banks of the Merrimack, Pemigewasset, and Connecticut rivers. Many segments of the trail are in place and new sections are added annually. For details call 271-3627.

HISTORIC HOMES AND SITES

New Hampshire residents have a strong appreciation for the state's history. Most communities have historical societies, and throughout the state many historic buildings and sites are open to the public. Most are listed in this guide. The largest concentration of historical houses is in Portsmouth, home of the large **Strawbery Banke** restoration and eight other houses open to the public. Along New Hampshire highways roadside markers recount short tidbits of local history. A copy of the roadside marker guide is available from the **New Hampshire Preservation Office** (271-3483). *New Hampshire Architecture* (University Press of New England) is a fine guide to historical and significant buildings.

HONEY

More than 200 members of the New Hampshire Beekeepers Association have hives throughout the state, and their honey is usually for sale at farmer's markets, some country stores, and at roadside stands.

HORSEBACK RIDING

Rising insurance costs are narrowing trail riding options, but you can still ride a horse through the woods at **Morning Mist Farm** in Henniker (see "The Concord Area") and a variety of instructional programs and serious treks are offered at **Honey Lane Farm** in Dublin. If you just want the sense of being on a horse (no experience necessary) contact the **Castle in the Clouds** in Moultonborough (see *To See* in "The Lake Winnipesaukee Area"), **Waterville Valley**

and **Loon Mountain** in the Western Whites, and the **Mount Washington Hotel** in Bretton Woods (see "Mount Washington's Valleys").

HUNTING

New Hampshire has long been a popular state for hunting. Licenses are required and are available from some 450 sporting goods and country stores, or contact the **New Hampshire Fish and Game Department** (271-3421), 2 Hazen Drive, Concord 03301.

ICE CREAM

It's hard to beat **Annabelle's Ice Cream,** located on Ceres Street in Portsmouth, open from spring through late fall. Former President George Bush liked their flavors so much that he had them make and serve red, white, and blueberry ice cream at the White House for the Fourth of July. Another popular homemade brand of ice cream is served at **Lagos' Lone Oak Dairy Bars** on old Route 16 in Rochester and Route 1 in Rye.

INFORMATION

We describe regional information sources at the head of each chapter. The **New Hampshire Office of Travel & Tourism Development** maintains a toll-free hotline (1-800-258-3608) with recorded info, varying with the season. You can also call 271-2343 or write to the Office, Department of Resources and Economic Development, PO Box 856, Concord 03302-0856. Request a copy of the *Official New Hampshire Guidebook* and a highway map. The guidebook includes year-round listings of the basics: golf courses, alpine and cross-country ski areas, covered bridges, scenic drives, events, fish and game rules, state parks, and state liquor stores. It also includes paid dining and lodging listings. Maps and pamphlets are also available in the state's full-service rest areas. (See *Rest Areas.*)

NH OFFICE OF TRAVEL & TOURISM

LAKES

Central New Hampshire is open, rolling country, spotted with lakes. **Winnipesaukee** is by far the state's largest, most visitor-oriented lake, and it is surrounded by smaller lakes: **Winnesquam, Squam, Wentworth, Ossipee**. Traditionally this has been New Hampshire's Lakes Region, but we've added the Western Lakes because there are so many west of I-93 as well: **Sunapee** and **Newfound** for starters, **Little Sunapee, Massasecum, Pleasant, Highland,** and **Webster** when you start looking for places to swim. Outdoorsmen are also well aware of the grand expanses of **Umbagog Lake** in Errol and of the **Connecticut Lakes** in New Hampshire's northernmost North Country. *Ponds and Lakes of the White Mountains* by Steve B. Smith (Backcountry Publications) describes more than 100 lakes and ponds, "from wayside to wilderness," including many bodies of water hidden deep in the woods (with detailed directions on finding them).

LIBRARIES

Every New Hampshire city and town has a public library, and there are many college and private libraries as well. In the seacoast, the **Portsmouth Public Library** and **the Portsmouth Athenaeum,** and the **Exeter Public Library** and **Exeter Historical Society** are centers for regional history and genealogical research. The **University of**

New Hampshire's **Dimond Library** has an extensive New Hampshire special-collections section and all of the resources one would expect to find in a major educational institution. In Concord, the **State Library** and the **New Hampshire Historical Society,** located side by side on Park Street, are centers for New Hampshire research. **Peterborough's public library** was the first in New Hampshire, and it and the nearby **Peterborough Historical Society library** have important regional collections. In Keene, the **Historical Society of Cheshire County Archive Center** and the **Keene State Library** are the best sources for local research. **Baker Library at Dartmouth College** is one of the fine institutions in the east. Among its many resources is an extensive White Mountains collection.

LLAMA TREKS

White Mountain Llamas in Jefferson (see "Along Route 2") is a source of one- to four-day treks. Similar treks in the Evans Notch area of the White Mountains, just over the Maine border, are offered by the **Telemark Inn & Llama Farm** in West Bethel.

LOTTERY

New Hampshire's is the oldest legal lottery in the country. Since 1964 it has funded more than $186 million to local education. For details from out of state, phone 271-2825; from in state, 371-3391.

MAGAZINES AND NEWSPAPERS

For such a small state, New Hampshire has an abundance of periodicals. The *Manchester Union-Leader* (Box 780, Manchester 03105), is the largest daily, and its strong conservative editorial policy has made it well known throughout the country. It is the best source of statewide news, but there are also dailies in Portsmouth, Dover, Laconia,

Conway, Claremont, Lebanon, Keene, Nashua, and Concord. Many of the larger towns also have weekly newspapers. The *Granite State Vacationer* (Box 519, Dover 03820) is a recreation newspaper, published 27 times each year and distributed free at roadside rest areas and information centers. It and several regional, free, tourist-oriented periodicals are good sources of information about local events and activities.

MAPLE SUGARING

When cool nights and warm days during late February through April start the sap running in maple trees, maple-syrup producers fire up their evaporators to begin making the sweet natural treat. Most producers welcome visitors and many offer tours, sugar-on-snow parties, and breakfast (pancakes with maple syrup, of course). For a list of maple-syrup producers, contact the **New Hampshire Department of Agriculture** (271-3551), Box 2042, Concord 03302-2042.

MARIONETTES

New England Marionettes (924-4022) in Peterborough claims to be America's largest marionette company presenting opera on a consistent basis. The theater at 24 Main Street features plush plum seats and a miniature but ornate stage designed to create the illusion that the marionettes—all made on the premises and deftly manipulated—are human-scale. Performances are adult-geared (although operas for children are occasionally presented) and are Thursday through Sunday. (See *Entertainment* in "Peterborough, Keene, and Surrounding Villages" for details.)

MOOSE

The state's largest animal is becoming more common and is often seen along roadsides, especially in the mountainous northern half of the state. Stay very alert when driving, since moose may unexpectedly walk into the road without looking. The state has recorded nearly 200 vehicle-moose collisions.

MOUNTAINTOPS

The summits of some New Hampshire mountains are more popular than others mainly because they offer better views, great hiking trails, or ways to ride to the top. The most popular, of course, is Mount Washington, at 6,288 feet the highest peak in the Northeast. The **Mount Washington Auto Road** is an 8-mile graded road on which you can drive your own car or ride in a chauffeured van. The **Mount Washington Cog Railway** offers an unusual steam-powered ride to the summit. Across Route 16 from Mount Washington, the **Wildcat Mountain gondolas** whisk you to the top of that wooded peak for a spectacular view of the Presidential Range, and the **Loon Mountain "Skyride"** (via gondolas) is to a summit complete with cafeteria, cave walk, and hiking trails. Both here and at **Mount Sunapee** (where a chair lift hoists you to the summit) cookout-style suppers are offered throughout the summer. The **Cannon Mountain Tramway** in Franconia offers its riders a view of the Franconia Range, the state's second highest group of

ROBERT J. KOZLOW

mountains. Although it is not a mountaintop, **Castle in the Clouds** (Route 109, Moultonborough), gives nonhikers the best view of Lake Winnipesaukee. For purist hikers **Mount Lafayette** is the favored summit in Franconia Notch. **Mount Moosilauke,** westernmost of the White Mountains, is also a spectacular summit. Lower mountains can nonetheless provide worthy views: **Mount Chocorua** rises beside Route 16 in Tamworth; although only 3,400 feet high, it is a challenging hike but with a great vista from its summit. **Mount Major** (Route 11, Alton) has an easy walk to its open summit. **Mount Monadnock** dominates the view throughout southwestern New Hampshire, but if you are not up to the hike, drive to the top of nearby **Pack Monadnock** (Miller State Park), Route 101, Peterborough. For those who like a challenge, the **Appalachian Mountain Club** has an informal 4,000 Footer Club; become a member by climbing all 48 New Hampshire mountains more than 4,000 feet high. The peaks are listed in the AMC *White Mountain Guide*. Some rugged folks have climbed all 48 in the winter; others have done it twice, with their dogs, or some other unique way.

MUSEUMS

Aside from art museums and children's museums (see *Art Museums and Galleries* and *Children, Especially for*), New Hampshire offers historical museums and houses (described here region by region). **Canterbury Shaker Village** in Canterbury (see "The Concord Area") is an outstanding museum village. The **New Hampshire Farm Museum** in Milton tells the history of farming in the state. The **Montshire Museum** in Norwich, Vermont (just across the river from Hanover, New Hampshire, where it began) is the most outstanding science museum in northern New England, well worth a stop for inquiring minds of all ages.

NH OFFICE OF TRAVEL & TOURISM

MUSIC

Music festivals are described under *Entertainment* and/or *Special Events* in each chapter. Check out the **New Hampshire Music Festival** in Centre Harbor (see "The Lake Winnipesaukee Area"), year-round performances at the **North Country Center for the Arts** in Lincoln, summer concerts at **Waterville Valley's Music Festival Concert Series,** the **Prescott Park Festival** in Portsmouth, the **Mount Washington Valley Arts Festival,** and the **Cochico Arts Festival** in Dover. The Monadnock Region is a traditional center for outstanding music; **Monadnock Music** is a series of two dozen summer concerts, operas, and orchestra performances staged in town halls, churches, and schools, and the **Apple Hill Chamber Players** in Nelson offers free faculty concerts. Band music is another sound of summer in New Hampshire. The **Temple Band**, also based in the Monadnock Region, claims to be the oldest town band in the country.

PARKS

New Hampshire has one of the oldest and best state park systems in the country. High mountains; lake, ocean, and river shores; unique stands of flowering shrubs and trees; historic buildings; and geological and archaeological sites comprise the diverse locations of the nearly 50 parks. Swimming, fishing, picnicking, camping, and hiking are among the many activities enjoyed in these parks. See *Campgrounds* for camping information or contact the **New Hampshire Division of Parks** (271-3254), 105 Loudon Road, Concord 03301. The 768,000-acre **White Mountain National Forest** runs through the middle of New Hampshire from east to west. The largest national forest in the east, it is managed for multiple-use activities including lumbering as well as recreation. Several ranger stations are located along major highways to provide information and assistance for forest users. The **Saco Ranger Station** (447-5448), at the Conway exit of the Kancamagus Highway, is open seven days a week, 8–4:30, or contact **WMNF headquarters** (528-8721), Box 638, 719 Main Street, Laconia 03247. Almost all cities and towns have parks, many of which include tennis courts open to the public.

PICK-YOUR-OWN

(See *Apple and Fruit Picking.*)

RENTAL COTTAGES, CONDOMINIUMS

Cottages are particularly plentiful and available in the Lake Winnipesaukee and the Western Lakes areas (contact the local chambers), and the same condominiums that cost $150-plus per night at Waterville Valley and Loon Mountain during ski season are a fraction of the price in summer when golf, horseback riding, hiking, and a variety of other activities make them increasingly attractive. The Mount Washington Valley Chamber of Commerce (356-3171; 1-800-367-3364) also keeps year-round tabs on condominiums and other family lodging. In the Seacoast Region, contact the Hampton Beach Chamber of Commerce (926-8717; 1-800-GET-A-TAN) for information about condo and cottage rentals.

REST AREAS

The state operates 17 highway rest areas. Three are open 24 hours a day: Hooksett (I-93 northbound and southbound) and Seabrook (northbound on I-95). The complete list of rest areas is printed on the official New Hampshire highway map, which is available at any information center or from the **New Hampshire Office of Travel and Tourism Development** (271-2343), Box 856, Concord 03302.

ROCK HOUNDING

Ruggles Mine in Grafton (see "The Western Lakes") is said to offer 150 kinds of minerals and gemstones. Commercial production of mica began here in 1803, and it's an eerie, interesting place that has gotten many a rock hound hooked.

SKI CONDITIONS

For alpine ski conditions call 1-800-258-3608. For cross-country conditions call 1-800-262-6660.

SKIING, CROSS-COUNTRY

New Hampshire offers more than 1,300 km of trails. The **Jackson Ski Touring Foundation** is the state's largest, with 150 km of varied trails including a run down the backside of Wildcat Mountain (accessible from the alpine summit via a single ride on its gondola). **Bretton Woods Ski Touring Center** offers a similar run from the top of its alpine area and a total of 88 km of trails.

PETER E. RANDALL

The **Mount Washington Valley Ski Touring Foundation** offers another 60 km, and the AMC in Pinkham Notch offers cross-country workshops and guided tours on national forest trails, too. Farther south both **Loon Mountain** and **Waterville Valley** offer major cross-country centers that tie into national forest trails. **Norsk** in New London is the outstanding cross-country center in central New Hampshire (in terms of size, elevation, and grooming) and **Windblown Ski Touring Center** in New Ipswich is favored by Bostonians; it's high, handy, and quite beautiful. In 1994 the New Hampshire Office of Travel and Tourism's **cross-country snow report** line is 1-800-262-6660. The centers are described region by region within this book. Also look for the free New Hampshire Ski Map (see *Downhill Skiing*), available from the state's Office of Travel and Tourism (see *Information*). Information about 10 of the larger ski-touring centers is available from Ski New Hampshire: 745-9396; 1-800-88-SKI-NH (out-of-state).

SKIING, DOWNHILL

New Hampshire boasts 17 major downhill ski areas. It's worth noting that on weekends their proximity to Boston puts their lifts (and lift tickets) at a real premium, but on weekdays they tend to be relatively empty. This pattern is beginning to alter as several "areas" become full-fledged "resorts." **Loon Mountain** in Lincoln and **Waterville Valley** (see "The Western Whites"), the state's largest areas, now offer a variety of activities to attract "ski weekers" as well as day trippers and weekenders. New Hampshire's areas may also just represent the world's largest concentration of snowmaking. The quality of the snowmaking itself varies, but most of New Hampshire's alpine slopes are now dependably white from Christmas through Easter. There's some discussion between Vermont and New Hampshire about whether alpine skiing was first introduced to this country in Woodstock (Vermont) or in Jackson (New Hampshire); the **New England Ski Museum** in Franconia Notch favors the New Hampshire version of regional ski history. We have described each ski area as it

ROBERT J. KOZLOW

appears, region by region. In 1994 the state-wide **snow phone** is 1-800-258-3608. Request a copy of the free New Hampshire Ski Map; it profiles the ski areas and includes winter events and attractions. Out-of-state phone is 1-800-22-SKI-NH for general information (lift-ticket prices, facilities, etc.) on all ski areas; in-state the Ski New Hampshire phone is 745-9396.

SLED DOG RACES

The world championships are in **Laconia in February** and climax in a series of colorful local meets.

SLEIGH RIDES

A number of New Hampshire inns and farms offer sleigh rides and hayrides in-season. Several are listed in this guide and others are found in "New Hampshire's Rural Heritage," a pamphlet from the New Hampshire Department of Agriculture (271-3788), Box 2042, Concord 03302-2042.

SNOWMOBILING

With some 6,000 miles of trails, New Hampshire offers the snowmobiler vast opportunities for winter fun. *Note:* Large portions of the WMNF are off limits to snowmobiling, trail bikes, or off-road vehicles, but most state parks do permit off-road vehicles on marked trails. For maps and regulations, contact the **Bureau of Off-Road Vehicles** (271-3254), Box 856, Concord 03302; the **New Hampshire Snowmobile Association** (224-8906), Box 38, Concord 03301; or chambers of commerce in Twin Mountain, Colebrook, Lincoln–North Woodstock, or North Conway. For snowmobile **snow conditions,** call 244-4666 or (from outside NH) 1-800-258-3609.

SOARING

Glider lessons and rides are offered in Franconia at **North Country Flying Service** (823-8881).

SOCIETY FOR THE PROTECTION OF NEW HAMPSHIRE FORESTS

Founded in 1901 to fight the systematic leveling of the state's forests by lumber firms, SPNHF was instrumental in securing passage of the 1911 Weeks Act, authorizing (for the first time) the federal purchase of lands to create national forests. One direct result is the 729,353-acre White Mountain National Forest. The group is also largely responsible for Mount Monadnock's current public status, and it now holds 57 properties for public use that total more than 18,000 acres. Many are described within this book, especially within the Monadnock Region, which harbors a large percentage. Stop by SPNHF headquarters (224-9945) in East Concord (just off I-93, Exit 15) or write SPNHF, 54 Portsmouth Street, East Concord, to obtain a copy of the society's "Lands Map & Guide" to their properties. If you are a hiker, fisherman, or cross-country skier, it is a valuable key to real treasure.

SUMMER THEATER

New Hampshire offers some outstanding summer theater. The **Barnstormers** in Tamworth, the **Peterborough Players** in Peterborough, and the **New London Barn Playhouse** in New London all rank among New England's oldest, best respected "straw hat" theaters. The **Weathervane Theater** in Whitefield, the **American Stage Festival** in Milford, the **Hopkins Center** at Dartmouth College in Hanover, the **Arts Center at Brickyard Pond** in Keene, and the **Prescott Art Festival** in Portsmouth also stage lively summer productions. Children's performances are staged at **Waterville Valley** during its Summer Concert Series. See *Entertainment* for each region. (Also see *Marionettes*.)

TRAILS, LONG DISTANCE

New Hampshire from the road is beautiful, but unless you see its panoramas from a high hiking trail, you miss its real magnificence. Long-distance hiking trails now crisscross the state. The longest, most spectacular, and most famous, the **Appalachian Trail,** cuts diagonally across the White Mountains, entering the state in Hanover on the west and traversing Franconia Notch, Mount Washington, and Pinkham Notch on its way into Maine. Detailed maps and guides as well as a free pamphlet guide "The Appalachian Trail in New Hampshire and the White Mountains" are available from the Appalachian Mountain Club Headquarters (617-523-0636), 5 Joy Street, Boston, MA 02108; also from the AMC Pinkham Notch Camp (see *Hiking*). The **Metacomet Trail,** running 14 miles south from Little Monadnock; the **Wapack Trail,** which heads south along ridges from North Pack Monadnock; and the **Monadnock-Sunapee Trail,** a 47-mile footpath, are also well mapped. (Also see *Hiking* within each region.)

ROBERT J. KOZLOW

WATERFALLS

The White Mountains have the best waterfalls to view and all are described in *Waterfalls of the White Mountains* (Backcountry Publications), which lists 30 trips to some 100 waterfalls.

I. THE SEACOAST

Whaleback Lighthouse in Portsmouth

ROBERT J. KOZLOW

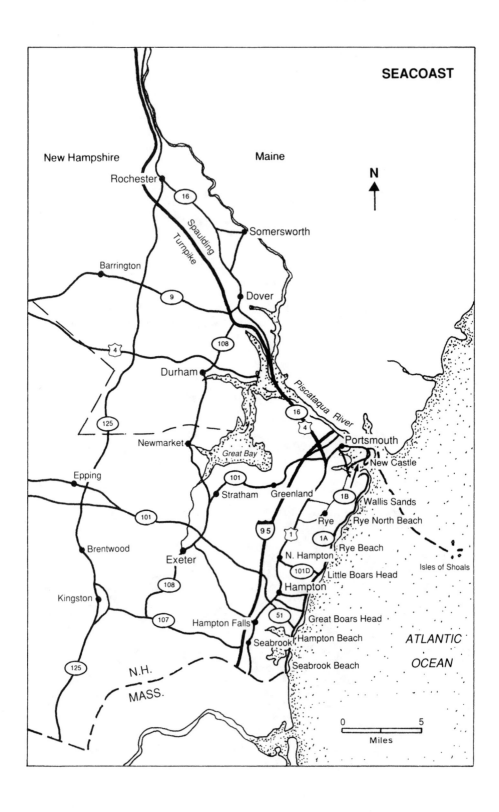

Introduction

With only 18 miles of oceanfront, New Hampshire's seacoast is often overlooked by visitors who are more impressed with neighboring Maine's more than 2,500 miles of coastline. In its small coastal area, however, New Hampshire has more than enough historical sites, beaches, restaurants, and events and attractions to keep her guests busy for many days and returning again and again for more.

At opposite ends of the seacoast are Portsmouth and Hampton Beach, near to each other in mileage but much farther apart in ambience and style.

Settled in 1630, Portsmouth was the colonial capital and an important seaport during the Georgian and Federal eras, periods that have given the city its distinctive architectural character. With fine inns and restaurants, a number of original and restored historical houses open to the public, theater, dance, music, and a superb waterfront park, Portsmouth is New Hampshire's most delightful and interesting city, loved and appreciated by its residents and visitors alike.

Hampton Beach has been one of New England's most popular seaside resorts since the development of the electric trolley at the turn of the century. Too bad the trolleys don't operate any more since the automobile traffic, especially on weekends, is one long snarl. Sand and sun, pizza and fried dough, and lively entertainment characterize Hampton Beach, where more than 200,000 people can be found on a summer holiday weekend. For many people, a week at Hampton Beach has been an annual family tradition for half a century or more.

Between these two extremes are mostly small towns (less than 1,000 to 12,000 population) with white churches, town commons, colonial architecture, and an ambience that is attracting many new residents and straining the capacity of these towns to manage the growth that has characterized this area since the end of World War II. The recent closure of Pease Air Force Base and conversion of its property to industrial development and to a public airport with daily service bodes well for the future and might ultimately offset the decline in activity at the Portsmouth Naval Shipyard, a facility that regularly faces the threat of closure. The seacoast's superb location and abundant educational, cultural, physical, and human resources seem to be more than adequate to continue the region's reputation as one of the top places in the country to live and work (and vacation).

GUIDANCE

Seacoast Council on Tourism (436-7678; outside NH 1-800-221-5623), 1000 Market Street, Portsmouth 03801. Publishes a handy guide. (Also see chambers of commerce under sectional listings.)

GETTING THERE

By plane: **Pease International Tradeport,** Portsmouth, is served by **United (Airlines) Express** (1-800-241-6522) with daily flights to Newark, and **Business Express, the Delta Connection** (1-800-345-3400), has daily flights to Boston, LaGuardia (NYC), and Newark. Pease has the following rental car agencies: **National** (334-6000; 1-800-227-7368), and **Budget** (427-0355; 1-800-527-0700). **Boston's Logan Airport, Portland's Jetport,** and **Manchester Airport** are each an hour's drive from the seacoast.

By car: I-95, the state's first superhighway, built in the 1950s, bisects the seacoast, connecting New Hampshire to the seacoast regions of Massachusetts and Maine. From the west, Routes 4 and 101 connect the seacoast with the central regions of the state while Route 16 is the road from the mountains.

By bus: **Greyhound Bus Lines** (436-0163) stops daily in Portsmouth's Market Square, connecting the seacoast with nationwide bus service. **Coach Company** (431-0163) has twice-daily trips to Boston. **C&J Trailways** (431-2424, 742-2990) provides many trips daily, connecting Logan Airport and downtown Boston with Dover, Durham, and Portsmouth (Pease) New Hampshire; Newburyport, Massachusetts; and Portland, Maine. **Hampton Shuttle** (926-8275; outside NH 1-800-225-6426), a reservation-only shuttle service, makes eight trips daily from Hampton, Exeter, and Seabrook to Logan Airport.

Portsmouth and Vicinity

For more than 300 years, the seacoast's largest community has been influenced by its maritime location. "We came to fish," announced Portsmouth's first residents in 1630, but shortly the community (first called Strawbery Banke) became a center for the mast trade, supplying long, straight timbers for the Royal Navy. Portsmouth's captains and crews soon roamed the entire world in locally built vessels, hauling cargoes to and from New England, the Caribbean, Europe, and the Far East. In the years before and after the revolutionary war, wealthy captains and merchants built many of the fine homes and commercial buildings that characterize Portsmouth today.

Unhappy with the demands of the British government, Portsmouth residents were quick to voice opposition to the crown. Before Paul Revere rode to Lexington and Concord, he first galloped to Portsmouth, warning the patriots to raid nearby Fort William and Mary and to remove the gunpowder before the British came from Boston to strengthen the undermanned fort. John Paul Jones lived in Portsmouth while overseeing the construction of two major warships during the Revolution. Built on the banks of the Piscataqua River were 28 clippers, unrivaled in construction, beauty, and speed as they hauled passengers and merchandise around the world.

The Portsmouth Naval Shipyard, founded in 1800, has long been associated with submarines, turning out 100 vessels to aid the Allied cause in World War II. Portsmouth's red and green tugboats symbolize the city's current maritime activity. Oil tankers and bulk cargo vessels continue to ply the river, halting traffic as they pass through bridges, creating a bustle of activity now missing from so many other old New England seaports, which have lost their commercial ship traffic.

The result of this 300-year maritime heritage is present in the city's architecture; in its active waterfront, which is used for international, commercial, and recreational boating; and in the many cultural activities that involve its riverfront location. Once an old swabby town, complete with rundown bars and a decaying city center and surrounding neighborhoods, Portsmouth has been transformed into an exciting city as its residents have begun to appreciate its historical traditions and classic architecture. Portsmouth's renaissance continues, fueled by fine

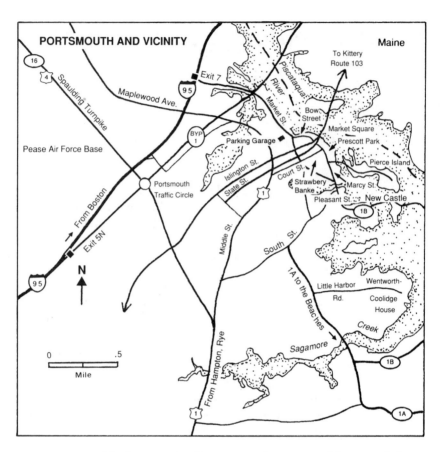

PORTSMOUTH AND VICINITY   Maine

To Kittery
Route 103

Exit 7

Spaulding Turnpike
Maplewood Ave.

Bow Street

Market Square

Prescott Park

BYP 1

Parking Garage

Pierce Island

Pease Air Force Base

Islington St.

Court St.

Strawbery Banke

Marcy St.

Portsmouth Traffic Circle

State St.

Pleasant St.   New Castle

From Boston

1B

Exit 5N

Middle St.

South St.

N

1A to the Beaches

Little Harbor Rd.

Wentworth-Coolidge House

Creek

0   .5
Mile

From Hampton, Rye

Sagamore

1B

1A

restaurants (the best north of Boston, and some would say "including" Boston), inns, music, dance, theater, and, seemingly, a festival every month of the year.

The Piscataqua River, one of the fastest-flowing navigable rivers in the world, separates New Castle, Portsmouth, and Newington, New Hampshire, from Kittery and Eliot, Maine. It is crossed by three main bridges. The lowest is Memorial Bridge, near the center of town, which raises its draw many times daily for commercial and recreational vessels. Residents and visitors alike usually stop to watch as the little tugs shepherd huge ocean-going vessels past this bridge. Next upstream is the Sarah Mildred Long Bridge, once the busiest bridge for motor vehicles but no longer now that the I-95 bridge just upriver carries most of the through traffic. The Piscataqua drains the Great Bay, a large, relatively shallow tidal bay known for its wildlife and winter ice fishing (see "Durham, Dover, and Vicinity," *Green Space*).

GUIDANCE

Greater Portsmouth Chamber of Commerce (436-1118), 500 Market Street, Box 239, Portsmouth 03802. A busy and active promoter of local tourism, the chamber has a year-round information center on Market Street, a short walk west of downtown. It serves Portsmouth and adjacent communities on both sides of the Piscataqua River. There is also a summer information kiosk in Market Square.

GETTING AROUND

By taxi: There are taxi stands on Market Square, across the street from the church. **A-1 Taxi** (436-7500), **Allied Taxi** (436-7111), **City Cab** (431-2345), and **Colonial Taxi** (436-0008) are among the several companies available.

By bus: **COAST** (Cooperative Alliance for Seacoast Transportation) (862-1931), the local bus transportation, connects Portsmouth and major outlying shopping centers with Durham, Dover, Newmarket, Rochester, and Somersworth, New Hampshire, and Berwick, Maine. A main stop is in Market Square.

By car: When traveling on I-95, take Exit 7, Market Street, which leads directly downtown, past the Chamber of Commerce Information Center, to Market Square.

PARKING

Although Portsmouth's traffic is not worse than any other city, it does have limited on-street parking, and its meter maids are superefficient in providing a written welcome to the city. Meter parking is limited to two hours, so seek out the parking garage, situated just off Market Square in the middle of town, or the large lot off Pleasant Street, adjacent to the South Mill Pond. All of Portsmouth's points of interest and finest restaurants are within an easy walk of both places. Portsmouth is best enjoyed on foot, anyway.

MEDICAL EMERGENCY

Portsmouth Regional Hospital (436-5110), 33 Borthwick Avenue, Portsmouth 03801. The hospital offers 24-hour emergency walk-in service. Portsmouth ambulance: 436-1127. Rye ambulance: 964-8683.

VILLAGES

Portsmouth is surrounded by four small towns: Newington, Greenland, Rye, and New Castle. **Newington,** upriver from Portsmouth, is the commercial and industrial center of the region. It has two major shopping malls, and many other shops, plus a large power plant, oil storage tanks, and other industries. Most of this commercial-industrial complex is located between the river and the Spaulding Turnpike (Routes 4/16). The residential area and village are south of the turnpike, by Pease Air Force Base, whose construction in the 1950s cut the town of Newington in half. **Greenland** is south of Newington, another residential town with a picturesque village green. East along the Piscataqua is the small island village of **New Castle**. Winding, narrow streets lined with eighteenth- and nineteenth-century homes combine to give New Castle the appearance of a town unchanged since the turn of the century. The historic Wentworth-by-the-Sea Hotel has been closed for a number of years, but the adjacent large marina keeps the town's tourist image alive even though New Castle no longer has lodging facilities. Next to New Castle is the largest of the four towns, **Rye,** once a popular summer retreat when it had several large hotels. Those old structures are gone now, and its summer residents live in oceanfront cottages. Several of the finest residential developments have been built in Rye, and it is a popular address for many seacoast executives. Route 1A along the coast of Rye is a fine bike route, passing several state parks, restaurants, and a few motels.

Also not to be missed is the **Isles of Shoals,** a historic nine-island group, about 10 miles off the coast and visible from Route 1A. Summer ferry service provides tours around the islands and a three-hour stopover on Star Island.

TO SEE

St. John's Episcopal Church (436-6902), Chapel Street, Portsmouth. Open Sunday and other times by applying at the church office in the adjacent building. Built in 1807, this church is a prominent city landmark, located beside the river. Its classic interior has wall paintings, religious objects, and interesting plaques. Its adjacent 1754 graveyard is the resting place of many of the city's colonial leaders, including Benning Wentworth, Royal Governor, 1741–1766.

Newington Historical Society, Nimble Hill Road, Newington 03801. Open Thursday 2–4 in July and August. The Old Parsonage, built 1710, has local artifacts and a special children's room with antique toys. Across the street is the 1712 Old Meetinghouse, in continuous use since that time but structurally altered, and nearby is the Langdon Library with an extensive genealogical collection.

Piscataqua Gundalow Project (Box 1522, Portsmouth 03802), Prescott Park, Marcy Street, Portsmouth. From the mid-1600s through the midnineteenth century, unique flat-bottomed workboats called gundalows hauled cargo between Portsmouth and upriver ports such as Exeter, Newmarket, Durham, Dover, and Berwick. Powered by the tides and lanteen sails, which could be lowered quickly to pass under bridges, the gundalows were important to the local economy and became familiar vessels on the river. Replaced by the railroad, the gundalow passed into history until the 1980s, when a nonprofit organization constructed this reproduction vessel for use as an educational tool to focus attention on the heritage of the river, Great Bay, and the seacoast environment. During July the gundalow is tied up at Prescott Park and is open for tours on weekends. At other times, it travels to surrounding ports. The tour schedule is posted at the **Sheafe Warehouse.** Fee charged for tour.

Port of Portsmouth Maritime Museum and Albacore Park (436-3680), Market Street, Box 4367, Portsmouth 03802. Open daily March through November, 9:30–4. Tour the *U.S. Albacore,* an important experimental submarine built in the 1950s at the nearby Portsmouth Naval Shipyard. This 205-foot submarine was used for 20 years as the design model for the contemporary nuclear United States fleet. The tour includes a memorial park and gardens, a short film, a picnic area, a gift shop, and the submarine. Fee charged.

Portsmouth Athenaeum (431-2538), 9 Market Square, Portsmouth 03801. Research library open Tuesday and Thursday 1–4, Saturday 10–4, and by appointment. Reading Room open to the public for tours Thursday 1–4. This three-story brick Federal building, with its four white pilasters, is the architectural anchor for Market Square. Built in 1805, after one of Portsmouth's disastrous fires, the building has, since 1823, been the home of the Athenaeum, a private library and museum. Genealogy, maritime history, biographies, and Civil War memorabilia are among its important holdings. Throughout the building are fully rigged ship models, half models, and paintings. Free.

Strawbery Banke (433-1100), ticket office off Marcy Street, Box 300, Portsmouth 03802. Open May through October and first two weekends in December, plus special winter and off-season group tours available. In the early 1960s the 10-acre site, which is now this nationally known and respected restoration project, was supposed to be razed for an urban renewal project. Local protests stopped the demolition, saving more than 30 historically significant buildings. The museum now has 42 buildings, including several moved to this site to protect them from demolition elsewhere in the city. Most of the buildings are on their original foundations, which makes this a unique project when compared to other historical restorations composed of new re-creations or buildings assembled from many places. As the location of Portsmouth's first settlement in 1630 and a residential area until the early 1960s, Strawbery Banke reflects the living 300-year history of this neighborhood, not just one era. Furnished houses have rooms reflecting life from the seventeenth through the midtwentieth centuries, depicting a variety of lifestyles, from wealthy merchants and professional people to sea captains, poor widows, and ordinary working families. Other houses have exhibits, displays, and craftspeople who offer their work for sale. The December candlelight stroll is a popular holiday attraction, and there are other special events throughout the year, including militia musters, horticulture and fabric workshops, and small craft displays—the latter complementing the institution's wooden boat shop. Extensive eighteenth- and nineteenth-century gardens enhance the grounds. The Washington Street Eatery, one of the city's best spots for gourmet sandwiches, soups, and light meals, is on the grounds. Picnic area and gift shop.
(Also see *Green Space.*)

HISTORIC HOMES

John Paul Jones House (436-8240), Middle and State streets, Portsmouth 03801. Open May 15 through October 15, Monday through Saturday 10–4, Sunday in July and August 2–4. The museum house of the Portsmouth Historical Society, this home was the residence of Captain John Paul Jones when he lived in Portsmouth overseeing the construction of two revolutionary war frigates, *Ranger* and *America*. A traditional Georgian house, built in 1758, it has furnished period rooms and a small museum. Fee charged.

Governor John Langdon Memorial (436-3205), 143 Pleasant Street, Portsmouth 03801. Open June through October 15, Wednesday through Sunday 12–5. One of New England's finest Georgian mansions, the house was built in 1784 by John Langdon, a wealthy merchant who was an important figure in the Revolution and later a United States senator and governor of New Hampshire. George Washington was entertained in this house, which is now owned by the Society for the Preservation of New England Antiquities. Extensive gardens are behind the house. Fee charged.

Moffat-Ladd House (436-8221), 154 Market Street, Portsmouth 03801. Open June through mid-October, Tuesday through Saturday 10–4, Sunday 2–5. Built in 1763, this house was the residence of wealthy eighteenth-century shipowners and merchants and is furnished in that period to reflect the family's lifestyle. William Whipple, a signer of the Declaration of Independence, lived here. Its great hall is a masterpiece of detailed woodworking. Internationally famous gardens fill the backyard, and don't miss the summer-long book sale in the carriage house. Owned by the Society of Colonial Dames. Fee charged.

Rundlett-May House (436-3205), Middle Street, Portsmouth 03801. Open June through mid-October, Wednesday through Sunday 12–5. Built in 1807, this Federal mansion remained in the builder's family until just a few years ago, when it was acquired by the Society for the Preservation of New England Antiquities. Although it has many fine Federal pieces built especially for the house, it does reflect the continuous ownership of successive generations of a family who valued the original features of the house and adapted their lifestyle with an appreciation for the past. The stable is impressive as are the extensive gardens and grounds, which retain much of their original layout. Fee charged.

Warner House (436-5909), 150 Daniel Street, Portsmouth 03801. Open June through mid-October, Tuesday through Saturday 10–4, Sunday 1–4. The finest New England example of an eighteenth-century urban brick dwelling, this house was built in 1716 and during its early years was the home of leading merchants and officials of the royal provincial government. It has outstanding murals painted on the staircase walls, splendid paneling, and period furnishings. Benjamin Franklin was said to have installed the lightning rod on the west wall. Owned by the Warner House Association. Fee charged.

Wentworth-Gardner and Tobias Lear Houses (436-4406), Gardner and Mechanic streets, Portsmouth 03801. Open mid-June through mid-October, Tuesday through Sunday 1–4. Built in 1760, the Wentworth-Gardner House is one of the perfect examples of Georgian architecture found in America. Built by Madam Mark Hunking as a gift to her son Thomas (brother of the last royal governor), its exquisite carving took 14 months to complete. It has been beautifully restored and furnished. Adjacent is the Tobias Lear House, built in 1740, the childhood home of George Washington's private secretary. The president enjoyed tea in the parlor in 1789. Not completely restored, the Lear House is occasionally open to the public. Both houses are owned by the Wentworth-Gardner and Tobias Lear Houses Association. Fee charged.

Richard Jackson House (431-3205), Northwest Street, Portsmouth. Open by appointment only; allow one-day notice. This is New Hampshire's oldest house, built in 1664 with later additions. It has few furnishings and is of interest primarily for its seventeenth-century architectural details. It is most picturesque in May when its apple orchard is in bloom. Owned by the Society for the Preservation of New England Antiquities.

Wentworth-Coolidge Mansion Historic Site (436-6607), Little Harbor Road (off Route 1A), Portsmouth 03801. Open weekends Memorial Day through late June, then daily until Labor Day. Owned by the state, this rambling 40-room mansion is one of the most interesting and historic buildings in New Hampshire. It was the home of Royal Governor Benning Wentworth, whose term from 1741 until 1766 was the longest of any royal governor in America. Council meetings were held in an ornately paneled room overlooking the channel between Portsmouth and Little harbors. Its lilacs, which bloom in late May, are said to be the first planted in America. Although the house is not furnished, its extensive woodwork is an exquisite display of Portsmouth craftsmen of the period. Fee charged.

FOR FAMILIES

Water Country (436-3556), Route 1, 1 mile south of town, Portsmouth 03801. Open weekends Memorial Day to mid-June, then daily until Labor Day. June and September, 11–6, July and August, 9:30–8. Called New England's largest water park, this complex has seven large water slides, a huge wave pool, and a new Raging Rapids ride plus Adventure River ride, bumper boats, fountains, and a kiddie pool. One admission covers all day for all rides; tube and boat rentals, additional. Discount admission after 4:30 P.M.

The Children's Museum of Portsmouth (436-3853), 280 Marcy Street, Portsmouth 03801. Open Tuesday through Saturday 10–5, Sunday 1–5, Monday 10–5 during school vacations and the summer. Housed in an old meetinghouse in the city's historic South End, this colorful museum is exciting for children of all ages. Many of its exhibits reflect the area's maritime heritage. Kids can explore the yellow submarine or ride in the lobster fishing boat, and there are many other hands-on exhibits, changing displays, and organized activities. Children and adults, $3.50. Children under 9 must be accompanied by someone age 12 or older. Memberships also available.

HISTORIC CEMETERIES

North Cemetery, Maplewood Avenue, Portsmouth. Dating from 1753, this cemetery holds the remains of prominent people from the revolutionary war to the War of 1812. Diverse headstones reveal the skill of early stonecutters.

Point of Graves Cemetery, off Marcy Street, Portsmouth. Adjacent to Prescott Park, this old cemetery was established in 1671. Although most of the oldest stones have sunk from sight, many old and uniquely carved stones remain.

TO DO

BOAT EXCURSIONS

Isles of Shoals Steamship Company (431-5500; 1-800-441-4620), Barker Wharf, 315 Market Street, Box 311, Portsmouth 03802. Open daily mid-June through Labor Day and Memorial Day weekend; special fall schedule until September 28 and whale-watch cruises beginning in mid-April. This is the Isles of Shoals ferry, hauling passengers and freight to Star Island and providing one of New England's finest narrated tours. The 90-foot *Thomas Laighton* is a replica of a turn-of-the-century steamship, the type of vessel used when the islands were the leading New England summer colony, attracting the era's most famous artists, writers, poets, and musicians. The boat docks at Star Island, home of the Star Island Conference Center, a summer religious institution meeting here since the turn of the century. On the 11 A.M. ferry trip, a maximum of 100 visitors can leave the *Laighton* for a 3-hour stopover, returning to the mainland on the 3 P.M. boat, which docks in Portsmouth at 4:30 P.M. Buy tickets early for this cruise since it often sells out. Bring your picnic lunch and plenty of film for the camera. Since the *Laighton* is the supply line for the conference center, delivering food, drinking water, supplies, mail, and oil for the island's generators, it operates rain or shine. The trip to the islands takes about an hour, the round trip about three hours. In addition to the daily Isles of Shoals cruises, the *Laighton* is also used for dinner cruises, including clambakes and big-band dance cruises. The 71-foot *Oceanic* is used for whale-watching (an all-day, offshore trip), special lighthouse cruises, the nightly sunset cruise to the islands, and weekend cocktail and dance cruises.

Portsmouth Harbor Cruises (436-8084; 1-800-776-0915), 64 Ceres

Stone church on Star Island

Street, Oar House Dock, Portsmouth 03801. Open early June through Labor Day with a reduced schedule until late October. The 49-passenger *Heritage* offers a variety of daily narrated cruises, which, depending on the tide, tour the harbor, and wend down the Piscataqua, past the two lighthouses, around New Castle Island, through Little Harbor, and back to the dock. Several trips circle the Isles of Shoals, and fall foliage trips travel the winding rivers and expanse of Great Bay. Our favorite is the 5:30 sunset cruise—no narration, just a cool drink and a quiet ride after a hot summer day. Several trips regularly sell out, so buy tickets early. Also available is a large sailboat for single-day or overnight charters.

New Hampshire Seacoast Cruises (964-5545, 382-6743), Rye Harbor State Marina, Route 1A, Box 232, Rye 03870. Open daily July through Labor Day; weekend whale-watches May, June, September, and October. Ride the 150-capacity *Granite State* for a six-hour whale-watch or a two-hour cruise around the Isles of Shoals.

Atlantic Fishing Fleet (964-5220), Rye Harbor Marina, Route 1A, Box 678, Rye 03870. Open Wednesday and weekends in April for all-day fishing, two half-day trips daily Memorial Day through Labor Day and weekends through early October, and night fishing in season. The speedy 70-foot *Atlantic Queen II* is designed for all-weather ocean fishing. Offshore trips seek cod, cusk, pollock, and haddock. Rods for rent.

BUGGY RIDES

The Portsmouth Livery Company (427-0044), 319 Lincoln Avenue, Portsmouth 03801. Open daily May through October; November through April open Friday through Sunday and Monday holidays, weather permitting. You will find Ray Parker and his horses and buggies in Market Square next to the North Church. Day and evening sightseeing tours are offered, ranging in length from 15 minutes to 35 minutes. The latter includes a ride through historic Strawbery Banke. A gourmet picnic ride for two with lunch served at a scenic picnic area, then a return ride is also offered.

GOLF

Portsmouth Country Club (436-9719), Country Club Drive (off Route 101 south of Portsmouth), Greenland 03840. Open mid-April to mid-November. Designed by Robert Trent Jones, 18 holes, the longest course in New Hampshire with several picturesque holes on the shores of Great Bay. Cart rentals, full bar and food service, and pro shop. Call for starting times.

Wentworth-by-the-Sea (433-5010), Wentworth Road (Route 1B), Portsmouth 03801. Open April to mid-November. Designed by Donald Ross, a beautiful, challenging 18-hole course with several holes bordering picturesque Little Harbor. Pro shop, cart rentals, full-service bar and restaurant. Open to the public weekdays and weekend afternoons. Call for starting times.

FARMERS' MARKETS

Farmers' Market (778-3702), Parrott Avenue, Portsmouth. Saturday 9–1, June through mid-October. Fresh, locally grown veggies and fruits in season, home-baked goods, and crafts. Seacoast Grower's Association.

GREEN SPACE

☞∅**Prescott Park,** Marcy Street, Portsmouth. Open year-round. Marcy Street was once an area of bawdy houses, bars, and run-down businesses. The Prescott sisters, who were born in this section of the city, inherited millions of dollars and sought to clean up the waterfront by creating a park, which they gave to the city. Supported by a substantial trust fund, the park is famous for its beautiful gardens, but it also includes boat wharves, an amphitheater, picnic areas, sculpture, fountains, and the historic 1705 Sheafe Warehouse with exhibits. From July through mid-August it is the location of the daily Prescott Park Arts Festival (donation requested), offering outdoor summer theater, varied musical performances, an art exhibit, and children's theater and art programs. At the east end of the park, cross the bridge to adjacent Pierce Island, home of the state's commercial fishing pier, and walk out to Four Tree Island, a picnic ground, nearly in the middle of the river.

Urban Forestry Center (431-6774), Elwyn Road, off Route 1 south of Portsmouth. Open year-round; summer 8–8, winter 8–4, office hours Monday through Friday 8–4. This large site, bordering tidal Sagamore Creek, has nature trails, herb gardens, hiking, cross-country skiing, and snowshoeing, and offers environmental programs throughout the year. Free.

Fort Constitution, off Route 1A, New Castle. Open year-round 10–5. Turn in at the United States Coast Guard Station and park where indicated. This historic site was first used for fortifications in the early 1600s, but today it reflects the revolutionary and Civil War periods. In December 1774, after being alerted by Paul Revere, local patriots raided the fort, overwhelmed its few defenders, and removed its powder and some weapons before British warships from Boston could reinforce the garrison. This is considered to be the first overt act against the king and predated the war's outbreak by some four months. The powder was used against the British at the battle of Bunker Hill. The last royal governor, John Wentworth, and his family fled their home in the city and remained in the fort before leaving the rebellious province for the last time. Restored and maintained by the state, the fort's entrance portcullis reflects the colonial period, while the fortifications along the water date from the Civil War although there were no battles here. Adjacent to the fort is the picturesque and still important Fort Point lighthouse, and just offshore is the Whaleback lighthouse. Ten miles at sea the Isles of Shoals is visible. Free.

Fort Stark, Wild Rose Lane, off Route 1A, New Castle. Open weekends and holidays, May through October, 10–5. To protect the important Portsmouth Naval Shipyard during World War II, the military occupied several points at the mouth of the river. One was Fort Foster, across the river from Fort Constitution, and Fort Stark was another. Although used as a fort from 1746, the site today reflects its World War II service. Free.

New Castle Great Common, Route 1A, New Castle. Open year-round; a small fee is charged to nonresidents during the summer. Another World War II site, this was Camp Langdon, an army base. It was acquired by the town of New Castle as a recreation area and the site for a new office complex. There are rest rooms, picnic tables, a small beach, and a pier for fishing. Overlooking the mouth of the river and its two lighthouses, this area is one of the scenic highlights along the coast.

Odiorne Point State Park, Route 1A, Rye. Open year-round; park fees charged in the main season, June through September. This 137-acre oceanfront park is the site of the first settlement in New Hampshire in 1623. Later, fine mansions were built here; then the site was taken over during World War II and named Fort Dearborn, with huge guns placed in concrete bunkers. As a park it has handicapped-accessible nature trails, a boat-launching ramp, picnic tables, and a fine nature center— open late June to late August—operated by the University of New Hampshire. The center has exhibits and offers varied daily nature programs using the park, its nearby marsh, and the ocean's intertidal zone. No swimming.

Rye Harbor State Park and Marina, Route 1A, Rye. Open year-round; fee charged in the summer season for the park and boat launching. The

PETER E. RANDALL

Boats moored in Rye Harbor

state's smallest state park, this jewel occupies an ocean point just south of Rye Harbor. It has picnic tables, a playground, a jetty for fishing, a view of the picturesque harbor, and cooling ocean breezes on hot summer days. Around the corner is the Rye Harbor State Marina with a launching ramp and wharves, where you can buy tickets for deep-sea fishing, whale-watches, or sight-seeing boat rides.

BEACHES

Wallis Sands State Park, Route 1A, Rye. Open weekends mid-May through late June, then daily until Labor Day. A large, sandy beach with lifeguards, rest rooms, parking, and a snack bar. Fee charged.

Jenness State Beach, Route 1A, Rye. Another large, sandy beach with lifeguards, rest rooms, and parking meters. A snack bar is across the street.

LODGING

BED & BREAKFASTS

Sise Inn (433-1200; outside NH 1-800-232-4667), 40 Court Street, Portsmouth 03801. Open year-round. The city's most luxurious accommodation, the Sise Inn is a beautifully restored, furnished, and decorated 1881 Queen Anne–style mansion with a new matching addition. The 34 rooms, including several suites, have private baths, mostly queen-size beds, TVs, VCRs (with free cassettes), telephones, alarm clocks, radios, tables, and comfortable chairs. Several rooms also have cassette tape players and whirlpool baths; one has a fireplace; and another, a skylight and a private staircase. With several meeting rooms, the inn was designed for the business traveler, but vacationers are welcome to share the Victorian luxury as well. A continental breakfast is served. Rates are $89–175.

The Inn at Christian Shore (431-6770), 335 Maplewood Avenue, Portsmouth 03801. Open year-round. Antiques furnish this lovely in-town Federal house, restored and operated as a B&B since 1979 by Louis Socia. There are six rooms (one is for a single), four with private baths, all with air-conditioning and TV. Hearty gourmet breakfasts are served before a roaring fire under a candelabra with exposed old beams. Rates are $60–75.

Governor's House B&B (431-6546), 32 Miller Avenue, Portsmouth 03801. Open year-round. Once the home of New Hampshire Governor Charles Dale, this 1917 Georgian colonial has been turned into an attractive five-room in-town inn by John and Nancy Grossman. Four of the rooms, each with a different motif, feature unique hand-painted ceramic tiles in the bathrooms. Canopy, four-poster, and cannonball beds in each room. The former servants' quarters have been turned into a two-room suite. There's a clay tennis court in the backyard. $90–140 with full breakfast, $20 less November through May.

Martin Hill Inn (436-2287), 404 Islington Street, Portsmouth 03801. Open year-round. The city's first B&B, this classic inn is composed of adjacent 1820 and 1850 houses joined by a brick garden path overlooking an extensive garden. The main inn has three guest rooms with period furnishings and canopy or four-poster beds. The Guest House has four rooms, three of which are suites and one with an attached greenhouse. It has period furnishings and queen-size canopy, spindle, or iron and brass beds. All rooms have private baths, air-conditioning, writing tables, sofas, or separate sitting areas. A no-smoking inn. Full breakfast served in the elegant dining room. Jane and Paul Harnden, innkeepers. Rates are $78–105, depending on the room and season.

Leighton Inn (433-2188), 69 Richards Avenue, Portsmouth 03801. Open year-round. This 1809 Federal in-town home has three rooms, all with private baths and furnished with antique and period pieces. The comfortable common room has a fireplace. A continental breakfast buffet is served on the screened porch; in winter the kitchen is a cozy spot for starting the day. A short walk to Portsmouth sights. Diane Kelley Teft, innkeeper. Rate is $80.

The Inn at Strawbery Banke (436-7242), 314 Court Street, Portsmouth 03801. The most in-town of Portsmouth's B&Bs, this circa-1800 house, with a more recent addition, has seven individually furnished rooms, all with private baths, some with queen-size beds, others with a double and a single. Upstairs and down common rooms with TV and books. Bright cheery breakfast room overlooks the gardens of the John Langdon mansion. A short walk to Strawbery Banke and Prescott Park. Full breakfast. Sarah Glover O'Donnell, proprietor. Rates are $65–90.

The Captain Folsom Inn (436-2662), 480 Portsmouth Avenue, Greenland 03840. Open year-round. Built in 1758 and overlooking one of the state's prettiest village greens, this mansion has been lovingly restored and furnished with antiques by Faith and Bob McTigue. The six rooms, some with shared baths, have antique double beds (two rooms with twins), and handmade quilts. There are comfortable sitting rooms, a wraparound screened porch, and an outdoor pool. Afternoon tea and after-dinner refreshments served. A full breakfast is served in an elegant dining room, where, by advance reservation, Faith also serves dinners she has cooked in her large colonial kitchen with its huge open-hearth fireplace and beehive oven. Rates are $65–85.

Rock Ledge Manor (431-1413), 1413 Ocean Boulevard (Route 1A), Rye. Open all year. On the ocean with views to the Isles of Shoals, this Victorian has four rooms, two with private baths, two with half baths and a shared full bath. Have a full breakfast and relax on the veranda overlooking the sea. Convenient to Portsmouth and beaches, good biking from the door. $60–85, depending on the room and season.

MOTELS

Portsmouth is well supplied with motels, most of which are located on Route 1 south of the city and at the traffic circle intersection of I-95, Route 1 bypass, and Routes 4/16 (Spaulding Turnpike). Among these motels are the **Anchorage Inn** (431-8111), **Comfort Inn** (433-3338), the **Meadowbrook Inn** (436-2700), **Howard Johnson Hotel** (436-7600), and **Holiday Inn** (431-8000). Downtown on Market Street (Exit 7 off I-95) is the new, full-service **Sheraton Portsmouth** (431-2300) with 148 rooms, restaurant, and lounge, within walking distance to everything.

WHERE TO EAT

Portsmouth is famous for its numerous quality restaurants, the best collection of fine dining north of Boston. Several of the top restaurants are located in the Old Harbor area where Bow, Ceres, and Market streets intersect. Here six-story warehouses, the largest structures north of Boston when built in the early 1800s, have been remodeled as restaurants and shops. A treat for summer and early fall visitors are the five outdoor decks located here on the waterfront, open for lunch and late into the evening (until the legal closing for serving liquor). Everything from snacks to sandwiches and full dinners is available on the decks. View the tugboats and watch large oceangoing ships pass, seemingly within an arm's length.

DINING OUT

Blue Strawbery (431-6420), 29 Ceres Street, Portsmouth. Open year-round, Tuesday through Thursday seating at 7:30 P.M., Friday and Saturday at 6 and 9 P.M., Sunday at 6 P.M. Winter: same hours, but closed

Tuesday and Wednesday. Confirmed reservations only. When this restaurant opened in 1970, even its three partners wondered if Portsmouth could support an expensive gourmet restaurant seating only 40 diners, located in a warehouse on the city's rundown waterfront. Today the restaurant is nationally known; one of the original three partners is still there; and the place is justly recognized as one of the catalysts that began Portsmouth's cultural and fine-dining renaissance in the 1970s. All diners are seated at the appointed hour and served a six-course, eight-item dinner. The rich American gourmet menu changes daily but always offers a choice of fish, meat, and fowl entrées. For a representative meal, begin with hot wine broth supreme soup and an appetizer of sea scallops wrapped in bacon with Benedictine and shallots served with toast rounds, then cleanse your palate with a mixed salad and sage blue-cheese dressing. Your entrée might be half a roast duck with a green peppercorn honey-lemon glaze; halibut, sea scallops, and shrimp baked in a duxelles Pernod lime butter; or beef Wellington with a lightly gingered Madeira wine and mushroom sauce. Vegetables are potatoes roasted in garlic and duck stock with zucchini and carrots sautéed in olive oil. Dessert is always the same: strawberries with sour cream and brown sugar. Fine wine and cocktails are also offered. $39 prix fixe; no credit cards.

The Dolphin Striker (431-5222), 25 Bow Street, Portsmouth. Lunch 11:30–2, Sunday brunch 11:30–3, dinner 5:30–9:30 and until 10:30 on Friday and Saturday. On the waterfront in a restored warehouse, this is an old favorite specializing in stuffed haddock, shrimp scampi, grilled salmon served on spinach with a fresh herb mayonnaise. Filet mignon and breast of chicken sautéed with garlic topped with a wine glaze with tomatoes and green onions round out the menu. On the lower level is the Spring Hill Tavern, a lounge with entertainment and walls covered with photographs and other items celebrating the city's maritime heritage. Moderate.

Porto Bello (431-2928), upstairs at 67 Bow Street, Portsmouth. Open Tuesday through Saturday 4:30–9:30 P.M.; reservations appreciated. No smoking. This small, second-floor restaurant specializes in traditional Italian cuisine representing many regions of the country. The four-course menu offers the chance to sample a variety of dishes. Begin with antipasto, then try a pasta dish, followed by meat or seafood, and a rich dessert. Moderate.

Oar House (436-4025), 55 Ceres Street, Portsmouth. Lunch 12:30–4:30, Sunday brunch until 3:30 P.M., dinner 5–9 P.M. and until 10 P.M. on Friday and Saturday. Valet parking. Another longtime favorite on the waterfront in a remodeled warehouse and our choice for chowder. Seafood is featured and varies from bouillabaisse and baked stuffed lobster to broiled scallops and Oar House Delight, a sautéed combination of shrimp, scallops, and fresh fish topped with sour cream and crumbs baked in the oven. Sirloin with peppercorn sauce, rack of lamb, veal Barbara (medallions of veal dipped in egg wash, sautéed in butter, and topped with fresh crab, avocado, cheddar cheese, mushrooms, and green onions), and a daily varied chef's chicken are also offered. The Oar House deck, open Memorial Day through early autumn, is our favorite for picturesque riverside relaxing and dining. Moderate.

Sakura (431-2721), 40 Pleasant Street, Portsmouth. Lunch Tuesday through Friday 11:30–2:30, dinner 5–10. Fine Japanese dining with a long sushi bar where you can watch the chefs prepare creative and tasty portions of sushi and sashimi. We like the dinner box (the meal is actually served in a portioned box) with miso soup, rice, salad, and a choice of two portions of sushi, sashimi, tempura, teriyaki, and other specialties. Although fish is featured, there is beef and chicken teriyaki and sukiyaki (slices of beef and vegetables with soup and rice). For a special occasion, try "Heaven"—12 pieces of sushi and 2 rolls with 10 pieces of sashimi. Japanese beer, sake, and plum wine also served. Moderate.

Chiangmai Thai Restaurant (433-1289), 128 Penhallow Street, Portsmouth. Lunch Monday through Saturday 11:30–2:30, dinner Monday through Thursday 5–10, Friday and Saturday until 10:30, Sunday 5–9:30. An extensive menu of authentic Thai cooking with curries and both hot and spicy dishes. (Their dinner soups are not recommended for first timers!) Chicken, seafood, and vegetarian entrées are featured in a variety of colorful dishes; some entrées allow you to create your own meal. Tasty Thai spring rolls and hot and sour soups highlight the appetizers. Lunch specials, appetizers from $3.25, all entrées under $13.95.

The Metro (436-0521), 20 Old High Street, Portsmouth. Open for lunch Monday to Friday, dinner Monday to Saturday, closed Sunday. Located just off Market Square, this is one of the city's most elegant restaurants, with rich paneling and a brass rail in the bar. Begin with New England clam chowder or have Caesar salad tossed at your table, then try veal Metro (medallions of veal sautéed with mushrooms and Marsala, baked with mozzarella cheese), or seared scallops with pesto on lemon black-pepper linguine, or fresh lobster served differently daily. Also filet mignon, roast lamb, roast pork, swordfish, or shrimp. Homemade desserts include their own ice cream and fresh fruit sorbets. Handicapped accessible, parking adjacent. Lunch inexpensive, dinner moderate to expensive.

Café Mirabelle (430-9301), 64 Bridge Street, Portsmouth. Open daily for lunch and dinner, Sunday brunch. A cozy restaurant with many plants and large windows. Begin with grilled shrimp and scallops Chesapeake style (on a bed of fresh tomato, garlic, and olive oil *coulis*) or baked Brie, then select *gateau de poulet* (chicken, smoked bacon, leeks, and goat cheese in phyllo dough served on a bed of tarragon cream sauce), *magret* of duck (duckling pan sautéed medium rare and served with balsamic vinegar and raspberry demiglaze), roast pork or lamb, grilled fish, or Alfredo du jour (vegetables in a Parmesan cream sauce over fettuccine). Some of these same entrées are also served at lunch along with specialty sandwiches, burgers, salads, soups. Lunch inexpensive; dinner moderate; also a Sunday through Thursday four-course special dinner for $10.95.

Café Avellino (427-2453), Route 1A, Rye. Open Tuesday to Thursday 5–9:30; Friday and Saturday until 10, Sunday 11–9. Fine Italian dining in a romantic room with candlelight and Chianti. Begin with one of seven appetizers, for example *mozzarella in carrozza* (slices of mozzarella in bread lightly fried in egg batter and served with marinara), then select a main entrée with veal, chicken, steak, fish, or pasta. *Frutti di mare* is assorted seafood and vegetables in a red or white sauce served over pasta; *lasagna melanzane* is thinly sliced eggplant layered with mozzarella and Parmesan cheese in a light tomato sauce; *vitello alla Ricardo* is sautéed veal, porcino mushrooms, sun-dried tomatoes, and cream finished with a brandy demiglaze. Special fish, pasta, and ravioli dishes change daily. Entrées moderately priced.

The Carriage House (964-8251), 2263 Ocean Boulevard, Rye Beach. Open daily at 5 P.M. Built as a restaurant in the 1920s, the Carriage House has been a favorite gourmet restaurant for two decades, offering quality Continental cuisine at reasonable prices. Specialties are an Indian curry of the day, Sicilian *coniglio* (rabbit), and grilled rack of lamb. There are six pasta entrées, salmon poached with vermouth in parchment, sole Oscar, seafood-stuffed chicken, veal Marsala, roast duckling, Szechuan-spiced chicken or beef, and several steaks. Appetizers, salads, and desserts to match. Prices moderate.

Joseph's at Rye Harbor, Oyster Bar and Grill (964-8080), Route 1A, Ocean Boulevard, Rye. Open all year, dinner 5–10, Sunday dinner 12–9, Sunday brunch 12–4. Joseph is one of the seacoast's best-known chefs, and this newly opened restaurant continues his reputation for fine dining. Oysters and littleneck clams are available on the half shell; then select an appetizer such as pan-fried calamari with hot cherry peppers. Entrées range from dry-aged New York sirloin and steak *au poivre* to chargrilled swordfish, scallops gratinée, grilled salmon, and grilled, roasted free-range chicken. A specialty is grilled jumbo lobster. All courses are à la carte, including vegetables. Entrées moderate to expensive.

Saunders at Rye Harbor (964-6466), off Route 1A at Rye Harbor, Rye. Open all year. Luncheon 11:30–3, dinner 5–10, Sunday 12–9. This well-known restaurant has offered harborside dining for over 75 years. The specialty is lobster (boiled, baked, or broiled stuffed), served fresh from saltwater tanks, but the diverse menu also includes chicken with lemon and herbs, Saunders jambalaya (lobster, crab, scallops, shrimp, sausage, vegetables, and creole sauce over rice), a variety of fresh fish, and land 'n' sea (prime rib with shrimp, scallops, or sautéed lobster). Saunders' deck overlooking picturesque Rye Harbor is one of the best spots on the seacoast for a relaxing lunch or beverage. Live music on the deck on

Sunday afternoons in July and August. On Friday nights from January to April the dining room is a supper club with live entertainment. Dinner prices moderate, lobster dishes at market price.

EATING OUT

☞ **Yoken's Thar She Blows Restaurant and Gift Shop** (436-8224; 1-800-552-8484), Route 1, Portsmouth. Open daily 1–8 P.M.; closed Monday, except on holidays and from Memorial Day to Columbus Day. The state's largest and best-known family restaurant, Yoken's, with its spouting-whale neon sign, has become a landmark since it first opened with a 20-stool counter and 99-cent dinners in 1947. Today it seats 750 and serves more than two million meals a year. Reasonable price for a complete dinner has been the trademark here since it first opened. Lobster; fried, baked, and broiled seafood; entrée salads; and roast beef, roast turkey, liver and onions, and a few Italian dishes provide something for everyone. The 20-entrée luncheon menu, served until 4 P.M., offers choice of appetizer, dinner, beverage, and dessert, all for under $6. The Spouter Gift Shop, open at 11 A.M., with 20,000 square feet of space, is the largest in New England, selling everything from tourist mementos to fine china, collectible glass and figurines, handbags, cards, T-shirts, and more. Menu prices range from $4.95 to $11.50.

Poco Diablo (431-5967), 37 Bow Street, Portsmouth. Open daily 11:30 A.M.–9 P.M., Friday and Saturday until 11 P.M. A popular Mexican restaurant with a dining room overlooking the tugboats and the river. Most any Mexican item you can imagine is here (sizzling fajitas a specialty), plus Mexican beer, sangria, and the best margaritas in the city. Their riverside deck opens as early as April and closes when it's too cool to use it (usually mid-October). Sunday brunch served when the deck is closed. Prices range from $5.95 to $11.25. Lighter menus served in the downstairs bar and on the deck.

The Stockpot (431-1851), 53 Bow Street, Portsmouth. Open daily 11 A.M.–11:30 P.M. This is a popular spot on the waterfront for lunch and light dinners. Homemade soups, a variety of salads and sandwiches, broiled scallops, and paella (a Spanish dish with chicken, mussels, crab, shrimp, chorizo, and veggies served over rice). A small deck, open whenever it is warm enough to use it, offers relaxing dining with views past the tugboats and up the river. Most dinners are under $10.

The Ferry Landing (431-5510), Ceres Street, Portsmouth. Open April 15 through September from 11:30 A.M.–9 P.M., the bar until 11 P.M. Light seafood dishes of many varieties, sandwiches, chowder, and burgers are served in this 100-year-old building, which was the original ferry landing before the bridges were built. Hanging out over the river, right beside the tugboats, the place is mostly a deck. It is always busy (especially the bar on weekends) during its summer season. Prices range from $3.50 to $12.50.

The Portsmouth Brewery (431-1115), 56 Market Street, Portsmouth.

Open daily 11:30 A.M.–12:30 A.M., dinner 5–11 P.M., Sunday brunch 10–2. A lively spot best known for its microbrewery producing six varieties of beer, including Old Brown Dog, Pale Ale, Amber Lager, and Black Cat Stout, and seasonal special ales. The menu is varied and includes soups, salads, chili, pizza, hot and cold super sandwiches, and nine dinner entrées. Special dishes, changing monthly, might include spicy poached salmon or Thai curry chicken. Lunch is inexpensive, dinners $8.95–13.95. Jazz for Sunday brunch and live music in the downstairs lounge Wednesday through Saturday.

Szechuan Taste and Thai Café (431-2226), 54 Daniel Street, Portsmouth. Open daily 11:30–10; Friday and Saturday until 11; Sunday brunch buffet. A popular downtown restaurant with a large Chinese menu, now serving Thai dishes as well. Moderate.

The Press Room (431-5186), 77 Daniel Street, Portsmouth. Open Tuesday through Saturday 11:30 A.M.–1 A.M., Sunday 5–11 P.M. Inexpensive, light meals, nachos, pizza, salads, soups, and sandwiches. The food is good and served with draft beer, but the music is the best in the city. This Irish-style pub has live music most of the time. Acoustic guitar, folk, Irish, blues, jazz, and country sounds in an informal atmosphere make this a popular spot with the locals.

Celebrity Sandwich (433-7009; 433-2277 is the hot line for daily specials), 171 Islington Street, Portsmouth. Open Monday through Saturday. Over 100 sandwiches, each named for a different celebrity, served in an art deco dining room. Box lunches, soups, salads, and desserts, too. Eat in or take out.

House of Commons (436-8451), 44 Bridge Street, Portsmouth. Open Monday through Saturday 11–6, until 7 on Friday, Sunday 12–3. This eatery and tea room features many British specialties including meat pies, ploughman's lunch (fruit, cheese, salad, and rolls), salads, and gourmet sandwiches. Choose from several varieties of tea served in your own pot. Plain and fruit scones and crumpets served all day, high tea from 2 until closing. Inexpensive.

The Golden Egg (436-0519), 960 Sagamore Avenue, Portsmouth. Open daily 6 A.M.–2 P.M. The seacoast's favorite breakfast spot, famous for its varied and unusual omelets, especially the changing daily specials written on the blackboard. Try one, and lunch will not be necessary. There is great granola, hot oatmeal, fresh-baked muffins, pancakes, French toast (with whipped cream and raspberry sauce), plus eggs any way you want them, including three variations of eggs Benedict. The trick on the weekend is to get there after the golfers and before the late sleepers! Homemade soups and sandwiches for lunch.

Ray's Seafood Restaurant (436-2280), Route 1A, Rye. Open daily, 11 A.M. to closing. For more than 30 years a seacoast favorite, specializing in fresh fried seafood, lobsters, and steamers. Dinners and lobsters cooked to go. Moderate.

LOBSTER

Lobsters are a seacoast specialty and almost every restaurant has a lobster dish. Live or cooked lobsters to go are available at several places. The **Sanders family of Portsmouth** is the largest local dealer. Their main lobster pound is at 54 Pray Street (436-3716), open Monday through Saturday 8 A.M.–6 P.M., Sunday 10 A.M.–5 P.M.; and they own the **Old Mill Fish Market** (436-4568) nearby at 367 Marcy Street, open daily 9 A.M.–6 P.M. The latter shop has all kinds of fresh fish in addition to live or cooked-to-order lobsters. Sanders can ship a mini-clambake anywhere in the country.

ICE CREAM AND SNACKS

Ceres Street Bakery (436-6518), 51 Penhallow Street, Portsmouth. Open 5 A.M.–5:30 P.M., Saturday until 4 P.M., closed Sunday. Our favorite bakery. Has the best bran muffins anywhere but also brioches, croissants, cookies, and a host of breads, cakes, and other diet busters. A few mostly vegetarian soups, quiches, and salads are served for lunch. Many local restaurants serve Ceres Street Bakery breads.

Café Brioche (430-9225), 14 Market Square, Portsmouth. Open daily 7 A.M.–6 P.M., Sunday until 5 P.M. A French-style bakery with breads and sweets, serving homemade soups and a variety of sandwiches plus espresso and cappuccino. Especially popular in the warm weather when their outside tables give Market Square a European-plaza atmosphere.

Annabelle's (431-1988), 49 Ceres Street, Portsmouth. Open for lunch until late in the evening, closed in the winter. Imaginative and tasty handmade ice cream comes from this popular local landmark. At the request of George Bush, they made and served red, white, and blueberry at the White House for the Fourth of July. Sandwiches and soups are secondary to the sundaes, sodas, banana splits, and hand-scooped cones.

Lagos' Big Scoop, Route 1, Rye. Open from spring through early fall. They have a long list of ice cream flavors (and huge portions) and also serve fried foods and sandwiches.

ENTERTAINMENT

Portsmouth's busiest performance season is September through May except for the Prescott Park Arts Festival, which has theater and music outdoors July through mid-August. The night scene is active all year with nearly a dozen restaurants and lounges offering live music weekends and several other nights: jazz, blues, big band, folk, and country music.

Seacoast Repertory Theatre (433-4472; 1-800-639-7650), 125 Bow Street, Portsmouth. Professional theater in the former Theatre-by-the-Sea building. Several different plays are performed September through early June. Also presents youth theater.

The Music Hall (436-2400), 28 Chestnut Street, Portsmouth. Built in 1878 as a stage theater and, more recently, revised as a movie theater, this restored hall has been acquired by a nonprofit group and offers a variety of dance, theater, and musical performances throughout the year. Tony Bennett, Pearl Bailey, international classical music, Sesame Street, magic shows, bluegrass, and jazz are among the recent offerings. Three to four events are held each month September through May.

Pontine Movement Theatre (436-6660), 135 McDonough Street, Portsmouth. This nationally known company with guest performers offers four productions between fall and spring but no summer performances.

The Press Room (431-5186), 77 Daniel Street, Portsmouth. Open Tuesday through Saturday 11:30 A.M.–1 A.M., Sunday 5–11. This Irish-style pub has lots of live music. Acoustic guitar, folk, Irish, blues, and country sounds in an informal atmosphere make this a popular spot with the locals. Friday 5–8 P.M. is a country jam session, the only thing like it in the state, when an ever-changing group of amateurs and professionals joins a group of regulars playing country tunes, sea chanties, and music from the British Isles. Sunday night is jazz with many nationally known performers sitting in with the best house combo in the region.

SELECTIVE SHOPPING

Portsmouth is filled with small shops, especially in the waterfront area bounded by Market, Bow, and Ceres streets. Here rows of mostly Federal-era brick buildings have been remodeled and restored and now offer the shopper everything from upscale clothing and antiques to natural foods, candles, secondhand clothing, jewelry, a fine children's shop, and even a Christmas shop. With several of the city's best restaurants and five waterfront decks, this is a busy and lively place until late in the evening since several shops are open until 11 P.M.

ART GALLERIES

New Hampshire Art Association-Robert Levy Gallery (431-4230), 136 State Street, Portsmouth. Open all year, Wednesday through Sunday 11–5. Members exhibit oils, watercolors, acrylics, photographs, prints, and sculpture.

BOOKSTORES

Two great antiquarian bookshops are located in Portsmouth near Strawbery Banke. The **Book Guild of Portsmouth** (436-1758), 58 State Street, specializes in maritime and local books while the **Portsmouth Book Shop** (433-4406), 110 State Street, leans more to travel and literature.

SPECIAL EVENTS

Summer in the seacoast offers a nearly unlimited number of special events and activities for people of all ages. Check with local chambers of commerce, the Portsmouth Children's Museum, and Strawbery Banke for varied activities.

February: Annual **African-American Heritage Festival** (929-0654), seacoast-wide. Various organizations sponsor a variety of musical, art, theater, and other events in several seacoast locations. Coordinated by the Blues Bank Collective.

April: **New England Blues Conference** (929-0654), Portsmouth. Blues workshops, conferences, and concerts.

Late May: **Prescott Park Chowder Festival.** For a small donation, sample the city's best restaurant chowders.

Second Saturday in June: **Market Square Day** (436-5388). The center of Portsmouth is closed to traffic, and the streets are lined with booths selling food, crafts, and much else; as many as four stages provide continuous entertainment. More than 30,000 people jam the city for this free event. A popular clambake is held the night before at the Port Authority; purchase tickets in advance.

Mid-June: **Blessing of the Fleet,** Prescott Park. The Piscataqua River's commercial fishing fleet, with all boats decorated, converge for a water parade and traditional blessing for safety at sea.

Late June: **Portsmouth Jazz Festival** (436-7678), Harbour Place. A fundraiser for local charities. On the waterfront with two stages offering continuous music from noon until 8 P.M., showcasing New England's best performers.

Fourth of July through mid-August: **Prescott Park Arts Festival,** on the waterfront, Portsmouth. A daily variety of outdoor theater and musical events beginning late in the afternoon. Come early, bring a picnic basket, and spend a few enjoyable hours at one of New England's most popular summer festivals. Donation requested. There also are art shows and art classes for kids.

Mid-July: **Bow Street Fair** (433-7272). A colorful weekend street fair with music and booths selling food and crafts.

Mid-August: **Candlelight house tour** (436-1118). An evening tour of Portsmouth's historic houses, all lit by candles.

Labor Day weekend (Saturday and Sunday): **Blues Festival** (929-0654), Harbour Place, Portsmouth. Blues on an outdoor, waterfront stage, in several bars, and a gospel blues church service.

Columbus Day weekend: **Chili Cook-off,** Prescott Park. Sample the culinary skills of the city's best chili cooks.

Early December: **Candlelight Stroll** (433-1100), Strawbery Banke. See Strawbery Banke's historic houses by candlelight.

December 31: **First Night** (436-5388). A nonalcoholic, family-oriented New Year's Eve celebration held annually in Portsmouth, late afternoon to midnight, with a wide variety of musical performances and other entertainment. Most events are held in downtown churches.

Hampton, Hampton Beach, Exeter, and Vicinity

The two large towns of Hampton and Exeter were founded in 1638, but while Hampton has retained little of its architectural heritage, Exeter's streets are lined with old houses and buildings.

Hampton was mostly a farming town with a small, beachside tourist community until the beginning of the twentieth century, when trolley lines connected the town and its beach with the large cities of the Merrimack Valley and cities in Massachusetts and central New Hampshire. The low-cost trolley transportation made the beach an inexpensive and accessible place for the urban workers to bring their families for a day or a week. A large casino was built to provide these visitors with games to play, lunches, and ballroom dancing, though not on Sunday. Hampton is now a fast-growing residential community. After World War II the population was about 2,300; now it is 12,000 people, and much of its open space has been developed except for large family holdings west of I-95. Hampton has a small shopping district, a movie complex, and several good restaurants.

While Hampton village was small, **Hampton Beach** boomed and became one of the leading family vacation centers in New England. Now, during peak summer weekends, more than 200,000 people jam the beach, nearly covering the long, sandy oceanfront from one end to the other with blankets. Young people seem to predominate, but there are plenty of older folks who would not consider any other place to spend their summer free time. The center of the beach is still the 90-year-old Casino, complete with restaurants, shops, penny arcades, and a nightclub offering nationally known entertainment.

Often overlooked by residents and visitors alike is **Hampton River.** Here 3 family-owned fishing party businesses have been serving the public for more than 50 years, recently expanding to include whale-watches and some sight-seeing cruises. Surrounding the harbor is the state's largest salt marsh, once thought of as a swamp and earmarked to be dredged and filled to create a lagoon-style seasonal home development. Although Hampton Beach development has pushed into the fringes of this 1,300-acre marsh, people now know the importance of the tidal wetlands as a source of nutrients for a wide variety of marine life, and the marshes are protected from filling by state and local laws. As a green space, the marsh is used by fishermen, boaters, and bird-watchers; and it is about the only piece of ground left on the seacoast that still looks today about the way it was when settlers arrived in the 1600s. South of the Hampton River bridge in Seabrook, bordering the marsh, is a recently protected sand dunes natural area.

West of Hampton is **Exeter,** with a much larger commercial area, one of the country's premier prep schools, and a marvelous architectural diversity that reflects its past as a center of government and education as well as the economic success of its residents, especially when Exeter had a small industrial center. Exeter also has about 12,000 people, although its growth has been slower than Hampton's. During the Revolution, Exeter was the center of government and many of its citizens were promi-nent participants in the rebellion. Several historic houses open to the public date from those times. The falls of the Squamscott River helped to power textile mills, giving the community an important economic base. Exeter is also the center of Rockingham County government, with a courthouse and the offices of the registers of deeds and probate, two places well used by visitors seeking genealogical information.

Phillips Exeter Academy, one of America's leading preparatory schools, has a list of alumni whose members have achieved the highest levels of prominence in literature, business, and government service. Prominent visiting lecturers in all fields, who often speak or perform for the public, and a fine art gallery contribute to the cultural and edu-cational atmosphere of the town and the area. Many students from sur-rounding towns attend the academy as day students. The academy's buildings reflect nearly three centuries of architectural design, contrib-uting to the great diversity of Exeter's cityscape. The academy is in the center of the **Front Street Historic District,** where a wide variety of architectural styles ranges from colonial residences of the 1700s to twentieth-century institutional buildings. Notable are the First Parish Meetinghouse, a variety of Victorian buildings, and the contemporary Phillips Exeter Academy Library designed by Louis Kahn.

Historic Route 1 bisects the seacoast from south to north. On the Massachusetts border is **Seabrook,** home of the controversial nuclear power plant, a huge facility that pays most of the town's taxes, giving Seabrook one of the lowest property tax rates in the state. The low prop-erty tax, combined with the state's lack of a sales tax, has fueled com-mercial development in Seabrook; most of the retail shoppers come from heavily taxed Massachusetts. **Seabrook Beach** is a heavily devel-oped residential area with little public access to the ocean since parking is limited, but many summer homes here are available for weekly rentals.

Seabrook's unplanned growth is in contrast to neighboring **Hamp-ton Falls,** a residential community whose many farms are now being subdivided into exclusive home developments. North of Hampton along Route 1 is **North Hampton,** also primarily a residential community but with a large colony of summer mansions along the coast in the section called Little Boar's Head.

Adjacent to Exeter, and extending west to the Merrimack Valley, are mostly small towns, once farming communities, now being heavily developed with residential subdivisions. Among these towns are **Stratham, Kensington, Epping, Newfields, Brentwood, Fremont, Danville, the Kingstons,** and **Nottingham**. Since New Hampshire has no sales or income taxes, and once had low property taxes, the seacoast area towns have been rapidly growing into popular bedroom communities for people who work in the Boston area, many of whom grew up in Massachusetts but moved north to escape the congestion of urban life for the peaceful countryside. The attractions of the seacoast and its proximity to metropolitan Boston are certain to make the area a magnet for new residents and for visiting tourists.

GUIDANCE

Hampton Beach Area Chamber of Commerce (926-8717; outside NH 1-800-GET-A-TAN), 180 Ocean Boulevard (winter and business office: 836 Lafayette Road, Box 790), Hampton 03842. A seasonal information center is open daily at the state park complex in the middle of Hampton Beach. The chamber runs daily summer events at the beach and seasonal programs in Hampton village and publishes a free accommodations and things-to-do guide.

Exeter Area Chamber of Commerce (772-2411), 120 Water Street, Exeter 03833.

GETTING AROUND

By car: Route 1 (Lafayette Road) between Seabrook and Portsmouth is lined with strip development and on summer weekends is especially snarled with traffic. If you want to go to Hampton Beach just to see the sights and the latest bathing suits, we do not recommend the weekends when traffic entering the beach from I-95 or Route 1A south may be backed up for several miles.

By taxi: **Coastal Taxi** (926-4334) serves Hampton and the adjacent towns. **Exeter Cab** (778-7778) serves Exeter and offers Logan Airport service.

By trolley: A seasonal trolley service serves Hampton Beach, running the length of Ocean Boulevard, with stops in Hampton village and the North Hampton Factory Outlet Center.

PARKING

Municipal and private parking lots behind Hampton's main beach, just a short walk to the sand, are the best places to park if you are not staying at beach lodgings. The parking meters are part of the state park and are closely monitored, so keep them filled with quarters to avoid an expensive ticket.

MEDICAL EMERGENCY
  Exeter Hospital (778-7311), 10 Buzzell Avenue, Exeter 03833; offers 24-hour emergency walk-in service. Exeter ambulance: 772-1212. Hampton ambulance: 926-3315.

TO SEE

Fuller Gardens (964-5414), 10 Willow Avenue, Little Boar's Head, North Hampton 03862. Open early May through mid-October, 10 A.M.–6 P.M. One of the few remaining estate gardens of the early twentieth century, this beautiful spot was designed in the 1920s for Massachusetts Governor Alvin T. Fuller, whose family members still live in many of the surrounding mansions. There is an ever-changing display here as flowers bloom throughout the season. Among the highlights are 1,500 rose bushes, extensive annuals, a Japanese garden, and a conservatory of tropical and desert plants. Nominal fee charged.

The Science and Nature Center at New Hampshire Yankee (1-800-338-7482), Route 1, Box 300, Seabrook 03874. Open 10–4, Monday through Saturday, March through Thanksgiving; Monday through Friday the rest of the year. The Seabrook Nuclear Power Plant has been a continual controversy since it was proposed more than 20 years ago. The best off-site view of the plant is from Route 1A at Hampton River, where it rises above the marsh on the western shore of the estuary. After demonstrations, construction delays, lengthy and complex legal proceedings, and the bankruptcy of its prime owner, the plant finally began producing power in 1990. The center is its educational facility and has a variety of exhibits about electricity, nuclear power, and the environment, especially the nearby marsh habitat, which you can view on a mile-long nature trail. Free admission.

Tuck Memorial Museum, 40 Park Avenue, Hampton 03842. Open mid-June to mid-September, Tuesday through Friday 1–4 P.M. The museum of the Hampton Historical Society has local memorabilia, especially related to early families, the trolley era, and Hampton Beach. Adjacent is the **Hampton Firefighter's Museum** with a hand engine, other equipment, and a district schoolhouse, all restored. Free admission.

Exeter Historical Society (778-2335), 47 Front Street, Exeter 03833. Open Tuesday, Thursday, and Saturday 2–5 P.M. Located in the former 1894 town library, this society has research materials for local history and genealogy, artifacts, photographs, maps, and changing exhibits.

Atkinson Historical Society, 3 Academy Avenue, Atkinson 03811. Open Wednesday 2–4 P.M. The Kimball-Peabody Mansion houses a collection of local artifacts plus extensive genealogical materials.

Fremont Historical Society, Route 107, Fremont 03044. Open second and fourth Sundays, June through August. The museum was the town library, built 1894, and measuring only 20 feet by 14 feet. From 1965 until 1981 it was a first-aid society, lending its rural residents hospital equipment.

Sandown Historical Society and Museum (887-6100), Depot Road, Box 33, Sandown 03873. Open Sunday 1–5 P.M., May 30 through November 1. Local history and railroad artifacts; wheelchair access plus rest rooms, picnic tables, and a nearby public swimming beach.

Stratham Historical Society (778-0403), Portsmouth Avenue, Stratham 03885. Open 2–4 P.M. on Thursday and the first Sunday of each month. The former Wiggin Library has recently been acquired by the historical society. Local artifacts and some genealogical materials.

HISTORIC HOMES

American Independence Museum (772-2622), One Governor's Lane, Exeter 03833. Open Tuesday through Sunday 10–4, May through October 15; Tuesday and Saturday 12–4, November through April 15. Also known as Cincinnati Hall, and one of New Hampshire's most historic buildings, part of this place was constructed in 1721. It served as the state treasury from 1775 to 1789 and as governor's mansion during the 14-year term of John Taylor Gilman. The Gilman family members were political and military leaders during the revolutionary war, when Exeter served as the revolutionary capital. The house has recently been restored, and its diverse exhibits revitalized.

Gilman Garrison House (436-3205), Water Street, Exeter 03833. Open June through October; Tuesday, Thursday, Saturday, and Sunday 12–5 P.M. A portion of this house was built in 1660 as a garrison out of log construction, but most of the building reflects the eighteenth century with fine paneling, especially in the governor's council meeting room. Owned by the Society for the Preservation of New England Antiquities. Fee charged.

Moses-Kent House (772-2044), corner of Pine and Linden streets, Exeter 03833. Open Tuesday 1–4 P.M., June through September. Built in 1868, this is the finest of three mansard-style houses in the historic district. The continuous occupation by one family is responsible for the remarkable state of preservation in the house. In the museum rooms are original furnishings from 1903.

HISTORIC SITES

Fremont Meetinghouse and Hearse House, Route 107, Fremont. Open May 30 and the third Sunday in August or by appointment; inquire locally. Built in 1800, this unique meetinghouse, unaltered since it was built, contains an early choir stall, slave pews, and twin porches. The Hearse house, built in 1849, has a hand engine built in that same year.

Sandown Meeting House, Fremont Road, Sandown. Owned by the Old Meeting House Association, this is the finest meetinghouse of its type in New Hampshire, unaltered since it was built in 1774. Its craftsmanship and architectural details are nationally recognized. One can easily imagine our colonial ancestors listening to a fire-and-brimstone sermon from the preacher standing in the wine-glass pulpit. Open on Old Home Day, the second Sunday in August, or by appointment. Inquire locally about a caretaker.

Old South Meetinghouse (Route 1) and **Boyd School** (Washington Street), Seabrook 03874. School opens the third Sunday in August. The old school has exhibits and local artifacts relating to salt-hay farming, shoemaking, and decoys used for bird hunting. The church is open by appointment only; inquire locally. Built in 1758, it has been altered inside.

SCENIC DRIVE

Follow Route 1B through New Castle, then connect with Route 1A through Rye, North Hampton, and the north end of Hampton Beach. The ocean is in view most of the way, and there are several restaurants and beaches. This route is also popular with bicyclists.

TO DO

Hampton Beach is an attraction by itself. The center of activity is the Casino, a historic rambling complex with arcades, gifts, specialty shops, and a nightclub. Adjacent is the Casino Cascade Water Slide. Nearby, along the half-mile business district, is the first seasonal McDonald's plus other fast-food takeouts, more arcades, shops, gift and clothing stores, miniature golf, and bike rentals. Across the street from the Casino is the ocean and the state park complex with the chamber of commerce information center, rest rooms, first-aid room, and the bandstand, which offers free concerts and talent shows throughout the summer. There are fireworks on the Fourth of July and every Wednesday night during July and August, the heart of the season; but many places are open weekends beginning in April, then open daily in June. A few of the newer, larger hotels are open year-round, and some have restaurants and lounges.

BOAT EXCURSIONS

Smith and Gilmore Fishing Parties (926-3503), Route 1A, Hampton Harbor, Hampton 03842. All-day fishing, on Wednesday and weekends April through Columbus Day; daily half-day trips May through September; night fishing June through August; weekend evening whale-watches July and August; fireworks cruises, Wednesday July through August. Three modern, speedy vessels provide a variety of fishing experiences for this longtime family-operated business. A specialty is a 24-hour overnight fishing trip, 50–90 miles offshore to New England's famed fishing banks; limited to 40 people. A great trip for seeing offshore birds. The business also has a bait-and-tackle shop, rowboats to rent for Hampton Harbor flounder fishing, and a restaurant.

Al Gauron Deep Sea Fishing (926-2469), State Pier, Hampton Harbor, Hampton 03842. All-day fishing, spring through Columbus Day; two

Hampton Beach

half-day trips daily; bluefish trips; night fishing; fireworks cruises on Wednesday night; evening whale-watches. Four modern, speedy vessels including the 90-foot *Northern Star*. Family-owned and-operated for half a century.

Eastman's Fishing Parties (474-3461), Seabrook Harbor, Route 1A, Seabrook 03874. Open April through October. All-day fishing, half-day and evening fishing, morning and afternoon whale-watch trips. The oldest of the family-operated fishing businesses on the seacoast. The Lucky Lady fleet has three modern, speedy vessels. Tackle-and-bait shops plus a full restaurant and pub with patio dining overlooking the harbor.

GOLF

East Kingston Country Club (642-4414), Route 107, East Kingston 03827. Open whenever weather conditions permit. 18 holes, cart rentals, snack bar.

Exeter Country Club (778-8080), Jady Hill Road (off Portsmouth Avenue), Exeter 03833. Open May through October. Eighteen holes, cart rentals, full bar, and food service.

Sagamore-Hampton Golf Course (964-5341), North Road (off Route 1), North Hampton 03862. Open mid-April to mid-December. Eighteen holes, no motorized carts allowed, pro shop, light food, and beverages. A busy recreational course, inexpensive.

ORCHARDS, PICK-YOUR-OWN, FARMERS' MARKETS

Applecrest Farm Orchards (926-3721), Route 88, Hampton Falls 03844. Open year-round, but the best times to visit are in May when apple blossoms cover the hillsides and in late summer through fall when apples are harvested. Pick your own apples and enjoy weekend festivals in season. Also pick your own strawberries, raspberries, and blueberries. Cross-country ski in winter. The Apple Mart and gift shop are open year-round.

Raspberry Farm (926-6604), Route 84, Hampton Falls 03844. Open first week in July through October. The state's largest grower, with 6.5 miles of rows in which to "pick your own" blackberries, black raspberries, and raspberries plus a farm stand with vegetables and baked goods.

Farmers' Markets are open Tuesday afternoon June through October at Sacred Heart School, Route 1, in Hampton and Thursday afternoon at Swasey Parkway in Exeter. Local homegrown vegetables, herbs, flowers, fruit, and plants plus baked goods and crafts.

RACING

Seabrook Greyhound Park (474-3065), Route 107, Seabrook. Open daily. Pick your racing greyhound and make a wager while watching this fast-paced sport. Lounge, snack bars, restaurant, and free parking.

GREEN SPACE

North Hampton State Beach, Route 1A, North Hampton. A long, sandy beach with lifeguards, parking meters, and rest rooms. A small takeout food stand is across the street. For one of the area's most scenic walks, park here, then proceed north past the old fish houses, which are now summer cottages, and a beautiful garden maintained by the Little Boar's Head Garden Club. A sidewalk follows the coast for about 2 miles to the Rye Beach Club.

Hampton Central Beach, Route 1A, Hampton. From the intersection of High Street and Route 1A, south through the main section of Hampton Beach, is a state park with lifeguards, metered parking, and rest rooms. North of Hampton's Great Boar's Head the beach is much less crowded but at high tides has limited sand area. South of Great Boar's Head the beach is opposite the business and touristy area of the beach. At the main beach is an information center, first-aid room, and rest rooms. Opposite the Ashworth Hotel is the New Hampshire Marine Memorial, a large statue and plaque dedicated to state residents in the merchant marine service who were lost at sea during World War II.

Hampton Beach State Park and Harbor, (925-3784), Route 1A, Hampton. Fees charged for the beach and boat launching in season. At the mouth of Hampton River is this long, sandy beach with some of the state's last oceanfront sand dunes. There is a bathhouse with dressing rooms, rest rooms, and snack bar. Twenty RV sites with full hookups are available on a first-come, first-served basis. Across Route 1A is the harbor, with a boat-launching ramp and the state pier.

Swasey Parkway, off Water Street, Exeter. A small park beside the

Squamscott River in downtown Exeter. Picnic area and playground.

Sandy Point Discovery Center (868-1095), Depot Road, just off Route 101 in Stratham. Part of the Great Bay National Estuarine Research Reserve (see "Durham, Dover, and Vicinity," *Green Space*), this new education center is set up primarily for school groups, but it has self-guiding nature trails, including a 1,600-foot boardwalk on the tidal marsh and a launch ramp for car-top boats.

Kingston State Beach, off Route 125, Kingston. Open weekends beginning Memorial Day, daily late June through Labor Day. A small state facility on Great Pond, this park has a long, sandy beach, picnic groves, and a bathhouse. Fee charged.

LODGING

Hampton and Hampton Beach offer a nearly unlimited number of rooms for tourists, especially at the beach and along Route 1 between Hampton Falls and North Hampton. The **Hampton Beach Area Chamber of Commerce** (see *Guidance*) provides a guide to most of the motels, but we have listed a few lodgings below. Both Hampton and Seabrook beaches have numerous cottages to rent by the week, and Hampton also has many condo units. Seabrook Beach is just residential and thus quieter than Hampton, and its beach is uncrowded. For information try **Harris Real Estate** (926-3400), **Preston Real Estate** (474-3453; 926-2604), or **Famous Door Real Estate** (926-4403).

BED & BREAKFASTS

Inn at Elmwood Corners (929-0443; 1-800-253-5691), 252 Winnacunnet Road, Hampton 03842. Open year-round. Located 1.5 miles from the beach, this B&B was a boardinghouse at the turn of the century. Its energetic owners have renovated and remodeled the place into an attractive and comfortable village inn. All the rooms have queen-size beds and are furnished country-style with stenciling, handmade quilts, curtains, and braided rugs. Five rooms share three baths (robes provided for these rooms); two rooms are suites with full kitchens and private baths. The guest sitting room has a TV and books. Homemade cookies served nightly. John and Mary Hornberger, innkeepers. Full breakfast. Rates are $50–90, depending on season and accommodations.

The Victoria Inn (929-1437), 430 High Street, Hampton. Open year-round. This recently renovated former guest house has six rooms, three with private baths; beds are doubles, queens, and kings; and all rooms have air-conditioning and overhead fans. Two sitting rooms, one with TV, and a glassed-in porch where the full gourmet breakfast is served. Half mile from the beach. Linda and Leo LeBlanc, innkeepers. Rates are $55–95, depending on season and accommodations.

HOTELS

Ashworth By The Sea (926-6762; 1-800-345-6736), 295 Ocean Boulevard, Hampton 03842. The only full-service oceanfront hotel has been a beach landmark and the finest beach lodging since the early 1900s. With the addition of a modern new wing and remodeling of the original hotel, it is now open year-round. Most of its 105 rooms have queen- or king-size beds; others have 2 doubles. There is a lounge with nightly entertainment, three restaurants (see *Dining Out*), indoor and outdoor pools, and private sun decks overlooking the ocean. Summer rates are $95–174; off-season is $55–119; discounts for multi-night stays.

Hampton House (926-1033; 1-800-458-7058), 333 Ocean Boulevard, Hampton 03842. Open year-round. Fifty-one spacious, modern, ocean-front rooms. All rooms have two doubles or a king-size bed, air-conditioning, TV, telephone, private balcony, and refrigerator. On-site parking, elevator. Coffee shop. Summer rates are $105–155; off-season is $50–80.

Oceanside Hotel (926-3542), 365 Ocean Boulevard, Hampton 03842. Open mid-May to mid-October. This turn-of-the-century summer home, located across the street from the ocean, has undergone many changes, but its interior has been maintained and tastefully furnished to reflect its Victorian beginnings. This is not typical Hampton Beach lodging. There are 10 rooms, all with private baths, all distinctly decorated, many with antiques and period pieces, including 2 with canopy beds; a lovely Victorian common room; and 2 porches. Midsummer rates (late June through early August) are $95–110; discounts for multi-night stays and before or after midsummer. Café serves breakfast July and August; complimentary continental breakfast at other times. No smoking.

The Inn of Exeter (772-5901; 1-800-782-8444), 90 Front Street, Exeter 03833-0508. Open year-round. In the middle of the Front Street Historic District, this comfortable, three-story, brick Georgian-style inn and restaurant is owned by Phillips Exeter Academy. The 50 rooms include several family suites, all with TV, radio, and telephones, with new traditional antique and reproduction furnishings. All size beds available. The fine restaurant serves three meals daily and Sunday brunch (see *Dining Out*). Afternoon tea served daily 3–5 P.M. Lounge, living room fireplaces. Rates for two: $72–100; suites from $125.

HOUSEKEEPING UNITS

Seaside Village (964-8204), One Ocean Boulevard, North Hampton 03862. Open May through September, weather permitting. This is about the only place on the New Hampshire seacoast with lodging right on the sand, with no street to cross. There are 19 units, 13 of which are full housekeeping, and 6 motel units (for 2 to 4 people) with only refrigerators and hot plates. Housekeeping guests bring towels and linens and rent Saturday to Saturday. Except for eight new housekeeping units that have private master bedrooms and a loft for the kids, the other units are older and not fancy. Nevertheless, many of the units are rented by the end of one season for the next season to come. Doris Godfrey, host. Housekeeping units are $450–750 per week; motel units are $60–75 per night for two to three people, three-night minimum.

WHERE TO EAT

DINING OUT

Ashworth By The Sea (926-6762; outside NH 1-800-345-6736), 295 Ocean Boulevard, Hampton 03842. Open year-round. A full-service, oceanfront hotel, the Ashworth has been a beach landmark, and its restaurant is the best on the main beach. Six lobster entrées, baked and broiled seafood, and steaks are menu features (dinners range from $9.95). An all-you-can-eat buffet ($12.95) is offered Tuesday through Saturday evening in July and August, the peak beach season.

The Inn of Exeter (772-5901; 1-800-782-8444), 90 Front Street, Exeter 03833-0508. Open year-round. Breakfast, lunch, and dinner served. The moderately priced Continental menu changes four times a year and ranges from fresh loin of venison and veal Roquefort to scampi Provençal and seafood primavera. Sunday brunch, 10–2, is a local favorite.

Ron's Beach House (926-1870), 965 Ocean Boulevard, Hampton. Open daily; lunch and Sunday brunch 11–3, dinner 5–10, lounge open until midnight; deck open Memorial Day weekend through at least Labor Day. Reservations recommended. Considered the best restaurant at this end of the seacoast, Ron's specializes in fish—as many as 14 different varieties are regularly offered, and each can be prepared steamed, baked, blackened Cajun-style, or charbroiled. A favorite entrée is cioppino, a Portuguese stew with lobster, clams, fish fillets, and shrimp; another is Norwegian pasta with salmon and fettuccine of the day. Chicken, veal, and steaks complete the menu. For appetizers there is a raw bar, in-house smoked fish, several salads, and chowders. Sunday brunch ranges from eggs Benedict with lobster to Swedish fruit pancake. Located north of the main section of Hampton Beach, Ron's is on the trolley route. Prices are moderate.

Lamie's Inn and Tavern (926-0330), 490 Lafayette Road, Hampton. Open all year. Breakfast, lunch, then dinner served until 9 Monday to Thursday, until 10 Friday and Saturday; 12–8 on Sunday. Founded in 1931, this is one of the oldest restaurants in the area, and when Route 1 was the main road between Boston and Portland, the place was open 24 hours a day on major weekends. With huge beams, pine paneling, tavern tables, and a large fireplace, Lamie's has a colonial atmosphere, but its menu has a Continental accent to the mostly New England fare. Try fried clams or scallops brochette (placed on a skewer with scallions and bacon), baked lobster pie or beef au poivre with creamy peppercorn sauce, or Shoal's baked seafood delight (clams casino, scallops, scrod, and stuffed shrimp). Also several veal and pasta dishes, plus lamb, dinner sandwiches, a variety of soups and salads. Lunch, complete dinners, or à la carte are all inexpensive to moderate. A 32-room motor inn with colonial decor is attached.

The Widow Fletcher's Tavern (926-8800), 401 Lafayette Road, Hampton. Open Monday through Thursday 11–9, Friday and Saturday until 9:30 (one-half hour later during the summer); Sunday brunch 11–3. This remodeled in-town home is decorated with eclectic folk art and antiques; it has a popular lounge and a diverse menu. Caesar salad supreme is a meal in itself. Try open-flame Thai shrimp as an appetizer; for an entrée, select shrimp and cheese tortellini, swordfish prepared differently daily, English-cut prime rib, roast duck, or grilled pesto chicken. There are many other seafood, beef, and chicken choices. Inexpensive to moderate.

The Starving Chef (772-5590), 237 Water Street, Exeter. Open for lunch, dinner, and Sunday brunch. The chef certainly is not starving here, especially since the recent move from a storefront to the restored eighteenth-century Tilton-Tattersal House. Creative cuisine is the specialty, and it ranges from Greek and Italian to East Indian and Asian entrées with some traditional New England favorites such as broiled swordfish and baked scrod. We like chicken devannandah (Indian spiced chicken and mild sausage with Chinese cabbage, red pepper, onion, eggplant, pea pods, and bean sprouts seasoned with sherry, soy, and chili sauce and served with jasmine rice). There's also roast duck with raspberry sauce, three veal entrées, steaks, rich desserts, and a variety of special coffees. Changing art from local artists adorns the walls. Prices moderate. Special Starving Starving menu at $12.95 or $24.95 for two.

The Half Barn (778-7898), Route 108, Newfields. Open Thursday through Saturday at 6 P.M. Built in 1793, this half barn (built shorter than it is wide) has been restored and turned into an intriguing, antiques-filled restaurant. The menu is not large, but there are nightly specials, including chef's choice chicken and veal dishes. Broiled haddock, roast duckling, rack of lamb, steaks, and broiled scallops en casserole are featured. Prices moderate.

EATING OUT

Galley Hatch (926-6152), Route 1, Hampton. Open daily 11 A.M.–10 P.M., Friday and Saturday until 11 P.M. A large and popular seacoast restaurant with a diverse and reasonably priced menu. Fish, chicken, steaks, pastas, and vegetarian entrées plus pizza, salads, and sandwiches. Many offerings are prepared to be heart healthy. Breads and pastries are made in their own bakery, which is open to the public. Two lounges; light meals served in the lounge until closing. Weekend entertainment. Next door is the Hampton Cinema complex. Prices range from under $8 to $16.

Abercrombie & Finch (964-9774), 219 Lafayette Road, North Hampton. Open daily 11:30–9, Sunday brunch 9–1. Locally popular restaurant and lounge with a large menu ranging from salads, soups, and sandwiches to full dinners. Several vegetarian entrées, plus steaks, quiche of the day, lobster pie, baked scrod, stir fry, and fried seafoods. Dinners $5.95–12.95, New England Sunday brunch buffet (eggs and omelets cooked to order) $6.95.

LOBSTER AND SEAFOOD

Fried seafood, chowder, steamed clams, and lobster in the rough are seacoast specialties. Local favorites include the following places: **Little Jack's Seafood** (926-0444), 539 Ocean Boulevard, Hampton Beach, open late spring through Labor Day. **Brown's Seabrook Lobster Pound** (474-9858), Route 286, Seabrook Beach, open year-round (weekends from mid-November to mid-April). Its screened dining room is on the marsh beside the Blackwater River. **Newick's Fisherman's Landing** (926-7646; 1-800-649-7646), 845 Lafayette Road, Hampton. Open winter and spring Wednesday through Sunday 11:30 A.M. to 8 P.M. or 9 P.M., open daily in the summer and early fall. Fish, clams, scallops, shrimp served deep-fried, broiled, or baked plus lobsters cooked any way you want them. (Also see Newick's in Dover.) Fresh fish market and lobsters packed to travel. Seniors and children's menu.

Lobsters are a seacoast trademark. For live or cooked lobsters, try the **New Hampshire Lobster Company** (926-3424), located at the Smith & Gilmore Pier at Hampton Harbor, open daily 9–5, summer until 6 P.M.; or **Al's Seafood** (946-9591), Route 1, Lafayette Road, North Hampton, open daily. Al's is a lobster pound and fish market with a small seafood restaurant, offering mainly fried seafood, but in warm weather, under a porch they serve "lobster in the rough."

ENTERTAINMENT

Hampton Playhouse (926-3073), Winnacunnet Road, Hampton. Open July and August, Tuesday through Saturday at 8 P.M., Sunday at 7 P.M., Wednesday and Friday matinees at 2:30 P.M., children's shows on Saturday at 11 A.M. and 2 P.M. For over 40 years this theater—in a remodeled, air-conditioned barn—has provided popular summer entertainment, often headlined with well-known stars. Most of the shows are musicals or comedies, with some version of burlesque, complete with risqué comics and dancing girls, a regular summer highlight.

SELECTIVE SHOPPING

North Hampton Factory Outlet Center, Route 1, North Hampton. More than 35 stores offer bargains in clothing, books, records, luggage, footwear, housewares, and gifts.

League of New Hampshire Craftsmen (778-8282), 61 Water Street,

Exeter 03833. Open Monday through Saturday 10–5. More than 200 craftsworkers are members of the league, supplying a wide variety of distinctive handmade items.

Exeter Handkerchief Fabrics and Custom Draperies Co. (778-8564), Lincoln Street, Exeter 03833. Open Monday through Saturday 9–5. A huge selection of yard goods and patterns make this place a "must stop" for the sewers in the family.

SPECIAL EVENTS

Summer in the seacoast offers a nearly unlimited number of special events and activities for people of all ages. Check with local chambers of commerce for varied activities.

Mid-May: **New Hampshire Towing Association Wrecker Rodeo** (926-8717), Hampton Beach. Scores of wreckers parade and compete for prizes.

Early June: **Hobie Cat Regatta** (926-8717), Hampton Beach. A weekend of racing just off Hampton Beach makes a colorful spectacle.

Late June: **Exeter Criterium** (778-0595), Exeter. Bicycle road race through the streets of Exeter.

Late June through early August: **Concerts in the Park** (778-0595), Swasey Park, Exeter, every Thursday.

July and August: **Hampton Beach Fireworks,** every Wednesday night. **Hampton Beach Concerts,** every Sunday at 7 P.M.

Fourth of July: **Kingston Fair**, Route 125, Kingston. A Fourth-of-July weekend country fair.

Mid-July: **Stratham Fair,** Route 101, Stratham. A weekend, agricultural country fair with horse and cattle pulling, midway, children's events, fireworks.

Mid-August: **Annual Children's Festival** (926-8717), Hampton Beach.

September: **Seacoast Seafood Festival** (926-8717), Hampton Beach. Sample a variety of seafoods prepared by area restaurants.

Durham, Dover, and Vicinity

Durham is the home of the University of New Hampshire, and its beautiful campus dominates the center of the town. Paul Creative Arts Center with its galleries, music, dance, and theater and intercollegiate athletics has the most to offer visitors, though these activities tend to happen during the school year, September through May. **Dover,** long an important mill town, is not a tourist center, but it does have a summer arts festival, theater, and several fine restaurants and B&Bs.

GUIDANCE

Greater Dover Chamber of Commerce (742-2218), 299 Central Avenue, Dover 03820.

University of New Hampshire main switchboard (862-1234) can provide details of various events or direct your questions to the proper office.

GETTING THERE

By car: From Portsmouth, follow the Spaulding Turnpike (Routes 4/16) north, then Route 4 west for Durham, or remain on the turnpike and take one of the three Dover exits.

By bus: **C&J Trailways** (431-2424; 742-2990) provides many trips daily connecting Logan Airport and downtown Boston with Dover, Durham, and Portsmouth, New Hampshire; Newburyport, Massachusetts; and Portland, Maine.

GETTING AROUND

By bus: **COAST** (Cooperative Alliance for Seacoast Transportation) (862-1931), local bus transportation connects Portsmouth and major outlying shopping centers with Durham, Dover, Newmarket, Rochester, and Somersworth, New Hampshire, and Berwick, Maine.

MEDICAL EMERGENCY

Wentworth-Douglas Hospital (742-5252), 789 Central Avenue, Dover 03820, has 24-hour emergency walk-in service. Dover ambulance: 911. Durham ambulance: 862-1212.

TO SEE

Woodman Institute (742-1038), 182 Central Avenue, Dover. Open Tuesday through Saturday 2–5 P.M. This three-building complex is Dover's historical museum. The Woodman House (1818) is a research library that has galleries and natural-history and war-related museum rooms. The 1813 Hale House is a historical museum with period furniture. The Damm Garrison, built in 1675, is a unique building that was used as a home and fortress by early settlers. Free.

Durham Historic Association (868-5560; 868-5436), Main Street, Durham. Open September through May, Tuesday and Thursday 2–4; June through August, Monday through Friday 2–5.

Lee Historical Society, Mast Road, Lee. Open first Saturday after Labor Day. Local artifacts, including farm tools, household items, and antique photographs, are housed in an old railroad freight station, moved to this site between the town library and the police station.

New Market Historical Society (659-7420), Granite Street, Newmarket 03857. Open Thursday 2–4 P.M., Memorial Day through Labor Day. The old Granite School Museum has old tools and local artifacts plus photographs of Newmarket mills and shoe shops.

TO DO

Rose City Junction (749-1100), corner of Main and Washington streets, Dover. Open Wednesday through Sunday 6 P.M.–12 A.M. The Old West has arrived on the seacoast with the opening of the largest country-and-western ballroom north of New York City. Located in an old downtown mill, the complex has a 2,500-square-foot ballroom, a restaurant (see *Dining Out*), and an apparel shop. Free dance instruction, live bands on Friday, Saturday, and Sunday nights, and dance workshops two Saturdays per month. $3 cover charge.

Farmers' Market, Welby Drug parking lot, Dover. Wednesday afternoon, June through October. Locally grown veggies and fruits, home-baked goods, and crafts.

GOLF

Hickory Pond (659-6565), Route 108, Durham. Open spring through early fall. This is a nine-hole, par-3 course. Pro shop. Inexpensive.

Nippo Lake Golf Course (664-2030), Province Road (off Route 126), Barrington 03825. Open April through November. Nine holes, cart rentals, full bar and food service year-round; call for starting times on weekends.

Rochester Country Club (332-9892), Route 125, Gonic 03867. Open mid-April to mid-November. Eighteen holes, cart rentals, full bar and food service, and pro shop; call for starting times on weekends.

Rockingham Country Club (659-6379), Route 108, Newmarket 03857. Open mid-April to mid-November. Nine holes, cart rentals, pro shop, full bar and food service; call for starting times on weekends and holidays.

Sunningdale Golf Course (742-8056), Green Street, Somersworth 03878.

Open mid-April to mid-November. Nine holes, cart rentals, full bar and light food.

GREEN SPACE

Great Bay National Estuarine Research Reserve (868-1095), 37 Concord Road, Durham. Great Bay, with some 4,500 acres of tidal waters and tidal wetlands and 800 surrounding upland acres, has been designated as part of the national estuarine research system. Famous for winter smelt fishing, oystering, and waterfowl, the bay is a unique resource in the midst of the rapidly growing towns of the seacoast. Some 23 rare or endangered species, including wintering-over bald eagles, depend on the shallow bay as a refuge. It is an important stop for migrating birds of all species. Its status as a research reserve will help to continue the scientific studies conducted since 1970 by the University of New Hampshire's Jackson Estuarine Lab on **Adams Point.** From Route 108 in Durham, follow Bay Road to Adams Point, where there is a launch ramp and a self-guiding nature trail. Return to Bay Road and follow it south to Newmarket, an especially scenic drive with views across the bay. Just across the bay from Adams Point is the Great Bay National Wildlife Refuge, part of the recently deactivated Pease Air Force Base and not yet open to the public. The public is welcome at the new **Sandy Point Discovery Center** on Depot Road, just off Route 101 in Stratham. Nearby on Route 108 in Stratham is **Chapman's Landing**, a launching site with rest-room facilities. There is another launch ramp in the middle of **Newmarket** on Route 108. Although the bay has a large surface area, its average depth is only 8 feet, making navigation in larger boats a challenge. Some of the Portsmouth tour boats offer fall foliage cruises on the bay and its tributaries. The bay drains through the Piscataqua River, the boundary between Maine and New Hampshire.

Hilton Park is located on Dover Point, bisected by the Spaulding Turnpike. It has a boat-launching ramp, picnic tables, outdoor grills, and play area.

LODGING

HOTELS

The New England Center (862-2800), 15 Strafford Avenue, Durham 03824. Located on the campus of the University of New Hampshire, this contemporary conference center (also open to the public) has 115 rooms, 61 of which are located in the newest of the 2 green, ceramic brick towers that make up the complex. All rooms have wall-to-wall carpet, air-conditioning, TV, and phones, and the new wing has two queen-size beds in each room. All rooms have dramatic views across the campus or into the treetops of this heavily wooded site, and there is daily bus service to Logan Airport in Boston. Breakfast, lunch, and dinner available next door at the Woods Restaurant (see *Dining Out*). Rates are $75–120 but vary by season and accommodations.

BED & BREAKFASTS

Pinky's Place (742-8789), 38 Rutland Street, Dover 03820. Open year-round. Two rooms in this restored Victorian share a bath. Located in a quiet residential neighborhood, it has a cozy living room and a tree-shaded porch. Full gourmet breakfast. Pinky and Bill Kram, hosts. Rates are $50 per room.

The Silver Street Inn (743-3000), 103 Silver Street, Dover 03820. Open year-round. This in-town Victorian B&B was built in the 1880s by a wealthy industrialist. It has been furnished to match the ornate architectural details, such as Spanish mahogany, Austrian crystal doorknobs, Italian slate, and French Caen stone for the fireplaces. Ten rooms (all but one with private bath) have air-conditioning, cable TV, and telephones. One downstairs room is handicapped accessible and has double and queen-size beds. The dining and living rooms and the ornate library are comfortable and have fireplaces. Full breakfast; served in rooms by request. Rates are $59–98.

Highland Farm (743-3399), 148 County Farm Road, Dover 03820. Open year-round. This interesting brick Victorian country house is on the outskirts of the city in a unique pastoral setting. There are nature trails for walking or cross-country skiing along the nearby Cocheco River. Four guest rooms share two baths. Beds include a queen-size with a canopy. Most rooms have a queen-size bed or a double and a single. Common rooms include a living room, library, and the dining room. Furnishings are antiques, enhanced by the unusual woodwork and architectural design of this house. Full breakfast. Rates are $60–65 per night.

WHERE TO EAT

DINING OUT

The Woods Restaurant and Wine Bar (862-2815), 15 Strafford Avenue, Durham. Open year-round for breakfast, lunch, and dinner. Dinner is 5:30–9 P.M., Friday and Saturday until 10 P.M. Sunday brunch 11–2. Part of the New England Center, this is one of the popular restaurants in the region. It's as well known for its fine food as for its distinctive architecture, which features angled walls and huge windows that place diners seemingly in the midst of the surrounding forest. Veal, roast stuffed leg of lamb, Norwegian salmon, and filet mignon are specialties, matched by varied appetizers, such as oysters on the half shell, and rich desserts. Sunday brunch has been called the best in New Hampshire by a statewide magazine. Prices are moderate.

Firehouse 1 (742-2220), 1 Orchard Street (adjacent to the municipal park-

PETER E. RANDALL

Thompson Hall, the administrative center of the University of New Hampshire

ing off the lower square), Dover. Open daily 11:30 A.M.–9 P.M., Friday and Saturday until 10 P.M., Sunday buffet 9 A.M.–1 P.M. Reservations recommended. Housed in a remodeled 1830s firehouse, this is Dover's best restaurant. The dinner menu is quite diverse, featuring steaks, haddock, veal, rainbow trout, fresh pasta dishes, Szechuan chicken, and seafood lo mein. Appetizers include seafood chowder, wonton ravioli, and baked stuffed mushroom caps. The bar is open until legal closing. Lunch is $5–9, dinner $10–15, dinner/comedy night $65 per couple, wine- or beer-tasting dinners $65–75 per couple; Monday and Thursday are pasta nights, $4.99.

Alexander's Italian Restaurant (742-2650), 489 Portland Avenue (Route 4), Rollinsford. Tuesday through Thursday 11:30–9, Friday until 10, Saturday 4–10, Sunday 12–8. This popular restaurant is located just west of downtown Dover. For antipasti select red peppers and anchovies or

eggplant parmigiana, then try calamari with linguine in red sauce, octo-
pus with linguine, or shrimp with garlic and butter on linguine. Meat
entrées range from veal parmigiana and roast veal to chicken cacciatore,
pork chops, and New York strip steak. Also pizza (white with fontina
cheese), lasagna, and fettuccine carbonara. Entrées inexpensive to moderate.

EATING OUT

Newick's Lobster House and Restaurant (742-3205), Dover Point Road,
Dover. Open daily 11:30 A.M.–8 P.M., Friday and Saturday until 9 P.M.,
closed Monday from after Columbus Day until Memorial Day weekend. Fresh fish and lobster right off the boat are the specialties at this
large, very popular restaurant overlooking Great Bay. Not fancy dining,
but you can have deep-fried (in cholesterol-free vegetable oil) fish of all
kinds with combinations of scallops, oysters, haddock, clams, or shrimp.
Portions are huge. For those with lighter tastes, try boiled lobsters,
steamers, or broiled, baked, or stuffed fish dinners. Also chicken, sandwiches, chowders, and lobster stew. Expect a wait at weekend dinner
times. (Newick's Fisherman's Landing in Hampton is also operated by
Jack Newick.) Prices range from $4.50 to $16.95.

The Desert Moon Café (749-1100), at Rose City Junction, corner of Main
and Washington streets, Dover. Open Wednesday through Sunday 5–9
P.M. A Wild West restaurant to go with the country-and-western ballroom. BBQ beef, pork, and chicken, plus baby-back ribs, T-bone steaks,
Pecos chile, High Noon tenderloin fillet, or Ol' Billy Bob's golden fried
chicken. Plus sandwiches, appetizers, and such western beverages as
Texan Tornado, Tallahassee Mule, or Longbranch Mudslide. $6.95–
13.95.

ENTERTAINMENT

✑ **Cochecho Arts Festival** (742-2218), Cochecho Falls Millworks Courtyard,
Dover. Open June through early September. In the center of Dover
beside the Cocheco River is a huge textile mill complex, recently
remodeled into a business center. The courtyard is the location for Friday
night, Wednesday noon, and occasional Sunday evening concerts featuring a variety of regional music groups. Children's concerts and programs
are held Tuesday at noon at nearby Henry Law Park.

✑ **Hackmatack Repertory Theatre** (749-3996), 425 Central Avenue, Dover
03820. Open September through May. The professional cast produces
nine varied shows including Shakespeare, musicals, drama, mysteries,
and popular plays. A six-week summer children's workshop offers lessons
and the chance for the young people to perform. The group runs a
summer theater (207-698-1807) in nearby Berwick, Maine, during July
and August.

SELECTIVE SHOPPING

Calef's Country Store (664-2231), Routes 9 and 125, Barrington. Open daily. Since 1869, five generations of Calefs have operated this old-fashioned country store. Penny candy, Cheddar cheese, maple syrup, Barbados molasses, jams and jellies, pickles and crackers in the barrel, dried beans for baking, hand-dipped candles, pumpkins in the fall, gifts, and more.

Tuttle's Red Barn (742-4313), Dover Point Road, Dover. Open daily 10–6. Tuttles have lived on this site since 1632, making this the oldest continuously operating family farm in America. Once just a seasonal farm stand operating from the large, old red barn, it has been expanded as a market and garden center. In season much of the produce, especially sweet corn, comes from the surrounding fields, but they also have plenty of fresh vegetables and fruit, breads, and cheeses.

SPECIAL EVENTS

June: ✍ **Somersworth International Children's Day,** an all-day event with four entertainment stages including one for children, a crafts fair, food booths, hands-on crafts tent for children, and an activities section for children.

Late June to early September: **Cochecho Arts Festival** (742-2218), Dover. Music and children's programs, several times weekly.

September: **Lee Fair Day,** Mast Road, Lee. A community fair with exhibits, games, and food.

Mid-September: **Rochester Fair,** 72 Lafayette Street. A 10-day fair with a midway, agricultural exhibits, and pari-mutuel harness racing.

Late September through early October: **Apple Harvest Day,** Dover.

II. THE MONADNOCK REGION

Peterborough, Keene, and Surrounding Villages

PETER E. RANDALL

The Old Meetinghouse in Jaffrey Center

Peterborough, Keene, and Surrounding Villages

Mount Monadnock towers a dramatic 2,000 feet above the surrounding roll of southwestern New Hampshire. Not only is the mountain visible from up to 50 miles in every direction, it's as much a part of the dozens of surrounding towns as the steeples on their meetinghouses.

Uplands around the mountain, in turn, rise like a granite island a thousand feet above the rest of southern New Hampshire. Hardy spruce, fir, and birch are the dominant trees, and the rugged terrain has deflected both developers and interstate highways.

Depending on where you draw the line, the Monadnock Region as a whole encompasses some 40 towns, all characterized by narrow roads, quintessential New England villages, and mountain vistas.

A region of rushing streams, this entire area was once spotted with small nineteenth-century mills, and many of these buildings survive. Harrisville, with its two cupola-topped mills graceful as churches, is said to be the country's most perfectly preserved early-nineteenth-century mill village. Larger brick mill buildings in South Peterborough and in Keene now house shops and restaurants, and a half dozen old mills are still producing a wide variety of products: paper, light bulbs, and matchbooks for starters.

Mount Monadnock itself spawned the region's tourism industry early in the nineteenth century. Early settlers had trimmed its lower beard of hardwood and spruce, planting orchards and pasturing sheep between tidy stone walls, right up its rocky shoulders. Then they took to burning the summit. The idea was to kill off the wolves, but the effect was to expose the mountain's bald pate. Once this bare spot was created, alpine flora (usually found only on mountains twice as high) took root, and hikers could enjoy not only the high-altitude landscape but also the spectacular view.

"Grand Monadnock" quickly became a famous freak. By 1823 a shed, the Grand Monadnock Hotel, was selling refreshments just below the summit, and a rival, Dinsmore's Comfortable Shantee, opened high on the mountain a few years later. By the 1850s local farmers and innkeepers had blazed trails up every side of Monadnock, and from 100 to 400 people could be found hiking them on any good day.

In the 1850s the mountain had inspired works by Henry David Thoreau and Ralph Waldo Emerson, and around the turn of the century, Dublin became known as a literary and art colony—writers included Samuel Clemens and Willa Cather, artists included Abbot Thayer, Frank Benson, and Rockwell Kent. In 1908 the MacDowell Colony in Peterborough became one of the country's first formal retreats for musicians, artists, and writers. The region's cultural climate remains rich, expressed through the unusual number of art galleries and musical and theatrical productions.

Most of the nineteenth-century summer hotels around Mount Monadnock are long gone, but a half dozen of the region's earlier stagecoach taverns survive, and over the past few years a couple dozen attractive bed & breakfasts have opened.

So the Monadnock Region is once more a destination area. But even innkeepers will tell you that a resort area it isn't. Residents take pride in the fact that Mount Monadnock is the world's second most heavily hiked mountain (after Mount Fuji in Japan), but everyone wants to keep the region's roads as delightfully little-trafficked as they are.

While Mount Monadnock itself is unquestionably the region's spiritual and physical hub, there's some rivalry between Keene and Peterborough for recognition as its commercial center. In fact they are twin centers: Keene for the western region, Connecticut River Valley towns, and Peterborough for the hillier eastern side of the region.

Keene (population 22,351) is the shire town of Cheshire County, home of Keene State College and the place most residents of southwestern New Hampshire come to go to the movies or the hospital or to seriously shop. Peterborough (population 5,162) prides itself on having "the first tax-supported Free Public Library in the world," on having inspired Thornton Wilder to write *Our Town,* and on serving as home for one of New England's oldest summer theaters and the nation's only marionette theater devoted primarily to opera. It also offers some unexpectedly fine shopping and dining.

The Monadnock Region remains pristine in part because of its location: too near Boston to be generally viewed as a place to spend the night, too far from Manhattan to draw the New Yorkers who tend to get no farther east than Vermont. So it happens that despite its beauty, its ski areas and cross-country ski centers, its hiking trails, biking routes, and wealth of antiques shops, and the quality of lodging and dining, prices are relatively and refreshingly low.

GUIDANCE

The Monadnock Travel Council, composed of the area's four chambers of commerce, publishes a useful brochure/guide to the region, available at all local chambers.

Greater Keene Chamber of Commerce (352-1303), 8 Central

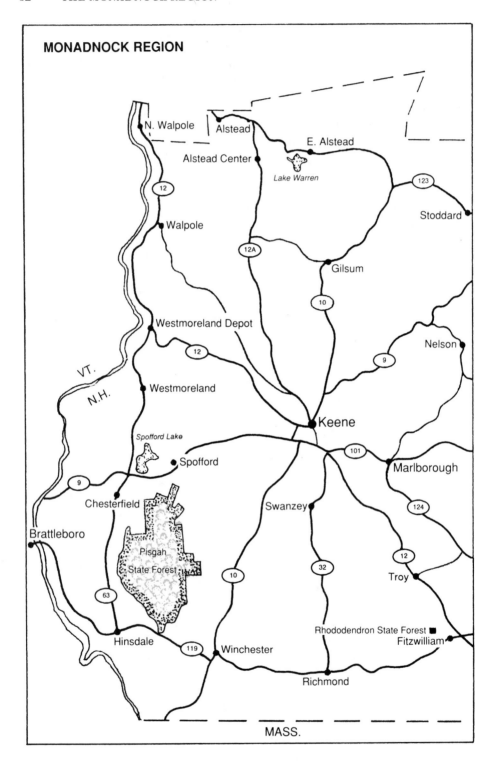

MONADNOCK REGION

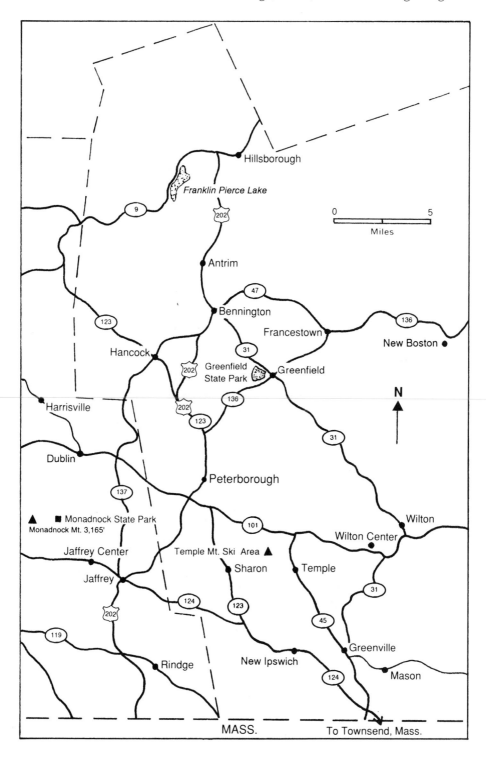

Square, Keene 03431. The Keene chamber's easy-to-find, walk-in office is also a source of brochures and detailed information about the western and Connecticut River Valley sides of the region.

Peterborough Chamber of Commerce (924-7234), PO Box 401, Peterborough 03458, publishes a booklet guide to the 20 central and eastern towns in the region, and the walk-in information center (with a rest room) at the junction of routes 101 and 202 is unusually friendly and helpful.

Hillsborough Chamber of Commerce (464-5858) publishes a brochure and maintains a walk-in information office in one of the Greek Revival Dutton houses on West Main Street.

Jaffrey Chamber of Commerce (532-4549), PO Box 2, Jaffrey 03452, offers local guidance.

GETTING THERE

By air: Jaffrey Municipal Airport (532-7763) is private and Dillant & Hopkins Airport in Keene (357-9835) has scheduled service only from Newark, New Jersey; contact **Colgan Air,** 1-800-272-5488.

By bus: **Vermont Transit Lines** (1-800-451-3292; in Keene 352-1331) stops in Keene (Gilbo Avenue), Troy, and Fitzwilliam en route from Boston to Montreal. The Fitzwilliam stop is right at the Fitzwilliam Inn, putting this exceptional town within reach of car-free urbanites.

GETTING AROUND

By taxi: **Countryside Limo Service** (924-7229).

By car: While the beauty of this region is its winding country roads, it's also worth noting the straightest, quickest routes: **Route 101**, which becomes Route 9 west of Keene, bisects the region from east to west, linking on the eastern end via Route 101A and Route 3 with Boston. By the same token, **Route 202** serves as a north/south spine linking I-89 north of Hillsborough with Route 2 (via Route 140) in Massachusetts. These two high roads cross at the lights in Peterborough, site of the region's prime information center (see *Guidance*). **Route 12** also links with Route 140 to form an obvious route (the one the bus takes) from Boston via Fitzwilliam and Keene to southern Vermont.

MEDICAL EMERGENCY

Cheshire Medical Center (352-4111), 580 Court Street, Keene.

Monadnock Community Hospital (924-7191), Old Street Road, Peterborough, has a 24-hour emergency department.

VILLAGES

Each of these small centers fits everyone's vision of what a New England village should look like. Each has a town clerk, listed with directory assistance, who can furnish further information.

Alstead. There are actually three Alsteads (pronounced "Aalsted"), a grouping of quiet hill towns in the northwestern corner of the region, not far from the Connecticut River. From the handsome old white houses and the Congregational Church in East Alstead, Route 123 dips down by Lake Warren—into Mill Hollow, by eighteenth-century waterpowered Chase's Mill, and by Vilas Pool, an unusual dammed swimming area with an elaborate island picnic spot, complete with carillon. The center of Alstead includes a general store and the Shedd-Porter Memorial Library, a domed neoclassic revival building given by native-son John Shedd. Shedd was an associate of Marshall Field, who gave an almost identical library to his home town of Conway. Turn left at the library and follow Hill Road up into Alstead Center, another hilltop cluster of old homes. It's a quick ride back to Keene via Route 12A.

Dublin. The flagpole in the middle of the village sits 1,493 feet above sea level, making it New Hampshire's highest village center. But the best views (a mile or so west on Route 101) are of Mount Monadnock rising above Dublin Lake. Large old summer homes are sequestered in the greenery around the lake and on wooded heights that enjoy this view. The original offices of *Yankee Magazine* and *The Old Farmer's Almanac* are in the middle of the village, as is the "oldest public library in the United States supported by private funds."

Fitzwilliam. The buildings gathered around this handsome green include an elegantly steepled town hall, an inviting double-porched inn, and a number of pillared and Federal-style homes, one now a library and another a friendly historical society called the **Amos J. Blake House,** open Memorial Day to Labor Day on Saturday 10–4 and Sunday noon–4. The Blake House has a small country store selling local food and crafts and the 13 rooms include a law office, old-time schoolroom, military room, and a vintage 1779 fire engine.

The town hall was first built as a Congregational Church in 1816 and then totally rebuilt after lightning struck it the following year. The spire is four-tiered: a belfry above the clock tower, then two octagonal lanterns topped by a steeple and a weather vane. The facade below is graced by a Palladian window and slender Ionic pillars set in granite blocks quarried right in town. Of course, the bell was cast by Paul Revere. Laurel Lake on the western fringe of town is a favorite local swimming hole, and Pinnacle Mountain, just down the street from the Fitzwilliam Inn, offers inviting walks in summer and cross-country skiing in winter. For a description of **Rhododendron State Park** on the edge of town, see *Green Space*. (Also see *Antiques* under *Selective Shopping*.)

Francestown. Named for Governor Wentworth's wife, Francestown has an almost feminine grace. The white-pillared 1801 meetinghouse stands across from the old meetinghouse at the head of a street lined on both sides by graceful Federal-era houses. One of these is now the George Homens Bixby Memorial Library (closed Monday) with wing chairs, oriental rugs, and a children's story corner that many a passing adult would like an excuse to curl up in. Pick up a guide to local antiques shops in the Francestown General Store. Contra dances are held the second Saturday of every month in the town hall. Crotched Mountain is just up the road (see *Hiking*).

Greenfield. Greenfield is best known for its state park, with Otter Lake as its centerpiece, and for the Crotched Mountain Rehabilitation Center, which sits high on the shoulder of the mountain and has spectacular views. The village itself is appealing. The vintage 1795 Congregational Church is the oldest meetinghouse in New Hampshire, serving both as a church and a town hall. It stands tall with maples in front and a grave-yard curving up the hill behind. It was built from local timber by Hugh Gregg, whose descendant, former governor Judd Gregg, lives here in town. The heart of the village is Carbee's Corner, a mansard-roofed complex across from the church and a source of penny candy, locally made quilts, and Swedish oatmeal cookies. The parakeets are a nice touch and the coffee shop can come in handy.

Harrisville. What excites historians about this pioneer mill village is the uncanny way in which it echoes New England's earliest villages. Here life revolved around the mills instead of the meetinghouse: the mill owner's mansion supplanted the parsonage and the millpond was the common. What excites most other people about Harrisville is its beauty. This little community of brick and granite and white-trimmed build-ings clusters around a millpond and along the steep Goose Creek Ra-vine below. The two mills have cupolas, and the string of wooden work-ers' houses, "Peanut Row," is tidy. Two decades ago when the looms ceased weaving, townspeople worried that the village would become an industrial version of Old Sturbridge Village. Instead, new commercial uses have been found for the old buildings, a few of them appropriately filled by **Harrisville Designs** (see *Special Programs* and *Selective Shopping*), founded by John Colony III the year after his family's mill closed. "Wool has been spun here every year since 1790," he notes.

Hancock. The John Hancock Inn, one of the oldest continuously operating inns in New England, forms the centerpiece of this village, and Norway Pond shimmers on the edge. There's also a green with a bandstand. A number of the aristocratic old homes have been occupied by "summer people" since the mid-nineteenth century. The **Harris Center for Conservation Education** (see *Hiking*) offers guided and unguided walks and workshops.

The Hillsboroughs. One of the region's more confusing but rewarding towns, once you figure out how it fits together. The oldest part of town, **Hillsborough Center**, a photogenic grouping of more than a dozen late-eighteenth- and early-nineteenth-century mansions, is up School Street beyond the **Fox State Forest** (see *Green Space*) from **Bridge Village**, a classic little mill town with an unusual number of surviving wooden nineteenth-century woolen and hosiery mills along the

Contoocook River. Note "The Dutton Twins," two Greek Revival 1850s mansions (one now houses the chamber of commerce) on Main Street. The **Franklin Pierce Homestead** (see *Historic Homes and Museums*) is in **Hillsboro Lower Village** (continue west on West Main Street, which is also Route 9, past the Sylvania bulb plant and turn north on Route 31). There's public swimming at neighboring **Franklin Pierce Lake** (Route 31/9). If you are heading south from here, we suggest continuing on Route 31, the scenic way to Antrim.

Jaffrey Center. Jaffrey itself is a workaday town, but Jaffrey Center, west on Route 124 just east of Mount Monadnock, is a gem. Its centerpiece is a white, steepled meetinghouse built in 1773, the site of the summer lecture series known as the Amos Fortune Forum Series (see *Entertainment*). Willa Cather, who spent many summers in attic rooms at the Shattuck Inn writing two of her best known books, *My Antonia* and *Death Comes to the Archbishop*, is buried in the cemetery here. So are Amos Fortune (1710–1801), an African-born slave who bought his freedom, established a tannery, and left funds for the Jaffrey church and schools; and "Aunt" Hannah Davis (1748–1863), a beloved spinster who made, trademarked, and sold this country's first wooden bandboxes. The Monadnock Inn, in the middle of the village, welcomes visitors year-round.

Mason. Another picture-perfect cluster of Georgian- and Federal-style homes around a classic Congregational Church, complete with horse sheds and linked by stone walls. A historic marker outside one modest old house explains that this was the boyhood home of Samuel Wilson (1766–1844), generally known as "Uncle Sam" because the beef that he supplied to the army during the War of 1812 was branded "U.S."

Nelson. This quiet gathering of buildings includes an 1841 Greek Revival and Gothic Revival church and an early, plain-faced but acoustically fine town hall that's the site of contra dancing every Monday night and the third Thursday of every month, sponsored by the Monadnock Folklore Society (see *Entertainment*).

Stoddard. Sited on a height-of-land that's said to divide the Connecticut and Merrimack river watersheds, Stoddard is known for the fine glass produced in three (long-gone) nineteenth-century factories. The Stoddard Historical Society is open Sunday 2–4 P.M. in July and August.

Temple. The common, framed by handsome old homes and a tavern, is classic. Known for its glass works in the eighteenth century, Temple is now known chiefly for its band, founded in 1799 (see *Entertainment*).

Walpole. A particularly handsome village of large white-clapboard houses, some dating from the 1790s and more from the early and midnineteenth century when Walpole was a popular summer haven with three large inns. Louisa May Alcott summered here and Emily Dickinson visited; current residents include filmmaker Ken Burns. It's now well off the beaten tourist track but offers pleasant lodging, dining, and golf. Summer band concerts are staged on the common, and the historical museum (displaying costumes, dolls, paintings, and tools) is open weekends May through October. The village is set high above Route 12, with long views off across the Connecticut River to southern Vermont. Search out the common with its fine Unitarian Church.

Wilton Center. Just off Route 101, but seemingly many miles away, is a ridge line of grand old houses ranging from eighteenth-century to late-nineteenth-century summer homes. Continue through the center of town, and follow signs to the **Frye's Measure Mill** (654-6581; 654-5345), a red-clapboard and shingled nineteenth-century mill, its works still waterpowered, turning out Shaker-style boxes. The Museum Shop is open May through December 15, 10–5, Saturday 12–5; tours are offered June through October, Saturday, 2 P.M.

TO SEE

Cathedral of the Pines (899-3300), marked from Route 119, a few miles east of Route 202, Rindge. Open May through October, 9 A.M. to dusk. Tall pine trees shelter the simple wooden benches, and the backdrop of the ridge-top stone altar is Mount Monadnock, rising grandly beyond intervening, heavily wooded hills. The roadside farmhouse and its 400 acres had been the summer home for Douglas and Sibyl Sloane for quite some time before the 1938 hurricane exposed this magnificent view, and their son Sandy picked the site for his future home. When Sandy was shot down over Germany in 1944, his parents dedicated the hilltop "cathedral" to his memory. In 1956 the United States Congress recognized it as a national memorial to all American war dead. It's used for frequent nondenominational services and for weddings (performed in the nearby stone Hilltop House in case of rain). On the stone Memorial Bell Tower at the entrance to the pine grove, four bronze bas-reliefs, designed by Norman Rockwell, honor American women. A museum in the basement of the Hilltop House is a mix of religious and military pictures and artifacts, thousands of items donated by visitors from throughout the country. Visitors are welcome to stroll the extensive grounds. Please: no dogs, no smoking, no picnicking (the Annett Wayside Area is a mile up the road). The Cathedral House Bed & Breakfast (899-6790) caters wedding receptions and is otherwise geared to the many weddings in the adjoining "cathedral."

HISTORIC HOMES AND MUSEUMS

The Barrett Mansion (878-2571), Main Street, New Ipswich. Open June to October, Tuesday, Thursday, Saturday, and Sunday noon–5 P.M.; admission $2. One of New England's finest Federal-style rural mansions, built in 1800 as a wedding gift. The bride's father is said to have boasted he would furnish as large a house as the groom's father could build. Both fathers outdid themselves, and it remained in the family until

On the historical marker:

PIERCE HOMESTEAD

The Pierce Homestead was built in
1804 by Benjamin Pierce, a general
in the American Revolution, twice
governor of New Hampshire (1827-28,
1829-30), and father of Franklin
Pierce, the 14th President of the
United States (1853-57). Franklin
Pierce was born in Hillsboro November 23, 1804 and the family occupied
this dwelling shortly thereafter.

PETER E. RANDALL

Franklin Pierce Homestead in Hillsborough

1948. The rich furnishings are mainly Empire and Victorian, and they
offer a sense of the surprisingly early sophistication of this area.

Franklin Pierce Homestead (464-5858), 3 miles west of town near the
junction of Routes 9 and 31, Hillsborough. Open daily in July and August, 10–4, Sunday 1–4; weekends only in June and September to Columbus Day. This is the restored, vintage 1804 home of the fourteenth
president of the United States (1853–1857), the only one from New
Hampshire. The hip-roofed, twin-chimney house was built in 1804 by

Benjamin Pierce, Franklin's father, two-time New Hampshire governor. It is beautifully restored to illustrate the gracious home Benjamin knew as a boy.

Jaffrey Civic Center (532-6527), just west of the junction of Routes 202 and 137, Jaffrey. Open year-round, Monday through Saturday 1:30–5 P.M. A historical society collection with information about past Jaffrey personalities like Willa Cather, Amos Fortune, and Hannah Davis (see Jaffrey Center under *Villages*) and changing exhibits by local artists. Films are also occasionally shown. Note the "Buddies" World War I monument outside carved from one block of granite.

Peterborough Historical Society and Museum (924-3235), Grove Street, Peterborough. September through June open Monday through Friday 10–4; also open Saturday 1–4 in July and August; $1 admission over age 12. An unusually large and handsome facility with an intriguing upstairs exhibit of the town's past products—from thermometers to soapstone stoves. Even a quick visit will help fill in the obviously missing buildings along Grove and Main streets. Note the photos of the big old Tavern Hotel that stood at the head of Grove Street and in the middle of Main Street until 1965; of the Depot; and of the Phoenix Cotton Mill that used to stand near the middle of town. Two of the old mill houses have been preserved behind the museum, one depicting a mill girls' boardinghouse and the other a family home. An early general store and kitchen can be seen in the museum's basement. There is also an extensive research library.

Swanzey Historical Museum, Swanzey. Open daily summer through foliage season, Monday through Friday 10–5 P.M., Saturday and Sunday 10–6. Exhibits include a steam fire pumper made in Manchester and an authentic stagecoach.

Horatio Colony House Museum (352-0460), 199 Main Street, Keene. Open June through mid-October, Tuesday through Saturday 11–4 and Saturday year-round; free. A Federal-era home filled with elegant family furnishings and souvenirs collected by Horatio and Mary Colony from their extensive travels throughout the world. Special collections include cribbage boards, walking sticks, Buddhas, beer steins, paperweights, and thousands of books.

The Wyman Tavern (352-1895), 39 Main Street, Keene. Open June to Labor Day, Thursday through Saturday 11–4: $2. This was the scene of the first meeting of the trustees of Dartmouth College under President Eleazar Wheelock in 1770, and it was from this site that 29 of Keene's Minutemen set out for Lexington in April 1775.

Historical Society of Cheshire County (352-1895), 246 Main Street, Keene. Open Tuesday noon–5 and Thursday 1–4. Primarily an archival library, the building also contains the Monadnock Room, hung with paintings by members of the Dublin art colony, and another room with works by muralist Barry Faulkner.

Thorne-Sagendorph Gallery at Keene State College (358-2719), Keene. An extensive permanent collection of nineteenth-century landscapes and changing exhibits recently resettled in a new museum on campus.

COVERED BRIDGES

The Swanzey area, just south of Keene, boasts one of the densest concentrations of covered bridges in the country. My favorite is the white, red-roofed **Winchester-Ashuelot** built in 1864 across the Ashuelot River just off Route 119 in Ashuelot. The 1830s **Winchester-Coombs** bridge across the Ashuelot is west of Route 10, 0.5 mile southwest of Westport. The 1860s **Swanzey-Slate** bridge across the Ashuelot is east of Route 10 at Westport. The 1830s, 155-foot **Swanzey–West Swanzey** bridge across the Ashuelot is east of Route 10 at West Swanzey. **Swanzey–Sawyer's Crossing**, rebuilt in 1859, bridges the Ashuelot 1 mile north of Route 32 at Swanzey Village. The **Swanzey-Carlton** bridge across the South Branch of the Ashuelot River is east of Route 32, 0.5 mile south of Swanzey Village. Off by itself 1 mile east of Route 202 or 3.5 miles west of Greenfield is the **Hancock-Greenfield** bridge, built in 1937, which spans the Contoocook.

FOR FAMILIES

- **Friendly Farm** (563-8444), Route 101, Dublin. Open daily 10–5 (weather permitting), late April to Labor Day, then weekends through mid-October. Admission. Operated since 1965 by Allan and Bruce Fox, this 7-acre preserve is filled with barnyard animals: cows, horses, pigs, goats, sheep, donkeys, chickens, geese, turkeys, rabbits, and a working beehive. Feeding and cuddling welcome. Don't forget your camera. (Honest, we usually don't go for these things but the photo of Chris's presently 165-pound son feeding a Friendly Farm goat when he was a cute little thing is one of her most prized possessions.)

- **Monadnock Children's Museum** (357-5161), 147 Washington Street, Keene. Open Tuesday through Friday 10–5, Saturday 10–4, Sunday 1–4; $2.50 per person; no child or family rate. The museum, a vintage 1840s house with translucent minerals lit up in its stairs, has a real tree house to climb into and a variety of engaging and changing exhibits based on a specific culture and a lively calendar of special events. It's a great resource for Keene residents (who can pay $40 for an annual membership), but a visitor with three children might feel shortchanged.

TO DO

AIR RIDES

Silver Ranch Airpark (532-8870), Route 124, Jaffrey, offers scenic plane rides and charters.

BICYCLING

The Monadnock Region's many miles of back roads and widely scattered

Mount Monadnock from Dublin Lake

lodging places endear it to bicyclists of all abilities. *Peterborough Bike Tours* by Ann Harrison describes 10 one-day tours ranging from 14 to 50 miles; it's available, along with reasonably priced lodging, from the Hosteling International (see *Other Lodging*). Nine tours in the region are described in *30 Bicycle Tours in New Hampshire* (Backcountry Publications).

Spokes & Slopes (924-9961), 109 Grove Street, Peterborough. Rental bicycles, both mountain and touring bikes.

Tory Pines Resort (588-2000), Route 47, Francestown, rents mountain bikes.

Summers' Backcountry Outfitters (537-5107), West and Ashuelot streets, Keene, rents a variety of bikes.

Monadnock Bicycle Touring (827-3925), Keene Road, Harrisville. Based at the Harrisville Squires' Inn (see *Lodging*), they offer self-guiding on- and off-road tours or jaunts from 10 to 30 miles (from Harrisville). Inn-to-inn tours can be arranged.

The Pedl'ing Fool (464-5286), 77 West Main Street, Hillsboro, no longer rents but sells and repairs bikes and topographical maps showing local tours. Guided tours can also be arranged.

BOATING

Boat rentals are available at **Greenfield State Park** (547-3497), which also offers a boat launch on Otter Lake. Canoes can be rented from **Sum-**

mers' **Backcountry Outfitters** (357-5107) across from the Colony Mill Marketplace in Keene.

Pellitier's Sport Shop (532-7180), Jenny Hill Road, Jaffrey, rents canoes and is a good source for boating and fishing advice and licenses.

Public boat landings can also be found (ask locally to find them) in Antrim on Franklin Pierce Lake, Gregg Lake, and Willard Pond; in Bennington on Whittemore Lake; in Dublin on Dublin Lake; in Francestown on Pleasant Pond and Scobie Lake; in Hancock on Norway Pond; in Jaffrey on Frost Pond; and in Rindge on the Contoocook River, Emerson Pond, Grassy Pond, and Pool Pond. A popular canoe route begins in Peterborough, where the Contoocook River crosses under Route 202, with a takeout at Powder Mill Pond in Bennington. The Audubon Society of New Hampshire's Willard Pond is rich in water wildlife.

CAMPING

Greenfield State Forest (547-3497) offers 252 tent sites, handy to a public beach and nature trails.

Monadnock State Park (532-8862) offers 21 sites. Private campgrounds are listed in the regional brochure (see *Guidance*).

GOLF

Angus Lea (464-5405), Routes 9 and 202, Hillsboro.

Bretwood Golf Course (352-7626), East Surry Road, Keene. Twenty-seven holes, par 72; driving range, pro shop, golf carts, snack bar.

Keene Country Club (352-0135). Eighteen holes, par 72.

Monadnock Country Club (924-7769), Peterborough. A nine-hole course with back tees for the second nine.

Shattuck Inn Golf Course (532-4300), Jaffrey Center. Eighteen holes, public welcome.

Tory Pines Resort (588-2923), Route 47, Francestown. Eighteen holes, Don Ross design, par 72.

Hooper Golf Club (756-4020), Prospect Hill, Walpole. Nine holes. Lodging available.

Woodbound Inn Golf Club (532-8341), Woodbound Road, Jaffrey. Nine holes, rental clubs, par-3 course.

GREYHOUND RACING

Hinsdale Greyhound Park (336-5382; 1-800-NH-TRACK), Route 119, Hinsdale. Year-round racing, dining room, club room.

HIKING

(Also see *Green Space*.)

Mount Monadnock (532-8862), Mount Monadnock State Park. Marked from Route 124, just west of Jaffrey Center. "Monadnock" is said to be Algonquin for "mountain that stands alone," and in the early nineteenth century the name spread from this mountain to designate every solitary prominence in the world that rises above its surroundings. To distinguish it from all others, purists now call this mountain "Grand" Monadnock. It acquired its bald summit in the 1820s (see the introduction to this chapter) and has been one of the country's most popular hiking mountains ever since. In 1885 the town of Jaffrey managed to acquire 200 summit acres, and, with the help of the Society for the Protection of New Hampshire Forests (SPNHF), which still owns 3,672 acres, much of the rest of the mountain was gradually acquired. The state park on the western side of the mountain is 900 acres. There are 40 miles of trails and a half dozen varied routes up to its 3,165-foot summit. First-timers, however, are advised to follow either the White Dot or White Cross trails from the state park in Jaffrey. Detailed information about the mountain is available at a small museum, the Ecocenter. There are also rest rooms, a snack bar, and picnic grounds. The park and its 21-tent campground (see *Camping*) is open year-round, and 12 miles of marked cross-country trails are maintained. Admission is $2.50 for visitors over age 11 on weekends, $2 on weekdays. Dogs are not permitted on the trails.

We strongly recommend buying a copy of the fourth edition of *Monadnock Guide* by Henry I. Baldwin (revised and edited by Martha Carolson, published by SPNHF), an excellent detailed guide to the mountain's history, flora, and fauna, as well as trails. *Grand Monadnock* by Julia Older and Steve Sherman (Appledore Books) is also a must for the mountain habitués.

Harris Conservation Center (525-3394), follow signs from Hancock Village. A nonprofit land trust with 7 miles of hiking trails, including two mountains with summit views; guided hikes and snowshoeing treks offered on weekends.

Crotched Mountain. Three trails lead to this 2,055-foot summit. The start of the Bennington Trail is marked 3 miles north of Greenfield on Route 31. The Greenfield Trail starts just beyond the entrance to Crotched Mountain Rehabilitation Center (also Route 31). The Francestown Trail starts beyond the entrance to the Crotched Mountain Ski Area on Route 47 and follows the easiest ski trail.

Long-distance trails. Hikers are advised to pick up trail maps to the following trails from the Mount Monadnock State Park Ecocenter (see Mount Monadnock, above).

Metacomet Trail. The northernmost 14 miles of a trail that theoretically leads to Meriden, Connecticut. The two most popular sections are Little Monadnock, accessible from the parking lot at Rhododendron State Park in Fitzwilliam, and Gap Mountain, accessible from trailheads on Route 124 west of Jaffrey Center from a spot just east of the Troy town dump. The trail is marked with white rectangles and is famed for its abundance of wild blueberries in July.

Monadnock-Sunapee Trail. The 47-mile northern continuation of the Metacomet Trail, originally blazed in the 1920s by the SPNHF, was reblazed in the early 1970s by Appalachian Mountain Club volunteers. It descends Mount Monadnock on the Dublin Trail, then cuts across Harrisville, through Nelson Village, up and down Dakin and Hodgeman hills in Stoddard, up Pitcher Mountain (a rewarding stretch to do from Route 123 in Stoddard), up Hubbard Hill (prime blueberry picking), then up 2,061-foot Jackson Hill, through Washington, and then up through successive, high ridges in Pillsbury State Park to Sunapee. Sounds great to me, but since I've never done it, be sure to pick up a detailed trail map from the Ecocenter, which displays a bas-relief of the entire trail.

Wapack Trail. A 21-mile ridge-line trail with many spectacular views from North Pack Monadnock in Greenfield to Mount Watatic in Massachusetts. The trail crosses roads about every 4 miles. Just west of Miller State Park on Route 101 turn right on Mountain Road, continue until the road makes a T, then turn right. After the road turns to gravel, look for a trail to the right. You will see a parking area. A 45-minute climb here yields great views.

HORSEBACK RIDING

Honey Lane Farm (563-8078; 1-800-897-8080), Dublin. One of New England's leading equestrian centers, set in 100 acres on the shoulder of Mount Monadnock, specializing in multi-day adult lodging and riding packages Memorial Day through October, four-day inn-to-inn treks ($995–1,195) for experienced riders, and multi-day programs with a combination of lessons and treks geared to ability; $165 per day includes food and lodging (private baths, a pool, Jacuzzi).

Rabbit Hollow (239-4569), Winchester. Trail rides.

Silver Ranch (532-7363), Route 124, Jaffrey. Trail riding; $30 per hour, $50 for two hours; all-day rides with picnic lunch, $160; also carriage and hayrides.

(Also see Morning Mist Farm in "The Concord Area.")

SPECIAL PROGRAMS

Harrisville Designs (827-3996), Harrisville 03450. Weekend and multi-day weaving workshops are held throughout the year; some are simply introductions to weaving, others are specialized and advanced courses. The workshops are held in the Weaving Center overlooking the mill-pond, and lodging is available in nearby B&Bs and in the Cheshire Mills Boardinghouse, built in 1850 for transient weavers. Daylong workshops are also offered; request a schedule.

Sargent Camp (525-3311), Windy Row, Peterborough 03458. A variety of outdoor skills and environmental programs are offered. Housing is in heated cabins and in dorms; family-style meals are served.

SWIMMING

While the region is spotted with clear lakes and ponds, public beaches are jealously town-held; understandably, given their proximity to Boston. Guests at local inns and B&Bs, of course, have access to local sand and water.

Contoocook Lake, Jaffrey. A small but lovely strip of soft sand along

Squantum Road, east of the junction of Routes 124 and 202; take Stratton Road to Squantum.

Franklin Pierce Lake, Antrim, has a public beach.

Greenfield State Park (547-3479), off Route 136 in Greenfield, offers the only truly public beach, and it's mobbed on summer Sundays. $2.50 per person.

Manahan Park, Hillsboro. A town beach that offers swimming on Pierce Lake, just off Route 9 across from the Franklin Pierce Homestead.

Otter Brook Dam and Lake, Route 9 in Roxbury. A man-made lake with lawns and sandy beach.

Pearly Pond in Rindge adjacent to the Franklin Pierce College campus is good for swimming and picnicking.

Spofford Lake, Route 9 in Spofford. Town-run beach.

Surry Mountain Dam and Lake, Route 12A in Surry. Also offers picnicking and a sand beach. Free.

Thordike Pond, near main entrance to Monadnock State Park on the Dublin/Jaffrey Center road. Public beach.

Vilas Pool, just off Route 123 in Alstead. Open in summer Wednesday through Sunday. A dammed pool in the Cold River with bathhouse and picnic area.

Warren Lake in Alstead has swimming from the public landing.

CROSS-COUNTRY SKIING

(Also see *Green Space*.)

Windblown (878-2869), Route 124 west of the village, New Ipswich. Since 1972 Al Jenks has been constantly expanding and improving his high, wooded spread that straddles the Wapack Trail. Thanks to the elevation and northerly exposure, this 40-km network frequently has snow when the ground is bare just 10 miles away. There's an unusual variety to the trails: easy loops from the ski shop and around Wildlife Pond; wooded, more difficult trails up on the Wapack; backcountry trails, including a climb to Mount Watatic (1,800 feet high); and a long, 75-foot-wide open slope for practicing telemarking. Hot soups, sandwiches, and home-baked munchies are served at the shop; warming hut and a couple of cabins. Open daily, weather permitting. Rentals, instruction. $10 trail fee weekends, $9 midweek.

Temple Mountain (924-6949), Route 101 east of Peterborough. A well-maintained network: 20 km of groomed trails that tie into the Wapack Trail's 20 more miles. Snowmaking and lighting on a 1.5-km loop. The trail fee also includes one ride to the top on an alpine lift, but you have to come down the ski trail. Rentals, instruction, telemarking, and guided tours. Food available in the base lodge (see *Downhill Skiing*). Skiers can also use Temple Mountain's nursery. $7 weekends, $6 midweek.

The Inn at East Hill Farm (242-6495), Jaffrey Road, Troy. Some 13 miles of trails meander gently around this property with its great view of Mount Monadnock. Rentals and instruction are offered, and informal meals are available at the inn. A warming hut on the trail, with fireplace and wood stove, serves hot drinks on weekends. $4 trail fee.

Woodbound Inn (532-8341), Jaffrey. Fourteen km of wooded trails, rental equipment. $8 trail fee.

Mount Monadnock State Park (532-8862), Dublin Road from Route 124, Jaffrey Center. A 12-mile, well-marked but ungroomed system of trails web the base of the mountain. Loops from 1 mile to more than 7 miles. Winter camping is also available. The entrance fee is $2.50 per visitor over age 11; $2 weekdays. No dogs allowed.

DOWNHILL SKIING

Temple Mountain Ski Area (924-6949), Temple Mountain, Route 101, Peterborough. One of New England's oldest ski areas, Temple has been in business every winter since 1937. Thanks to its elevation (1,460 feet at the base), exposure, and a natural snow pocket, the skiing is frequently better here than farther north. A quad chair services the summit, accessing all trails. This is a true family area, owned and managed by Peterborough native Sandy Eneguess.

Trails: 17.

Lifts: 1 quad, 1 double, 2 T-bars, 2 rope tows.

Vertical drop: 600 feet.

Snowmaking: 100 percent of the terrain.

Night skiing: 10 trails.

Services: The base lodge is new but still small and friendly, and the West Lodge warming hut is still vintage 1930s. Ski school, rentals, lounge, child care from three months. Kids' Ski School packages, snowboarding.

Rates: $28 for adults, $22 for juniors (age 14 and under) and seniors on weekends; $20 and $18 midweek; $16 for night skiing; multi-day and half-day rates.

SLEIGH RIDES

Silver Ranch (532-7363), Route 124, between Jaffrey and New Ipswich, has a variety of sleighs: large pungs for groups, classic small sleighs for couples and families. A 45-minute ride through the woods. Warm drinks and square dancing can be arranged for larger parties.

Inn at East Hill Farm (242-6495), Jaffrey Road, Troy. Sleigh rides offered along with cross-country skiing to nonguests. (Also see *Lodging.*)

GREEN SPACE

(Also see *Swimming.*)

Pack Monadnock Mountain in Miller State Park (924-7433), Route 101, 3 miles east of Peterborough. For those who don't feel up to climbing Mount Monadnock, this 2,300-foot-high summit is a must. A 1.5-mile winding, steep, but paved road leads to the top where there are walking trails, picnic sites, and views of Vermont to the west and (on a good day)

Boston skyscrapers to the south. Opened in 1891, this was New Hampshire's first state park.

Chesterfield Gorge, Route 9, Chesterfield. Open weekends from Memorial Day, daily from late June to mid-October. Footpaths along the gorge were carved by a stream that cut deep into ledges. The 0.5-mile trail crosses the stream several times, and there are plenty of picnic tables within sound and sight of the rushing water. Nominal fee on weekends and holidays.

Rhododendron State Park, Route 119 west of the village, Fitzwilliam. The wild rhododendron grow up to 30 feet high and are salted along paths above wildflowers and ferns and under pine trees. It is one of those deeply still and beautiful places. These *Rhododendron maximum* bloom in mid-July. A great place for a picnic.

The Heald Tract, off Route 31 near Greenville. A new Society for the Protection of New Hampshire Forests (SPNHF) preserve with fairly flat trails, pond views.

Shieling Forest, off Old Street Road, Peterborough (marked from Route 202 north of town). This is one place you can walk your dog. There are 45 acres of tree-covered ridges and valleys.

Fox State Forest (464-3453), Center Road, Hillsboro. Twenty miles of trails within 1,445 acres of woodland. A detailed booklet guide is available from the state's Division of Forests Office in Concord.

MacDowell Reservoir (924-3431), Peterborough. Good for picnicking, boating, fishing. Maintained by the United States Army Corps of Engineers.

In Keene

Drummer Hill Preserve, off Elm Street. Logging roads wind through 140 acres of public and private conservation land.

Horatio Colony Trust, off Daniels Road (take a left, 0.5-mile west of the blinking light on Route 9). A 450-acre bird and animal preserve with marked trails through the woods.

Bear Den Geological Park, Route 10, Gilsum. Look for a large pull-off area on the right (heading north). This is a geologically fascinating area, with glacial potholes and caves.

Pisgah Natural Area, off Route 63, 2 miles east of Chesterfield. Other than a parking lot and pit toilets, the park has no facilities. It does offer old logging trails (good for hiking and cross-country skiing) and ponds to satisfy the adventurous fisherman. In all, this is a 13,000-acre wooded wilderness.

Society for the Protection of New Hampshire Forests (SPNHF) properties. New Hampshire's oldest and largest conservation organization (the one for actually preserving Mount Monadnock itself), SPNHF owns and manages 16 properties in the region, among them:

    Charles L. Pierce Wildlife and Forest Reservation, Stoddard. From Route 9 in Stoddard, follow Route 123 north approximately 2 miles; turn right at fire station; cross bridge. At junction go straight on dirt road approximately 1 mile; park on lot 300 feet beyond woods road on left. The 5-mile Trout-n-Bacon Trail, beginning at a small brook to the left of the road, offers outstanding views from Bacon Ledge and leads to Trout Pond. This is a 3,461-acre preserve with more than 10 miles of hiking trails and woods roads that wind over ridges, through deep forest, and around beaver dams. SPNHF also owns the 379-acre Thurston V. Williams Forest and the 157-acre Daniel Upton Forest in Stoddard.

Gap Mountain Reservation, Jaffrey. From Troy, follow Route 12 south 0.4 mile; turn left on Quarry Road; continue past transmission lines. At a sharp left in the road, a woods road continues straight uphill. Park and hike up the hill. Near the top, trail markers bear left through the woods. Gap Mountain is a favorite with berriers and picnickers. The 1,107-acre preserve includes three peaks, two bays, and a rich variety of plants and wildlife.

McCabe Forest, Antrim. Route 202 north from Antrim 0.2 mile; right on Elm Street Extension; right to the parking area. This former 192-acre farm has 2 miles of trails, including a fine self-guided interpretive trail, and a variety of wildlife.

LODGING

Keene and Western Monadnock Region

☞ **The Amos A. Parker House** (585-6540), Fitzwilliam 03447. This a standout. It sits right on Route 119 (little trafficked after dark), but the back deck overlooks a deep, formal, and flowery garden with a lily pond and rock fountains; mountains extend the view. All rooms have private baths and some have working fireplaces; all are furnished with carefully chosen antiques. A downstairs suite, great for honeymooners, has its own fireplace, bath, and kitchenette. Guests can relax in the formal front parlor, with its original hearth and wainscoting, or in the informal den, filled with books and magazines. Memorable breakfasts, featuring delicacies like stuffed French bread and soufflés, are served on fine china in the dining room. An enthusiastic transplant from the Midwest, innkeeper Freda Houpt is unusually knowledgeable about the area and an outstanding hostess. $65–85 double. No credit cards please.

✎ **Hannah Davis House** (585-3344), 186 Depot Road, Fitzwilliam 03447. A few doors up from the Amos Parker House, Kaye and Mike Terpstra have turned an 1820s Federal-style house into another outstanding bed & breakfast. Guests enter through a cheery country kitchen and gather in the sunny sitting and breakfast rooms. All three of the upstairs bedrooms have been nicely furnished. My favorite is Chauncey's Room, with the queen-size antique iron bed and working fireplace. There is also a downstairs suite and a loft room in the old carriage house, with a queen-size bed, a sleeper sofa, and cathedral ceiling: a find for families. $55–95 per room includes a full breakfast.

Chesterfield Inn (256-3211; 1-800-365-5515) Route 9, West Chesterfield 03466. The original house served as a tavern from 1798 to 1811, but the present inn is pure 1980s. Vermont architect Rodney Williams has created many windowed spaces, and the 13 guest rooms all have phones, controlled heat or air-conditioning, optional TVs and wet bars; some have working fireplaces, others have Jacuzzis. Innkeepers Phil and Judy Hueber have created a popular dining room (see *Dining Out*) in an entirely separate wing that guests access through the kitchen. The inn is set back from busy Route 9, the main road between Keene and Brattleboro, Vermont. $110–165 double includes a full breakfast.

The Fitzwilliam Inn (585-9000), Fitzwilliam 03447. The three-story, double-porched, Greek Revival inn serves as a centerpiece for one of New England's most handsome towns, and it's the kind of place anyone feels comfortable walking into. We must admit to using this route, as Vermont Transit does, between Boston and Vermont; and we know that we can always duck into the rest room right next to the front desk or use the phone or simply sit for a few minutes in one of the friendly old parlors. Built in 1830, the inn has been in the Wallace family for more than 20 years and involves 4 generations of the family (at age 90 plus, Grannie Wallace still keeps the ledgers and shucks all the beans). Innkeeper Barbara Wallace, a former well-known soprano soloist in Boston, is known locally for her outstanding desserts. The inn offers 28 guest rooms (15 with private bath), simply but nicely furnished, some with stenciling and matching stenciled curtains; some with, others without bath. Families may want to note the large third-floor rooms with shared bath ($40 double, $10 per extra person, cribs $3 extra). Three meals a day are served (see *Dining Out*) and the pub is inviting. Amenities include a summer pool, winter ski-touring, and Sunday afternoon chamber concerts. Since Vermont Transit stops here daily en route from Boston to Montreal, this is one country inn accessible to car-free urbanites. From $40 to $55 double.

Darby Brook Farm (835-6624), Alstead 03602. Open May through October. Alstead is in the little-touristed northwestern corner of the region, handy to canoeing on the Connecticut River; there's also a choice of swimming holes in town. Howard Weeks has summered all his life in this Federal-style house that's been changed little by the three families who have owned it since the 1790s. Weeks has devoted his retirement to maintaining the house and its 10-acre hay field, the apple orchard up above the field, and the berry bushes and sizable vegetable garden just behind the house; also the animals: five sheep and some chickens and turkeys. The two large front rooms share a bath but have working fireplaces, set in their original paneling, and the $50 double ($25 single) rate includes tax as well as a full breakfast, served in the elegant old dining room.

Fitzwilliam Inn

Josiah Bellows House (756-4250; 1-800-358-6302), PO Box 818, North Main Street, Walpole 03608. Built in 1813, this is one of the grander, more historic houses in the region. Set on 6 acres, it is within walking distance of an unusually beautiful village (see *Villages*) and sweeping views off across the Connecticut River to Vermont. There are two large guest rooms with private baths, one of them with an iron bedstead, marble-topped cottage furniture, and a Franklin fireplace. Two smaller rooms share a bath. Innkeeper Lois Ford is best known for her cookies, irresistible confections like the almond crescents, oatmeal raisin, and frosted chocolate cookies she ships worldwide. Ask about the ghost. Tax as well as a full breakfast is included in $60–70 double per room; no smoking or children, please.

The Carriage Barn Guest House (357-3812), 358 Main Street, Keene 03431. Hidden away behind an imposing house, within walking distance of the college, downtown shops, movies, and restaurants, a Civil War–era barn now holds four attractive guest rooms and a cheerful breakfast room. $45 single and $55 double, includes tax as well as breakfast. No children under five years.

Goose Pond Guest House (352-2828), East Surry Road (a right off Court Street, 2 miles north of Central Square), Keene 03431. Zoning precludes a sign out front, but it's hard to miss this big, vintage 1790, white home (on a knoll on the left) with the Sise family name on the mailbox. Just one room (really a suite) is available, $60 single, $65 double, includes a private breakfast. The Bretwood Golf Course (27 holes) is just up the road.

Old Mill House (847-3224), Munsonville 03457. The old cotton mill across the road is gone, but this early-nineteenth-century mill boardinghouse continues to welcome guests. Susan and Walter Lawton offer seven rooms sharing two baths. Granite Lake, good for boating in summer and ice-skating in winter, is just across the road. $45 double, $35 single; extra person in the room, $12. A full country breakfast is included.

Inn at East Hill Farm (242-6495), Troy 03465. The setting is spectacular, on a back road between Troy Village and Route 124, with Mount Monadnock rising above the pond out back. This isn't a fancy place. Over the years (since 1973) David and Sally Adams have created a lively, friendly family resort. The core of the complex is an 1830s inn with a fireplace in its living room and six guest rooms including Grandmother's Attic, a suite with TV. The old-style cottages, all nicely furnished and spanking clean, each have two or three bedrooms, a living room, and one or two baths; Trailsend, a lodge with large, motel-style rooms, overlooks the pond and mountain. Amenities include a basic indoor and two outdoor pools, a lake beach, tennis, shuffleboard, boats, and waterskiing, plus the barn full of animals. The large dining room is usually open to the public for lunch and dinner, but call ahead to make sure it hasn't been reserved by a bus group. Off-season the inn is also frequently filled with square-dancing groups. Winter rates: $56 per person midweek, $144 per adult per weekend with meals.

Peterborough Area

The Birchwood Inn (878-3285), Route 45, Temple 03084. Henry Thoreau is counted among past guests at this small brick inn, built around 1800 in the center of a tiny backroad village. Since 1980 Bill and Judy Wolfe have taken personal pride in both the kitchen and the seven guest rooms (five with private bath), each decorated around a theme and each very different; the one ground-floor room is wheelchair accessible. There's a cheerful BYOB bar and a fine little dining room with 1820s murals by Rufus Porter (see *Dining Out*). Temple Mountain, good for both alpine and Nordic skiing, is just 3 miles away. $60–70 double, breakfast included.

The Monadnock Inn (532-7001), Box B, Jaffrey Center 03454. Sally Roberts has kept the hearths burning, pub humming, and dining room popular for 18 years in this landmark, the last survivor among many right around Mount Monadnock itself (see *Dining Out*). This white, wooden landmark sits in the middle of one of the region's most beautiful villages, giving it a friendly heart. The 15 rooms are homey, nothing fancy, and some bathrooms are shared. $40–45 single, $55–65 double.

Harrisville Squires' Inn (827-3925), Keene Road, Box 19, Harrisville 03450. A roadside mid-1800s house on the outskirts of a gem of a village. Innkeepers Pat and Doug McCarthy go all out for bicyclists, offering a series of self-guided tours—on- and off-road, some loops, some to other inns. The inn is on the Monadnock-Sunapee Trail (see *Hiking*), and Doug will happily provide shuttle service. The comfortable living room with fireplace and five guest rooms (two with private bath) are furnished thoughtfully. Breakfast is a production, maybe pumpkin bread or ginger pancakes with lemon sauce or stuffed French toast. It's served (along with dinner by special arrangement) at the long oak table in the beamed dining room that seems to form the center of the house. In winter Doug regularly grooms the cross-country ski trails that web the 30 acres out back. Pat, a justice of the peace, both performs and caters weddings. $50 for a room with private bath, from $30 with shared bath.

The Benjamin Prescott Inn (532-6637), Route 124, East Jaffrey 03452. This stately 1850s farmhouse has been meticulously restored. Each of the 10 guest rooms has a private bath and charm of its own, and a few of the rooms, especially the upstairs suite with views out across the fields, are ideal for honeymooners. Another downstairs suite is ideal for families. A full breakfast is served in the attractive lemon-colored dining room and sitting rooms. Hosts Barry and Janice Miller are adept at helping guests find their way around on two or four wheels. $60–75 single, $60–130 double.

The Inn at New Ipswich (878-3711), PO Box 208, Porter Hill Road, New Ipswich 03071. A handsome 1790s farm, just far enough away on Route 124. Two of the six guest rooms have fireplaces and all but one (frequently paired to form a suite) have private bath; breakfast is served by the hearth in the old keeping room. Innkeepers Ginny and Steve Bankutt are recent and enthusiastic Monadnock Region converts, happy to steer guests to local sites. Windblown, the area's outstanding cross-country ski center, is a few minutes' drive. $44 single, $65 double; includes a full breakfast. No smoking and no children under age eight, please.

Apple Gate B&B (924-6543), 199 Upland Road, Peterborough 03458. A nicely sited 1832 country house, not far from the Sharon Arts Center, which Ken and Dianne Legenhausen have turned into a delightful B&B. It's all very tasteful yet cozy—the double parlor, fireplace in the living room, and the low-beamed dining room. All four guest rooms, ranging from an inviting single to spacious doubles, have private baths. $55 single, $70 double; includes a full candlelit breakfast. No children under 12 and no smoking, please.

The John Hancock Inn (525-3318; 1-800-525-1789), Main Street, Hancock 03449. Built in 1789, this pillared inn is said to be the state's oldest, but its look is nineteenth century, thanks to two-story pillars and a mansard roof. It sits in the center of a picture-perfect village with Norway Pond shimmering at one end of the street. Owing to a recent change in ownership many rooms have been renovated and the tavern is now very inviting. The 11 upstairs guest rooms (all with private baths) are furnished with canopied and 4-poster beds, braided and hooked rugs, rockers and wing-backs; rooms on the third floor are smaller than the rest. You might want to request the Mural Room, with its walls painted by nineteenth-century artist Rufus Porter. The new innkeepers are Linda and Joe Johnston; no children under age 12. $88–108 double, $10 extra for a port-a-crib.

Woodbound Inn (532-8341; 1-800-688-7770), Woodbound Road, Jaffrey 03452. A rambling old 40-room family- and group-geared inn on a small lake with its own 9-hole golf course, tennis, and cross-country skiing, presently owned by the bank but open for business as usual. $75 per couple for bed & breakfast, $110 per couple MAP.

Auk's Nest (878-3443), East Road in Temple (mailing address is RFD #1, Wilton 03086). Anne Lunt's 1770s cape sits at the edge of an apple orchard. It's filled with books and antiques, offers a low-beamed living room with a Rumford fireplace and two guest rooms. Breakfast is served in a sunny, stenciled dining room or, in summer, on the screened-in porch overlooking a meadow. Walks, tennis, swimming, and skiing are all within minutes. Both pets and children are welcome by prior arrangement. From $40 single to $60 double, full breakfast included.

Eastern Monadnock Region

Stepping Stones Bed & Breakfast (654-9048), Bennington Battle Trail, Wilton Center 03086. This remarkable house, flower- and sun-filled, at once unusually cozy and airy, is hidden away in a bend off a back road to a picture-perfect old village. There are three guest rooms with handwoven rugs and throws and down comforters, two with shared bath. A full breakfast is served in the solar garden room, with its many books and plants. There's also a friendly living room with more books, pillows, TV, stereo, and fireplace, and a weaving room. The gardens are inviting and extensive, reflecting Ann Carlsmith's skill as a landscape designer. Breakfast is served on the porch or terrace, weather permitting. $35 single, $45–50 double; full, imaginative breakfast included.

Final Folly (654-2725), 203 Wilson Road, Wilton Center 03086. This is probably the most elegant B&B in southern New Hampshire. Or maybe all of New Hampshire. George and Joan Andersen, previous owners of a B&B near Philadelphia, have renovated and expanded this classic 1790s Federal-era home on the edge of a classic village. George, an electrical engineer in his previous life, has also added intricate moldings, built-in bookcases and detailing to the library, a formal room with a grand piano, matching in tone and antiques the parlor and dining room. You appreciate these formal rooms all the more because there are informal options: a new post-and-beam wing with a kitchen-cum-family room with fireplace and a glorious high-ceilinged sun porch and patio. There are three guest rooms, all carefully furnished and color coordinated, full of fascinating detail and art. Baths are outside the rooms; the one for the largest room is at the top of the main staircase (robes are provided), and the other two—which can be shut off to form a suite—share. $50–65.

The Inn at Crotched Mountain (588-6840), Mountain Road, off Route 47, Francestown 03043. The 1820s brick inn is now a centerpiece for wooden wings, but it still contains a gracious parlor and two dining rooms. The Pine Room also serves as a small gathering space for guests, away from dinner patrons (see *Dining Out*). The real beauty of this place, aside from its food and the warmth of its longtime innkeepers John and Rose Perry, is its setting at 1,300 feet, high on a ridge with sweeping views. Four of the 14 rooms have working fireplaces and all have private baths. Amenities include a pool, tennis courts, and cross-country skiing. $60–70 double, B&B and midweek rates also available; add 15 percent for service. Dinner is served Friday and Saturday.

The Inn at Maplewood Farm (464-4242), 447 Center Road, PO Box 1478, Hillsborough 03244. The setting is very special: just up a country road from Fox State Forest and just below Hillsborough Center, one of the smallest and most picturesque villages in New England. Jayme and Laura Simoes have turned this classic old farmhouse into a welcoming haven with six guest rooms with private or semiprivate baths. Guests have access to mountain bikes and a canoe (for use on a nearby lake), and your hosts can also advise on nearby cross-country ski trails, swimming, and antiquing (their own barn is a seasonal antiques shop). $55–60 per room.

The Greenfield Inn (547-6327), Greenfield 03047. Vic and Barbara Mangini have turned this Victorian village mansion into a romantic bed & breakfast. There's a wood stove and organ in the parlor, and each of the nine guest rooms has its own name and lacy decor; all rooms are furnished with antiques and 1890s touches. If the Casanova Room with its delicate pink lace spread isn't your style, you can opt for the smaller, less frilly rooms, which are perfectly comfortable (we like Sweet Violet's). Most rooms have TVs and there's a "guest pantry" with sodas and munchies. A cottage is available by the week, and a glass-walled deckhouse lends itself to guest meetings and wedding receptions. Rates are $49–99 per couple with a full breakfast. Ask about packages designed as getaways for working couples.

Ram in the Thicket (654-6440), Maple Street, Wilton (the mailing address is Milford). This large white-clapboard house on a quiet side street in Wilton Village is best known for its fine dining, but there are also nine rather funky guest rooms, one with a working fireplace and private bath, another with a canopy bed and claw-foot tub in its bathroom, and some appealing third-floor rooms (the Apricot Room is small but has a great cottage-furniture bed and dresser) that share a bath and a shower room (yes, a little room that's all shower). $60–75 per room includes an "expanded continental" breakfast served in a cheery breakfast room with hearth studded with Delft tiles.

Maplehurst Inn (588-8000), Main Street, Antrim 03440. This rambling old village inn has had a series of owners in recent years. Each of the 14 guest rooms now has a private bath, and each is comfortably but eclectically furnished. One front room has a canopy bed and working fireplace, but we would pick a rear room to be away from Route 202 (Main Street). There's a combination bar/TV room, a more private living room for guests, and a public dining room that's getting good reviews at this writing. $60–95 per room depending on the room and season.

OTHER LODGING

Hosteling International (formerly AYH) (924-9832), 52 Summer Street, Peterborough 03458. Ann and Peter Harrison have built a new wing onto the back of their old house. Downstairs is a comfortable living room and communal kitchen and dining space; upstairs the rooms are both dorm-style and double, all bunk beds and futon beds equipped simply with pillows or blankets. You can bring your own sleeping bag or rent linen. This is one of a sadly shrinking number of hostels in New England and one of the best. (Also see *Bicycling*.) $14 for nonmembers, $11 for members.

Equestrian Center at Honey Lane Farm (563-8078), Box 353, Dublin 03444. This unusual complex doesn't fit in any other category, but it's a real find for horse lovers, even those who don't know how to ride. $165 per day includes food and lodging (private baths, twin or queen-size beds, a pool, Jacuzzi) as well as riding. (See *Horseback Riding*.)

WHERE TO EAT

DINING OUT

In and Around Keene

Henry David's (352-0608), 81 Main Street, Keene. Open daily 11:30 A.M.–11 P.M. Somehow it's difficult to imagine its namesake—Henry David Thoreau—eating amid this downtown restaurant's glitz and greenery, but Henry's maternal grandmother did build a part of the 1770s house that's now a part of this 1980s complex with its central atrium and skylights. Good for oversized sandwiches at lunchtime and a varied dinner menu ranging from prime rib to Mexican and oriental dishes. Moderate to expensive.

Tony Clamato's (357-4345), 15 Court Square, Keene. Italian trattoria decor and menu with pasta specialties like angel-hair carbonara and homemade lasagna, slightly more ambitious dishes like *zuppa di pesci* and scallops Mussolini. Moderate.

One Seventy-Six Main (357-3100), 176 Main Street, Keene. Open 11:30 A.M.–11 P.M. daily; until midnight Saturday, 10 P.M. Sunday. Brunch Saturday and Sunday 11–4. "Casual gourmet dining," featuring Mexican food on Monday and Tuesday, Italian on Wednesday, seafood on Thursday and Friday. Moderate.

Chesterfield Inn (256-3211), Route 9, Chesterfield. Open for dinner Tuesday through Saturday 5:30–9, nightly in foliage season. Chef Carl Warner has an enviable reputation for imaginative dishes and the setting is an eighteenth-century tavern. The menu changes every two months. Moderate to expensive.

✐ **The Fitzwilliam Inn** (585-9000), Fitzwilliam. Open daily for all three meals. Baskets dangle from the low beams in the old dining room. The dinner menu is fairly traditional, but there may be some surprises like shrimp Baton Rouge (large shrimp in casserole with blue cheese, cream cheese, parsley, and vermouth with a side of pasta) and chicken Florentine. There's also a children's menu and a large selection of luncheon entrées like homemade quiche and Laurel Lake (crabmeat with melted Swiss cheese on a toasted muffin), as well as sandwiches. Moderate.

Major Leonard Keep Restaurant (399-4474), Route 12, Westmoreland. Open for lunch and dinner; closed Tuesday and in February. A traditional go-out-to-eat place for locals, an oldie country atmosphere with an all-American menu ($15–20): baked stuffed shrimp, Yankee pot roast, fresh fish. Moderate.

The Homestead Inn (756-3320), off Route 12, Walpole. A historic house, built in 1752 by Colonel Benjamin Bellows, founder of Walpole, a major stop during pre–Civil War days on the Underground Railroad. Under longtime ownership, a rather staid but dependable restaurant open Thursday through Saturday 5–9; Sunday 12–4. The menu includes veal Oscar, broiled Boston scrod, and coquilles Saint-Jacques. Moderate.

In and Around Peterborough

Latacarta (924-6878), 6 School Street, Peterborough. Open for lunch Tuesday through Friday 11–5, Saturday 12–5; and for dinner Tuesday through Thursday 5–9, Friday and Saturday 5–9:30, Sunday 5–7. Sunday brunch is 11–5. Hiroshi Hayashi is a master chef who has turned an old movie theater into a restaurant. Fans of Hayashi's "nouvelle naturale" cuisine drive up for dinner from Boston (his previous restaurant was on Newbury Street). Fresh, natural ingredients are stressed, and there's little salt or sugar in eclectic dishes like fresh salmon lightly baked with herbs, served with sautéed snow peas, mushrooms, and tomatoes in a fresh dill sauce, and served with salad, fresh vegetables, and rice ($14.75); teriyaki beef, served in traditional teriyaki sauce with sake and soy sauce; or a vegetarian dish of vegetables and tortellini with olive oil, parsley, and pine nuts. Pastas and Mexican dishes are also featured, and both soups and salads are specialties. The wine list is respectable. Dinner entrées are moderate, lunch entrées $4.75–6; a pub menu ($6.25–7.70) is served all evening in the small lounge.

The Folkway (924-7484), 85 Grove Street, Peterborough. Open Tuesday through Saturday 11:30 A.M.–midnight, and for special Sunday concerts. A restaurant and gathering place to hear folk music and jazz during the late 1970s and 1980s, this landmark closed in 1988 when its founder,

Widdie Hall, died of cancer. In the summer of 1990 it was reopened as a nonprofit foundation with the aim of perpetuating the tradition of fine music and food. Right on the main street with parking in the rear, the restaurant is in a Victorian house with garden dining in warm weather—an attractive place to lunch on vegetarian chili with house salad, a chicken teriyaki sandwich, or a Brie turnover followed by fettuccine with shrimp and scallops or vegetable pot pie. Call to inquire about live entertainment and the cover charge. Sunday jazz brunches are an institution. Moderate.

The Boiler House at Noone Falls (924-9486), Route 202 south of Peterborough. Open for lunch Tuesday through Friday 11:30–2, dinner Tuesday through Saturday 5:30–9, and Sunday brunch. Overlooking the waterfall beside the former textile mill in which it is housed, a fairly formal dining room with iffy service but a locally respected chef. Venison, lamb, duck, and sautéed fresh fish are staples. Rack of lamb is a specialty. The wine list is both extensive and expensive. Lunch is also served on an outside terrace in summer. Moderate to expensive.

☞ **The Birchwood Inn** (878-3285), Route 45, Temple. Open for breakfast every day but Monday and for dinner every night but Sunday. BYOB. Innkeeper Bill Wolfe is the chef and with the help of his wife, Judy, makes everything from scratch on the premises—the reason for the low prices and strong local following. The dining room is small (so be sure to reserve ahead), candlelit, and decorated with murals painted in the 1820s by itinerant artist Rufus Porter. The four-course dinner is reasonably priced. The blackboard menu always lists a choice of chicken, duckling (a specialty) or veal, red meat, and fish. Homemade breads, soups, and delectable desserts like chocolate hazelnut torte and Temple trifle are all made daily from scratch. The inn's reasonably priced, multi-course breakfasts are also worth noting for those Mount Monadnock–bound hikers who like getting up and out, eating an hour or so later. Moderate.

The Monadnock Inn (532-7001), Route 124, Jaffrey Center. Rated a shade higher than other local inn dining rooms (in our unscientific, local opinion poll), this homey dining room offers a large selection—from pasta (different each day) to chicken Mandalay (dredged in curried flour, then sautéed with ginger, apricot and orange marmalade, white wine, and butter) to filet mignon. Entrées include soup or salad, vegetable, starch, and breads. Lunch choices are very reasonably priced. Moderate.

Del Rossi's Trattoria (563-7195), Route 137, Dublin. Open Tuesday through Saturday for lunch and dinner. A real find. David and Elaina Del Rossi have created a genuine Italian trattoria in a pleasant old house just north of Route 101. The lunch menu changes daily, always includes a choice of salads, a quiche, and homemade pasta. Dinner might be veal Marsala, spicy shrimp marinara, or haddock Parmesan. Live folk music is featured Friday and Saturday nights. Wine and beer are reasonably priced.

The John Hancock Inn (525-3318), Main Street, Hancock Village. Open for all three meals daily. An eighteenth-century inn with dimly lit dining rooms. Dining reviews at this writing, both for food and service, are mixed. The à la carte menu features entrées like lotus salmon (tournedos of salmon encrusted in the inn's own fresh herbs, pan seared, and finished with lemon dill sauce) and Shaker cranberry pot roast. Moderate to expensive.

Woodbound Inn (532-8341), Woodbound Road, Jaffrey. A pleasant country inn dining room with a moderately priced à la carte menu: traditional fare like grilled New York sirloin and chef's catch of the day and some Italian and vegetarian dishes. Moderate.

Eastern Monadnock Region

The Inn at Crotched Mountain (588-6840), Mountain Road, Francestown. Open for dinner Wednesday through Saturday 6–8:30, weekends only off-season. Reserve. Rose Perry hails from Indonesia, and her native specialties add an exotic touch to the otherwise traditional menu: New York sirloin and eggplant parmigiana. The liver, onion, and bacon gets rave reviews from liver lovers. Nightly specials may include stuffed sole in puffed pastry; swordfish sautéed oriental-style with tomatoes, pepper, and onion; and cellophane noodle soup. The entrée price includes a soup, salad, breads, and vegetable. Moderate to expensive.

Pappa Tecci's Ristorante (588-4477), 584 Francestown Road (Route 47), Bennington. Open daily except Monday 5–9; Sunday 4–8. Stand-up comedy acts on most weekends. All regions of Italy are represented on a menu that runs from *antipasti* like marinated shrimp and deviled lobster cakes through *zuppe* like minestrone with prosciutto and *insalate* like a full antipasto to *primi piatti* like *Agnello fritella* (lamb loins with olives, artichokes, and tomatoes wrapped in a *fritella* with a rich brown sauce) and *saltimbocca Maiale* (fresh pork cutlet layered with prosciutto and mozzarella cheese, finished with Marsala sauce). All entrées come with soup or salad and a side of pasta. Or you can sup on pastas ranging from Alfredo or pesto to cannelloni. House wine is available by the glass and carafe. Decor is pleasant and local reviews are rave. Moderate.

The Maplehurst Inn (588-8000), Main Street, Antrim. Open for dinner and Sunday brunch. Attractive, old-fashioned dining rooms and an à la carte menu featuring classics like filet mignon, roast rack of lamb, and blackberry peppercorn duckling. Moderate to expensive.

Rynborn Restaurant (588-6162), Main Street, Antrim. Open daily for lunch 11:30–3, dinner 5–10; Sunday brunch 11–2, dinner 4–8. Just across the street from the Antrim Inn. An informal, chef-owned restaurant with a series of small dining rooms—the nicest overlooking a pond in back—a friendly pub, and a growing reputation for its live blues. The dinner menu is large and varied. Appetizers include a heaping bowl of mussels poached

Mailboxes in East Alstead

in white wine and garlic, and the two dozen entrées include steak au poivre, veal Marsala, and breaded veal topped with crabmeat, hollandaise, and a touch of Parmesan cheese. Moderate. (Also see *Eating Out*.)

Ram in the Thicket (654-6440), Maple Street, Wilton. Open Friday and Saturday 5:30–9:30; otherwise 5:30–8:30, but always call ahead. A Victorian mansion complete with a crystal chandelier and oriental rugs is the relaxed setting for unusual, memorable meals mixing Greek, Indonesian, Mexican, and Continental dishes, combining ingredients in salads and entrées that may never have been combined before. What's more, they work. You might begin with Plimouth pâté (ground turkey, pork, and smoked ham infused with brandy, studded with hazelnuts, garnished with mustard and fresh cranberry mustard) and dine on lamb Norwich (rack of lamb roasted with carmelized onions and hazelnut crumb crust). There's also an inviting pub room. The owner-chefs are the Rev. Dr. Andrew and Priscilla Tempelman. Dinners include appetizer, salad, homemade breads, and vegetable. Moderately expensive.

Pickity Place (878-1151), Nutting Hill Road (2.5 miles off Route 31), Mason. Open year-round, daily for three lunch sittings: 11:30, 12:45, and 2:00. Reserve ahead because there are just 12 tables in this 200-year-old house. Homegrown herbs are the draw here and you come for "herbal lunches." The set menu changes each month. At this writing it happens to be a bell pepper soup followed by a choice of glazed baked ham or walnut/broccoli crêpe, with a carrot/sprout salad and summer squash, all garnished with edible flowers, washed down with herbal tea. The prix fixe includes homemade breads and dessert. Children can have a Little Red Riding Hood basket of sandwiches and fruit; the reason they come is to see "Grandmother's bed" in the Red Riding Hood Museum. Moderate.

Café Pierrot (654-9411), Pine Valley Mill, Main Street, Wilton Village. Closed Monday, otherwise open for lunch and dinner. This former mill room makes a spacious, informal dining room. Dinner entrées might include chicken with grain mustard and trout almondine, served with salad and vegetable. Also pasta, pizzas, stir fry, and reasonably priced turnovers stuffed with beef, chicken, or spinach and feta. A variety of live folk, jazz, and blues is the big draw Thursday through Saturday; an entertainment schedule is usually available for the upcoming month. (Also see *Eating Out.*)

The Gibson Tavern at Tory Pines Resort (588-2000). The centerpiece 1790 mansion of a golf-resort development, with a handsome dining room that's open for lunch during golf season and otherwise sporadically at this writing.

EATING OUT

In and Around Keene

Lindy's Diner (352-4273), Gilbo Avenue just off Main Street across from the bus station, Keene. Open daily 6 A.M.–9 P.M., until 10 P.M. on Saturday. Arietta Rigopoulos takes particular pride in her chowders and chicken pies.

The Bench Café (357-4353), Colony Mill Marketplace, Keene. Open daily for lunch and dinner. The only real restaurant in the marketplace, it's now a cousin to a trendy Manchester, Vermont, place by the same name. It's attractive, predictable, fairly fast service, and just what you may want if you're shopping or passing through. Entrées include Mexican and Cajun dishes and grilled specialties like baby-back ribs.

The Stage Restaurant (352-9626), 30 Central Square, across from the County Courthouse, Keene. Open Monday through Saturday 7–9:30, Sunday 8–3. A trendy café with a playbill decor and a large menu: burgers, sandwiches, pasta, and salads.

Casey J's, Junction of Routes 12 and 119, Fitzwilliam. Open for all three meals. The former Troy Diner moved down the road in December of 1993 to reemerge as a spiffy new family restaurant, one that promises quickly to become a regional landmark. The rolls, cakes, pies, soups, and lasagna are all homemade and the hams, turkeys, and roasts are home-baked. The shrimp scampi and the chicken teriyaki stir fry, not to mention the Szechuan chicken stir fry, also get rave reviews, as do the fried fish and seafood. Leave room for the key lime pie.

☞ **Monadnock Mountain View Restaurant** (242-3300), Gathering Mall, Route 12, Troy. Open daily, Sunday brunch a specialty. A dependable lunch or dinner stop with the best Mount Monadnock view of any area restaurant. A large bar and lounge. Good sandwiches; dinner entrées like veal Marsala, Cajun-fried shrimp, tortellini. Bargain-priced Sunday brunch.

Gap Mountain Bakery (242-3284), on the Common, Route 12, Troy. Open 8 A.M.–7:30 P.M. The bakery is a source of outstanding morning muffins (made with honey), Sunberry bread and oatmeal cookies, also distinctly less healthy but addictive chocolaty whoopee pies. Subs, pizzas, soups, and salads are served at lunch and gourmet coffees are on tap.

Bread Tree Bakery (357-7588), 28 Washington Street, Keene. Open weekdays, 7 A.M.–6 P.M., Saturday 7 A.M.–5 P.M., Sunday 8 A.M.–1 P.M., a bakery café featuring a bread of the day, homemade soup, and lunch specials.

Barney's (756-3703), Walpole Village. Open 7 A.M.–9 P.M. year-round. A welcome oasis in the middle of this picturesque village, a café with homemade bagels, muffins, and pastries, also soups, "quiche puffs," and a variety of Barney's bagel concoctions like broccoli and cheese, eggplant, and primavera.

In and Around Peterborough

Twelve Pine (924-6140), 1 Summer Street, Peterborough. Open Monday through Friday 11–6, Saturday 11–3. The aroma is a mix of coffee, spices, and baking, which—combined with the array of salads, quiche, calzone, and soups—is something to savor before deciding on any one thing. This tiny house expands the definition of a take-out place, and Daniel and Jan Thibeault have a strong local following. Ideally, this is the source of a classy picnic to be consumed in one of the settings we've listed under *Green Space;* practically, it's a source of outstanding chicken burritos or egg rolls to be consumed on the steps of the neighboring Unitarian Church, by the neighboring Contoocook River, or maybe in the small riverside park behind the library.

The Café at Noone Falls (924-6818), Route 202 south of Peterborough in the renovated Noone Falls mill. Open Monday through Friday 7 A.M.–8 P.M., Saturday 9–4. Quick, delicious, and fun, one of the most popular eating spots around. One whiff of the stuffed croissants and you know this is no ordinary fast-food place; soups, breads, pastries are all made from scratch and the salads are good, too. There's usually plenty of seating space at the garden café–style tables.

✏ **Aesops Tables at the Toadstool Bookstore** (924-1612), 12 Depot Square, Peterborough. Open 8:30–4 weekdays, 10–3 Saturday. Oilcloth-covered tables and mismatched chairs fill an inviting corner of this outsized bookstore, a former A&P. The blackboard menu lists sandwiches and café fare like bagels, raspberry squares, and Brazilian chocolate cake. There's a play corner for small fry and a choice of gourmet coffees on tap.

The Peterborough Diner (924-6202), Depot Street, Peterborough. Open Monday through Saturday 6 A.M.–9 P.M., Sunday 6 A.M.–1 P.M. A 1950s green-and-yellow diner featuring homemade soups, pies, daily and nightly specials, wine, beer. Choose a counter or wooden booth.

Nonies (924-3451), Grove Street, Peterborough. Open from early morning to 2 P.M. Doughnuts made daily, full breakfasts, soups, sandwiches, local gossip.

Eastern Monadnock Region

☞ **Sampan Chinese Restaurant and Lounge** (464-3663), Route 9, Hillsborough. Open for lunch and dinner except Sunday. The attractive decor suggests the quality of this place, one of the better places to eat in the area. Dishes are all cooked to order so you can request holding on the MSG, sugar, and salt. Lunch plates are under $5.

Pat's Millview (646-3188). Open for breakfast and lunch. Friendly, diner atmosphere in a house: fresh soups like ham and bean, omelets like vegetable and cheese served for both meals; giant muffins are the specialty; superb corn bread.

✐ **Rynborn Restaurant** (see *Dining Out*) in Antrim is a good lunch bet for soups and salads, burgers, or an open-faced Reuben. Children's menu.

✐ **Café Pierrot** (see *Dining Out*), Pine Valley Mill, Wilton. The lunchtime atmosphere is different from dinner. Note the children's corner to keep youngsters happy while parents gab.

☞ **Wilton Diner** (654-6567), Main Street, Route 31 (next to the fire station), Wilton Village. How good can a burger or a cup of corn chowder or a BLT be? Not much better than you'll find in this classic little diner with the sink at the end of the Formica counter. There are also some booths and small tables for two. Window boxes and curtains suggest a female touch. Specialties include an authentic, bargain-priced Wednesday night smorgasbord, Friday chowder, and superlative pies (we recommend the walnut and blueberry).

Parker's Maple Barn and Sugar House (878-2308), Brookline Road, Mason. Tuesday through Friday 8 A.M.–9 P.M., Saturday 7 A.M.–9 P.M., Sunday 7 A.M.–8 P.M. Dinner reservations recommended. Best known for its breakfast featuring Parker's own maple syrup. The dinner menu is "home-cooked meat and potato."

ENTERTAINMENT

DANCE

Monadnock Folklore Society (352-8616), Nelson. Call for the current calendar of events. It always includes Monday night contra dancing in the Nelson Town Hall; also other events in this elegantly simple old building and in similar settings throughout the region.

LECTURE AND PERFORMANCE SERIES

Amos Fortune Forum Series. Ongoing since 1947, Friday evenings in July and August at the Jaffrey Center Meeting House.

Monadnock Summer Lyceum (924-6245), Unitarian Church, Main Street, Peterborough. Every Sunday in July and August at 11 A.M.

MUSIC

Monadnock Music (924-7610), Box 255, Peterborough. This is a prestigious series of some two dozen concerts, operas, and orchestra performances staged by highly professional artists in town halls, churches, and schools; also under a tent high on Crotched Mountain. Some are free, others range in price from $8 to $21.50; all are in July and August. The three major locations are the Jaffrey Center Meeting House, the Pine Hill School in Wilton, and under a tent at the Crotched Mountain Foundation in Greenfield, site of most larger orchestral and opera performances (the audience is invited to bring a picnic to enjoy the spectacular view). Call or send for the current calendar, or check local listings.

Apple Hill Chamber Players (847-3371), Apple Hill Center for Chamber Music, Apple Hill Road, Nelson 03455. Tuesday evenings at 8 P.M. In June, July, and August faculty concerts are free. This noted group also performs throughout the country and world.

Temple Band (878-2829). Said to be the oldest town band in the country, performs at the Sharon Art Center, the Jaffrey Bandstand, and a number of scheduled festivities throughout the summer. Past masters of oompahpah.

Jaffrey Bandstand. Performances Wednesday evenings in the summer.

(Also see The Folkway, Del Rossi's Trattoria, Rynborn Restaurant, and Café Pierrot under *Dining Out*.)

THEATER

Peterborough Players (924-7585), Middle Hancock Road, Peterborough. Since 1933 this professional group has performed everything from Will Shakespeare to Tom Stoppard. One of New England's better-known summer theaters.

New England Marionette Opera (924-4333), Marionette Theatre, 24 Main Street, Peterborough. Thursday, Friday, Saturday performances at 8 P.M., Sunday matinees. Year-round schedule. Billed as America's largest marionette theater devoted primarily to opera, an adult-geared presentation that's winning high praise and a loyal audience from throughout the Northeast. The theater, featuring plum seats in a brick 1840s Baptist church, is a gem in itself and is designed in a way to create the illusion that the marionettes, deftly manipulated by strings, are human-scale. Puppets and their costumes are made on the spot, and visitors are welcome to drop in and see what it's all about. Tickets are $20 per adult, $18 for students. Performances scheduled for 1994 include *The Magic Flute* in English and *Porgy and Bess*.

American Stage Festival (673-7515), Milford. Summer productions usually include a classic, like Shakespeare or Molière, and new plays. The Young Company stages children's matinees. Tickets $16–20.

The Arts Center on Brickyard Pond at Keene State College in Keene and Franklin Pierce College in Rindge. Both stage musical, theatrical, and dance performances. Check local listings.

Tensing Theatre (924-6878), 6 School Street, Peterborough. Classic and art films are shown by the Peterborough Community Film Society on a wide screen Thursday through Sunday 7:30 P.M. in the old village cinema, now part of the Latacarta (see *Dining Out*); inquire about dinner/theater packages. Pick up a schedule at the restaurant.

The Colonial Theater (352-2033), 95 Main Street, Keene. A majestic, magical old theater featuring both current and classic films and live performances.

SELECTIVE SHOPPING

ANTIQUES

Listing every antiques store in the Monadnock Region would fill the rest of this book. Be it said that antiquing is BIG but composed of many small shops, thickest in the Francestown and Fitzwilliam areas. Free, frequently updated flyers describing these shops and their whereabouts are available locally. **Fitzwilliam Antiques** at the junction of Routes 12 and 19, houses the merchandise of 43 dealers, and there are a half dozen more dealers in Fitzwilliam. **Antiques at Colony Mill** (358-6343) represents more than 100 dealers. *The Directory of New Hampshire Antiques Dealers*, available from most chambers of commerce and antiques shops, lists dozens of dealers in this area.

ANTIQUARIAN BOOKSHOPS

Homestead Bookshop (876-4213), Route 101 just east of Marlborough Village next to Wilber Brothers Supermarket, Marlborough. Open daily; 45,000 volumes specializing in juvenile series, town histories, older fiction.

Hurley Books (399-4342), east side of Route 12 (just north of Route 63), Westmoreland. Open by appointment or chance; 35,000 volumes specializing in religious, farming, and gardening.

Rainy Day Books (585-3448), Fitzwilliam. Open May to mid-November, Thursday through Monday 11–5:30. Specialties include mountaineering, fiber arts, cooking.

Eagle Books (357-8721), 19 West Street, just off Central Square, Keene. Open daily except Sunday and holidays; 12,000 volumes specializing in WPA writers' project books.

ART GALLERIES

The Sharon Arts Center (924-7256), Route 123, Sharon. Open Tuesday through Saturday 10–5, Sunday 1–5, Monday seasonally. The three parts to the center are the Killian Gallery, showcasing quality painting, sculpture, and furniture, most of it for sale; the Handcraft Shop, one of the most extensive crafts shops in the state; and studio space, the scene of classes and workshops in a variety of arts. The museumlike complex is the setting for frequent lectures and concerts.

Tensing Gallery (924-6878) above the Latacarta restaurant, Peterborough. Changing shows.

Peter Pelletier Fine Art (924-7558), 32 Grove Street, Peterborough. Open year-round, Tuesday through Saturday 12–5. A serious gallery specializing in nineteenth- and early-twentieth-century landscape paintings.

Crescent Pond Studios (446-7072), Chalet Drive off Shedd Hill Road, Stoddard. Noted landscape and portrait artist Richard Whitney and still-life artist Sandy Sherman welcome visitors by chance or appointment in their studio overlooking Crescent Pond, set in 81 acres of woodland. From Route 3 take Route 123 to Stoddard, then 1.8 miles to Shedd Road and 2.1 miles to Chalet Drive; go to the end of the road.

Peter Granucci (352-6828), Hammon Hollow, Riverrun Farm, Gilsum. Nationally recognized for his portraits and landscapes, Granucci welcomes visitors. Please call ahead.

BOOKSHOPS

The Toadstool Bookshops (924-3543), 12 Depot Square, Peterborough, and in the Colony Mill (352-8815), Keene. Outstanding bookstores with a wide range of general titles, including many regional and art books. Under *Eating Out* note Aesops Tables, a café in the Peterborough store, which is immense, a former A&P.

CRAFTS

The Sharon Arts Center. (See *Art Galleries*.) This is also the region's leading crafts shop.

Granite Lake Pottery (847-9908), Route 9, Munsonville. Open year-round, daily except Sunday. Hand-thrown dinnerware and accessories from mugs to lamps to bathroom sinks (the sinks are a specialty).

Five Wings Studio (585-6682), East Lake Road, Fitzwilliam. Susan Link makes and sells her attractive dinnerware—porcelain with an oriental look—and two stoneware lines; also table lamps.

Harrisville Designs (827-3996), Harrisville. Tuesday through Saturday 10–5. Handweaving looms are designed and made here, priced from $400 to $3,000. Check out the new children's weaving looms and kits. A variety of yarns and weaving accessories are also sold in the Weaving Center, housed in an 1850 brick storehouse by the millpond. (Also see *To Do—Special Programs*.)

Frye's Measure Mill (654-6581), Wilton Center. Open May through December 15, Tuesday through Saturday 10–4. Mill tours are conducted on Saturday at 2 P.M., June 15 to October 15. Housed in part of a nineteenth-century mill that retains its original machinery, some still waterpowered to make woodenware. Quilts and coverlets, salt-glaze pottery, and other country folk art are also sold.

Parkside Gallery (464-3322), 17/19 West Main Street, Hillsborough. Open daily. A mix of antiques, crafts, and gifts.

The Artek Company Store (588-6825), Elm Avenue, Antrim. Open Monday through Saturday from 10 A.M. until 4 or 5 P.M. Quality reproductions of museum-quality scrimshaw, decorative boxes, carved jewelry, Christmas ornaments, sculpture.

Artistic Walnut, Fitzwilliam Village (next to the Fitzwilliam Market), offers a limited but quality selection of crafted items.

River Place Crafts (654-9411), Soughegan Marketplace at Pine Valley Mill, Milford. A quality and varied selection of crafted items.

SPECIAL STORES AND COMPLEXES

☞ **Eastern Mountain Sports** (924-7231), Vose Farm Road, off Route 202 north. Open Monday through Friday 9–9. Founded in Wellesley, Massachusetts, in 1967, specializing in quality and hard-to-find equipment and clothing for backpacking and climbing enthusiasts, EMS now has 48 stores across the country. This is corporate headquarters and one of the largest stores, the only one with a discount corner. Pick up a pamphlet guide to hiking and other outdoor sports possibilities in the Monadnock Region.

Brookstone (924-8485), Vose Farm Road, off Route 202 north. Open Monday through Saturday 9–6; Sunday 12–6. A retail branch of a well-known chain featuring labor-saving devices, tools, and housewares.

Colony Mill Marketplace (357-1240), 222 West Street, Keene. Open daily 10–9, Sunday 11–6. This nineteenth-century brick woolen mill now houses 33 shops and a food court. The anchor store is Cherry, Webb & Touraine and the most interesting is Country Artisans, a large, handsome crafts gallery displaying batik, kites, quilts, pottery, weaving, ironwork, lamps and shades, toys, etc., etc. **Toadstool Bookstore** is also here.

Ashwood Basket Corp. (924-0000), 350 Union Street, Peterborough. Classic picnic baskets, hampers, even bassinets; a variety of sturdy products made on the premises, sold throughout the country.

Joseph's Coat (924-6683), 26 Main Street, Peterborough. Quilting is what this place is about, but there are a variety of sewing workshops; handmade clothes.

Keene Mill End Store (352-8683), 55 Ralston Street, Keene. A great source of curtains and custom blinds as well as a vast array of fabrics and trims.

The Oasis (352-5355), 45 Central Square, Keene. An appealing New Age store selling crystals, clothing, candles, cards, jewelry, a large selection of self-help books, notions of all kinds.

Thistledown (588-3192), Mountain Road, Francestown. Open Wednesday through Sunday 10–5. Handmade baskets, salt-glazed pottery, reproduction furniture, dried flowers, herbs all make for a worthwhile stop.

Herb Barn (532-8486), 80 Main Street, Jaffrey. Open weekends 10–4. Extensive gardens and selection of herb products. Guided garden viewing with plant identification and folklore followed by a "garden tea" is available by reservation.

Pickity Place (878-1151), Nutting Hill Road, Mason. A large herb garden and gift shop, catalog. (Also see *Dining Out*.)

Steele's, 40 Main Street, Peterborough. In business since 1860, the nicest kind of stationery, card, and generally useful supply store.

SUGARHOUSES

Maple sugaring season in the Monadnock Region is March to mid-April, but farmers may not be "boiling" (40 gallons of sap boil down to 1 gallon of syrup) every day so be sure to phone ahead to make sure there's something to see—and something to eat. Most maple producers offer "sugar parties": sugar on snow (usually crushed ice these days) and maybe the traditional accompaniment (a pickle). Most sell a variety of maple products.

Bascom's Sugar House (835-2230; 835-6361), between Alstead and Acworth off Route 123A. One of the largest maple producers in New England, a huge sugarhouse and warehouse set high on Mount Kingsbury. Visitors are welcome to tour the plant, which uses unusual reverse-osmosis evaporators. Sugar parties on weekends.

Chadwick Farm (532-8811), south of Route 202 (Gilmore Pond Road to Peabody Hill Road to Chadwick Road), Jaffrey.

Dan's Sugar House (532-7379), Jaffrey. (See Chadwick Farm above.) Follow signs at Gilmore Pond Road.

Bacon's Sugar House (532-8836), Dublin Road, just south of Monadnock State Park entrance, Jaffrey Center. The familiar plastic jug now used by 75 percent of the country's maple producers was invented in 1973 by Charles Bacon, who welcomes visitors on weekends. Flanked by two cross-country networks, this vintage 1910 sugarhouse stands on a farm that's been in the family since 1780.

Barrett's Sugar House (352-6812), Route 12 northwest to Wyman Road, Keene. Old brick schoolhouse converted into a sugarhouse.

Parker's Maple Barn and Sugar House (878-2308), Mason (signs from Route 13 in Brookline). Big dining barn. (See *Eating Out*.)

Fisk's Little Sugar House (654-9784), Dale Street just off Route 31, Wilton. Specializing in maple candy.

Stuart & John's Sugar House and Pancake Restaurant (399-4486), junction of Routes 12 and 63, Westmoreland. Open weekends in spring and fall; syrup available year-round.

PICK-YOUR-OWN AND FARM STANDS

High Hopes Orchard (399-4305), 582 Glebe Road, Westmoreland. Peaches in August, apples and pumpkins (wagon rides) in September and October; gift shop, cider, homemade pies, apples, donuts, and apple gift packs August through December.

Alyson's Orchard (756-3424), Route 12, Walpole. A 600-acre farm specializing in peaches, also plums, apricots. Inquire about Rochambeau Lodge, a group-geared (seven bedrooms, shared kitchen) facility on the farm.

SPECIAL EVENTS

May: **Spring Concert**, Monadnock Chorus and Orchestra.

Late June: The annual **Rock Swap** in Gilsum (behind the elementary school on Route 10) attracts 8,000–10,000 mineral buffs.

July: (See *Entertainment* for music, theater, and lecture series in July and August.) **July Fourth celebrations,** Noaning on the Common, an old-fashioned community picnic, Peterborough.

Third week of July: **Fitzwilliam Antiques Fair,** more than 40 dealers.

*At the July full moon: **The Old Homestead,*** a pageant/play is performed in the Potash Bowl, a natural amphitheater in Swanzey.

August: **Festival of Fireworks,** Jaffrey Airport. **Oak Park Festival,** Greenfield. **Medal Day,** MacDowell Colony, Peterborough. **Old Home Days,** Hancock. **Summerfest,** Peterborough.

September: **Labor Day Festival,** Francestown. Annual **Benefit Auction,** Peterborough Players. Annual **Balloon Festival,** Monadnock Travel Council.

October: **Foliage Festivals** in Francestown, Greenfield. **Antique Auto Show** and **Octoberfest** at Crotched Mountain Foundation. German music, food, and classic cars. Biannual **Quilt Show,** Monadnock Quilters Guild. Annual **Book Fair,** MacDowell Colony.

November: **Monadnock Music Christmas Fair,** Peterborough Elementary School.

December: **Christmas Teas** at the Sharon Arts Center. **Messiah Festival** at Franklin Pierce College. **Monadnock Chorus & Orchestra Christmas Concert** at Peterborough Town Hall.

III. THE MERRIMACK VALLEY

The Manchester Area
The Concord Area

ROBERT J. KOZLOW

Canterbury Shaker Village scene

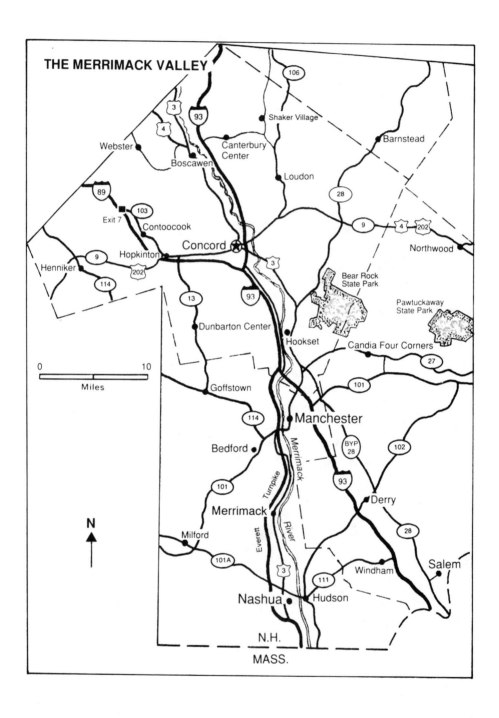

THE MERRIMACK VALLEY

Introduction

The Merrimack, New England's second-longest river, was an early New Hampshire highway, and today it's paralleled by I-93, New Hampshire's north-south transportation spine. One of the state's first settled corridors, the Merrimack Valley has recently been enjoying another migrational rush from hundreds of companies and thousands of families moving north from Massachusetts to take advantage of New Hampshire's tax breaks (no sales or income tax).

Relatively few visitors, however, venture farther into this area than the fast-food chains just off I-93. The very way the highways slice through and around both Manchester and Concord does little to encourage exploration. Manchester's proud, old, brick shopping streets, its Currier Gallery of Art, and its Amoskeag Mills—once the world's largest textile "manufactury"—are rewarding stops. So are Concord's state capitol building, the neighboring New Hampshire Historical Society, and downtown shops. The headquarters for the New Hampshire Audubon Society (just off I-89) and the Society for the Protection of New Hampshire Forests (just off I-93) are also well worth the small detours they require.

Other genuine finds are salted around this little-touristed central New Hampshire corridor. Canterbury Shaker Village, just 15 miles north of Concord, remains a working Shaker community in addition to being one of New England's most interesting museums. "America's Stonehenge" is at Mystery Hill in North Salem. The town of Henniker offers skiing, some fine lodging, dining, and shopping. There are also numerous state parks with sandy beaches.

The Manchester Area

Manchester is by far New Hampshire's largest city (roughly 100,000 people). It's also arguably New England's most interesting "mill city," an image many current residents reject.

When white men first traveled up the Merrimack, they found a large Native American village at Amoskeag Falls. In 1650 the English missionary John Eliot set up one of his "Praying Indian" communities and called it Derryfield. The natives were later displaced by a white settlement early in the eighteenth century. By 1810 local judge Samuel Blodgett foretold the community's future, suggesting that its name be changed from Derryfield to Manchester, the world's biggest manufacturing city (in England).

This early-American Manchester population was just 615, but Judge Blodgett raised money to build a canal around Amoskeag Falls to enable flat-bottomed boats to glide downstream and onward, via the Middlesex Canal, into Boston. Both the canal and the town's first cotton mill opened in 1809.

It was a group of Boston entrepreneurs, however, who put Manchester on the map. By the 1830s these "Boston Associates" had purchased waterpower rights for the entire length of the Merrimack River and had begun developing a city full of mills in Lowell, Massachusetts, 32 miles downriver from Manchester. Incorporating themselves as the Amoskeag Manufacturing Company, they then bought 15,000 acres around Amoskeag Falls and drew up a master plan for the city of Manchester, complete with tree-lined streets, housing, churches, and parks.

Like Lowell, Manchester enjoyed an early utopian period during which "mill girls" lived in well-regulated boardinghouses. It was followed by successive periods of expansion, fueled by waves of foreign immigration. With direct rail connections to Quebec, Manchester attracted predominantly French Canadian workers but Polish, Greek, and Irish communities were (and are) also substantial.

At its height in the early twentieth century, the Amoskeag Manufacturing Company employed 17,000 workers, encompassed 64 mill buildings lining both sides of the Merrimack River for a mile and a half, and contained the world's largest single mill yard. The total mill space

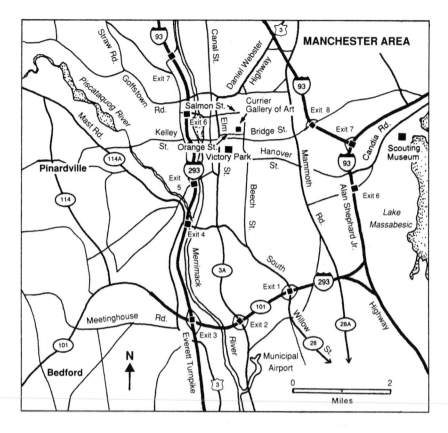

equaled that of the present World Trade Center in New York City. Imagine this space filled with the noise and movement of nearly 700,000 spindles and 23,000 looms!

Life for workers was unquestionably hard. The tower bells rang each morning at 4:30, and the first call for breakfast was 5:30; the workday began at 6:30, lasting until 7:30 in the evening. But it's a way of life that many workers remember fondly in the oral histories recorded in *Amoskeag: Life and Work in an American Factory-City* by anthropologist Tamara Hareven and photographer Randolph Langenbach. Based on interviews with thousands of former Amoskeag employees, this interesting book, published in 1978, vividly conveys what it was like to live within Manchester's tightly knit ethnic circles, reinforced by a sense of belonging to a full city of workers united like one family by a single boss.

The Amoskeag Manufacturing Company went bankrupt in 1935, and the following year the mills were shut down. In desperation a group of local businessmen formed Amoskeag Industries, Inc., purchased all the mills for $5 million and managed to lease and sell mill space to diversified businesses.

"Diversify" has been the city's slogan ever since. Having once experienced complete dependency on one economic source, Manchester now prides itself on the number and variety of its industries and service businesses as well as on its current status as a financial and insurance center. New business and residential buildings rise high above the old mill towers.

Loosely circled by hills and with buildings that rise in tiers above the mills on the eastern bank of the Merrimack, Manchester is an attractive city with a Gothic Revival town hall, handsome nineteenth-century commercial blocks, and the gemlike Palace Theater. The Currier Gallery of Art, one of the country's outstanding small art museums, is also located here.

Still, it's puzzling that while a half dozen other New England mill cities have opened visitors centers and museums, Manchester has done nothing to dramatize its story. Even as historic mill buildings in Lowell were being restored, the graceful curve of the Amoskeag's mile-long river wall was broken and the canals filled in. Check with the Manchester Historical Society and with the Currier Gallery of Art about both printed and walking mill-yard tours.

GUIDANCE

Greater Manchester Chamber of Commerce (666-6600), 889 Elm Street, Manchester 03101. Upstairs over Dunkin' Donuts at the corner of Hanover and Elm, the chamber office stocks brochures and sells a city map for $2.

Greater Nashua Chamber of Commerce (891-2471), 1 Tara Boulevard, Suite 211, Nashua 03062.

GETTING THERE

By bus: From the **Manchester Transportation Center** (668-6133), Canal and Granite streets, you can get anywhere in the country; Concord Trailways, Vermont Transit Lines, and Peter Pan all stop regularly.

By plane: The **Manchester Airport** (624-6559) with its brand new terminal is the largest airport in the state. It's served by United Airlines (1-800-241-6522) Northwest Airlink (1-800-225-2525), Continental (1-800-525-0180), and USAir (1-800-428-4322), with nonstop flights to Washington, New York, Chicago, Philadelphia, Pittsburgh, and Boston. Hertz, Budget, Avis, and Thrifty Car Rental are all here and offer free airport transfers. For parking information call 641-5444.

By car: The biggest problem with Manchester is finding your way in. It's moated by interstate highways 93 and 293 more effectively than it ever was by canals and mill walls. The simplest access to downtown is via the Amoskeag Bridge on I-293, Exit 6 to Elm Street. Approaching the city from the south, however, we actually prefer taking Exit 6 off I-93 and following Hanover Street across town. A handy map, available from the chamber of commerce (see *Guidance*), pinpoints parking garages, and there are reasonably priced (warning: and well-monitored) meters.

GETTING AROUND

Hudson Bus Lines (424-2446), 22 Pond Street, Nashua, offers limousine service between pick-up points in Concord, Manchester, Nashua, downtown Boston, and Logan International Airport.

MEDICAL EMERGENCY

Catholic Medical Center (668-3545), 100 MacGregor Street, Manchester.

TO SEE

MUSEUMS

Currier Gallery of Art (669-6144), 192 Orange Street, Manchester. Open Tuesday through Saturday 10–4, Thursday until 9 P.M., Sunday 1–5. Admission: $4 per adult, $3 per senior, student with ID; under age 18, free. Free admission Thursday 1–9. A fine landscape by Claude Monet; an 1850s painting of the spa at Clarendon Springs, Vermont, by James Hope; a spooky 1935 Edward Hopper Maine coastal scene titled *The Bootleggers;* a 1940s painting by Sheeler of the Amoskeag mills; and a downright engaging picture of Daniel Webster are a few of the unexpected treasures you might find displayed from the Currier's extensive collection of works, which range from a thirteenth-century Tuscan Madonna and Child to twentieth-century works by Rouault, Picasso, Wyeth, and Matisse. Silver, pewter, art, glass, furniture, and textiles are also displayed, and special exhibits are frequently outstanding.

The Zimmerman House, a Usonian home designed in 1950 by Frank Lloyd Wright—his only house open to the public in New England—is also maintained by the Currier. Guided tours are offered from the museum Thursday through Sunday year-round; $6 per adult, $4 for seniors and students includes museum admission. Inquire about seasonal "Twilight Tours." The Currier is in a residential neighborhood on the site of the Victorian home of Moody and Hannah Currier, the couple who gave it and who specified in their will that their house be torn down to make way for the museum. The trick to finding it is beginning at either highway exit from which it's marked (the Amoskeag Bridge exit on Route 293 and the Wellington Street exit on I-93), following the Indian trail of signs. (Also see the map for Manchester in this chapter.)

Science Enrichment Encounters (669-0400), 324 Commercial Street, Manchester. Open Monday through Friday 9–5 for school groups; Thursday 5–9; Saturday and Sunday noon to 5 for the public. Experience weightlessness, experiment with a momentum machine, giant bubbles, gyroscopes, microwaves, and more.

The Lawrence L. Lee Scouting Museum (669-8919), Bodwell Road, Manchester. Open daily July and August, 10–4; September to June, Saturday 10–4. Exhibits include original drawings and letters of scouting founder Lord Robert Baden-Powell and exhibits about scouting

Amoskeag Canal, *1948, by Charles Sheeler, from the collection of the Currier Gallery of Art, in Manchester*

throughout the world. The library of 3,000 books and bound periodicals also relates to scouting.

Manchester Institute of Arts and Sciences (623-0313), 148 Concord Street, Manchester. Open Monday, Friday, and Saturday 9–5. Just across Victory Park from the historic association, this arts center stages frequent gallery exhibits; also sponsors concerts, films, and lectures.

The Nashua Center for the Arts (883-1506), 14 Court Street, Nashua, displays contemporary art, including photography and sculpture, in its gallery. It also sponsors a January-to-May "Downtown Live" performance series and a Saturday program of children's entertainment. In summer it sponsors outdoor performances in Holman Stadium.

HISTORIC MUSEUMS AND SITES

Manchester Historical Association (622-7531), 129 Amherst Street, Manchester. Open Tuesday through Friday 9–4, Saturday 10–4. Free. Special exhibits vary, and the permanent collection includes Native American artifacts (in the basement), photographs, and furniture. The research library contains Amoskeag Manufacturing Company records, city records, and family papers. Inquire about frequent lectures and workshops, also walking tours of the Amoskeag Mills (see below) as well as residential neighborhoods in the city.

The Amoskeag Mill Yard. Bounded by the Merrimack River and by Granite, Franklin, Market, Canal, and West Salmon streets, the buildings of the former Amoskeag Manufacturing Company still represent one of the country's leading examples of nineteenth- and early-twentieth-century industrial architecture. The four- and five-story-high mills stand in two rows along the east bank of the river. Built variously from the 1830s to 1910, they look fairly uniform because as the older mills were expanded, their early distinctive features were blurred. The adjoining blocks lined with tidy, brick mill housing, however, reflect a progression of styles from the 1830s to 1920. The two large mills on the west side of the river were once connected to these by tunnels and bridges. Stand on Granite Street (by the Granite Street Bar & Grill) and look up the long brick column of buildings for a sense of nineteenth-century Manchester. Inquire at both the Currier Gallery of Art (see *Museums*) and the Manchester Historical Association (see above) about guided tours of the former mill yard.

Nashua, New Hampshire's second-largest city, has its share of monumental **mill buildings** along Water and Factory streets, built by the Nashua Manufacturing Company, which was chartered in 1823 to produce cotton fabric.

"Mystery Hill" (893-8300; if no answer: 432-2530), off Route 111, North Salem. Take I-93 Exit 3 and follow Route 111 five miles east to Island Pond Road, then Haverhill Road to the entrance. Open daily June to Labor Day, 9–5; in May and September, 10–4; weekends in April and November. $5 per adult, $4 per senior, $3 per student, $1.50 per child. Billed as "one of the largest and possibly the oldest megalithic . . . sites in North America." The intriguing stone formations may or may not have been built by Celts 4,000 years ago, but it's a sight to see.

Stark House (622-5719; 623-2985), 2000 Elm Street, Manchester. Tours by appointment only. An eighteenth-century house built by Archibald Stark, a community leader and father of Major General John Stark, who commanded the battle of Bennington.

The Nashua Historical Society (883-0015) exhibits its collections in the Florence Speare Memorial Building, 3 Abbott Street, and maintains the Abbott-Spalding House on Abbott Square. Open seasonally; call for hours.

Robert Frost Farm (432-3091), 2 miles south of Derry on Route 28. Open June to October, daily 10–6. An 1880s clapboard house, in which the poet lived between 1901 and 1909, is filled with original furnishings. An interpretive nature trail runs through surrounding fields and woods, past the "mending wall." Frost did the bulk of his writing here.

Taylor Up and Down Saw Mill, Island Pond Road, Derry. A waterpowered up-and-down sawmill that processed logs into boards; open usually in spring when the water level is high enough to power it. Call the Department of Resources and Economic Development (271-3456) for details.

Old Sandown Railroad Museum (887-3259; 887-4611), Route 121A, Sandown. Open June to October, Saturday and Sunday 1–5. Railroad memorabilia, telegraph equipment, old magazines, posters, photographs, and Civil War letters are among the exhibits.

Milford Historical Society (673-3385), 2 Union Street, Milford. The Carey House is open June to September, Saturday 2–4. Milford is an old shopping and mill town with an ornate, Victorian-style town hall.

OTHER SITES

Anheuser-Busch Brewery (889-6631), Route 3, Merrimack (between Manchester and Nashua). At least two Clydesdales are always on view here; tours of the brewery are offered May to October, daily 9:30–3:30; otherwise, Wednesday through Sunday 9:30–3:30.

COVERED BRIDGE

Hopkinton-Rowell's covered bridge is on Contoocook Road, north of Route 127, at West Hopkinton.

FOR FAMILIES

Canobie Lake (893-3506), Exit 2, I-93, Salem. Open daily Memorial Day to Labor Day, weekends mid-April to Memorial Day. One of New England's biggest amusement parks: more than 40 rides, including a big roller coaster, extensive Kiddieland, swimming pool, wild log flume ride, and excursion boat and mini-train ride around the park.

The Children's Metamorphosis (425-2560), 217 Rockingham Road, Londonderry. Take Exit 5 off I-93, then go 1 mile north on Route 28. Open Tuesday through Saturday 9:30–5, Sunday 1–5, and Friday evening until 8. Geared to ages two to eight, 12 exhibit areas including a nature center, a construction site, a grocery store, a hospital emergency room, a "sticky" room, a world cultures room, and a "climbing hall." Admission: $3.50 per person, $6.50 per family.

SCENIC DRIVE

Goffstown to New Boston. Both Goffstown and New Boston are unusually handsome towns and the ride between is one of the most pleasant around. The road follows the winding Piscataquog River, a good stream for fishing and canoeing. Take Route 114 west from Manchester and Route 13 to New Boston.

TO DO

CANOEING

Detailed boating maps ($2.95) and guides ($1.95) of the Merrimack River are available from the **Merrimack River Watershed Council,** 694 Main Street, West Newbury, MA 01985. For information about local rentals and events, try 224-8522 or the council's headquarters at 508-363-3777.

Robert Frost Home in Derry

GOLF
Candia Woods Golf Club (483-2307), High Street, Candia. Eighteen holes, open to the public.

Valley View Golf Club (774-5031), Dunbarton. Nine holes.

HORSE RACING
Rockingham Park (898-2311), Routes 28 and I-93, Salem. Major-league thoroughbred racing.

GREEN SPACE

Bear Brook State Park (485-9874), off Route 28 in Allenstown. Open mid-May to mid-October. Take the Hooksett exit off I-93. The park has 9,600 heavily forested acres with 6 lakes, swimming, rental boats, picnicking for up to 1,500 visitors under tall pines, a physical fitness course, nature trails, fishing (Archery Pond is reserved for fly-fishing), camping with 81 tent sites on Beaver Pond (where the swimming beach is reserved for campers). The Bear Brook Nature Center also has programs, 2 nature trails, more than 30 miles of hiking trails in the park with separate marked routes for ski-tourers and snowmobilers in winter. Very crowded on summer weekends but not too bad midweek. Fee.

Pawtuckaway State Park (895-3031), off Route 156, Nottingham. Open mid-May through mid-October. At Raymond, 3.5 miles north of the junction of Routes 101 and 156. The attraction is a small beach on 803-acre Lake Pawtuckaway with good swimming, a bathhouse, a 25-acre picnic area, and hiking trails. Rental boats are available; outboard motors are permitted; and the lake is stocked for fishing. Horse Island and

Big Island, both accessible to cars, have a total of 170 tent sites, many right on the water; campers have their own boat launch. Trails lead up into the Pawtuckaway Mountains. Both cross-country skiing and snowmobiling are popular here in winter.

Silver Lake State Park (465-2342), Route 122, Hollis. A great beach with a bathhouse, concession stand, picnic tables, and a diving raft. More than 100 picnic sites are scattered through the pine groves. Summer weekend crowds come from Nashua but midweek is pleasant. Fee.

Clough State Park (529-7112), between Routes 114 and 13, about 5 miles east of Weare. Open daily late June to Labor Day. The focus here is 150-acre Everett Lake, created by the United States Army Corps of Engineers as a flood-control project. The 50-acre park includes a sandy beach and bathhouses, a picnic grove, and playground. Motorized boats are not permitted, but there is a boat launch and rental boats are available. Fee.

LODGING

INNS

Bedford Village Inn (472-2001), 2 Old Bedford Road, Bedford 03102. Just 12 rooms carved out of an old barn, all with 4-poster beds, large-screen TVs, Jacuzzi baths, and all rooms opening onto a central meeting space. Rates are $110–165.

Highlander Inn and Tavern (625-6426), 2 Highland Way, Manchester 03101. Near the airport, an attractive motel with a good restaurant and outdoor pool. Rates are $70–90.

☞ **The Fairfield Inn** (424-7500), Route 3, Exit 11, Nashua 03054, is an opulent 114-room motel, managed by Marriott. Despite the reproduction antiques, designer wallpapers, and pool, it's $40.95 per room at this writing.

MOTELS

Most chain motels are represented in this area.

Holiday Inn (625-1000), 700 Elm Street, Manchester. Rates are $75–86 for the only rooms right downtown within walking distance of shops and museums.

WHERE TO EAT

DINING OUT

✐ **Café Pavone** (622-5488), 75 Arms Park Drive, Manchester. Open Monday through Saturday for dinner, weekdays for lunch. A trendy trattoria down below Canal Street in the mill complex, featuring semolina pasta made fresh daily. Specialties include homemade fettuccine served in a light cream and cheese sauce with shrimp, lobster, and scallops, and pasta primavera with fresh sautéed vegetables in a light tomato cream. All pastas come with a cup of minestrone soup or an Italian green salad. All heavier entrées—which range from eggplant parmigiana to veal saltimbocca —come with a pasta marinara. Children's menu. Moderate.

Bedford Village Inn (472-2001), 1 Old Bedford Road, Bedford. Open for lunch and dinner daily, Sunday from 3 P.M. This beautifully restored (some say over-restored), eighteenth-century house has been the talk of Manchester since its owners went broke investing millions renovating it. The dining rooms are elegant (request one of the smaller rooms in the house itself), and there's also a cheery tavern with its own less-expensive menu. Fare is traditional New England. Chicken New Hampshire is a specialty. Moderate to expensive.

Levi Lowells (429-0885), 585 Webster Highway, Merrimack. Three attractive dining rooms with fireplaces and a large menu that ranges from French nouvelle to "upbeat New England." Entrées range from braised chicken to roast lamb noisettes and include beef Wellington, a carefully cooked and garnished roast duck, and haddock poached in wine and butter that is finished with smoked Maine shrimp in cream sauce. For appetizers try New England crabcakes or mushroom strudel. Generally ranked among the best places to eat in southern New Hampshire. Moderate to expensive.

Ya Mama's (883-2264), 41 Canal Street, Nashua. Open for lunch Thursday and Friday, for dinner Tuesday through Saturday. Word is getting out about this small, superb Italian restaurant owned and run by Michael and Michelle Ferrazzini. Just 40 people can be seated in the cheery, informal dining room, where both northern and southern Italian dishes are lovingly prepared. Moderate.

Lord Jeffrey's (673-7540), The Meeting Place, Route 101, Amherst. A classic, cozy dining room with romantic atmosphere. Specialties include lobster bisque and lobster Savannah, chateaubriand served tableside, and flaming desserts. Moderate to expensive.

EATING OUT

Shorty's Mexican Roadhouse (424-0010), 450 Charles Bancroft Highway (Route 3A), Litchfield. Open daily from 11:30 A.M., Sunday from 1 P.M. This is a local favorite: a 1940s roadhouse atmosphere with Mexican reliables like tacos, fajitas, and enchiladas; also dinner specials like chicken mole and grilled fish with salsa. Entrées from $5; same menu all day.

Granite Street Bar & Grille (622-0900), 50 Phillipee Cote Street, Manchester. A pleasant, pubby atmosphere and standard menu.

Tiya's Restaurant (669-4365), 8 Hanover Street, Manchester. A clean, attractive Thai eatery well-sited right downtown near the corner of Elm and Hanover. You can get a tuna salad or Reuben, but stir-fry dishes like shrimp, scallops, sea legs, broccoli, pepper, and mushrooms are the same price. House specialty is *pad thai:* stir-fried egg, chicken, bean sprouts, and spicy sauces garnished with crushed peanuts.

The Black Forest (672-0500), Salzburg Square, Route 101, Amherst.

Open 9–5 daily. One in a lineup of Austrian-style facades in this shopping mall; known for its pastries, which you can buy to go; also good for omelets, quiche, soups, good shopping-out fare.

ENTERTAINMENT

⊘ **The Palace Theater** (668-5588), 80 Hanover Street (PO Box 3006), Manchester 03105. Opened in 1915, reopened and restored in 1974, this 883-seat theater is a beauty—with small, glittering chandeliers, bright local art, and an intimate feel. Its own resident company mounts six productions a year, and during the summer Stage One Productions (see below) uses the facility to stage musicals. Magic shows, children's theater, ballet, and opera are also frequently performed. Phone for the current program.

Stage One Productions (669-5511), at the Palace Theater, performs dinner theater during winter months and musicals during the summer.

American Stage Festival Theater (673-7515), Milford, stages a series of summer productions, mid-July to early August.

Currier Gallery of Art (669-6144), 192 Orange Street, Manchester. Concerts are held in the museum's central courtyard once a month, October to April.

⊘ **The Nashua Center for the Arts** (883-1506), 14 Court Street, Nashua. The center sponsors a January-to-May "Downtown Live" performance series and a Saturday program of children's entertainment. In summer it sponsors outdoor performances in Holman Stadium.

SELECTIVE SHOPPING

ART GALLERIES
Art 3 Gallery (668-6650), 44 West Brook Street (off Canal), Manchester. Contemporary and traditional work by a range of artists.

CRAFTS
Craftings (623-4108), 71 Hanover Street (next to the Palace Theater), Manchester. An outstanding selection of handcrafted gifts and furnishings from throughout New England.

SPECIAL STORES
☞ **McQuades** (625-5451), 844 Elm Street, Manchester. Open 9:30–5:30 Monday through Saturday, 12–5 Sunday, and until 9 P.M. Thursday and Friday. The nicest kind of family-owned clothing store. Coffee is always hot for shoppers and caged birds are chirping. The bargains in the basement range from coats to comforters with plenty for both adults and children. In this the largest of the three McQuades (there's one on Concord's Main Street, another in Nashua's Simoneau Plaza), cash and checks are still shunted from cash registers through tubes.

MALLS

Reluctantly we include directions to malls along Manchester's "strip" because that's what many out-of-staters are here for; New Hampshire's lack of sales tax has its appeal.

The Mall of New Hampshire, 1500 South Willow Street, has 88 stores including Lechmere, Filene's, and Sears.

K-Mart Plaza, 1535 South Willow Street, has a Filene's Basement store.

Willow Tree Mall, 575 Willow Street, and **TJ Maxx Plaza,** 933 South Willow Street, are also large.

The Bedford Mall, South River Road, Bedford, has 27 stores including Anderson-Little, Montgomery Ward, Jordan Marsh, and Marshall's.

SPECIAL EVENTS

May: **Hillsborough County Annual Sheep and Wool Festival** (763-5859), New Boston. **Little Nature Museum Open House,** Weare. Nature activities, guided walks, museum tours.

July: **Family Outdoor Discovery Day,** Bear Brook State Park Campground (see *Green Space*).

August: **Annual Antique Dealers Show,** Manchester.

September: **Riverfest,** Manchester. Three days with fireworks, live entertainment, canoe competitions, country fair exhibits. **Hillsborough County Agricultural Fair** (674-2510), New Boston. **Hanover Street Fine Arts Fair,** Manchester. **Deerfield Fair** (463-7421), Deerfield.

October: Annual **Weare Craft Bazaar,** Weare. **Head of the Merrimack Regatta** (888-2875), Nashua.

The Concord Area

The golden dome of the state capitol building still towers above downtown Concord. Since 1819, when it was built out of local granite by convict labor, this building has been the forum for the state's legislature—now numbering 400 members—said to be the fourth largest deliberative body in the world.

The Native Americans called this site Penacook, or "crooked place," for the snakelike turns the Merrimack makes here. Concord's compact downtown clusters along the western bank of the river, and it's encircled by the concrete wall of I-93 along the opposite bank.

Concord owes its prominence to two forgotten phenomena: the Middlesex Canal—opened in 1815 to connect it with Boston—and the steam railroad from Boston, completed in 1842. Today Concord remains an important transportation hub—the point at which I-89 forks off from I-93 to head northwest across New Hampshire and Vermont, ultimately linking Boston with Montreal.

Concord is really just a medium-sized town of 34,500 residents, and you are quickly out of it and in the countryside of East Concord at the Society for the Protection of New Hampshire Forests headquarters or in the western countryside at Silk Farm, New Hampshire's Audubon House.

While still very much in the Merrimack Valley, Concord—in contrast to Manchester—is just beyond southern New Hampshire's old industrial belt with its ethnic mix. Some of Concord's surrounding towns are as Yankee—and as picturesque—as any in New England.

Canterbury Shaker Village, a striking old hilltop community, is a gathering of white wooden buildings surrounded by spreading fields. Hopkinton, a proud early-nineteenth-century town, offers a different kind of serenity and some good antiquing. And Henniker is a mill town turned college town, with more to offer visitors than many resorts.

GUIDANCE

The Greater Concord Chamber of Commerce (224-2508), 244 North Main Street (just off Exit 15, I-93), Concord 03301. Open June to Labor Day, Monday through Friday 8–5. Easy to miss and with limited parking, but friendly and helpful once you get inside. The chamber

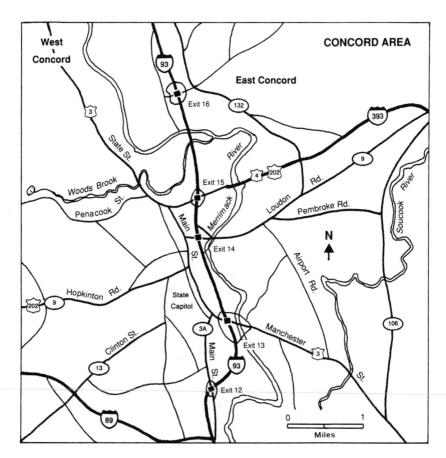

also maintains an information kiosk downtown near the statehouse, open weekends June to Labor Day, depending on the availability of volunteers.

GETTING THERE

By bus: The **Concord Bus Terminal** (228-3300), Depot Street, is served by Concord Trailways, Peter Pan Bus Lines, and Vermont Transit.

GETTING AROUND

By taxi: **AA Taxi** (225-7433), **A&P Taxi** (224-6573), **Central Taxi** (224-4077). **Hudson Bus Lines** (424-2446), based at 22 Pond Street, Nashua, offers limousine service between pick-up points in Concord, Manchester, downtown Boston, and Logan International Airport.

PARKING

Not a problem downtown.

MEDICAL EMERGENCY

Concord Hospital (225-2711), 250 Pleasant Street, Concord.

VILLAGES

Henniker. West of Concord at the junction of Routes 9/202 and 114 (take Exit 5 off I-89), the "only Henniker in the world" is a delightful little college town with an outstanding small ski area, cross-country ski center, and a number of interesting shops and restaurants. Well into this century Henniker was a bustling crossroads town with a thriving inn, a number of farms, and three mills on the Contoocook River—one mill making bicycle rims; another, handles; and the third, leatherboard for shoes. Several mills, however, were destroyed by a 1936 flood, and in the 1940s New England College was established. With a combined student and faculty of 1,000, the college now forms the heart of the town. The former Henniker Inn is the administration office, the art gallery next door showcases New England art, and shops and restaurants line a green strip along the Contoocook River across the street. A family ski area, a winery, two outstanding inns, and a wide scattering of shops and restaurants are also part of this unusual small town.

Hopkinton. Just west of Concord off I-89, with a Main Street that's lined with early white-clapboard mansions, Hopkinton is known for the quality and quantity of its antiques shops and for its old-fashioned State Fair, held Labor Day weekend. **The New Hampshire Antiquarian Society** (746-3825) on Main Street is open year-round, Monday 1–5 P.M. and 6:30–8:30 P.M. and Wednesday 9–11 A.M. and 1–5 P.M. The collection includes genealogical materials, paintings, and changing exhibits.

TO SEE

MUSEUMS

☞ **Canterbury Shaker Village** (783-9511), Shaker Road, Canterbury 03224. Open early May through October daily, Monday through Saturday 10–5, Sunday 12–5; weekends in April, November, and December. Admission: $7.50 per adult, $3.75 per child 6–16, $20 per family.

The single most rewarding sight to see in central New Hampshire, this complex of 24 buildings set in 644 acres conjures up a unique, almost vanished way of life that produced many inventions and distinctive art, food, and music. Between the 1780s and 1990 some 2,300 Shaker men, women, and children lived in this rural community, putting their "hands to work and hearts to God." In the 1850s, when this Shaker village owned 4,000 acres with 100 buildings, it was one of 18 such American communes extending from Kentucky to Maine to Ohio. Today just six communities survive in shape enough to tell their story, and Canterbury is one of the few settlements that has never been out of Shaker hands. In 1969 Eldress Bertha Lindsay (who died in 1990) had the foresight to incorporate the present buildings and property as a nonprofit museum.

The Christa McAuliffe Planetarium

The last village to assume the "Lead Ministry," Canterbury absorbed a number of brethren from other communities as they closed and so conveys a vivid sense of Shaker life from the 1880s on around the turn of the century. Visitors are guided through a dozen buildings, encouraged to lunch and on weekends to dine in the Creamery, generally recognized as one of the best places to eat in New Hampshire, and to follow the nature trail around Turning Mill Pond, one of the eight that once powered a variety of mills on a 4,000-acre spread. The vintage 1792 Meeting House now doubles as exhibit and performance space. The Laundry is immense and fascinating, and the brightly lit sewing room is furnished with exquisitely crafted tables, hung with the "Dorothy Cloaks" invented here, popularized by Mrs. Grover Cleveland, who wore one to her husband's inauguration in 1885. The infirmary is equally fascinating, restored to trace the evolution of medical care here. Herbs in the built-in drawers are left from the last time they were used, and the tools on the dentist chair are just as Elder Henry Blinn left them. (Also known as a cartographer and geologist, Blinn began practicing dentistry here in 1860.) In the School House it's easy to assume that the pupils are just out for recess and will be rushing back in, up the graceful staircase and into the bright, wood-paneled room that is filled with books, hung with maps. The blackboard bears a reminder written there by Sister Bertha: "No one will find a spirit-real heaven, until they first create earthly heaven."

Special evening dinners and candlelight tours of the village are also offered by reservation Friday and Saturday when the village is open. The village's Creamery restaurant, generally rated one of the best places to lunch in New Hampshire, is also open daily and for Sunday brunch when the museum is open. Note the many special happenings listed at the end of this chapter under *Special Events*.

Southbound on I-93 the village is marked from Exit 18. Northbound use Exit 15E and follow I-393 east for 5 miles; then Route 106 north for 7 miles and turn at the sign for Shaker Road.

Christa McAuliffe Planetarium (271-STAR), 3 Institute Drive, Concord. Take I-93, Exit 15, then east on I-393 to Exit 1 and follow signs. Open Tuesday through Sunday. Christa was a teacher at Concord High School when she was chosen from among 11,000 to be the first teacher-in-space. Dedicated to her memory, this facility, with its dramatic rendition of the universe, has the most sophisticated electronics system of any planetarium. Although geared primarily to schoolchildren, it has a variety of programs. There are several shows daily, but the general public must reserve in advance since seating is limited to 92 persons. $5 per adult; $3 for children, college students, and seniors.

New Hampshire Historical Society Museum and Library (225-3381), 30 Park Street. Open year-round Monday through Friday 9–4:30, Saturday and Sunday 12–4:30. Closed holidays; library closed Sunday. Free. A classic little museum building with a Concord Coach occupying center stage in the marble rotunda. Here you quickly learn that the Concord Coach, first manufactured in 1827 by wheelwright Lewis Downing and coach builder Stephen Abbot, was soon available in 14 styles. Over the next century more than 3,000 were made in town, each weighing some 2,400 pounds, costing between $775 and $1,250. A painting by John Burgum depicts "an express freight shipment of 30 coaches April 15, 1868, by Abbot, Downing & Co., Concord, NH, to Wells Fargo Co., Omaha, Neb." The picture vividly supports Concord's claim to having helped open up the West.

New Hampshire's only statewide historical society, this is a combination research library and museum, with limited exhibit space and changing exhibits. Fund-raising is currently under way to finance a Museum of New Hampshire History to be located in a stone warehouse behind the Eagle Hotel; due to open in spring 1995. The library will always remain in this classic 1911 building.

HISTORIC HOMES AND SITES

A leaflet describing a self-guided walking tour of Concord, "The Coach and Eagle Trail," is available from the chamber of commerce booth. It includes some of the following:

New Hampshire State House and The State House Plaza (271-2154), 107 North Main Street, Concord. Open year-round, weekdays 8–4:30. A handsome 1819 building, this is the oldest state capitol in which a legislature still meets in its original chambers. A visitors center contains dioramas and changing exhibits. More than 150 portraits of past political figures are displayed.

The Eagle Hotel, North Main Street, Concord. For more than 135 years the Eagle Hotel was the center of Concord's social and political happenings. Andrew Jackson, Benjamin Harrison, Jefferson Davis, Charles Lindbergh, and Eleanor Roosevelt were all guests. The hotel is now the Eagle Square Marketplace, mostly offices with a few shops and a restaurant.

The Pierce Manse (224-9620), 14 Penacook Street, Concord. Open mid-June to Labor Day, Monday through Friday 11–3, or by appointment. Closed holidays. Built in 1838 and moved to its present site in 1971, this Greek Revival structure was home for Franklin and Jane Pierce from 1842 to 1848, between the time Franklin served in the United States Senate and was elected fourteenth president of the United States. Exhibits include many items owned by the Pierce family prior to 1869.

Kimball-Jenkins Estate (225-3932), 276 North Main Street, Concord. Open for "tea and tours" May to October and for special monthly events throughout the year. Built in 1882, a high Victorian brick and granite mansion with hand-carved oak woodwork, frescoed ceilings, oriental rugs, and many original furnishings. Special events include an October Mystery Night, a December Victorian Christmas, and a March Gilbert and Sullivan dinner-theater night. Staff are all in Victorian dress, and any food served is from Victorian recipes.

WINERY

The New Hampshire Winery (428-WINE), 38 Flanders Road (the access road to Pat's Peak ski area, 2 miles south of the village off Route 114), Henniker. Founded in 1964 near Lake Winnipesaukee sold, and moved to Henniker in 1990, this remains the only grape winery in northern New England. The juice from a variety of local and California grapes is processed here into eight different wines, the specialty being French-style dry food wines; a dessert wine recently took top honors in international competitions. Open daily 10 A.M.–9 P.M.; visitors are welcome to tour and taste (closed certain holidays, so please call ahead). A gift shop features New Hampshire products as well as wine; bottles of wine are priced from $6 to $12.

COVERED BRIDGES

Hopkinton-Rowell, West Hopkinton. Built in 1853 across the Contoocook River; rebuilt in 1965.

Henniker-New England College. A single-span, 150-foot bridge across the Contoocook River on the New England College campus.

FOR FAMILIES

White's Farm (435-8258), marked from Route 28 (off Routes 4/202) in Pittsfield. Open May to September, daily 10–5. Mike White breeds miniature horses; the petting farm is a sideline. Visitors are welcome to pet the horses, miniature donkeys, goats, and pigs. You won't find any food or soft drink machines, just friendly animals and an atmosphere that will make you want to linger. $4 per adult, $2 per child ages 2–12.

TO DO

BICYCLING

The Biking Expedition (428-7500), 10 Maple Street, Box 547, Henniker 03242. The specialty is organized long-distance tours for children, but customized tours with a support van, camping, or inn-to-inn tours can be arranged in this area.

CANOEING

See "The Manchester Area" (*Canoeing*) for the Merrimack River Watershed Council.

Canterbury Canoes (783-4479), West Road, Canterbury 03224. Rentals.

Hannah's Paddles (753-6695), I-93, Exit 17, Route 4 West, Penacook. Offers rentals and a livery service for the Merrimack and Contoocook rivers.

Note that the Contoocook between West Hopkinton and Henniker is a popular white-water canoeing and kayaking stretch in spring.

CAR RACING

New Hampshire International Speedway (783-4931), Route 106, Loudon. Billed as "the country's newest auto racing facility," it offers a 55,000-seat grandstand and stock-car racing and is the scene of Sports Car Club of America Regionals, American Motorcyclist Association Championship Competition runs, and World Karting Association races. Call for current schedule.

FISHING

The New Hampshire Fish & Game Department (271-3211; 271-3421), 2 Hazen Drive, Concord, is a source of information about where to fish as well as how to obtain licenses. Trout fishing is particularly good in this area.

GOLF

Beaver Meadow Golf Course (228-8954), Concord. Eighteen holes.

Dustin Country Club (746-4234), Hopkinton. Nine holes.

Plausawa Valley Country Club (224-6267), Pembroke. Nine holes.

HORSEBACK RIDING

Morning Mist Farm (428-3889), 15 College Hill Road, Henniker. Trail rides by reservation for all levels of riders; also English riding lessons.

DOWNHILL SKIING

Pat's Peak (428-3245; snow phone: 1-800-258-3218), Route 114, Henniker. The mountain rises steeply right behind the base lodge. It's an isolated 1,400-foot-high hump, its face streaked with expert trails and a choice of intermediate and beginner runs meandering down one shoulder; a half dozen more beginner runs—served by their own lifts—down the other. Big, old fir trees are salted around the base area, and the summit and some of the intermediate trails—certainly Zephyr, the quarter-mile-long beginner's trail off the top—convey the sense of skimming through the woods. When it comes to expert runs Tornado and Hurricane are wide and straight, but Twister is an old-timer—narrow, twisty, and wooded. This is a family-owned, -run, and -geared ski area that's a great place to learn to ski.

Trails: 19.

Lifts: 6, including a double chair and a triple chair to the summit.

Snowmaking: 90 percent.

Night skiing: 12 trails, 5 lifts.

Services: Ski school, rentals, ski shop, lounge, cafeteria, child care, snowboarding.

Rates: $30, $22 for juniors, on weekends; $19 for all skiers midweek; $12 for everyone for night skiing.

GREEN SPACE

Audubon Society of New Hampshire Headquarters (224-9909), 3 Silk Farm Road (follow Audubon signs from I-89, Exit 2), Concord. Open year-round, Monday through Saturday. Exhibits, overview of Audubon centers and programs in the state, Discovery Room with a "touch table," research library, eyrie for spotting passing birds, and resident barred owls. The adjacent Silk Farm Wildlife Sanctuary offers two trails, one to Great Turkey Pond.

Society for the Protection of New Hampshire Forests Headquarters (224-9945), 54 Portsmouth Street (take I-93, Exit 15 east), East Concord. Open year-round, Monday through Friday 8:30–4:30. The passive solar building has exhibits and a gift shop; it sits above its 95-acre spread of pine, which stretches down to the river with views of the capitol beyond. A 2-mile nature trails leads down to the Merrimack.

Elm Brook Park and Wildlife Management Area, off Route 127, West Hopkinton. Swimming and picnic areas; built and managed by the United States Army Corps of Engineers.

Hannah Duston Memorial, west of I-93, Exit 17 (4 miles north of Concord), Boscawen. The monument is on an island at the confluence of the Contoocook and Merrimack rivers. It commemorates the courage of Hannah Duston, a woman taken prisoner from Haverhill, Massachusetts, during a 1696 Indian raid. She later made her escape, killing and scalping 10 of her captors (including women and children), at this spot on the river. The 35-foot-high monument, erected in 1874, depicts a busty lady with a tomahawk in one hand and what look like scalps in the other. Open all winter, but the trail from the parking lot is unplowed in winter.

LODGING

Colby Hill Inn (428-3281; 1-800-531-0330), just west of the village center, PO Box 778, Henniker 03242. Ellie and John Day with their daughter Laurel have turned this 200-year-old landmark around since purchas-

Concord Coach, on display at the New Hampshire Historical Society

ing it in 1990. Despite the popular public dining room (see *Dining Out*) there's privacy for inn guests: a comfortable living room with hearth off by itself and a game room. There are 10 rooms in the inn itself, 6 more in the neighboring Carriage House, all with private baths and phones, 2 with working fireplaces. All are wallpapered in flowers and furnished with antiques; some have twin, some double beds. Facilities include a pool, croquet and badminton, tennis across the street. A full breakfast is served in the glass-walled dining room, overlooking birds feeding in the barnyard. It's included in the rates: $85–140; add tax and 10 percent gratuity.

☞ **The Meeting House Inn and Restaurant** (428-3228), Flanders Road, Henniker 03242. Up a hill road, right across from the entrance to Pat's Peak, this is a 200-year-old farmhouse with 6 outstanding country-elegant but air-conditioned rooms, to which breakfast is delivered in a basket. The barn has been turned into one of the area's most popular dining spots (see *Dining Out*). Because the restaurant is in an adjoining but separate building, inn guests have their privacy and a common room with a TV and VCR; with the public they share access to the inn's tub and sauna (it's between the inn and restaurant). Rates are $65–83 double and $98 for the two-room efficiency suites. No smoking.

☞ **Wyman Farm** (783-4467), Wyman Road, Loudon 03301. Despite its urban address this is actually one of the most rural and remote-feeling hide-aways around—and one of the most beautiful. This eighteenth-century "extended" Cape rambles along the very top of a hill with lawns and fields that seem to roll away indefinitely. The hilltop farm is actually in Loudon, a 10-minute drive from Canterbury Shaker Village. The living room retains its small-paned windows and original woodwork, giving a sense of age and comfort. The farm has been in Judith Merrow's family for many generations, and accommodating guests has been a tradition since 1902 when this was "Sunset Lodge" and the going rate for room and board was $5 a week. Today Wyman Farm remains a bargain for the genuine luxury it offers. All three bedrooms have private baths and sitting areas, also air-conditioning. Breakfast is cooked to order from the menu guests receive when they check in, and it is served in a cheery dining area with a soapstone stove and grandfather clock. Rates are $45–65 per room.

Windyledge Bed and Breakfast (746-4054), Hatfield Road, Hopkinton. Dick and Susan Vogt offer three rooms, one with private bath and the other two sharing, all nicely furnished. From $45 single to $75 double.

WHERE TO EAT

DINING OUT

Crystal Quail Restaurant (269-4151), Pitman Road, Center Barnstead. Dinner by reservation, Wednesday through Sunday. BYOB. You may luck out and find a free table tonight, but this unusual restaurant—limited to just a dozen patrons per night who dine on five courses in the dining room of an eighteenth-century house—is frequently booked at least a week in advance. Three entrées are always offered, and one is always a game dish, not necessarily but frequently quail. Organically raised veal is another specialty, and there is often a vegetarian (organic) dish. Needless to say, everything is made from scratch, and the desserts are exquisite. Be sure to ask for directions—there is no sign outside, and Barnstead is one of those towns webbed with back roads; even owner-chef Harold Huckaby admits to not knowing them all. $40 prix fixe.

The Horseshoe Tavern (746-4501), Route 103, Hopkinton. Open for lunch Tuesday through Friday, dinner Tuesday through Sunday, and Sunday brunch. Chef-owned with a reputation for consistent high quality. The setting is an old house with one large and three smaller dining rooms—an elegant, intimate atmosphere overlooking a pond. The emphasis is on fresh ingredients, and the soups, salad dressings, and baking, as well as the sauces, are all made from scratch. Specialties include seafood and veal, prepared a variety of ways. Dinner entrées include salad and vegetables. Moderate to expensive.

Candlelight Evening at the Creamery (783-9511), 288 Shaker Road, Canterbury. Chef Jeffrey Paige has an excellent reputation for dishes like sherried pumpkin apple soup, corn and blueberry salad, and baked sole with salmon stuffing. The candlelight evening meals are by reservation only, Thursday through Saturday at 7 P.M. $32 prix fixe includes a guided, candlelight tour of Canterbury Shaker Village. (Also see *Eating Out.*)

Vercelli's Ristorante Italiano (228-3313), 11 Depot Street, Concord. Open Monday through Friday for lunch and dinner; also Saturday dinner. This gets top votes from many Concordians as the best place in town—spacious and fashionably pink, black, and green, with traditional Italian specialties and decadent desserts. Specialties include osso buco Milanese and *bistecca Fiorentina.* Moderate.

Thursday's (224-2626), 6–8 Pleasant Street, Concord. Open Monday through Saturday for lunch; also Sunday brunch. An informal, friendly dining room with excellent soups and stews, quiches, and crêpes. Light and reasonably priced dinner specialties include chicken Mandalay and vegetable and cheese strudel. Moderate.

Hermanos Cocina Mexicana (224-5669), 8 Pleasant Street (off North Main Street), Concord. Open for lunch and dinner except Sunday. A Mexican restaurant that gets high ratings for authenticity and incredible margaritas. Moderate.

The Meeting House Inn and Restaurant (428-3228), 35 Flanders Road (off Route 114, across from Pat's Peak), Henniker. Open for dinner Wednesday through Saturday 5–9:30 P.M., Sunday 4–8 P.M. You enter through an inviting, solar-sided pub—its walls hung with dozens of Baggies filled with sand that patrons have sent from all corners of the world. The attractive dining area fills this 200-year-old barn. Specialties range from breast of chicken Basque with sweet Italian sausage and pimentos in chicken stock and white wine to beef Wellington. Lunch can be a charbroiled Angus burger or ribs. The favorite dessert at all meals is mud pie. Moderate.

Daniel's (428-7621), Main Street, Henniker. Open for lunch Monday through Saturday, dinner nightly, Sunday brunch. An unusually attractive dining space that overlooks the Contoocook River; there's also a brick-walled lounge. Lunch can be a Mediterranean salad (fresh greens, roast turkey, smoked ham, and imported cheeses garnished with marinated vegetables) or simply a Cajun burger. For dinner you might try chicken Contoocook, a breast of chicken baked with an apple, walnut, and sausage stuffing and glazed with a maple cider sauce. Moderate.

Colby Hill Inn (428-3281), off Western Avenue, Henniker. Open Tuesday through Saturday 5:30–8:30 P.M., Sunday in-season. Candlelight makes the paneling and furniture glow, and the view of fields adds to the romantic old-country-tavern feel of this dining room. Chef Michael Mack's signature dish is chicken breast stuffed with lobster, leeks, and boursin cheese, served with a cream sauce. You might also want to try the seafood Provençal (shrimp, lobster, scallops, and mussels sautéed with mushrooms, tomatoes, olives, and white wine, then tossed with pasta). Leave room for dessert. Moderate to expensive.

Country Spirit (428-7007), junction of Routes 202/9 and 114, Henniker. Open daily 11–9, Friday and Saturday until 10 P.M.; closed Christmas and Thanksgiving. Walls are festooned with memorabilia from "the only Henniker on earth": old tools, signs, and photos. The ceiling of the tavern is literally wadded with dollar bills, all donated by patrons, which the restaurant passes on to charity at regular intervals. Specialties include the restaurant's own smoked meats, aged Angus sirloin, and fresh fish. Moderate.

EATING OUT

The Creamery (783-9511), 277 Shaker Road, Canterbury. Lunch Monday through Saturday. The soups and breads are outstanding, and all the Shaker-inspired dishes are imaginative and nicely herbed and spiced.

Tio Juan's (224-2821), 1 Bicentennial Square, Concord. Open nightly from 4 P.M. This former police station is now the downtown singles bar. A great place to dine in the old jail cells (very private) on Mexican fare: burritos, quesadillas, tacos, and enchiladas.

Capitol City Diner, just off I-93, Exit 13, Concord. Open daily 6 A.M.–9 P.M. A great highway stop; 1950s diner atmosphere under the same ownership as the Common Man (see *Dining Out* in "The Lake Winnipesaukee Area"). Specials like 99-cent hamburger nights and Saturday when you dine half-price if you come in a 1950s or 1960s car.

Intervale Farms Pancake House (428-7196), Route 114 and Flanders Road (bottom of Pat's Peak access road), Henniker. Open 5:30 A.M.– noon, until 1:30 on weekends. Shaped like a giant red sugar shack, this spacious, friendly family-run restaurant is one of the very best places for breakfast in the state, featuring the farm's own homemade syrup.

Red Arrow Lunch (626-1118), 61 Lowell Avenue, Concord. In business since 1903, a small, friendly diner, open most of the time, the kind of place with a brass hanger for your coat and a mug of coffee that's brought the moment you sit down. Specialties like meatloaf and chicken pot pie, hot sandwiches, and stuffed cabbage.

The Grist Mill Restaurant and Bow Mills Pub (226-1922), just off I-89 in Bow. This is a large, attractive new place built on an old mill site; a good way stop with an immense all-day menu, everything from a tuna salad sandwich to a Cajun-blackened 10-ounce sirloin.

SELECTIVE SHOPPING

ANTIQUES

Route 4 between the Epson Circle and the Lee Rotary, especially in **Northwood**, is widely known as **"Antique Alley."** The more than two dozen shops here represent up to 400 dealers; the primary customers are antiques-store owners and other dealers from throughout the country. This area is just far enough off the beaten tourist path to make for exceptional pickings. Along Route 4 in Northwood, **Tavern Antiques** (942-7630) represents 50 dealers, **Hayloft Antique Center** (942-5153) has 120 dealer spaces, the **Parker-French Antique Center** (942-8852) represents 130 dealers, and a half dozen more shops in town represent a full range of antiques, from country furniture to quilts, folk art, china, and jewelry.

BOOKSTORES

Book Farm (428-3429), 2 Old West Hopkinton Road (just off Route 202/9), Henniker. An inviting browsing spot with a wood stove and 30,000 titles, general interest and reflecting owner Walter Robinson's special interests: history, literary criticism, and biography.

Old Number Six Book Depot (428-3334), 26 Depot Hill Road, Henniker (up the hill from Town Hall). Open daily 10–5. General and scholarly stock in all fields.

34 Churchillbooks (746-5605), 181 Burrage Road, Hopkinton. The world's largest stock of books by and about Sir Winston Churchill.

Women's Words Books (228-8000), 902B Upper Straw Road, Hopkinton. All areas of women's studies.

The Book Mill (224-2770), 484 North State Street, Concord. Open Tuesday through Saturday 10–5:30. General stock.

CRAFTS

Canterbury Shaker Village (783-9511), Shaker Road, Canterbury. The museum shop features Shaker crafts (see *To See* and *To Do*).

The League of New Hampshire Craftsmen (224-1471) is headquartered at 205 North Main Street (a red colonial across from the chamber of commerce office just off I-93, Exit 15) in Concord. The gallery here is open weekdays and has changing shows. The league's downtown shop in Phoenix Hall, 36 North Main Street (228-8171), is open Monday through Saturday and has juried crafts in a range of media and prices.

Mark Knipe Goldsmiths (224-2920), 13 South State Street, Concord. Custom-made jewelry studio and gallery.

The Fiber Studio (428-7830), Foster Hill Road, Henniker. Open year-round Tuesday through Saturday 10–4. Wide selection of natural knitting and weaving yarns and spinning fibers; looms, spinning wheels, knitting machines, handwoven and knit items, workshops.

Country Quilter (746-5521), College Hill Road (follow signs from routes 202/9), Hopkinton. Open May to December, Tuesday through Sunday 10–5:30; closed Sunday rest of the year. Ready-made and made-to-order quilts, pillows, wall hangings, and handcrafts in a 200-year-old barn.

Heritage Herbs and Baskets (753-9005), Hannah Duston Road, Canterbury. Open May through October, 11–6 daily. Herb garden, a country barn stocked with herbs, handcrafted baskets, wreaths, books.

North Woods Chair Shop (783-4595), 237 Old Tilton Road, Canterbury. Open weekdays 12:30–4:30, Saturday 9–1. Handmade furniture and accessories.

SPECIAL SHOPS

The Fragrance Shop (746-4431), College Hill Road, Hopkinton. Open May to Christmas, Tuesday through Saturday 10–5. An eighteenth-century barn filled with potpourri, herb wreaths, crafts, and a display garden. Follow signs from Hatfield Road (see Country Quilter under *Crafts*).

Granite State Candy Shoppe (225-2591), 13 Warren Street, Concord. A great old-fashioned candy shop that's been in business since 1927, making its own mints and butter chocolate creams among a wide assortment of chocolates, all made on the premises. A number of customers are also hooked on the freshly roasted cashews.

Caring Gifts (228-8496), 18 North Main Street, Concord. Specializes in baskets filled with everything from toys to gourmet foods, depending on the need.

Rare Essentials (226-2407), 97 North Main Street, Concord. Housed in a former bank building, a boutique with imaginative and expensive women's clothing and accessories.

☞ **McQuade's** (228-5451), 45 North Main Street, Concord. Like the Manchester store, this family-run Merrimack Valley chain features caged birds and basement bargains.

The Golden Pineapple, off Routes 202/9, Henniker. A trove of unusual gifts.

Henniker Pharmacy (428-3456), middle of Henniker. This distinctive building marks the center of Henniker in more ways than one. Pharmacist and owner Joe Clement stocks fishing gear, stationery, grocery items, wine and beer, cards and much more. There's also a soda fountain/snack bar and, in the basement, a surprising selection of toys.

SPECIAL EVENTS

May: Annual **Herb Day,** Shaker Village, Canterbury. Plants, herbal crafts, garden tours, demos.

June: Annual **Farm Day,** Shaker Village, Canterbury. Plowing contest, working sheep dogs, horseshoeing, butter churning, hayrides. **New Hampshire Concord Coach & Carriage Festival,** early June at New Hampshire Technical Institute, Concord. Horse-drawn parade, rides, competitions.

July: **Fourth Fireworks,** Memorial Field, Concord. **Strawberry Festival,** Contoocook. A 5-km road race, a 5-mile canoe race, a parade, strawberries. **Fireman's muster,** Pembroke. **Old Fashion Bargain Days,** downtown Concord. Main Street closes to traffic for three days; entertainment. **Canterbury Fair,** Canterbury. Chicken BBQ, auction, antiques, juried crafts, Morris Dancers. Annual **Bean Hole Bash** Weekend, Northwood. Food, games, raffle, auction, flea market.

August: Annual **Hot Air Balloon Rally,** Drake Field, Pittsfield. Twenty balloons usually come; arts, crafts, entertainment. Annual **Northwood Community Craftsmen's Fair,** Northwood. Country fair, more than 60 craftsmen, music, food, folk dancers, flower show.

September: Annual Kiwanis **Antique & Classic Car Show,** New Hampshire Technical Institute, Concord. Annual **Wool Day** at Shaker Village, Canterbury. Natural dyeing, rag-rug weaving, fleece-to-shawl.

October: Annual **Harvest Day** at Shaker Village, Canterbury. Ox-cart rides, apple-head dolls, pumpkin paintings.

December 31: **First Night New Hampshire,** Concord. New Year's Eve, some 130 performances in 30 locations around the city.

IV. THE LAKES REGION

The Lake Winnipesaukee Area
The Western Lakes

PETER E. RANDALL

Chocorua Lake with Mount Chocorua in the background

The Lake Winnipesaukee Area

The Lake Winnipesaukee Area, that section of New Hampshire that surrounds Lake Winnipesaukee, is often described as a single place, but it has several different environments for visitors. East and north of the lake are mostly small towns where New Hampshire's rural character offers a quiet, pastoral landscape with fewer services for vacationers, except for Wolfeboro, which boasts that it was America's first summer resort.

Ironically, views of, and access to, the lake are limited unless one is a property owner or guest at a motel, cabin colony, exclusive club, or condominium development. Squam Lake, made famous to nonresidents by the movie *On Golden Pond*, is a pristine jewel that is relatively undeveloped and has only limited public access. Even some public beaches are restricted to town residents or property owners. In sharp contrast is the western side of Winnipesaukee from Alton Bay to Meredith. Although many sections are heavily developed, there are numerous broad lake views and Winnipesaukee's only waterfront state park. From the honky-tonk atmosphere of Weirs Beach to the more upscale environment of Meredith, the western side of the lake is a busy place in the summer, with enough activities to keep any vacationer on the go.

Between these two extremes are such smaller lakes as Wentworth, Ossipee, Crystal, Chocorua, Province, or Merrymeeting. Here are found less commercial development, more parks, and some of the better inns and restaurants.

There is a unique character to summers in the Lakes Region. Unlike North Conway or Hampton Beach, where hotels and motels host the majority of visitors, the Lakes Region's summer population leans more to property owners who have their own lakefront cottages (or mansions, in some cases) or to week-long renters of housekeeping cottages. Many families have owned their summer places for generations, and many renters-by-the-week have similarly returned to the same cottages for the same week year after year. Indeed, while there are numerous housekeeping colonies, we have not listed many because few of them have any weeks open for new vacationers.

Although winter brings skiing, snowmobiling, and ice fishing, the

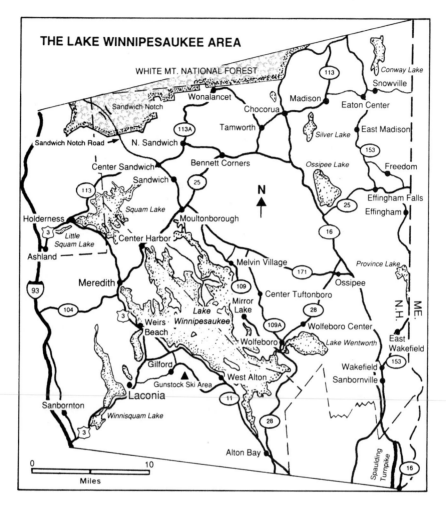

THE LAKE WINNIPESAUKEE AREA

Lakes Region is primarily a summer recreation area. Motels and some of the inns are closed between the end of foliage season and ice-out, but the off-season traveler will find ample accommodations and discover that the Lakes Region is a quiet alternative to the more-developed winter vacation areas of the state.

Historically, the summer residential pattern in this part of New Hampshire precedes the coming of Europeans to America. For centuries, Native Americans camped on lake shores to fish. Although they may have remained in the region during the winter, they moved away from the shores to avoid cold winds that still blow across ice-covered waters. Their old camping areas have become the sites of archaeological digs, and the Native American geographical names remain. Winnipesaukee, for example, means variously, "Smile of the Great Spirit" or "Beautiful water in a high place." One of their most popular locations was on the western side of the lake, where they set their weirs (today's Weirs Beach) to catch fish and eventually made a permanent settlement.

Although land grants were made in this region as early as 1748, it was not until the 1760s, and the end of the dangers caused by the French and Indian wars, that widespread settlement began in the Lakes Region. Royal Governor Benning Wentworth became a millionaire by granting new townships and retaining a portion of each grant for himself. It is his nephew John Wentworth, however, who deserves the credit for much of the early settlement in central New Hampshire and for beginning the summer vacation business there. In 1763 Wentworth began building a summer estate on his huge holding in today's Wolfeboro, and in 1769 he completed a road from Portsmouth to that farm, eventually extending it to Hanover, home of the then-new Dartmouth College. The so-called Governor's Road encouraged other wealthy seacoast families to build summer homes in the region. Thus the concept of a summer vacation place was born. The road also helped other settlers to move to the area. Wentworth and his family were forced to flee the colony in 1775 as the revolutionary war was beginning, abandoning his mansion, which later burned in 1820. It is now a historic archaeological site.

Although Wolfeboro remained a vacation area, the western side of Winnipesaukee developed more quickly, since it was on the main stagecoach route from the south and eventually was served by railroads pushing north toward the White Mountains. From those years until the early twentieth century brought the development of automobiles, the railroad-steamboat combination serviced lake visitors and residents alike. Various types of vessels have hauled freight and passengers around the lake since settlers first arrived here more than 250 years ago. Steamboats at one time dominated the traffic. Train passengers stopping at Weirs, Alton Bay, or Wolfeboro could transfer to boats bound for other land ports and islands all around the lake. Some boats offered direct service to various hotels or connected with smaller vessels sent to major ports from villages or hotels in some of the bays. This convenient transportation system led to the rapid residential development of the lake, so that by the late 1800s Winnipesaukee was a full-fledged recreation area. A section of the main street at Weirs Beach retains this turn-of-the-century Victorian atmosphere.

One of the more famous of the steamboats was the *Mount Washington,* a wooden side-wheeler in service from 1872 until it was destroyed by an off-season fire in December 1939. She was replaced by the present steel-hulled *Mount Washington II* a year later but remained in port for most of World War II when her engines were commandeered for the war effort. In 1946 she returned to service as the M/V *Mount Washington.* Lengthened in 1983 and changed to M/S (motor ship status), she continues today as the queen of the lake and a New Hampshire landmark.

The relative lack of commercial development on the eastern side of Lake Winnipesaukee dates back to the days when the railroads originally serviced only the western side of the lake, and much of the eastern shoreline was contained within large estates. Except for Wolfeboro, other eastern-shore towns remained small, mostly farming communities with a few guest houses, even as the large estates were eventually sold and subdivided for summer cottage lots. By 1895 a single railroad spur line reached Wolfeboro from a junction in Sanbornville, a stop on the Boston & Maine Railroad route between the seacoast and North Conway. This line ensured Wolfeboro's importance to the vacation business, but it did little to boost the fortunes of the surrounding towns, many of which still appear as they did at the turn of the century.

Just as it has been for nearly two and a half centuries since European settlement, Lake Winnipesaukee remains the centerpiece of the Lakes Region. The sixth largest natural lake completely inside United States borders, Winnipesaukee covers some 72 square miles and is 28 miles long and 13 miles wide. It has 274 habitable islands, ranging in size from mere piles of rocks to 1,000 acres, and contains 283 miles of shoreline; it is ringed by mountains—even Mount Washington can be seen. This is one of the most beautiful lakes in the world, and it is obviously a boat lover's paradise. On its shores are uncounted numbers of camps, cottages, year-round homes, condominiums, and mansions, and it appears that every one has at least one boat. With thousands of boats docked at marinas, there is an opportunity for anyone to launch a vessel at the many public and private launching sites. On major holiday weekends the lake often appears to be wall-to-wall boats. Everything from sailboards to schooners, from Jet-skis to high-speed runabouts, from canoes to luxury cabin cruisers can be seen among the more than 20,000 registered vessels using the lake. With all of this activity, there are marine patrol officers, speed limits at certain congested areas, and a goodly number of accidents each summer. No driver's license is required to operate a boat, but one must be 16 years old to operate one with more than 25 horsepower. This is not to suggest that boaters avoid the lake, only to use caution and constant vigilance. Also, keep an eye on the weather because high winds, sudden squalls, and thunderstorms can quickly whip the lake surface into waves as rough as the ocean, an especially dangerous situation for those in small boats who have no experience in such conditions.

There are more than two dozen other lakes of 100 or more acres (273 lakes and ponds of all sizes) in this region, so there are plenty of alternatives to boating, fishing, and other water sports. There are also mountains to climb, summer theater to attend, amusement parks and rides to enjoy, covered bridges to find, fruit to pick, horses to ride, slopes to ski, and racing sled dogs to watch. It is New Hampshire's most diverse recreational area, stretching from the foothills of the White Mountains nearly to the ocean. For family fun and recreation, it is a tough place to beat.

GUIDANCE

Lakes Region Association (253-8555), Box 1545, Centre Harbor 03226. For more than 50 years this association has produced its popular *Where to in the Lakes Region,* a handy guide to towns, accommodations, and attractions. Write for a copy or look for the guide throughout the region at rest areas and information centers.

Alton-Alton Bay Chamber of Commerce, Box 550 (summer office in the old railroad station, Route 11), Alton 03809.

Centre Harbor-Moultonborough Chamber of Commerce, Box 824, Centre Harbor 03226.

Greater Laconia Chamber of Commerce (524-5531; 1-800-531-2347), 9 Veterans Square, Laconia 03246. A summer information booth is maintained on Route 3, just south of Weirs Beach.

Meredith Chamber of Commerce (279-6121), Box 732 (office across from the town dock on Route 3), Meredith 03253-0732.

Greater Ossipee Chamber of Commerce (539-6201), Box 557B, West Ossipee 03814.

The Greater Wakefield Chamber of Commerce (522-9209), Box 111, Sanbornville 03890.

Squam Lakes Area Chamber of Commerce (968-4494), Box 498, Holderness 03245.

Squam Lakes Association (968-7336), Box 204, Holderness 03245. Contact this nonprofit association for hiking, boating, and wilderness information and maps.

Weirs Resort & Recreation Association (1-800-THE-WEIRS), Box 5336, Weirs Beach 03247. Free comprehensive guide to lodging, dining, and attractions.

Wolfeboro Chamber of Commerce (569-2200), Box 547 (in the old railroad station), Wolfeboro 03894.

GETTING THERE

By air: There is regular service to airports in Manchester (see "The Manchester Area") and Lebanon (see "Upper Valley Towns"), both of which are just a short drive via rental car from the Winnipesaukee Region.

By bus: **Concord Trailways** (1-800-852-3317), provides scheduled service from Boston's Logan Airport to central and northern New Hampshire via Londonderry, Manchester, Concord, Tilton, Laconia, New Hampton, Meredith, and Plymouth. Daily service varies.

MEDICAL EMERGENCY

Lakes Regional General Hospital (524-3211; 1-800-852-3311), Highland Street, Laconia 03246. Walk-in care 9–9, 24-hour emergency service.

Franklin Regional Hospital (934-2060), Aiken Avenue, Franklin 03235.

Huggins Memorial Hospital (569-2150), South Main Street, Wolfeboro 03894.

Moultonborough Medical Center (253-7721), Route 25, Moultonborough 03254.

VILLAGES

Alton Bay. One of the lake's early tourist centers, Alton Bay's waterfront area appears little changed from the turn of the century when train passengers transferred to steamboats. Concerts are held in the bandstand, and the old railroad station is the information center. Cottages around the bay shore evoke memories of the days when summer places were small houses, not condos. The chamber of commerce issues a detailed schedule of numerous summer events (see *Guidance*).

Freedom. The little village of Freedom is just off Route 153. We wandered through during the August Old Home Week when the many old, white-painted homes and public buildings were festooned with American flags. Apple pie and ice cream were the only missing elements.

Tamworth. Centered around the old Tamworth Inn and the Barnstormers is a fine collection of private and public buildings. Combined with a fast-running brook for swimming and a neat general store, the town has an "I'd like to live here" feeling about it. It is easy to see why Grover Cleveland, the two-term president, summered here; why his son Francis moved here to stay; and why Francis founded the Barnstormers some 60 years ago. A village of Tamworth, **Chocorua** sits astride busy Route 16. The view across the waterfall and its mill pond may look familiar; it has appeared in several national advertising campaigns. Have a tasty treat at the Dam Ice Cream Shop in the lee of the waterfall.

Wakefield. The sprawling town of Wakefield is composed of several villages: Union, Brookfield, Sanbornville, and Wakefield Corners, the latter now a historic district of 26 mostly white-painted eighteenth- and nineteenth-century houses and public buildings. Sanbornville is the commercial center and offers several shops, service stations, churches, and places to eat.

Melvin Village. Seemingly the antiques center of the eastern Winnipesaukee Region, the little town of Melvin Village still looks as it did in the nineteenth century when many of the houses lining the main street were built. Some of these homes now have antiques shops, and one business repairs antique motorboats.

Centre Harbor. At the head of Winnipesaukee is the winter home of the M/S *Mount Washington*. This town is bisected by Route 25, but it still retains its nineteenth-century character. The town was named for the Senter family, but the "S" became a "C," and "Center" became "Centre." There is similar spelling confusion with the names of many New Hampshire towns that end with "borough," often spelled "boro." Just one of the many little details that makes New England so interesting!

Center Sandwich. In all of New England there is not another village with such a distinguished reputation and tradition as a center for craftsworkers. Who would not want to live and work here among the picturesque white eighteenth- and nineteenth-century buildings in the village center—even the old gas station has been recycled as a frame shop. Just driving to the village is a relaxing experience, with its location off the main roads. Follow Route 113 east from Route 3 in Holderness or Route 109 north from Route 25 in Moultonborough. Or take one of the most scenic and rural drives in the state by joining Route 113 at Route 16 in Chocorua Village, then motor to Tamworth; follow 113A to Wonalancet and North Sandwich, and rejoin 113 to Center Sandwich. After following the country roads past old farms and mountain and lake views, the village is like a civilized oasis in the near-wilderness countryside. Shop for handmade crafts and lunch at the Corner House Inn. The Sandwich Fair, held on Columbus Day weekend, is the last one of the year. While the fair retains an old-fashioned feeling, the traffic clogging the winding roads to the fairgrounds is more like a city rush hour.

Tilton, west of I-93, is not exactly a quaint village, but it does boast that no other American town of its size has so many statues. From the interstate, one first notices the 55-foot-high granite Tilton (actually in Northfield) arch, an exact copy of a Roman memorial built in 79 A.D. Beneath it is a Numidian lion carved from Scottish granite, a tribute to Charles E. Tilton, the town's wealthiest midnineteenth-century citizen and a descendant of the first settler. He persuaded the town of Sanbornton Bridge to change its name to Tilton in 1869, a decision no doubt made easier by his gift of statuary. Such allegorical figures as America, Asia, and Europe can still be found around town along with Tilton's mansion, now the library of the private preparatory Tilton School, founded in 1845.

TO SEE

HISTORIC SITES

Governor Wentworth Historic Site, Route 109, Wolfeboro. Open in the summer months. This was the location of Royal Governor John Wentworth's summer estate, now owned by the state of New Hampshire, and the site of much archaeological work conducted under the auspices of the state Historic Preservation Office. Visitors are welcome. No facilities. (See the introduction to this chapter for background.)

Libby Museum, Route 109, 4 miles north of Wolfeboro Village. Open daily except Monday, Memorial Day through Labor Day 10–4. This natural history museum was built by a native in 1912 and is now operated by the town. It has a varied collection of mounted bird, fish, and animal specimens; Native American relics, including a dugout canoe; old maps and photographs; and eighteenth- and nineteenth-century country-living artifacts. Programs include nature walks, lectures, musical presentations, and art exhibits. Small fee.

Endicott Rock Historical Site, Route 3, Weirs Beach. A large boulder has been preserved here that dates to 1652, when a surveying party claimed this region for the Massachusetts Bay Colony. The second oldest historic landmark in the country, the site is named for Governor John Endicott, who ordered the survey. Adjacent is a city-maintained beach on Lake Winnipesaukee.

Ashland Historical Society, Whipple House Museum, 4 Pleasant Street, Ashland 03217. Open Wednesday and Saturday 1–4, July through Labor Day. Owned by the town of Ashland, the house was the home of a Nobel Prize winner for medicine, Dr. George Hoyt Whipple, and features exhibits related to his life, plus local artifacts. Next door is the Pauline Glidden Toy Museum.

Centre Harbor Historical Society, Plymouth Street (Route 25B), Centre Harbor 03226. An 1886 schoolhouse, open Saturday afternoon in July and August.

Freedom Historical Society operates the Allard house and barn on Maple Street. Open Tuesday, Thursday, Saturday, and Sunday 2–4, June through October 15. The collection includes household and barn artifacts and some genealogical items. Refreshments served on Thursday in July and August.

Harold Gilman Museum, Routes 11 and 140, Alton. Open Wednesday and Saturday, July through September, and the first Sunday of each month. An eclectic collection of country antiques including furniture, dolls, guns, china, glass, pewter, toys, clocks, and a working Regina floor model music box.

Madison Historical Society Museum, corner Route 113 and East Madison Road, Madison 03849. Open Tuesday and Sunday 2–4, April through September. A general collection of local artifacts, a turn-of-the-century kitchen, and a complete peddler's wagon with contents intact.

Meredith Historical Society, Winona Road, Meredith 03253. Open Saturday 1–4 in July and August, meetings first Tuesday of each month, April to December. Formerly the Oak Hill church, the museum has tools, costumes, photographs, "made-in-Meredith" items, and local historical information.

Ossipee Historical Society, Old Route 16, Center Ossipee 03814. The society opens Grant Hall, Tuesday and Thursday 1–4, in July and August.

Sanbornton Historical Society (286-7227), Sanbornton Square, Route 132, Box 2, Sanbornton 03269. The old Lane Tavern is open Sunday in July and August, 2–4.

Sandwich Historical Society (284-6269), Maple Street, Center Sandwich 03227. The Elisha Marston House is open June through September, Tuesday to Saturday (June and September, 1–5; July and August, 11–5), and the first Sunday of each month. On display are portraits by native Albert Gallatin Hoit, and there are special annual exhibits.

Tamworth Historical Society, Tamworth Village 03886. Meetings (held every third Wednesday April to October) of local, state, and, occasionally, national interest.

Tuftonboro Historical Society, Main Street (Route 109), Melvin Village 03850. Open July and August daily, except Sunday, 2–4. Photographs and literature relating to Lake Winnipesaukee and reference material on local families.

Thompson-Ames Historical Society, 24 Belknap Mountain Road, Gilford (mailing: Box 2532, Laconia 03247). Former church, now a museum open first Monday of each month, except in winter. Recently acquired an old Grange hall.

Wolfeboro Historical Society (569-4997), South Main Street, Wolfeboro 03894. Open July to August daily, except Sunday, 10–4:30. This is a three-building complex including the restored and furnished 1778 Clark House, an 1820 one-room school, and the replica 1862 Monitor Engine Company, complete with a restored 1872 horse-drawn, Amoskeag steam-pumper fire engine and an 1842 Monitor hand engine. When completed in 1983, this complex received a national award for historical excellence.

COVERED BRIDGES

A new **Graton covered bridge** just off Route 3 in Ashland was built for the town by resident Milton Graton, a renowned builder and restorer of covered bridges throughout the Northeast. The **Whittier bridge** crosses the Bearcamp River, just off Route 16 and north of Route 25, in West Ossipee. The **Cold River bridge** is a little difficult to find but well worth the effort. It is located off Route 113A just north of North Sandwich.

FOR FAMILIES

New Hampshire Farm Museum (652-7840), Box 644, Plumer's Ridge, Route 16 (Exit 18 off Spaulding Turnpike), Milton 03851. Open Tuesday through Saturday 10–4, mid-June to Labor Day, then weekends until mid-October. Museum office open weekdays 9–2, all year. Also inquire about special "Beat-the-Winter-Doldrums" scheduled for alternate Saturdays in winter. New Hampshire's rural agricultural heritage is maintained in this unusual collection of buildings, situated about midway between the Lakes Region and the seacoast. The huge barn is filled with wagons and a host of other farm artifacts, plus there are blacksmith and cobbler shops, a country store, and a furnished farmhouse, once the home of the Jones family. The best part of this museum occurs on most Saturdays and Sundays when there are special events. In 1990, 33

New Hampshire Farm Museum in Milton

different programs featured workshops and demonstrations of weaving, blacksmithing, beekeeping, ice-cream making, herbs, stone-wall repairing, chair-seating, rug-braiding, butter-making, fiber to fabric, and reed basket–making. Special days are devoted to pigs, sheep, dairy animals, goats, and even llamas. The second Saturday in August is an annual old-time farm day, with 60 farmers, artists, and craftspeople gathered to demonstrate their skills. A chicken barbecue is served. Fee charged. Detailed program of events available. The facility is also the museum of the Milton Historical Society.

The Museum of Childhood (522-8073), Wakefield (Mount Laurel Road, just off Route 16). Open daily except Tuesday, Memorial Day week to mid-October, 11–4, Sunday 1–4. Adults $3, children under nine $1.50. Town historian Elizabeth Banks MacRury and her sister Marjorie Banks accumulated more than 2,000 dolls and teddy bears plus music boxes, puppets, stuffed animals, and dollhouses in their lifetimes of collecting. Many of the dolls were picked up in their foreign travels. When this collection outgrew their home, they bought the house next door and in the spring of 1990 they opened this little museum to share their treasures with the public. The garage has been converted into Miss Mariah Plum's 1890 schoolroom, complete with old-fashioned desks, books, chalkboards, and the teacher herself.

Winnipesaukee Railroad (528-2330), South Main Street, RFD 4, Box 317, Meredith 03253. Open weekends (except Father's Day) from Memorial Day to late June, then daily until mid-October. Board from Meredith or Weirs Beach. Ride beside the lake on historic coaches of the 1920s and 1930s or connect with the M/S *Mount Washington* for a boat ride (see *Boat Excursions*). Fall foliage trips go north to Plymouth.

- **Science Center of New Hampshire at Squam Lakes** (968-7194), Box 173, junction of Routes 25 and 113, Holderness 03245. Open May through October 9:30–4:30, except 1–4 on Sunday in spring and fall. More than 50,000 children and adults each year benefit from programs operated by this nonprofit organization. While most of its activities are aimed at school groups, the center offers plenty to do and see in July and August. A 0.75-mile walking trail displays live bear, deer, bobcat, fox, bald eagle (and other birds of prey), and many other creatures. Hike through 200 acres of meadow and forest, past streams and brooks. A pontoon boat is used for exploring Squam Lake. Inquire about special summer family activities, which include two live animal programs daily. Gift shop. Fee charged.

- **Castle in the Clouds, Castle Springs** (1-800-729-2468), Route 171, Moultonborough 03254. Open weekends May to early June; then daily mid-June to mid-October. Built in the early 1900s at a cost of $7 million, this stone mansion is high on the side of the Ossipee mountains, overlooking Lake Winnipesaukee. Part of a 6,000-acre estate constructed by an eccentric multimillionaire, the castle has become a family recreation area. Castle Springs water is now bottled on the site. Tour the mansion, ride a paddleboat, take a hayride, picnic, or take a guided horseback trip on part of the 85 miles of graded carriage trails. Fee charged.

- **Centre Harbor Children's Museum and Shop** (253-TOYS), Route 25, Centre Harbor 03226. Open daily July through Labor Day, 9–8; Monday through Saturday the rest of the year, 9–5; Sunday 10–5. An interactive children's museum with a music room, a lake boat wheelhouse, country store, dress-up acting room, and similar things for kids. The toy shop has wooden toys, educational games, puzzles, and activity books. Fee charged.

- **Weirs Beach,** at the junction of Routes 3 and 11B, is the attractions center of the region, *the* place to go for many folks, and *the* place to avoid for others. It is difficult to be ambivalent about two water slides, miniature golf, a go-cart track, the country's largest arcade, and a strip of pizza parlors, fast-food spots, gift shops, and penny arcades. Right beside all of this activity is a summer religious conference center dating back to the turn of the century, a fine beach, one of the oldest historical markers in New Hampshire, the wharf for the M/S *Mount Washington* (see *Boat Excursions*), and the Winnipesaukee Railroad. Whatever you think about Weirs Beach, it is difficult to avoid passing through a section of it on the west side of the lake, so maybe you can stop for a while, have a pizza, let the kids take a few rides, and remember that you, too, were young once.

- **Surf Coaster** (366-4991), Route 3, Weirs Beach. Open weekends Memorial Day to mid-June, then daily until Labor Day. The largest water-slide complex in the region, with seven slides, changing rooms, and lifeguards. Pay once and slide all day. Also, two 18-hole miniature golf courses (additional fee).

- **Weirs Beach Water Slide** (366-5161), Route 11B, Weirs Beach. Open weekends Memorial Day to mid-June, then daily until Labor Day. This complex includes a variety of slides for beginners through experts. The Super Slide for experts is the longest in New England.
- **Funspot** (366-4377), Route 3, 1 mile north of Weirs Beach. Open all year, 24 hours a day, July through Labor Day. If you like games, there are 550 here, in the largest complex of its type in the country. From pinball to video and driving games, this has something for people of all ages, including both candlepin (a mostly New England game) and 10-pin bowling, driving range, and miniature golf.
- **Sumner Brook Fish Farm** (539-7232), Route 16, Ossipee. A former state fish hatchery, this is now a private business welcoming visitors to feed the fish, catch fish (rod rentals available, also fly fishing), or to purchase fresh or smoked fish. Fee charged, inexpensive.

SCENIC DRIVES

The northern and eastern sides of the lake abound with country routes. Our favorite is **Route 153** from Sanbornville to Conway, a wandering alternative to busy Route 16. **Routes 113** and **113A** from Tamworth to Holderness, **Route 109** from Wolfeboro to Sandwich, **Route 171** from Center Ossipee to Moultonborough, **Route 11** from Alton Bay to Glendale, and **Route 140** from Alton to Gilmanton are also favorite scenic drives.

TO DO

AIRPLANE RIDES

Laconia Airport (524-5003), Route 11, Laconia 03246, is an all-weather, paved runway facility with several air-taxi operators available for charter.

Lakes Region Airport (569-1310), off Route 109, Wolfeboro, is a community facility, with a paved runway, operated since 1939 by Ralph Horn. Adjacent is a seaplane base offering sight-seeing rides.

Moultonboro Airport (476-8801), Route 25, Moultonborough 03254. Sight-seeing rides.

Seaplane Services (524-0446), Route 3, Weirs Beach 03246. Daily seaplane, sight-seeing rides from the shores of Paugus Bay.

BOAT EXCURSIONS

Winnipesaukee

- **M/S *Mount Washington*** (366-5531), Lakeside Avenue, Weirs Beach 03246. Open late May through June 30 for two cruises daily, July 1 to Labor Day three cruises daily, then one cruise daily until late October. Special theme cruises and dinner and moonlight dancing cruises (two floors and two bands). For a first-time Lakes Region visitor, a ride on this famous vessel is a great introduction to Lake Winnipesaukee. Some 230 feet long with space for 1,250 passengers, the *Mount* cruises at 14 knots on a 3¼-hour,

50-mile route beginning at the Weirs, with stops at Wolfeboro and, on alternate days, Centre Harbor and Alton Bay. Round trips are available from all four ports. Depending on the schedule, dinner cruises depart from and return to Weirs Beach, Wolfeboro, or Alton Bay. Breakfast, luncheon buffet, snacks, and cocktails are served. Adult fares $12, children 5–12 $6, under 5 free. Reduced fares and special family package fares on new 2¼-hour cruises from Wolfeboro and Weirs. Dinner dance and theme cruises $25–32, reservations required, under age 21 not admitted unless with parent, guardian, or spouse over 21.

M/V *Sophie C* (366-5531), Lakeside Avenue, Weirs Beach 03246. Departs Weirs Beach. Open weekends only early May to early June, daily mid-June to the week after Labor Day, then weekends until Columbus Day. This is the floating United States Post Office and its cruises wind around the islands, into coves and channels, delivering mail to island dwellers, many of whom meet the boat at their wharfs. Depending on the day, there are two- or three-hour cruises, some with mail stops, some without. Also nightly sunset cruises (BYOB, complimentary snacks). Light refreshments are available. Adult fares $8, children 5–12 $4, under 5 free.

Queen of Winnipesaukee (366-5531), Lakeside Avenue, Weirs Beach 03246. Departs Weirs Beach. Open weekends (weather permitting) for two sailings mid-May through June and after Labor Day through mid-October; daily for three cruises July through Labor Day; also special BYOB evening cruises with complimentary snacks. This 46-foot sloop offers a wind-powered alternative to the motorboats plying the lake. Adult fares $9.50, children 5–12 $6, under 5 free, sunset $13.

M/V *Doris E* (366-5531), Lakeside Avenue, Weirs Beach 03246. Departs Meredith and Wolfeboro. Open July through Labor Day for one sunset and three daytime cruises (BYOB, complimentary snacks). Discover Meredith Bay and many islands on these 1¾-hour trips. On weekends the *Doris E* departs from Wolfeboro, and the *Sophie C* runs from Meredith. Light refreshments available. Adult fares $8, children 5–12 $4, under 5 free.

M/V *Judge David Sewall* (569-3016). Owned by the Wolfeboro Inn, this 65-foot vessel makes several narrated 1½-hour cruises daily from Memorial Day weekend through Columbus Day. Boarding is at the Wolfeboro town dock, snacks and beverages are available.

Squam Lake

Squam Lake Tours (968-7577), Route 3, PO Box 185, Holderness 03245. Open May through October, two 2-hour cruises daily, reservations suggested. See this pristine lake, the second largest in New Hampshire, aboard Captain Joe Nasser's 28-foot, canopy-top pontoon boat. He'll show you loons, Church Island, and the spot where *On Golden Pond* was filmed. Available for charters. Joe also runs a fishing-guide service.

Golden Pond Tour (968-3348) departs from the Manor on Golden Pond daily 10–4, Memorial Day through foliage season. Two-hour cruise in an all-weather boat to see loons, the islands, and the movie-filming location. Reservations suggested.

BOAT RENTALS

While many visitors are content to go swimming or take a cruise, other people bring their own boats or rent from a local marina. Listed are some of the businesses that provide motorboat rentals by the day or week and launching. Note that many motels and cottage colonies on the water also offer launching areas and limited dock space to their guests. Most towns provide public launching sites; inquire locally. Boat rentals usually require reservations.

Wolfeboro and East Side of the Lake

Goodhue and Hawkins Navy Yard (569-2371), Sewell Road, Wolfeboro.

Wolfeboro Marina (569-3200), Bay Street, Wolfeboro.

KRB Marine (544-3231), Melvin Village. Rentals only.

Melvin Village Marina (544-3583), Melvin Village. Launching only.

Wentworth State Beach and **White Lake State Park** (see *Green Space*).

West and North Sides of the Lake

Castle Marine (875-2777), Echo Lake Shores, Minge Cove, Alton Bay. Launching only.

Fay's Boat Yard (293-8000), 71 Varney Road, Smith Cove, Gilford. Also canoes.

Smith Cove Marina (293-2007), 17 Dock Road, Gilford.

Anchor Marine (366-4311; 524-3724), Winnipesaukee Pier, Weirs Beach. Rentals and tours.

Thurston Enterprises (366-4811), Route 3, on the bridge, Weirs Beach.

Meredith Marina (279-7921), Bay Shore Drive, Meredith Bay, Meredith. Also canoes.

The Sailing Center on Squam Lake (968-3654), PO Drawer R, Route 3, Holderness 03245. Sailboat, sailboard, motorboat, and canoe rentals by the half-day, day, or week. Also sailing instruction.

GOLF

Most courses in this region operate from mid-April through October, weather permitting, and all offer cart rentals.

Den Brae Golf Course (934-9818), Prescott Road, off Route 127, Sanbornton. Nine holes, driving range, full bar, and light food.

Indian Mound Golf Course (539-7733), off Route 16, Center Ossipee. Nine holes, full bar and food service.

Kingswood Golf Course (569-3569), Route 28, Wolfeboro. Eighteen holes, full bar and food service. This is a busy summer place, so call for tee times.

Laconia Country Club (524-1273), off Elm Street, Laconia. Eighteen holes, full bar and food service. Call for tee times; none available to the public on weekend mornings.

Lakeview Golf Course (524-2220), Ladd Hill Road, opposite Belknap

Mall, Belmont. Nine holes, sandwiches, and bar service. Great views of the lake from this hilltop course.

Mojalaki Country Club (934-3033), Prospect Street, off Route 3, Franklin. Challenging nine-hole course, food and bar service; tee times needed, especially on weekends.

Oak Hill Golf Course (279-4438), Pease Road, off Route 104, Meredith. Nine holes, full bar and food service. No tee times.

Pheasant Ridge Country Club (524-7808), Route 11A, Gilford. Nine holes, light food and bar service, tennis.

Province Lake Country Club (207-793-9577), Route 153, East Wakefield. Eighteen holes, full bar and food service; tee-time reservations available seven days in advance. The Maine–New Hampshire state line cuts through the course, and several holes line picturesque Province Lake.

Waukewan Golf Course (279-6661), off Routes 3/25, Centre Harbor. Eighteen holes, full bar and food service. No tee times, so plan ahead for busy weekend play.

White Mountain Country Club (536-2227), off Route 3, Ashland. Eighteen holes, full bar and food service, tee times suggested on weekends.

HIKING

Most people head for the White Mountains to hike, but the Winnipesaukee region offers a variety of trails with fewer hikers and splendid mountaintop lake views (although the peaks are not so high as those farther north). The ambitious hiker could follow connecting trails from Mount Chocorua to Waterville Valley. The standard reference is the *AMC White Mountain Guide,* although the Squam Lakes Association, which maintains many trails in this region, also has a guidebook (see *Guidance*). We have listed only a few of the many possible trails in the region. We do recommend one of these guidebooks because many of these trails are used less and marked less than the more famous trails farther north. All times shown are for the ascent only. Although brooks abound in the mountains, hikers should carry their own water. (Also see *Green Space.*)

Chocorua Region. Mount Chocorua is only 3,475 feet high, but its rugged, treeless summit makes it a popular destination, and it has many trails to the summit from a variety of points. The **Piper Trail** begins on Route 16 at a restaurant-campground-parking lot (fee charged for parking) a few miles north of Chocorua Lake. The well-trod trail is 4.5 miles long and requires about 3½ hours hiking time. The **Liberty Trail** begins on Paugus Mill Road, which is off Route 113A, southwest of the mountain. Some 3.9 miles long, requiring about 3 hours, 20 minutes, this oldest trail on the mountain passes the Jim Liberty cabin, a mountainside cabin with bunks. The **Champney Falls Trail** ascends the mountain from the Kancamagus Highway on the north and is described in "Mount Washington's Valleys." West of Chocorua are Mounts Paugus, Passaconaway, and Whiteface, all of which can be climbed from a parking lot off Ferncroft Road, at Wonalancet on Route 1

Sandwich Notch Region. Sandwich Notch Road connects C
wich with Route 49, the main road to Waterville Valley. 1
(elevation 2,620 feet) offers fine views of the Lakes Region ιυι υ....,
modest effort. On Sandwich Notch Road, about 2.6 miles from Center
Sandwich, watch for signs to Mead Base, a Boy Scout camp. The
Wentworth Trail is 1.6 miles long, and estimated hiking time is two
hours. Park in the field below the camp buildings and enter the woods
at a sign at the left rear of the main building. The **Algonquin Trail**
ascends Sandwich Dome (elevation 3,993 feet), also from Sandwich
Notch Road, about 3.7 miles south of the junction with Route 49. The
4.5-mile-long trail is rough but offers fine views from its rocky ledges.
Hiking time is 3½ hours.

Red Hill. A fine view of Lake Winnipesaukee is the prize at the end of the
Red Hill Trail. In Centre Harbor, at the junction of Routes 25 and
25A, take Bean Road for 1.4 miles, then follow Sibley Road (look for
the fire-tower sign) to a parking lot with a gate. Past the gate is a Jeep
road changing to the trail. The hike is 1.7 miles and requires just over
an hour. A famous Bartlett lithograph, often found in local antiques
shops, shows a gathering of Native Americans on Red Hill.

Belknap Range. On the west side of the lake is a low ridge of mountains
with many trails. A good starting point is the Gunstock Recreation Area
on Route 11A in Gilford (see *Green Space*). Several trails ascend beside
the ski slopes. Ask for a map at the camping area office.

Mount Major. Located just north of Alton on Route 11, this is everybody's
popular climb. **Mount Major Trail** is only 1.5 miles long and requires
about 1 hour, 20 minutes; views across the lake are impressive. Hike on
the right day and watch the M/S *Mount Washington* as she cuts through
the waters of Alton Bay.

SAILING

Winni Sailboard School (528-4110), 687 Union Avenue, Lake Opechee,
Laconia. Rentals of sailboards, rowboats, canoes, and paddleboats.

WATER SPORTS

Dive Winnipesaukee (569-8080), 4 North Main Street, Wolfeboro. Open
all year. Scuba instruction, rentals, guided dives, through-the-ice dives,
and air.

CROSS-COUNTRY SKIING

Deer Cap Ski Touring (539-6030), Route 16, Center Ossipee.

Gunstock Ski Area (293-4345), Route 11A, Gilford. This county-operated
area has both downhill and cross-country facilities plus ski jumping.

The Nordic Skier (569-3151), North Main Street, Box 269, Wolfeboro.
Open daily 9–5:30. Sales, rentals, and instruction for cross-country and
telemark skiing, also sales and rentals of toboggans, ski skates, and snow-
shoes. They also schedule moonlight tours and races and maintain a 20-
km trail network. Visit the shop for maps or suggestions for backcountry
skiing.

Perry Hollow Cross Country Ski Area (569-3151; 569-3055, ext. X-C), 2.5 miles south of Wolfeboro on Middleton Road. A country club with 20 km of trails and services maintained by the Nordic Skier (see above).

DOWNHILL SKIING

Gunstock Ski Area (293-4345; 293-4341; 1-800-GUNSTOCK), Route 11A, Gilford. This county-operated area has 7 lifts, 40 trails, and 98 percent snowmaking coverage, rentals, nursery, ski boarding, night skiing, and package plans, plus cross-country facilities and ski jumping.

GREEN SPACE

PARKS AND FORESTS

Gunstock Recreation Area (293-4341), Route 11A, Gilford. Operated by Belknap County, this 2,000-acre facility includes the Gunstock Ski Area and a large campground with related facilities. The 420-site campground has swimming, fishing, horseback riding, a store, and a playground. Extensive hiking trails lead to the summits of the Belknap Mountains, one of which is Gunstock. Trail maps are available. Warm-weather events include dances, crafts and woodsmen's festivals, and Oktoberfest. The ski area has 40 slopes and trails, 7 double chair lifts, and 2 ski jumps plus snowmaking and a cross-country center. The annual winter carnival is held in February.

Cate Park, Wolfeboro, on the waterfront by the town wharf. Occasional concerts and art exhibits in the summer, a delightful place to sit and relax any time.

Hemenway State Forest, Route 113A, Tamworth. Two trails here, one a short, self-guided nature trail, the other longer with a spur to the Great Hill fire tower offering views of the southern White Mountains. Brochures for both trails can usually be found in the summer in a box a few yards up each trail.

White Lake State Park, Route 16, Tamworth. Open late May through mid-October. Here is a picturesque sandy beach and a 173-site campground, one of the most popular in the state. Great trout fishing and rental boats available. Hike the 1.5-mile trail around the lake or climb nearby Mount Chocorua. The park's large stand of tall pitch pines is a national natural landmark. Fee charged; no reservations.

Chocorua Lake, Route 16, Tamworth. Just north of Chocorua Village, this location offers perhaps the most photographed scene in the country: rugged Mount Chocorua viewed across its namesake lake. This area gets its name from an old legend about a Native American who, after an altercation with early settlers, climbed the mountain, then leaped to his death to avoid capture. Most of the lakeshore has been preserved for its scenic beauty, and nary a summer cottage disturbs the pristine character of the place. At the north end of the lake, adjacent to the highway, is a popular swimming area and a place to launch a canoe or sailboard, but there are no public facilities, save a disgusting, smelly outhouse.

Sandwich Notch Road, from Center Sandwich to Route 49 in Campton. Sandwich Notch was once a farming region, but it has reverted to virtual wilderness and is now part of the White Mountain National Forest. The 11-mile road is sound but steep, rough, and slow-going; it is maintained that way to keep it from becoming too popular as a shortcut between the south and Waterville Valley. It is not winter-maintained. About 3.5 miles from Center Sandwich is Beede Falls in a town park. Several hiking trails lead from the road, including several for Sandwich Dome and Mount Israel.

Chamberlain-Reynolds Forest, College Road, off Route 3, 2 miles north of Meredith Village. Owned by the New England Forestry Foundation, this is a 150-acre managed woodland on the shore of Squam Lake. With beaches, trails, and picnic tables, it is a quiet spot to enjoy the country.

☞ **Stonedam Island Wildlife Preserve** (279-3246), operated by the Lakes Region Conservation Trust, Box 1097, Meredith 03253. Open weekends from July 4 through Labor Day, Saturday and holidays 10–5; Sunday noon–5. Stonedam Island is an undeveloped 112-acre preserve in Lake Winnipesaukee. A variety of family-oriented nature programs are offered to the public on weekends, but visitors are also welcome to walk the trails, relax under a tree on the shoreline, or pursue their own nature study. Transportation to the island is provided on weekends by Weirs Beach Boat Tours ($2 per person, call the preserve for departure schedules). Private boats may dock at the 60-foot pier on the northeast side of the island. Bring water, as none is available on the island; no pets, audio equipment, smoking, fires, or glass containers. Programs are free.

BEACHES

Ellacoya State Beach, Route 11, Gilford. Open weekends from Memorial Day, daily mid-June to Labor Day. The only state beach on Lake Winnipesaukee. A 600-foot beach with refreshment stand and changing rooms; handicapped accessible. The view across the lake to the Ossipee Mountains is one of the best in the region. Fee charged.

Wentworth State Beach, Route 109, Wolfeboro. Open weekends from Memorial Day, daily mid-June to Labor Day. This small park on Lake Wentworth has a bathing beach, play field, changing rooms, and shaded picnic area. Fee charged. Nearby is the Governor John Wentworth Historic Site.

LODGING

INNS

Wolfeboro and Vicinity

The Lakeview Inn (569-1335), 120 North Main Street, Box 713, Wolfeboro 03894. Open all year. Situated on a hill just a short distance north of the village, this is a combination restored old inn and adjacent two-level motel. All rooms have private baths, TV, and phones; a few have kitchenettes. Beds are doubles and queens (two beds in motel units). The inn features one of the area's best dining rooms (see *Dining Out*). $55–85 for two depending on the season.

The Wolfeboro Inn (569-3016; 1-800-451-2389), 44 North Main Street, Wolfeboro 03894. Open all year. This inn dates back to 1812; thanks to its 1988 expansion, it offers the region's finest accommodations and one of its better restaurants. Nine guest rooms are in the old front portion of the inn while the modern addition, built with a contemporary design to resemble an old barn, has 32 more rooms, including some suites with 4-poster beds. The country-style rooms have private baths and king, queen, double, or twin beds, with phones, TV, and individually controlled heat and air-conditioning. The deluxe water-view rooms in the addition have decks where one can watch lake activities or catch cooling breezes. Two rooms are handicapped accessible. The center sections of the three-story addition have open areas with chairs and reading nooks. The inn has a private beach on the lake; and, with the inn's village location, guests can leave their cars behind as they take a short walk to shopping or to the dock of the M/S *Mount Washington*. In season, guests are invited on a free morning lake cruise aboard the M/V *Judge David Sewall*, a 70-passenger reproduction of an old lake boat. It is also used for private charters. The inn also has conference facilities, a large dining room (see *Dining Out*), and Wolfe's Tavern, which is located in the old portion of the inn. $99–225 for two includes continental breakfast; MAP package plans available and discounts for weekday and three-day or longer stays.

North and East of the Lake

Stafford's in the Field (323-7766), off Route 113, Chocorua 03817. Open all year. Some 25 years ago Fred and Ramona Stafford bought an abandoned house in the countryside, where, with hard work and imagination, they have created one of New Hampshire's classic inns. They have 17 rooms, 6 with private baths, 1 with a fireplace, and 3 rooms in separate cabins. The eclectic furnishings are mostly cozy, older pieces, adding to the country character of the setting. Two common rooms have books and games; there is a short walk to Chocorua Lake for swimming and miles of trails for walking or cross-country skiing. Plan on some exercise to have plenty of room for Ramona's "on-the-gourmet-side" cooking, the inn's trademark (see *Dining Out*). MAP $120 (higher in foliage season) plus tax and 15 percent service charge.

The Tamworth Inn (323-7721; 1-800-642-7352), Main Street, Tamworth 03886. Open all year. Built in 1833, this village inn retains its nineteenth-century charm. There are 15 individually decorated rooms, including 4 suites, all with private baths. Beds range from kings to twins. There is a comfy pub, and the library has books, videos, and a fireplace. Summer guests enjoy the outdoor pool and strolling (or trout fishing)

DICK SMITH

The M/S Mount Washington *cruising on Lake Winnipesaukee*

beside the river. Just across the street is the Barnstormers' summer theater. Rates include a full country breakfast. The inn is popular locally for lunch and dinner (see *Dining Out*). Phil and Kathy Bender, innkeepers. $85–130 for two (higher during foliage season or holiday-skiing weeks), $110–160 MAP for two, plus tax and 15 percent service charge.

Corner House Inn (284-6219), Center Sandwich 03227. Open all year. Another New Hampshire favorite located in a special town, this popular place fills up quickly since it has only four rooms. It has been an inn for more than 100 years but has been owned for a decade by Don and Jane Brown, who have turned it into the kind of comfortable inn one dreams about. The four rooms, one with a private bath, are furnished with antiques and older pieces. You will find plenty to do in the shops of Center Sandwich. Nearby is Squam Lake for hiking and swimming. Full breakfast to guests; lunch and dinner also served in this popular restaurant. $60–70 for two.

Kona Mansion (253-4900), off Moultonborough Neck Road (turn at the blinker on Route 25 and follow the signs; mail: Box 458, Centre Harbor 03226). Open daily Memorial Day to Columbus Day and weekends earlier and later. More than 100 years ago, 16-year-old Herbert Dumaresq began working as an office boy for the Jordan Marsh Company, a large Boston department store. Thirty-three years later, he married the boss's daughter and became a partner in the business, which had become a leading New England retailer. Dumaresq used his fortune to buy up a large number of farms on Moultonborough Neck, creating a large summer estate where he built this mansion in 1900. The Crowley family bought the mansion and 130 acres of hilltop and lakefront in 1971, operating an inn since then. Drive up the hill to the mansion and enter a private country-club-like atmosphere, complete with a 9-hole, par-3 golf course, tennis courts, and lake boat dock. The inn has 10 rooms with twin or 1 or 2 double beds and private baths. On the lakefront are four housekeeping cottages with one to four bedrooms and 2 two- to three-bedroom chalets. Some of the inn rooms are small, but all are well decorated and comfortable. Relax in the lounge with a view across the lake to the Belknap Mountains. Breakfast and dinner served to the guests and the public (see *Dining Out*). EP $55–150; MAP for two (weekly only), $880–1,200; inquire about B&B rates. Cottages by the week, $400–675.

West and Northwest of the Lake

Red Hill Inn (279-7001), Route 25B and College Road (RFD 1, Box 99M), Centre Harbor 03226. Open all year. This inn has become another of New Hampshire's classics; but when Rick Miller and Don Leavitt bought the place in 1985, it was totally derelict, and friends suggested tearing it down. Built as a mansion in 1904 as part of a several-hundred-acre estate, the inn most recently was the administration building of the now-defunct Belknap College. When the school closed in 1974, the building was abandoned and eventually vandalized. The current owners immediately began transforming it into an inn and restaurant, a process that continues. Currently there are 10 rooms in the main inn. All have private baths, three have fireplaces, five have Jacuzzis, and several have separate sitting rooms. A separate stone cottage has three rooms (all with fireplaces, two with Jacuzzis), and the recently completed farmhouse has eight rooms (six rooms with Franklin fireplaces, two with Jacuzzis). Three rooms have twin beds; all the rest have doubles, and all have antique furniture and easy chairs. To feed these fireplaces (and another large one in the living room), the innkeepers annually cut some 35 cords of wood on the surrounding 50 acres. The hilltop location offers sweeping views of Squam Lake and the mountains, a panorama that improves in the winter when the Red Hill Cross-Country Ski Center opens (groomed trails and rentals). Dining is a highlight here as well, and the inn serves 3 meals daily, with menu items enhanced by more than 30 herbs gathered in the unique garden lining the path to the dining room patio. The lounge, with a 1940 Chris Craft runabout as the bar, offers guitar music on Saturday night (see *Dining Out*). B&B $65–135 for two. MAP five-day midweek packages begin at $450 for two; also three-day packages (three breakfasts, dinner one night) beginning at $199.95 for two.

The Manor on Golden Pond (968-3348; 1-800-545-2141), Shepard Hill Road and Route 3 (Box T), Holderness 03245. Built in 1903–1907, this inn is another of the region's many mansions built as summer estates by millionaires. Begin outside, where the 13-acre hilltop location provides a 65-mile panorama across Squam Lake and surrounding mountains. Inside, leaded glass windows, ornate woodwork, and detailed architectural elements remain from the past. No 2 of the inn's 17 rooms are alike, but all are furnished mostly with antiques (4-poster beds), have private baths, and some have fireplaces. Most rooms are large, especially the deluxe rooms which have king, queen, or two double beds, ceiling fans, air-conditioning, and lake views; some have balconies. Two large common rooms have fireplaces and plenty of books and games, and a second-floor library. Three detached housekeeping cottages are suitable for four, and another on the lakeshore has a fireplace and sleeps up to six. All have porches, living rooms, and kitchens. There are tennis courts and the manor's private 300-foot beach with a boat dock. Guests can enjoy special Squam Lake cruises. Breakfast and dinner served daily (see *Dining Out*). Rates for two: B&B $105–195, B&D $155–245; cottages are $800–1500 per week, no meals.

Inn at Mills Falls (279-7006; 1-800-622-MILL), Route 3, Meredith 03253. Open all year. Built around a tumbling waterfall adjacent to an old mill, this large, 54-room complex is perhaps the most upscale place to stay in the region. Each decorator-designed room has New Hampshire–made maple or Shaker pine furnishings with easy chairs and desks, air-conditioning, TV, and telephone. Beds are queens, twins, or a queen and a twin, and half the rooms have views out to Meredith Bay. There is an indoor pool, a spa, and a sauna plus 2 restaurants and 20 shops, galleries, and boutiques. EP, lake view, summer and fall, $87–157; off-season $77–142. Less for limited-view rooms; two- or three-night minimum for peak weekends. Packages for two nights $109–145 per person, including two breakfasts and one dinner.

BED & BREAKFASTS

Wolfeboro and Vicinity

Tuc' Me Inn (569-5702), 68 North Main Street, Wolfeboro 03894. Open all year. This nineteenth-century inn, with screened porches, a cozy music room, and a parlor with TV and guest telephone, is just two blocks from the downtown area. Seven rooms, three with private baths (the others share two full baths). Rooms have queen, double, and twin beds. Full country breakfast. Complimentary high tea served on request, 4:30–5:30. Innkeepers: Ernie, Terry, and Tina Foutz, and Idabel Evans. $75 for two for private bathroom, $69 for shared bathroom.

The Hardie House (569-5714), Route 109, Box 344, Mirror Lake 03853. Open all year. This 1850s guest house has been a B&B, operated by Cheryl Marsh and Harmon Hudson, since 1984. The six rooms are furnished with family antiques, double and twin beds (two rooms have one of each, just right for a family). A country location and one of the very few off-season places to stay on this side of the lake between Wolfeboro and Moultonborough. No pets or children under eight. $65 for two.

North and East of the Lake

Whispering Pines Bed & Breakfast (323-7337), 113A and Hemenway Road, Tamworth 03886. Open all year. This woodland inn is nestled into the edge of Hemenway State Forest. The inn has four rooms, one on the first floor with a private bath; the others share two full baths. Beds are doubles, queens, or a king that can be made up as twins. Most furnishings are antiques. A full breakfast is served in the paneled kitchen, which has a black kitchen wood stove. Hike or cross-country ski from the door, or swim in nearby Chocorua Lake. $55–80.

River Bend Country Inn (323-7440), Route 16, Chocorua. Open all year. Set 800 feet off the highway, this nine-room inn has a private, quiet location beside a babbling brook. Two rooms have private baths, one has a deck, and the other seven share three full and two half baths. One room has two doubles; other beds are queens and kings, and day beds can be moved in as needed. The country decor matches the style of this colonial reproduction building. Each of three common rooms has a fireplace and there is a small guest kitchen. Full gourmet breakfast served. $60–105.

The Wakefield Inn (522-8272; 1-800-245-0841), Mount Laurel Road (RR 1, Box 2185, Sanbornville 03872). Open all year. A centerpiece of the historic district, this three-story inn is a bed & breakfast. Open to travelers in one form or another since 1890, the inn is now operated by Lou and Harry Sisson. The seven guest rooms are reached by a unique hanging, spiral staircase. All the rooms, two of which are two-bedroom suites, have private baths, and the attractive furnishings feature Lou's homemade quilts. During the winter, Lou runs three-day quilt-making workshops. There is a large common room with a fireplace. Dinner served to guests on weekends as part of a package. $65 for two, $50 singles, B&B.

Freedom House B&B (539-4815), 1 Maple Street, Freedom 03836. Open all year. No smoking. Drive through quaint, quiet Freedom Village and you'll want to stay there for a while. Freedom has a town swimming beach, an antiquarian bookshop, and public tennis courts. The inn has six rooms, all of which share two full and two half baths, are furnished with antiques, and offer twin or double beds. Full country breakfast. Marjorie and Bob Daly. $60.

The Gilman Tavern (323-8940), Main Street, Tamworth 03886. Open all year. This eighteenth-century village tavern has been beautifully restored and furnished with antiques by Bill and Sue McCarthy. There are four rooms, one with a private bath. We loved the "Village Center" room with its stenciled floors and 1830s country furnishings including a canopy bed. Full breakfast served on the patio in warm weather. Afternoon refreshments are served to guests at 4 P.M. $60–85 for two.

Mount Chocorua View House (323-8350), Route 16, Box 348, Chocorua 03817. Open all year, winter by reservation only. New ownership and many changes for this 1845 colonial located just south of Chocorua village. Relax by the Franklin fireplace, then retire to an antique bed with a homemade quilt. Guests may use a kitchen where tea and coffee are available any time. Seven rooms share 3½ baths; continental breakfast. $49 for two, suite with private bath from $98.

Strathaven (284-7785), Route 113, North Sandwich 03259. Open all year. This is a special little B&B with a rural location and beautiful grounds that include extensive gardens, a pond for swimming or skating, and an English croquet court. There are four lovely rooms; two large rooms each have two double beds and a private bath, and two rooms share a bath. Many rooms feature antiques as well as Betsey Leiper's embroidery, a craft she teaches occasionally in week-long workshops at the inn. $55–60 for two with full breakfast.

West and Northwest of the Lake

Hedgecroft B&B (253-6328), Route 25B in the village (RFD 1, Box 547), Centre Harbor 03226. Open all year. Patte and Frank Fancher turned an 1820 village home into a three-room B&B. Two rooms have kings, the other has twin beds. The rooms share a bath. You can walk to the lakefront where the M/S *Mount Washington* docks (see *Boat Excursions*), shop in the new mall, or just relax on the inn's front porch hammock. $60 for two.

Watch Hill B&B (253-4334), Old Meredith Road, in the village (Box 1605), Centre Harbor 03226. Open all year. A professionally trained cook and former kennel owner, Barbara Lauterbach, bought one of the oldest houses (1772) in Centre Harbor and turned it into a comfortable B&B. Four rooms—one with a king, one with twins, two with queens—share two baths. Antiques furnish the house, and there is a cozy wood stove in the breakfast room, where Barbara applies her cooking talents. She also offers special cooking class weekends where guests can help plan and prepare the meals. $65 for two, discount for three nights or more.

Country Options (968-7958), 27–29 North Main Street, Ashland 03217. Open all year. Five rooms with two shared baths, furnished with antiques. Innkeepers Sandy Ray and Nancy Puglisi also operate a special-order bakery so one can imagine the treats offered for breakfast. For dinner, just walk across the street to the Common Man, a leading regional restaurant (see *Dining Out*). $45–50 for two.

The Glynn House Inn (968-3775; 1-800-637-9599), 43 Highland Street, Ashland 03217. Karol and Betsy Paterman have transformed this ornate, in-town, 1890 Queen Anne–style Victorian into an impressive B&B. The house retains all of its handsome, original woodwork and ornate oriental wallpaper. Each room is furnished to the period. Four rooms with private baths have queen-size beds, one has a fireplace, and the honeymoon suite has a canopy bed and Jacuzzi. Two rooms with double beds share a bath. Karol is a professional chef, having recently sold a local, popular restaurant, and his breakfast talents include eggs Benedict and apple strudel. B&B $65–95 for two.

The Inn on Golden Pond (968-7269), Route 3 (Box 680), Holderness 03245. Open all year. Bill and Bonnie Webb left other careers to open this large B&B in 1984. It is located right on Route 3, although well back from the road. Most of the nine rooms have queen-size beds, and all have private baths. All the rooms are furnished differently and have one or two easy chairs, a nice touch since so many places lack this amenity. You may wander the inn's 55 wooded acres or test your skills in table tennis or darts in the separate sports shed. The living room has a fireplace, and a second common room has cable TV. $85–135 for two. Children over 12 welcome.

Tuckernuck Inn (279-5521), 25 Red Gate Lane, Meredith 03253. Open all year. This is a five-room village inn, within walking distance to the shops and Lake Winnipesaukee. Each room is individual, but early-American decor is featured with stenciled walls and floors, quilts, and other antique touches. Two rooms have private baths, some have two double beds. There is a large fireplace in the living room along with a huge shelf of books and games to play. Breakfast is continental, but the selection of teas, coffee, hot muffins, fresh fruit, and cereals is more than filling. Paty Sariol, innkeeper. $55–65 for two.

Parade Rest B&B (524-3152), Parade Road, Laconia 03246. Open all year. Just two rooms with private baths, one with a kitchen, in a 1766 farmhouse out in the country. Watch for their sign; it's tiny. $65 for two with full breakfast, $55 per night for two or more nights.

Hickory Stick Farm (524-3333), Laconia 03246. Call for reservations and directions. Open Memorial Day to Columbus Day. Two rooms (one with a double, one with twin beds) furnished with antiques. The breakfast is served in a country kitchen. These two rooms are part of the region's best-known restaurant (see *Dining Out*). $70 for two.

Ferry Point House (524-0087), off Route 3 in Winnisquam (mail: RR 1, Box 335, Laconia 03246). Open Memorial Day through Labor Day, weekends through October. We found this place by accident, even though it has been open for five years and deserves to be better known. Make sure to get directions to their country location. They are situated on Lake Winnisquam and offer wide views from their 60-foot veranda and a waterfront gazebo. Guests may use the horseshoes, raft, paddleboat, or rowboat. The five rooms, all with private baths, have a lacy Victorian decor highlighted by old high-back beds and claw-foot tubs. Since the Damato family has published its own breakfast cookbook, be prepared for a gourmet start to your day. Try stuffed French toast, crêpes, cheese-baked apples, stuffed pears, and fresh breads and muffins. $70–80 for two.

Black Swan (286-4524), 308 Main Street, Tilton 03276. Open all year. An 1880s mill owner's mansion with seven guest rooms. Stained glass and ornate woodwork in the parlors and a spacious feeling to the bedrooms makes this a comfortable, interesting place to stay. Children over 12. Full breakfast. Bob and Janet Foster, innkeepers. $55–65 for two.

COTTAGES

✑ **The Anchorage** (524-3248), Route 3, Winnisquam (mail: RFD 1, Box 90, Laconia 03246). Open mid-May to mid-October. While this place is not fancy, it attracts a worldwide clientele, and cottages are booked early, often by folks who return year after year. With 35 acres and nearly a mile of shore on Lake Winnisquam, the Anchorage has 30 fully equipped (just bring groceries and a beach towel) housekeeping cabins that sleep from 2 to 8 people, plus 2 houses that accommodate 18. On the lakefront are three beaches, several boat docks, and rafts. Rowboats are free, or you can rent canoes or paddleboats, or fish from the shore for salmon and trout. Cook your catch on the charcoal grills while you watch the kids play lawn sports, use the playground and the ball fields, or run about with new friends through the fields, orchard, or woods. With no roads to cross, children can play safely all day. There are play areas for kids and adults and occasional organized cookouts and campfire sing-a-longs. Rates by the week, beginning on Saturday, late June through Labor Day, $415–1,250 per cottage. Houses $1,800–2,300; off-season $250–770. Minimum three-day stays also available off-season.

Ames Farm Inn (293-4321; 742-3962), 2800 Lake Shore Road (Route 11), Gilford 03246. Open late April (for fishermen) to first weekend in October. Tradition! This 300-acre inn and cottage community celebrated its 100th anniversary in 1990, having been operated by five generations of the Ames family. One guest, who has come to this inn for 64 years, probably knew them all. Another family of guests has stayed regularly for four generations. Needless to say, book early for the short peak season of July and August. Seventeen fully equipped housekeeping cottages are spread out on the lakefront. Each has one or two bedrooms, kitchenette, living room, and screened porch. The view across Lake Winnipesaukee stretches across the Broads for miles to the Ossipee Mountains and Mount Washington. Away from the shore are buildings with housekeeping apartments and 15 modern guest rooms with private baths. No charge to guests to launch and dock a boat. Some rental boats are available. The inn restaurant is open daily 8–2, from late June to Labor Day. Weekly rates; apartments and small cabin, $385; housekeeping cottages, $665 peak season, $350 off-season. B&B for the private rooms, weekly, $300 per person; three days and two nights, $100 per person.

MOTELS

If it's a motel you are after, Weirs Beach has a wide choice, especially along Route 3 (Weirs Boulevard), between the beach and Laconia. Some places are on Paugus Bay; others are across the street. The most luxurious is the **Margate** (524-5210; outside NH 1-800-MARGATE), a full resort with indoor pool, lake swimming, health club, tennis, and a restaurant ($55–164). Nearby are **The Naswa Lakeside Resort** (366-4341) and **Christmas Island Motel and Steak House** (366-4378). You'll also find many lovely inns, B&Bs, and cottages.

OTHER LODGING

Pick Point Lodges (569-1338), off Route 109 (6 miles north of Wolfeboro), Mirror Lake 03853. Open early May to late October. If a week on the lake is your idea of a perfect summer vacation, it is difficult to find a better place than this collection of cottages in a 113-acre pine forest with a half-mile of shoreline. Other people apparently agree since the place is 60 percent booked by Labor Day for the following summer, and many guests come back for the same week every summer. A perfect family spot—the kids can wander the woods on trails, use the playground, or swim in the lake. The 10 housekeeping cottages, 7 on the water, have 1 to 4 bedrooms each, with a fully equipped kitchen, 1 to 2 baths, cable TV, telephones, and all linens, towels, and blankets. Seven cottages have fireplaces, and all have king-size beds in the master bedrooms, with double and twin beds in other rooms. There is daily maid service (in season) and no tipping. Just bring your vacation clothes and wash them in the guest laundromat. The cottages rent weekly-only in the summer, when guests arrive on Saturday. Guests are welcome at complimentary breakfast on Sunday morning and the get-acquainted cookout on Monday night. Two rooms in the lodge (daily or weekly rates offered) have king-size beds and include daily breakfasts. In addition to indoor and outdoor tennis courts, the main lodge has four fireplaces, a large common room, books, and a game room for kids and adults. Weekly rates, early July to Labor Day, $1,300 (one to two persons) to $2,500 (four to eight persons); before and after Labor Day, rates range from $700 up. Daily rates available only in spring and fall.

WHERE TO EAT

DINING OUT
Wolfeboro and Vicinity
The Lakeview Inn (569-1335), 120 North Main Street, Wolfeboro. Open all year, nightly 5:30–10. Dining is in the restored rooms of this old inn. Highly regarded locally, this restaurant has a diverse menu of American and Continental entrées. Filet *boursin* Wellington ($16.95), scampi à la carbonara ($17.95), roast duckling ($14.95), and shrimp fantasia ($17.95) highlight the menu. Fresh baked breads and pastries, home-made soups. The adjacent lounge serves sandwiches, soups, salads, and lighter fare. Reservations suggested.

The Wolfeboro Inn (569-3016), 44 North Main Street, Wolfeboro. Open all year, Wolfe's Tavern from 11:30, the dining room 5–9:30. Located in the old section of the inn, the tavern serves a huge (70 items) variety of lighter fare, from hot and cold sandwiches and salads to soups, pizza, munchies, and dinners. More than 40 brands of beer, too. The dining room features New England–style cuisine with moderate prices.

The Cider Press (569-2028), Middleton Road, South Wolfeboro. Nightly, except Monday, 5:30–9; Sunday until 8. A popular rustic spot with barnboard walls, fireplaces, antiques, candlelight dining, and varied menu. Baby-back ribs, chicken Parmesan, lamb chops, fried shrimp, and roast duck are featured. Prices moderate.

East of Suez (569-1648), Route 28, South Wolfeboro. Open daily June through early September for lunch and dinner (closed Monday). Asian food of all descriptions is prepared by the Powell family. Japanese, Chinese, Philippine, Thai, Indian, and Korean specialties, huge portions, and moderate prices make this place a dining adventure. They have been here for over 20 years, yet remain a secret, even for many locals.

The Bittersweet Restaurant (569-3636), Route 28 (north) and Allen Road, Wolfeboro. Open daily all year, Monday to Friday noon–8:30; Saturday 5–9; Sunday brunch 11–2, dinner 5–8. Here's another old barn, furnished with antiques, recycled as a fine restaurant. The international cuisine ranges from grouper and Norwegian salmon with seafood mousse to stir-fry seafood and liver and onions. Moderate. The lounge has lighter, less expensive fare.

The Foxy Johnnie Restaurant and Firehouse Lounge (859-3381), off Route 11, New Durham. Open daily 5–9, Friday and Saturday until 10; Sunday 12–9. Part of this popular, rambling place was built in 1764, and many old elements remain, including the massive fireplace, hand-hewn beams, and wide floorboards. Roast beef and steaks broiled over live coals are the specialty. Several entrées including tenderloin and baked seafood such as haddock, shrimp, scallops, or mixed casserole. All steaks are served with sautéed mushrooms or pan-fried onions. Other entrées include sautéed lobster, fried seafoods, and veal parmigiana. Moderate to expensive.

North and East of the Lake

Stafford's in the Field (323-7766), off Route 113, Chocorua. Call for reservations. Three entrées are offered nightly in the summer, one entrée the rest of the year. Lamb with prunes, pork tenderloin, or sole Florentine might be offered along with homemade tasty soups, distinctively prepared vegetables, and scrumptious desserts.

The Tamworth Inn (323-7721), Main Street, Tamworth. Open all year for dinner, 6–8, Sunday brunch 11–2. This old inn's attractive dining room has a diverse, changing menu. Sample leg of lamb, beef Stroganoff, roast duckling, or chicken Tamworth. Appetizers include smoked trout, and provolone and pesto terrine. Fresh-made soups and homemade pies and cakes complete the menu offerings. Moderate. Lighter fare is served in the pub. Summer theater packages include room, dinner, and tickets to the Barnstormers (see *Entertainment*).

The Greenhouse (323-8688), Route 16, Tamworth. Monday through Friday 5–9, Sunday noon–8. Situated in the woods near White Lake State Park, this newly built restaurant specializes in European cuisine. Featured are schnitzel, sauerbraten, and *rolladen* (a traditional German beef roll stuffed with bacon, pickles, and onions), plus prime rib and steak au poivre. Chicken, seafood, and roast duck also offered along with homemade desserts. Two greenhouse dining rooms give the place its name. Inexpensive to moderate.

Corner House Inn (284-6219; 1-800-832-7829), Center Sandwich. Open all year: June through October, lunch 11:30–2:30 and dinner 5:30–9:30 daily; November through May, lunch and dinner Wednesday to Sunday. Reservations suggested. Candlelight dining, antiques, and local art, some of which are for sale, serve to accent the delicious dining found here. Fresh-made breads and ever-changing soups and desserts complement such menu highlights as chicken Oscar, veal Piccata, tournedos Normandy, double-thick lamb chops, shellfish sauté, and lobster and scallop pie. Prices moderate. Lunch ($1.95–$8.95) is not to be missed either, if one cares for fresh breads with large hearty sandwiches such as the black Angus: carved steak topped with onions, tomatoes, and buttermilk dressing on French baguette. Salads, quiche, crêpes, and soups, plus delicacies such as broiled scallops and Maine crabcakes with Cajun sauce, round out the menu.

The Woodshed (476-2311), Lee's Mill Road, off Route 109, Moultonborough. Open all year for dinner. To operate a successful restaurant in the countryside, on a side road, off a less-than-major route, in a small spread-out town, you must have atmosphere and good food. This place has both in abundance. What began as a small restaurant in an old farmhouse a decade or so ago has grown into a large operation using the barn, its loft, and even a screened-in patio. The barn is exquisite, retaining its old hand-hewn features and decorated with antiques and collectibles. An evening could begin at the raw bar for clams and oysters or peel-and-eat shrimp and escargot. Prime rib is the specialty, but how about a combination with king crab or lobster? After Cajun roast pork tenderloin, shrimp kabob, steak teriyaki, or chicken gourmet, no wonder the dessert menu begins with "We dare you?" Cheesecake, a one-scoop hot chocolate sundae, or Indian pudding can complete the repast. Moderate.

The Sweetwater Inn (476-5079), Route 25, Moultonborough. Open all year for dinner. Despite the name this is a restaurant only, specializing in Italian dishes with pasta made fresh daily. Generally prices are moderate, but this menu also includes 15 items priced between $4.95 and $9.95. One could order pizza or something traditional like chicken Parmesan, pasta with clam sauce, or Alfredo. Or you have other choices: fettuccine jambalaya with sautéed chicken, scallops, and Andouille sausage with garlic, sherry, onions, peppers, tomato, and Cajun spices; lobster ravioli; medallions of veal with shallots and fancy mushrooms; seafood paella; or chicken Veronique. Favorites like steak au poivre, baked haddock, and oriental stir fry round out the menu. The Belgium chocolate dessert specialty changes daily, and there are many delectables from the dessert tray.

Kona Mansion (253-4900), Moultonborough Neck Road (off Route 25), Centre Harbor. Open daily Memorial Day to Columbus Day, and weekends earlier and later. Salads, veal du jour, Delmonico steak, shrimp,

Winter scene in Tamworth

and chicken Kona (breast stuffed with spinach and cheese, topped with white wine sauce) are featured in this mansion overlooking the lake on Moultonborough Neck. Dine in the ornate Victorian spaces once used as the mansion's library, living, and dining rooms.

West and Northwest of the Lake

Red Hill Inn (279-7001), Route 25B and College Road (RFD 1, Box 99M), Centre Harbor. Open all year, lunch 12–2 summer and fall, Sunday buffet brunch 11–2, dinner 5–10. Gourmet dining with candlelight and fresh flowers. Everything is made fresh from scratch with noncholesterol butter seasoning for sautés. Try oven-fried rabbit, roast pheasant, broiled lamb chops, baked stuffed chicken breast, shrimp with lobster stuffing, or lemon-pepper scallops plus steaks, king crab legs, haddock, veal, and a variety of vegetarian dishes. Homemade dessert offerings change daily, and we haven't mentioned the appetizers, salads (12 dressings), and homemade soups and desserts, especially the berry pies. Inexpensive to very expensive.

The Manor on Golden Pond (968-3348; 1-800-545-2141), Shepard Hill Road and Route 3 (Box T), Holderness. Open daily for breakfast and dinner 5:30–9, weekends until 9:30, off-season until 8:30; Sunday brunch 11–2. Feel like a Victorian millionaire in the manor's ornate dining room while sampling roast duckling, pork tenderloin sautéed with ginger and tarragon, rack of lamb, veal with king crab and scallops in champagne basil cream, or sautéed chicken topped with spinach *boursin* and dill Havarti cheeses. Their apple pie has been judged the best in New England. Moderate to expensive.

The Common Man (536-4536), North Main Street, Ashland. Open daily for lunch and dinner; no lunch Sunday and Monday. Opened in 1971, this is the original, and still popular, restaurant in a group that has grown to include the Capital City Diner in Concord (see "The Concord Area"), the Common Man in Lincoln, and the Italian Farmhouse in Plymouth (see "The Western Whites"). The country decor features old posters, books, tools, and art, a comfortable feeling for relaxed dining. The varied menu ranges from pasta primavera and veal or chicken Oscar to chicken Kiev and crab and scallop pie. The "Grate Steak," a large planked steak with a medley of vegetables served family-style, can feed up to three people for $26.95. All the swordfish is served fresh, never from frozen, and the beef ages in their own walk-ins for three to five weeks. White chocolate mousse or brownie sundae, mud pie, or chocolate decadence cake. Moderate to very expensive.

Hickory Stick Farm (524-3333), Laconia. Open Memorial Day through Columbus Day daily at 5, except Monday; Sunday at noon. Also open Thursday, Friday, and Saturday nights in winter. Reservations are required, so ask for directions. Charlie and Dee, the first generation of Roeders, started this unique restaurant in 1950 and must have had plenty of courage since it is well off the beaten path. Success solved the location problem, however, as this place now has a national reputation, especially for their specialty, roast duckling. Scott Roeder and his wife, Mary, ran the business for many years and now son Greg is in charge. The main dining room has early-American decor, but the large screened gazebo overlooking the gardens is our favorite spot. For an appetizer, among other items, try duck-liver pâté, fried duck livers, or duck soup. Roast duck is prepared for one, or a whole duck for parties of two, three, or four ($27.50–43.80). Slow-roasted to remove the fatty layer under the skin, these 4- to 5-pound Wisconsin-bred ducks have crisp skin with moist, fork-tender meat beneath. Frozen, cooked duck with a packet of orange sherry sauce is available in their gift shop or by mail. Casseroles of seafood, scallops, or vegetables, baked chicken, filet Wellington, and rack of lamb are among other menu specialties. Dinners include orange curl rolls, a molded pineapple salad, or country green salad. Moderate.

Mame's (279-4631), Plymouth Street, adjacent to the Mill Falls Marketplace, Meredith. Open daily for lunch 11:30–3, dinner 5:30–9, and Sunday brunch 11:30–2. An 1825 brick house with barn, now with six dining rooms, Mame's offers varied and reasonably priced dining. Chicken baked in white wine with lemon and mushrooms, vegetable Alfredo, lobster-scallop divan, baked haddock, and roast prime rib are offered, along with the evening dinner special (soup to white chocolate for $9.95) and surf and turf for two at $19.95. Mud pie, liqueur parfaits, cheesecake, and more for dessert.

The William Tell Inn (293-8803), Route 11, West Alton. Open for dinner daily except Monday, spring to fall; Thursday to Sunday in winter. With a name from Switzerland and housed in a chalet, expect Swiss cuisine. One of the region's better restaurants, with a variety of Continental favorites served by owner-chef Peter Bossart and his wife, Susan. Weiner or Holstein schnitzel, roast duck, filet mignons of beef, veal, and pork charbroiled and served with various sauces, or boiled meats with sauerkraut and parslied potatoes provide hearty dining. The desserts feature dark Tobler chocolate imported from Switzerland. Moderate.

EATING OUT

Bailey's Dockside, Wolfeboro. On the water, off Main Street in the center of town. Open mid-May to mid-October for lunch and dinner. An old favorite located on the wharf where the M/S *Mount Washington* docks. Known for its ice cream. Also see Bailey's on South Main Street. Open all year for breakfast, lunch, and dinner—a tradition for more than 50 years.

Hart's Turkey Farm Restaurant (279-6212), Route 3, Meredith. Open all year at 11:15 A.M. for lunch and dinner. Turkey is the specialty but there are also steaks, seafood, and sandwiches in this large, popular restaurant, family-owned since 1954.

Pauli's Bakery (286-7081), 170 Main Street, Tilton. Open 6:30 A.M.–3 P.M., Monday through Saturday; also Thursday and Friday nights and Sunday brunch. Step into this perfectly ordinary-looking eatery and enjoy everything homemade from breads and quiches to soups and pies. Try strawberry waffles or crab and cheese omelets for breakfast; buffalo or venison stew or a smoked fish for dinner in this small oasis. A lunch special is chicken and crab (boneless breast of chicken sautéed and topped with sliced tomatoes, broccoli, crabmeat, and melted cheese).

ENTERTAINMENT

GALLERY

Belknap Mill Society (524-8813), Mill Plaza, Laconia 03246. Open all year, weekdays 9–5, Saturday 9–1. Built in 1823, this is the oldest unaltered textile mill in the country. There are tours of the building, but this mill, which was saved from demolition, is also the headquarters of the only year-round arts center in the region. Art exhibits and displays, music, lectures, and children's programs are among the many events open to all.

MUSIC

New Hampshire Music Festival (253-4331). This regional music institution begins in early July for six weeks; all performances held at 8. Chamber music on Tuesday at Boyd Hall, Plymouth State College; orchestral symphony Thursday at Newfound Regional High School, Bristol, and (repeat of Thursday) Friday at Gilford Middle-High School.

The Arts Council of Tamworth (323-8693), presents monthly (except summer) performances in the Tamworth-Sandwich area. Included are classical pianists, string quartets, and vaudeville.

SUMMER THEATER

The Barnstormers (323-8500), Tamworth 03886. Open July and August. New Hampshire's oldest professional theater celebrated its sixtieth anniversary in 1990. Director-founder Francis G. Cleveland stages outstanding plays with an equity cast. Musicals, some popular plays, and other lesser-known offerings. Dinner-theater packages available with the Tamworth Inn.

The Lakes Region Theater (279-9933), Route 25, Box 1607, Meredith. Professional summer-stock productions of Broadway plays presented in Inter-Lakes High School. Late June through August.

SELECTIVE SHOPPING

Annalee Dolls (279-6542; 1-800-433-6557), off Route 3 or Route 104, Meredith, also a shop in North Conway Village. Open all year (except two weeks in January); hours vary by the season. Dolls are for kids, of course, but these dolls are also among the more collectible items one can purchase today, so probably more golden-agers stop here than children. Annalee Thorndike began making her felt dolls in 1934; now she runs a major local industry employing more than 450 people; and her dolls are sold and collected nationally. For collectors, the best inventory is maintained here, including more than 1,000 different early dolls. You can see the finished pieces in the gift shop, the doll museum, and the Annalee Doll Antique and Collectible Doll Shoppe. Join the Annalee Doll Society and receive a free doll, membership pin, newsletter, and an invitation to the annual barbecue and doll auction held on the last Sunday of June. Small fee for the museum, dolls for sale; also a catalog.

Ayottes' Designery (284-6915), Center Sandwich. Open year-round, Thursday to Saturday 10–5, or by appointment. This is the home-studio-shop of renowned handweavers, Robert and Roberta Ayotte. They weave apparel, wall hangings, rugs, pillows, and placemats; they sell looms, accessories, and weaving supplies; and they display handmade crafts by others.

Basket World (366-5585), Route 3, Weirs Beach. Leave the kids across the street at the Funspot while you shop through this huge display of woven baskets, furniture, and other items.

Camelot Bookstore (569-1771), 16 North Main Street, Wolfeboro. A fine selection of local books and gifts.

Kelly's Gem Shop (323-8203), Route 16, West Ossipee. Open all year, Tuesday through Sunday 9–5. Sterling silver, turquoise, beads, earrings, jewelry, and mineral specimens from around the world. Most jewelry made by Russell and Marie Kelley.

Country Braid House (286-4511), Clark Road, Tilton. Open Monday to Saturday 9–4, Sunday by appointment. Pure wool rugs in a variety of patterns.

Hampshire Pewter (569-4944), 9 Mill Street (just off the main street), Wolfeboro. Open year-round daily except Sunday, 9–5. Beautiful pewter items, especially their Christmas tree ornaments. This company was founded in 1974 to revive a nearly forgotten early-American craft. Shop and tours.

Pepi Herrmann Crystal (528-1020), 3 Waterford Place, Gilford. Fine-quality, hand-cut crystal and giftware.

Keepsakes Quilting and Country Pleasures (253-4026), Route 25, Senter's Marketplace, Centre Harbor (mailing address: Box 1459, Meredith 03253). Open daily. Called New England's largest quilt shop, there is everything and anything a quilter could desire, including 3,500 bolts of cotton cloth, stencils, patterns, and kits. For the less ambitious, there are also ready-made quilts for sale. Free catalog.

League of New Hampshire Arts & Crafts. Shops in Center Sandwich (Sandwich Home Industries in the village) and Meredith (Route 3). Open daily late May through Columbus Day. Superb New Hampshire–made crafts of all types including lamps, furniture, prints, carvings, textiles, pottery, and much more. Demonstration programs in July and August. Sandwich Home Industries in Center Sandwich was started in 1926 to promote traditional crafts, and it became the founding member of the League of New Hampshire Arts & Crafts in the 1930s. Its present shop opened in 1934.

The Old Country Store, Route 25, Moultonborough. Open daily. Built as a stagecoach stop in 1781, this rambling old building has a small museum to go along with gifts, books, New Hampshire–made products, and typical country-store items.

The Old Print Barn (279-6479), Winona Road, off Route 104, Meredith. Open Memorial Day to Columbus Day, 10–6 P.M., by appointment at other times. The largest display of original prints in New Hampshire includes antique and contemporary work from 1600 to the present. We especially like the old New Hampshire views of the lakes and White Mountains, but one can find etchings, lithographs, and engravings covering virtually any subject from any continent as well as work by locally prominent and world-famous artists. The huge restored barn, with its detailed nineteenth-century craftsmanship, is impressive, too. Free, but it will be hard to resist buying a print!

The Sundial Shops (524-3322), 604 Main Street, Laconia (also in Gilford and Meredith). Local books plus chocolates and gifts.

Farmers' Market, Belknap Mill Plaza, Laconia. An outdoor market open Saturday 9–noon, mid-July through October.

SPECIAL EVENTS

Dozens of events are held each summer in the Winnipesaukee Region, too many to list here in detail, especially since some are one-time events.

We suggest checking with the local chambers of commerce (see *Guidance*), in the several free vacation newspapers found throughout the region, or with such organizations as the Lakes Region Association (569-1117), New Hampshire Farm Museum (652-7840), Belknap Mill Society (524-8813), and Gunstock Recreation Area (293-4341).

Early February: **World Championship Sled Dog Derby,** Opeechee Park, Laconia. Three days of racing by colorful teams of sled dogs.

Mid-February: **Winter Carnival** (569-2758), Wolfeboro Lion's Club. A week of events.

Mid-May: **Annual Winni Fishing Derby** (253-8689), Lake Winnipesaukee. A weekend fishing contest with cash prizes for the largest land-locked salmon or lake trout.

Early June: **Annual Barn Sale and Auction** (652-7840), New Hampshire Farm Museum, Milton. Call for detailed schedule of many summer events.

Late June: **Annalee Doll Auction and Barbecue** (279-6542), Annalee Dolls, Meredith.

July and August: **Alton Bay Band Concerts.** Several free concerts are held weekly during July and August, plus a week of events during Old Home Week in mid-August. Write the chamber of commerce for a full schedule of summer activities (see *Guidance*).

Early July: **New Hampshire Music Festival** (253-4331). A six-week regional tradition, all performances at 8. Chamber music on Tuesday, Boyd Hall, Plymouth State College; orchestral symphony Thursday at Newfound Regional High School, Bristol, and (repeat of Thursday) Friday at Gilford Middle-High School.

July Fourth: Region-wide celebrations with parades and fireworks, some special events, some events held the night before. Alton, Ashland, Laconia, Meredith, Tamworth, Wolfeboro.

Mid-July: **Arts and Crafts Street Fair,** downtown Laconia.

Late July: **Annual Antiques Fair and Show** (539-5126), Kingswood High School, Wolfeboro. **Family Fish and Game Day** (271-3254), White Lake State Park, Tamworth. **Antique and Classic Boat Show,** Weirs Beach. **Annual Flea Market and Chicken Barbecue,** East Alton.

Early August: **Huggins Hospital Street Fair** (569-1043), Brewster Field, Wolfeboro.

Mid-August: **Old Home Week** (539-6323), Freedom and Alton. **Miss Winnipesaukee Pageant** (366-4377), Funspot, Weirs Beach.

Late August: **Annual Lakes Region Fine Arts and Crafts Festival** (279-6121), Meredith.

Mid-September: **Annual Winnipesaukee Relay Race** (524-5531). Begins in Gunstock Recreation Area and teams of runners circle the lake. **Rochester Fair** (332-6585), Rochester.

Early October: **Annual Quilter Show** (524-8813), Belknap Mill Society, Laconia.

The Western Lakes

From Canaan Street Lake in the northwest corner to Bradford's Lake Massasecum in the southeast, from Lake Sunapee in the southwest to Newfound Lake in the northeast corner, this region is spotted with lakes big and small, all set in open, rolling countryside, each with a view of one of the area's three mighty mountains: Sunapee, Kearsarge, and Cardigan.

All three summits are rewarding hikes, and all the lakes offer attractive lodging as well as superlative swimming, fishing, and boating. But this entire area is far less well known than the Winnipesaukee Region, because the big old hotels here were replaced with second homes instead of with the cottage colonies and motels that took their place around Winnipesaukee. Still, these "summer people" continued to patronize summer theater, shops, ski areas, and restaurants. When lodging places began proliferating again—as they have over the past decade—these amenities were all in place.

But it's still all very low-key. The year-round hub of the area is the handsome old college town of New London, with a rambling, eighteenth-century inn and Colby-Sawyer College at its center and two small lakes (Little Sunapee and Pleasant) on its arms.

The region's most famous lake is Sunapee. Unusually clear (it is still a source of drinking water) and unusually high (1,100 feet), Lake Sunapee sits midway between the Connecticut River Valley and the Merrimack River Valley. Ten miles long and three miles wide, still sheathed almost entirely in green, it's unquestionably a special place.

Lake Sunapee, however, is a tease. Stand on the summit of Mount Sunapee (accessible by chair lift) and its 10-mile-long expanse shimmers below, seemingly inviting you to jump in. But back on level ground it's elusive. You can swim at the beach in Lake Sunapee State Park, choose from two excursion boats, or rent almost any kind of boat. But no road circles the lake because from the 1850s until the 1920s everyone came and went by train and got around the lake itself by steamboat. The largest cluster of hotels and busiest steamboat landing was Sunapee Harbor, still the summer focal point of the lake.

Newfound Lake (8 miles west of I-93), with 22 miles of shoreline, is even more low-key than Sunapee; and Mount Cardigan looms above

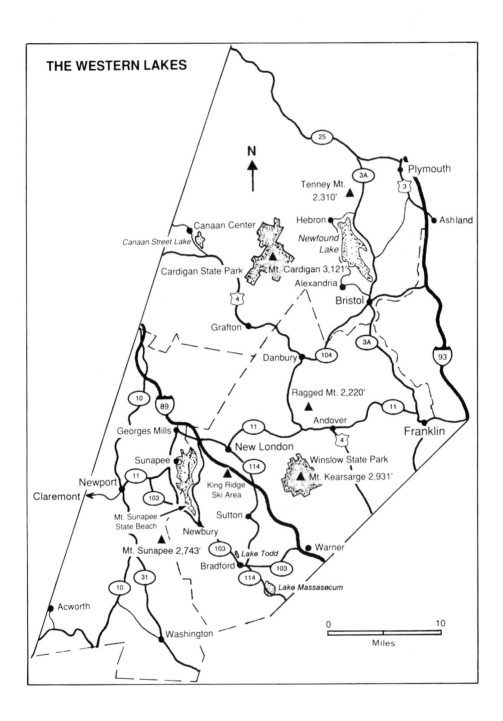

THE WESTERN LAKES

N

Plymouth

25

3A

3

Ashland

Tenney Mt.
2,310'

Canaan Center

Hebron

Canaan Street Lake

*Newfound
Lake*

Cardigan State Park

Mt. Cardigan 3,121'

Alexandria

Bristol

4

3A

Grafton

Danbury

104

93

Ragged Mt. 2,220'

10

89

Andover

11

Georges Mills

11

Franklin

Sunapee

New London

114

Winslow State Park

4

Newport

11

114

Mt. Kearsarge 2,931'

Claremont

103

King Ridge
Ski Area

Mt. Sunapee
State Beach

Sutton

Newbury

Warner

Mt. Sunapee 2,743'

103

Lake Todd

Bradford

103

31

114

Lake Massasecum

10

Acworth

Washington

0   10

Miles

its western shore as Mount Sunapee does above Lake Sunapee. Both Sunapee and Newfound offer sandy state beaches, as does smaller Kezar Lake in North Sutton, off I-89, Exit 10 (see *Swimming*). Other lakes accessible to guests at local inns include Canaan Street Lake in Canaan Center; Little Sunapee and Pleasant Lakes, both in New London; Lake Todd and Lake Massasecum in Bradford; Highland Lake in East Andover; and Webster Lake in Franklin.

Since its opening in 1968, I-89 has put New London and Sunapee less than two hours from Boston, but the increase in tourist traffic has not been dramatic. In winter, skiers tend to day-trip from Boston as well as Concord; and in summer, innkeepers complain, they whiz right on through to Vermont. Lodging prices are relatively low—even lower in the northern part of this region, backroaded when I-89 replaced Route 4 as the region's major east-west route.

In state of New Hampshire literature you'll find this area under "Dartmouth/Lake Sunapee," but we believe that these "Western Lakes" (west of I-93) deserve more recognition. While it is handy to the cultural happenings around the Dartmouth Green, the area is equally handy to attractions in the White Mountains, the Merrimack Valley, and the Monadnock Region. These Western Lakes are great spots to explore from. Or to just stay put.

GUIDANCE

The Lake Sunapee Business Association maintains a lodging reservations number (763-2495; 1-800-258-3530). It's based year-round at Mount Sunapee Ski Area. This does not represent all lodging, but it is the only umbrella information service for this area. There is also a seasonal information booth for Sunapee in Sunapee Lower Village.

The New London Area Chamber of Commerce (526-6575) answers phone queries year-round and maintains a helpful, walk-in information booth in the middle of Main Street, June to Labor Day.

The Newport Chamber of Commerce (863-1510) maintains a seasonal information booth in the center of town.

The Newfound Region Chamber of Commerce (744-2150) maintains a seasonal information booth on Route 3A at the foot of the lake.

King Ridge Ski Area in New London also maintains its own seasonal lodging service: 1-800-258-3530.

GETTING THERE

By bus: **Vermont Transit** (1-800-451-3292) stops at the New London Pharmacy on Main Street twice a day en route from Boston to White River Junction; direct service from Boston's Logan Airport.

By car: I-89 cuts diagonally across the heart of this region, putting it within 1½ hours of Boston; via I-91 it's also 2½ hours from Hartford.

By air: See "The Upper Connecticut River Valley" and "The Manchester Area."

MEDICAL EMERGENCY
New London Hospital (526-2911), County Road, New London, is a major facility. (Also see "The Upper Connecticut River Valley.")

VILLAGES

Andover. This is an unusually proud town, with Proctor Academy, established in 1848 (actually it moved to Wolfeboro in 1865, back in 1875), at its core. Hence the B&Bs and unusually good dining and shopping. The **Andover Historical Society Museum,** housed in a vintage 1874 Victorian-style railroad station on Route 4 in the tiny village of Potter Place (open weekends from Memorial Day to Columbus Day, Saturday 10–3, Sunday 1–3) is worth a stop. According to a historical marker in the nearby Route 11 rest area, Potter Place takes its name from Richard Potter, a nineteenth-century magician known throughout America. Highland Lake is in East Andover.

Bradford Center. Just off the main drag (Route 103), but it feels like a million miles. Coming north, the turn for River Road is a left just beyond the junction of Routes 103 and 114. You go through the Bement covered bridge (see *Covered Bridges*), built in 1854. Continue up the hill, up and up until you come to the old hill-town crossroads. Turn left and you will find the old schoolhouse and vintage 1838 meetinghouse with its two doors and Gothic-style tower topped with decorative wooden spikes (peculiar to New Hampshire) resembling upside-down icicles. The old graveyard is here, too. The present town hall was moved from this village down to what is now the business center of Bradford when the train arrived in the 1860s.

Canaan Center is a classic hill town: a proud, old agricultural community left high and dry when the railroad came through in the 1860s and the town's business shifted to the area (now the village of Canaan) 3 miles down the road, around the depot. Like Old Deerfield Village in Massachusetts, the houses here—a few eighteenth-century homes and the rest built before 1850—line one single street, and over the years the community itself has become known as "Canaan Street." Its unusual beauty—and that of its lake—was recognized early on; the train to Canaan soon began bringing summer tourists, hotels opened to accommodate them, and an elaborate pier was built. The **Canaan Historic Museum** (open Memorial Day to Labor Day, Saturday 1–4) displays souvenir dishes with "Canaan Street" and color pictures printed on them. After a long hiatus, this is, happily, one of the places you can once more find lodging. Now Canaan itself is off the beaten track. Look closely and you may find the old depot. A second story has been added, and it's now a laundromat.

Hebron is a classic gathering of white-clapboard houses around a common at the northwestern corner of Newfound Lake. The handsome, two-story meetinghouse was completed in 1803, and the Hebron Village School is housed in a churchlike building with a Gothic Revival steeple (upside-down wooden icicles again).

New London. Sited on a ridge, good for summer views and winter skiing (both cross-country and downhill), New London is the home of **Colby-Sawyer College** (526-2010), a four-year co-ed college founded as a Baptist academy in 1837. The 80-acre campus includes the Marion G. Mugar Art Gallery, with changing exhibits by recognized artists and by college faculty and students. The **New London Historical Society Museum and Library** (526-4978), off on Little Sunapee Road, is an ambitious gathering of eight restored buildings, including an 1835 cape with an attached el and barn; also a schoolhouse, country store, and blacksmith shop on 5 acres. Unfortunately the society has run out of volunteer steam and so is open only by appointment. New London is also home to the **Barn Playhouse** (see *Entertainment*), one of New England's oldest and best summer theaters. The town's hidden gems are Cricenti's Bog (see *Green Space*) and Little Sunapee Lake, site of Twin Lake Village, one of New England's most authentic and low-profile nineteenth-century family resorts.

Newport is an old mill town and commercial center with some elaborate nineteenth-century buildings like the **Newport Opera House** (863-1111) on Main Street, the scene of frequent concerts, plays, and dances. **The Richards Library Arts Center** (863-3040), 58 North Main Street, hosts continuous exhibits by local artists. The handsome brick **South Congregational Church** at the other end of Main Street (it's diagonally across from the Mobil Station), completed in 1823, is almost identical to the Unitarian Church (1824) in Deerfield, Massachusetts. No longer an outlet for the woolen mill across the street, **The Dorr Mill Store** (see *Selective Shopping*) is still well worth a stop.

South Sutton, off I-89, Exit 10, and south on Route 114, or 5 miles north of Bradford. A nineteenth-century mill-village center with a 1790s meetinghouse, a former general store, now the Old Store Museum, exhibiting (we're told) no less than 4,000 items, along with the 1863 schoolhouse, open to visitors in July and August, Sunday 1–4 or by appointment (927-4183; 938-5005).

Sunapee Harbor. In the Sunapee Historical Society Museum (see *Museums*) you browse through scrapbooks filled with pictures of the village's half dozen vanished hotels, most notably the 4-story, 100-room Ben-Mere, which sat until the 1960s on a knoll in the middle of "The Harbor." Local residents worry that most of the lakeshore is now privately owned and to this end the Sunapee Harbor–Riverway Corporation has been formed to revitalize the Harbor's adjacent waterway, which once fueled a tannery, a pulp mill, and clothespin and wooden hame (part of a harness) factories. To date the Corporation has restored several buildings in Sunapee Harbor, and worked to bring in restaurants, shops, and

MIKE ROUNDS

Ice harvesting in North Sutton

summer entertainment. Woodbine Cottage (see *Dining Out*) is the village's most amazing landmark.

Washington. A tiny gem of a village with a cluster of imposing buildings— a meetinghouse completed in 1789 (the Asher Benjamin–style steeple was added later), an 1840s Gothic-style Congregational church, and a two-story, 1830s schoolhouse—all huddled together on the north side of the common. According to a historical marker, this is the birthplace of the Seventh-Day Adventist Church (April 1842) and also the first town in the country incorporated (December 13, 1776) as "Washington."

TO SEE

MUSEUMS
(Also see *Villages*.)

Mount Kearsarge Indian Museum (456-2600), Kearsarge Mountain Road, Warner. Open May through October, Monday through Saturday 10–5; Sunday 1–5. $5 per adult; $3 for ages 6–12. This is one of the most impressive displays of Native American artifacts in the Northeast. Frankly, we weren't prepared for the quantity or quality of this collection, amassed by one man, Bud Thompson, over the past 40 years. With the skill of a professional curator (he was formerly with Canterbury Shaker Village), Thompson has transformed a former riding arena into a showcase for hundreds of priceless and even evocative pieces: dozens of intricate sweet-grass baskets from the Penobscots, carved ash baskets from the Passamaquoddies, and intricate quillwork from the

Micmacs, Seneca corn-husk masks, Anasazi pottery from Chaco Canyon in New Mexico (dating from somewhere between 800 and 1200 A.D.), Navajo Yei rugs, elaborate saddlebags beaded by the Plains Indians, cradle boards from Idaho, and much, much more.

"I don't want people bending and squinting over labels," Bud Thompson observes. Instead, guides elaborate on the various Native American pieces as well as the cultures they represent. One of the few modern pieces in this museum is an imposing, bigger-than-life statue of a Native American in full regalia, which Thompson bought many years ago at the annual League of New Hampshire Craftsmen's Fair at Mount Sunapee State Park.

"It wasn't until after I had settled on this site for the museum and positioned the statue at the entrance that its sculptor told me it was carved from a single tree he had cut from the slopes of Mount Kearsarge," Thompson relates. The museum stands at the base of Mount Kearsarge, near the entrance to Rollins State Park and its trails to the mountain's bald summit. (Also see *Hiking* and *Green Space*.)

Sunapee Historical Society Museum (763-4418), Sunapee Harbor. Open mid-June to Labor Day, Tuesday and Thursday through Sunday 1–4; Wednesday 7–9. A former livery stable, filled with photos of Sunapee's grand old hotels and steamboats. You discover that visitors began summering on Lake Sunapee as soon as the railroad reached Newbury in 1849 and that the lake's resort development was sparked by the three Woodsum brothers from Harrison, Maine (another lake resort), who began running steamboats to meet the trains. Soon there were 2 competing ferry lines (one boat carried 650 passengers) serving dozens of small landings on the shore and islands.

HISTORIC HOMES

Daniel Webster Homestead (934-5057 in summer; 271-3254 off-season), Flaghole Road, marked (badly) from Routes 11 and 127 in Franklin. You might want to call for directions and hours. This is a small clapboard eighteenth-century cabin filled with replicated furnishings. Webster (1782–1852), Dartmouth class of 1801, represented New Hampshire in Congress from 1813 to 1817 and Massachusetts in the Senate from 1827 to 1841. He was a legendary orator, involved in many major issues of his day.

The Fells Historic Site at the John Hay National Wildlife Refuge, Route 103A between Newbury and Blodgett Landing. For details and programs call 763-5041 or 763-5958. Tours are offered on weekends. "The Fells," former estate of statesman and author John Hay, sits high above the eastern shore of Lake Sunapee. Unfortunately, the 42-room mansion itself is unfurnished, but the estate is a delightful place to walk—from the exquisite "Alpine Garden," a half mile down along meadowlike lawn to the water. Be prepared for a walk from the parking area; it's a half-mile to the house.

COVERED BRIDGES

The Keniston bridge, built in 1882, spans the Blackwater River, south of Route 4, 1 mile west of Andover Village.

The Cilleyville bridge, now open to foot traffic only, was built across Pleasant Stream in 1887; it's now at the junction of Routes 11 and 4A in Andover.

Bement bridge, built in 1854, is on River Road in Bradford Center.

The Warner-Dalton bridge, originally built in 1800 and rebuilt in 1963, crosses over the Warner River, south of Route 103 in Warner Village (multiple king-post truss).

The Warner-Waterloo bridge, rebuilt in 1972, is 2 miles west of Warner Village, south of Route 103 (Town lattice truss).

FOR FAMILIES

Ruggles Mine (523-4275), off Route 4, Grafton. Open daily mid-June to October 9–5; until 6 in July and August; weekends only mid-May to mid-June. Admission $9 per adult, $4 per child age four and over. Children of all ages will love this place; you don't have to be a mineral buff. The eerie shape of the caves high up on Isinglass Mountain is worth the drive up the access road, and the view includes Cardigan, Kearsarge, and Ragged mountains. Commercial production of mica in this country began here in 1803. The story goes that Sam Ruggles set his large family to work mining and hauling the mica (it was used for lamp chimneys and stove windows) to Portsmouth; from there it was shipped to relatives in England to be sold. When the demand for his product grew, these trips were made in the dead of night to protect the secrecy of the mine's location. The mine has yielded some $30 million over the years. It was last actively mined by the Bon Ami Company—for feldspar, mica, and beryl—from 1932 to 1959. An estimated 150 different minerals can still be found; visitors are welcome to take home samples.

SCENIC DRIVE

Bradford Center to Washington to Sunapee. The most difficult part of this tour is finding the starting point, just west of the stoplight at the junction of Routes 104 and 114 in Bradford. The road immediately threads a covered bridge, then climbs 2.4 miles to Bradford Center (see *Villages*). Stop to see the original town buildings (just out of view on your left), but turn right and follow that road 1.8 miles until a sign on a tree points the way to East Washington—which brings you into the middle of another picturesque village from which the way is marked—it leads through a barnyard ("visitors welcome") on past Island Pond. Turn north (right) on Route 31 into Washington, a photographer's delight with its vintage 1787 meetinghouse, school, and Congregational church all conveniently arranged to fit in one picture. Continue north on Route 31 to Pillsbury State Park (see *Green Space*). Just north of Goshen village a right brings you back to Route 103 and Mount Sunapee. Be sure to stop at Nelsons Crafts along the way.

TO DO

BICYCLING
The Sunapee Off-Road Bicycle Association (763-2303) sponsors Wednesday evening rides.

Bob Skinner's Ski & Sports (763-9880) in Sunapee Harbor rents mountain bikes. Inquire about the many mapped local routes.

(Also see the Inn at Danbury under *Lodging*.)

BOATING
Sargents Marine (763-5032), Route 11 on Lake Sunapee, Georges Mills. Rents sailboats, canoes, boats, and motors. A great source of advice on where to fish.

Bob Skinner's Ski & Sports (763-9880) in Sunapee Harbor rents canoes and paddleboats.

Canoe put-ins can be found on Lake Sunapee; Pleasant Lake; Otter Pond in Georges Mills; Rand Pond in Goshen; Lake Todd, Blaisdell Lake, and Lake Massasecum in the Bradford area; Little Sunapee in New London; Kezar Lake in North Sutton; and Kolelemook Lake in Springfield.

Public boat launches in Sunapee Harbor, at Blodgett's Landing (shallow), at Sargents in Georges Mills, and at Sunapee State Park Beach (see *Swimming*).

BOAT EXCURSIONS
M/V *Mount Sunapee II* (763-4030), Sunapee Harbor. From weekends in mid-May through foliage season, twice daily from late June through Labor Day: 1½-hour narrated cruises of the lake. $9 per adult, $5 per child. This is unquestionably the best way to see Lake Sunapee. Captain Dave Hargboll never seems to tire of telling the history and pointing out the present sites to see. New London's long swath of eastern shore is entirely green, with rustic cottages hidden in woods above occasional docks. In Newbury on the south, you see Blodgett's Landing, a tight cluster of gingerbread cottages descended from the tents of the 1890s Sunapee Lake Spiritualist Camp Meeting Association. All children aboard are invited to take a turn at the helm.

M/V *Kearsarge* (763-5477), Sunapee Harbor. Summer months. A re-creation of a nineteenth-century steamer offers 1¾-hour cruises twice daily and a single dinner cruise.

Moonlight Miss (744-9254), Pasquaney Inn pier, Route 3A, Bridgewater. The 26-foot excursion boat offers narrated 1¼-hour tours of Newfound Lake. $8 adult, $5 children age five and over.

CHAIR LIFT
Mount Sunapee State Park (763-2356). Weekends Memorial Day to late June and after Labor Day through foliage season; daily 12–6 in the time between. $5.50 per adult, $2.50 per child. $9 adult, $5.50 per child buys a BBQ dinner in the summit restaurant. Definitely worth the ride. From

the 2,700-foot-high summit, lakes spread away to mountains on the north; and on the west, you can see all the way into Vermont—from Killington on down (on a clear day) to Mount Snow.

FARMS, PICK-YOUR-OWN

Bartletts Blueberry Farm (863-2583), Bradford Road, Newport. Blueberries.

Grandview Farm (456-3822), Walden Hill, Warner. Strawberries, blueberries, apples, peaches, plums.

King Blossom Farm (863-6125), Dunbar Hill Road, Grantham. Apples and raspberries.

Lavalley Orchard (863-6710), Newport. Apples.

Page Hill Farm (863-2356), Page Hill, Newport. Raspberries, apples.

Sugar Springs Farm (863-1928), Grantham. Strawberries, blueberries, raspberries, apples.

Windy Hill Farm (863-1136), Bascom Road, Newport. Raspberries.

FISHING

Dickie's (938-5393), Route 103 in South Newbury, is a source of fishing tackle and advice. Ditto for **Sargents Marine** in Georges Mills (see *Boating*).

Lake Sunapee is good for salmon, lake trout, brook trout, smallmouth bass, pickerel, perch, sunfish, hornput, and cusk. Otter Pond, Perkins Pond, and Baptist Pond yield bass, pickerel, and perch. Rand Pond, Croydon Pond, Long and Lempster ponds, and Sugar River are good for trout. Pleasant Lake has salmon, trout, bass. Inquire locally about what other lakes offer.

GOLF

Country Club of New Hampshire (927-4246), New London. $20 for 18 holes; cart rentals; reservations required.

Eastman (863-4500; 863-4240), Grantham. $32 for 18 holes; cart rentals; reservations required 2 days in advance.

John Cain Golf Course (863-7787), Newport. $22 weekdays, $25 weekends for 18 holes; reservations Friday through Sunday.

Maple Leaf (927-9806; 927-4419), Sutton area. Nine holes.

Twin Lake Village Golf Course (526-2034), Twin Lake Village Road, New London. Nine holes, par-3 course by the lake. $16.

HIKING

Mount Cardigan. From Mount Cardigan State Park (see *Green Space*) on the western side of the mountain, the West Ridge Trail takes you to the summit in just 1.3 miles. From Old Baldy, the principal peak, the view is of Mount Sunapee and of Mount Ascutney in Vermont. A ridge trail runs north to Firescrew Peak and south to South Peak. In all, a network of 50 miles of trails accesses the summit from various directions. Although this western ascent is the shortest and easiest, many hikers prefer the eastern climbs. You might ascend by the Cathedral Spruce and Clark trails (2.5 miles to summit; average time 2 hours, 10 minutes not including stops) or by the more difficult Holt Trail (1.9 miles to summit, *not* to be attempted in wet or icy weather), and return on the Mowglis and Mannin trails (3 miles from the summit). The Appalachian Mountain Club lodge, high on the mountain's eastern flank (posted from the village of Alexandria), is the departure point for these and other year-round ascents (see *Other Lodging*).

Mount Kearsarge. Serious hikers prefer the 2-mile ascent from Winslow State Park on the north side of the mountain to the mere 0.5-mile saunter up from Rollins State Park (see *Green Space*). The Northside Trail to the summit begins in the southeast corner of the picnic area, climbs through birch and spruce into fir, emerges on smooth ledges, then barren rocks. The view is one of the most spectacular in New England, especially for anyone familiar enough with the landscape to know what they're looking at. The sweep is from Mount Sunapee on the southwest to Moosilauke (the westernmost of the White Mountain peaks) to the Sandwich and Ossipee ranges and Mount Washington. This is a favorite hang-gliding spot. Round-trip time on the Northside Trail averages 1½ hours.

Mount Sunapee. The lazy man's way up to this outstanding summit view is via the aerial chair lift (see *Chair Lift*), but you can always walk down the 1.6-mile Solitude Trail to Lake Solitude and continue along the ridge to South Peak, then back to the base area via the Rim Trail. The most popular hiking trail up is the Andrew Brook Trail (1.8 miles to Lake Solitude) from a marked trailhead 1.2 miles up Mountain Road, well marked, in turn, off Route 103 roughly 1 mile south of Newbury. The most ambitious approach to Mount Sunapee is along the 47-mile Monadnock-Sunapee Greenway, which begins atop Mount Monadnock (see *Hiking* in "Peterborough, Keene, and Surrounding Villages"). The last and perhaps the most rewarding stretch of this trail is from Pillsbury State Park (see *Green Space*), which offers primitive camping and its own 20-mile system of trails.

SWIMMING

Sunapee State Park Beach (263-4642), Route 103, 3 miles west of Newbury. Open weekends mid-May to mid-June and Labor Day to mid-October, daily in between. A 900-foot stretch of smooth sand backed by shaded grass, picnic tables, a snack bar, bathhouse. $2.50 per person.

Wellington State Park (744-2197), Route 3A, 4 miles north of Bristol. Open weekends from Memorial Day, daily mid-June to Labor Day. This is a beauty: a sandy, half-mile-long beach on a peninsula jutting into Newfound Lake. Picnic tables are scattered along the shore, away from the bathhouse and snack bar, under pine trees. $2.50 per person.

Wadleigh State Beach (927-4724), on Kezar Lake, Sutton. Marked from Route 114. Open weekends from Memorial Day, daily mid-June to Labor Day. Smaller, less well known, and less crowded than nearby

Sunapee; a pleasant beach sloping gradually to the water. Facilities include a shaded picnic area, a bathhouse, and a large playfield. $2.50 per person.

Town beaches. Many more local beaches can be accessed by guests at local inns.

TENNIS

Dexter's Inn and Tennis Club (763-5571), Sunapee. (See *Inns*.)

King Ridge Racquet Club (526-9293), King Ridge Road, New London.

Colby-Sawyer College (526-2010), New London. Courts (and the Sports Center) are open to the public.

Newport High School courts are open to the public.

WINDSURFING

Mount Sunapee State Park Beach (763-2356). Rentals and lessons available.

CROSS-COUNTRY SKIING

Norsk (526-6040; 1-800-42-NORSK), Route 11 (2 miles east of I-89, Exit 11), New London. One of New England's most ambitious and successful cross-country centers. John Schlosser discovered the sport while attending the University of Oslo in 1972 and with wife, Nancy, opened Norsk—at the Lake Sunapee Country Club—in 1976. Thanks to its unusual elevation (1,300 feet) and regular grooming, Norsk's 95-km trail network frequently offers the best snow conditions south of the White Mountains. A favorite 6-mile loop is to Robb's Hut (open weekends 11–2:30) for lunch, and ambitious types can now take advantage of the 20-km Edge Loop. Trails begin on the golf course (where experiments with snowmaking are under way), but it's possible to quickly get into the woods—and stay there. Better skiers can actually access the system from the Outback parking area, 2 miles east on Route 11. The center itself was expanded and rebuilt in 1990, and the adjacent country-club restaurant caters to skiers. Trail fee $10 adults, $6 juniors; night skiing, lessons, and rentals offered.

Ragged Mountain Nordic Center (768-3600; 744-3391), Danbury. Fifteen km of tracked, groomed cross-country ski trails with views of Ragged Mountain and Mount Cardigan. $5 all day; rentals; Nordic and telemark lessons.

Snowhill at Eastman (863-4500), turn right off I-89 (you can't miss the sign), Grantham. Offers 30 km of groomed trails.

DOWNHILL SKIING

Mount Sunapee State Park (763-2356; snow phones 763-5626; 763-4020), Route 103, Newbury. This is a major ski area that is frequently less crowded than the competition. The base lodge is no-nonsense (no condominium models, either) and pleasant. The Summit Triple Chair accesses a half dozen swooping intermediate to expert runs, each at least a mile long. Off the North Peak Triple Chair, our favorite is Flying Goose—a quick, steep, and addictive run. The smaller North Peak

Lodge (at the opposite end of the parking lot) and the summit cafeteria help disperse the crowds at lunchtime. When all trails are open, skiers can choose from exposures on three peaks.

Trails: 37.

Lifts: 3 double chairs, 3 triple chairs, and 1 pony.

Vertical drop: 1,510 feet.

Snowmaking: 80 percent.

Ski school: With SKIwee and Little Indians (ages three to four).

Facilities: Two base lodges and summit cafeteria.

Rates: $34 weekends, $28 weekdays for adults, $24 and $20 for juniors; multi-day rates.

King Ridge (526-6966; snow phone 1-800-343-1312; lodging phone 1-800-258-3530), off I-89, Exit 11, New London. Founded by the nonprofit New London Outing Club in the late 1950s, King Ridge has managed to preserve a no-hassle, welcoming atmosphere despite the I-89 exit just down the road. It caters to families in unusual ways. Rental ski lockers mean you don't have to tote all those skis and boots every weekend, and there is ample, free storage space for day trippers. Brown baggers, instead of being relegated to the basement, enjoy a large, cheerful space with drink and soup service. The nursery accepts children from six months to five years old. The 20 trails are named for *Alice in Wonderland* characters like Mock Turtle and the March Hare, and a life-size Mad Hatter skis about. Trails are wide, gentle, and well groomed. If the family hotshot gets bored, there is snowboarding, a sport King Ridge takes seriously (rentals and lessons are offered). The base lodge is glass-faced to maximize the top-of-the-hill view, and it's comfortable and separate from the skiers' service lodge, which handles tickets, ski school, rentals, and a lodging service. At this writing King Ridge is "owned by the bank" but operating as well as ever.

Trails: 19.

Lifts: 1 triple, 2 doubles, a J-bar, a T-bar, and a rope tow.

Vertical drop: 710 feet.

Snowmaking: 90 percent.

Night skiing: 12 trails, 5 lifts.

Ski school: Group and private lessons.

Facilities: Base lodge, rental shop, nursery (six months to five years).

Rates: $30 adults, $22 juniors on weekends; $19 for all ages weekdays.

Ragged Mountain Ski Area (768-3475; snow phone 768-3971), off Route 4, Danbury. A pleasant intermediate mountain that's been upgraded in the past few years with snowmaking, a new lift, and a base lodge. Still, it's just enough off the beaten track and little-known enough to be relatively uncrowded.

Trails: 23.

Lifts: 3 double chairs and a T-bar.

Vertical drop: 1,250 feet.

Snowmaking: 90 percent.
Facilities: Ski school, ski shop, rentals, restaurant, lounge, child care.
Rates: $19.95 adults, $14.95 juniors on weekends; $14.95 and $9.95 on weekdays. A genuine family area.

Snowhill at Eastman (863-4241), off I-89, Exit 13, Grantham. Really just a weekend facility for this self-contained condo resort: a 243-foot vertical drop, one double chair and one novice lift, three trails. $14 adults, $10 juniors.

(Also see *Downhill Skiing* in both "The Western Whites" and "The Concord Area.")

GREEN SPACE

STATE PARKS

Mount Cardigan State Park, off Routes 4 and 118, 4½ miles east of Canaan. Open mid-May to mid-October. This western approach to the mountain includes a picnic area sited among pines and rocks. For more about the West Ridge Trail, the shortest and easiest route to the 3,121-foot-high summit of Mount Cardigan itself, see *Hiking.*

Pillsbury State Park (863-2860), Route 31, 3½ miles north of Washington. Open weekends from Memorial Day, daily from mid-June. Day-use and camping fees. What a gem! This 9,000-acre near-wilderness was once a thriving settlement with its share of mills. Today the dams are all that survive of "Cherry Valley." Camping is restricted to 20 superb primitive sites on May Pond, and there's both stream and pond fishing. Inquire about hiking trails to nearby mountains.

Winslow State Park (526-6168), off Route 11, 3 miles south of Wilmot. Open weekends from Memorial Day, daily from early June; fee. An auto road climbs to the 1,820-foot level of 2,937-foot Mount Kearsarge. There are picnic tables and comfort facilities, and you can inspect the cellar hole of a big nineteenth-century resort hotel, the Winslow House. A steep, mile-long trail leads to the summit for a 360-degree panoramic view. The park is named for Admiral John A. Winslow, commander of the sloop *Kearsarge* when it sank the Confederate gunboat *Alabama* in 1864. (Also see *Hiking.*)

Rollins State Park (239-8153), off Route 103, 4 miles north of Warner. Open weekends from Memorial Day, daily from early June through October. A 3½-mile road, built originally as a scenic toll road in 1874, leads to picnic sites roughly a half mile below the summit. A walking trail accesses the bald summit of Mount Kearsarge described above.

OTHER AREAS

Knights Hill Nature Park, County Road, New London. Sixty acres of fields and forest, fern gardens and a pond, a marsh, and a stream, all linked by easy trails. No dogs. Inquire at the town information booth about guided hikes.

Cricenti's Bog, Route 11, New London. A genuine bog with a nature trail. Wooden walkways thread a pond that's been filled with sphagnum moss and rare bog flora.

Audubon Society of New Hampshire Paradise Point Nature Center and Hebron Marsh Wildlife Sanctuary (744-3516), North Shore Road, East Hebron. This 43-acre preserve includes an extensive, rocky, and unspoiled stretch of shore on Newfound Lake. The property is webbed with trails and includes a nature center (open late June to Labor Day, 10–5 daily; also some spring and fall weekends) with hands-on and wildlife exhibits, a library, and Nature Store. During the summer a natural history day camp and a variety of workshops and special events are also staged. Hebron Marsh is another 1.4 miles down the road toward Hebron Center (drive past the red Ash Cottage and take the next left down the dirt road; park off the road on the left by the sign). The 36-acre property includes the field directly across the road from Ash Cottage down to the Cockermouth River and the field to the southwest of the cottage. The marshes are teeming with bird life; follow signs to the observation tower.

Sculptured Rocks, west of Groton Village on Sculptured Rocks Road. The parking area is roughly a mile in (the sign may be down off-season). The river has carved a deep chasm through which it tumbles from pool to pool. A path follows the water down, by waterfalls and pot holes that form a popular local swimming spot. Bring a picnic.

Profile Falls, Route 3A, 2.5 miles south of Bristol. A popular (and dangerous) local swimming hole. This is a 40-foot falls with the profile of a man silhouetted against the water at its base.

Grafton Pond, off Route 4A. A 935-acre Society for the Protection of New Hampshire Forests preserve. North from Wilmot take a sharp left at the Grafton-Sullivan county line; take the first left, then an immediate right, and park at the dam site. The only amenity is a public boat ramp. The pond has a 7-mile shoreline. Good boating and fishing.

(Also see Fells Historic Site under *Historic Homes*.)

LODGING

RESORTS

☞Twin Lake Village (526-6460), RR 1, Box 680, New London 03257. One 1890s resort that's still flourishing. Opened by Henry Kidder in 1897, it's presently owned and managed by 3 generations of Kidders and accommodates 160 guests between the rambling "Villa" and a number of Victorian houses scattered through surrounding trees. A nine-hole golf course stretches from the rocker-lined veranda down to the lake. All three daily meals and old-fashioned evening entertainment—maybe a suppertime picnic on Mount Kearsarge or a talent show by guests' children—are included in the weekly $320–575 rates.

Eastman (863-4444), PO Box 1 (just off I-89, Exit 13), Grantham 03753. Developed by an improbable consortium that includes Dartmouth College and the Society for the Protection of New Hampshire Forests; a second-home and condo community, scattered in clusters through 3,500 acres on Eastman Lake. Winter facilities include a small ski hill and an extensive ski-touring network. Summer renters can enjoy an 18-hole golf course, tennis, swimming, and boating (Sunfish, canoes, and rowboats can be rented). An indoor pool and a recreation barn are available year-round. Units are attractive; individually decorated condos with two to four bedrooms, decks, lofts, and woodstoves. Two-night and weekly rentals: from $360 for two bedrooms in summer, from $390 for winter weekends, from $760 for seven days in summer, from $835 in winter.

INNS
In the Lake Sunapee Area
Dexter's Inn and Tennis Club (763-5571; 1-800-232-5571), Stagecoach Road, Sunapee 03732. Open May through October. This hilltop house dates in part from 1801, but its present look is 1930s, when it became a summer home for an adviser to Herbert Hoover. In 1974 Frank and Shirley Simpson turned it into the gracious inn it's been ever since, now owned and managed by their daughter Holly and her husband, Michael Durfor. Tennis is a specialty of the house and the three all-weather courts are the stuff of tournaments (there's also a pro). A pool is set in the extensive, beautifully landscaped backyard, which also offers croquet and other lawn games. Fields across the road, in front of the house, slope toward Lake Sunapee in the distance. You can also see the lake from porch rockers and from many of the 19 guest rooms (each individually decorated, all with private baths). The best views are from the annex across the road. There's also a great view from the dining room, which is small and open to the public (there are four seatings per night; see *Dining Out*). Common spaces include a formal living room and a pubby, pine-paneled "cocktail lounge." Altogether this is one of those special places where you tend to want to stay put. $135–175 double per night, MAP plus 15 percent service. The B&B rate (available May, June, September, October) is less. Pets are permitted in the annex at $10 per day. Discounts for three nights or longer.

New London Inn (526-2791; from outside NH 1-800-526-2791), PO Box 8, Main Street, New London 03257. Built originally in 1792, this large (30 guest rooms) inn sits in the middle of New London, next to Colby-Sawyer College. It's always busy, but guests can usually find quiet space in a corner of the large, graciously furnished living room. The attractive, shop-studded street invites strolling. Since the Boston-Montreal bus stops at the pharmacy practically across the street, this is one place, theoretically at least, you can come without a car. Rooms are attractive, freshly papered, furnished in real and reproduction antiques. There's a sense of things well-managed by Rose and Jeff Follansbee. Although he is not "from" this area, Jeff's great-grandfather built the original Follansbee Inn in North Sutton. All three meals are served. $60–95 per room, EP (no meals) plus a 10 percent service charge.

The Inn at Sunapee (763-4444), Burkehaven Hill Road, Box 336, Sunapee 03782. An 1880s farmhouse set high on the loop road above Sunapee Harbor, facing Mount Sunapee across a pasture. The lobby walls and ceiling are tin, and the rooms in the main house all have charm; frankly, however, we wouldn't go for the three double rooms in the converted barn out back. Families can take advantage of two- and three-bedroom suites, and there are also double rooms with private baths. The pool is unheated and surrounded by a chain-link fence, and the tennis court is basic (but great for those of us who don't have "whites"; the inn supplies racquets and balls). Both the lounge and dining room overlook the meadow and mountain. $70 double B&B.

Colonial Farm Inn (526-6121; 1-800-805-8504), Route 11, New London 03257. Bob and Kathryn Joseph thoroughly renovated their fine 1836 center chimney before opening as a full-service inn in 1993. At this writing there are just four carefully decorated guest rooms. Dinner, by reservation to the public, is served Wednesday through Sunday evenings in the fireplaced dining rooms. A full breakfast is included in $56–95 double, $44–75 single plus 8 percent service.

☞ **Follansbee Inn** (927-4221), Route 114, PO Box 92, North Sutton 03260. Open except for parts of November and April. In summer the porch is filled with rockers, festooned with flowers, and a small blackboard displays the message of the day—on our last visit it was "Everyone is ignorant, only on different topics." The low-beamed living room is friendly, the airy dining rooms are comfortably furnished with antiques. On the upper floors the 23 guest rooms are divided by wide halls, and books are scattered around. This classic white, green-trimmed structure was built originally as an annex for the huge but long-gone Follansbee Inn that once stood across the street. The property abuts Kezar Lake, and guests can swim or boat; for those more comfortable with a lifeguard on duty, Wadleigh State Park is just down the road. Many guests also discover the joys of the 3-mile walk, bike, or jog around the lake. In winter there's cross-country skiing out the back door. Innkeepers Dick and Sandy Reilein are knowledgeable about everything and happy to give advice. No smoking and no children under age 10; no TV. $70–90 includes breakfast. Dinner is also served, and guests are encouraged to sit down together, a practice appreciated by single guests.

Seven Hearths Inn (763-5657; 1-800-237-5657), old Route 11, Sunapee 03782. Five of the seven hearths are in guest rooms, and yet another (in the Hearth Room) is a focal point for evening cocktails and hors d'oeuvres. The inn is unusually elegant throughout and facilities include a landscaped swimming pool. From $88 in winter and $118 in summer, B&B.

Back Side Inn (863-5161), RFD 2, Box 213, Newport 03773. Open year-round. A very pleasant place, set in four acres on a back road (across from our favorite shopping/browsing spot in the region: Nelson Crafts and Used Books [see *Selective Shopping*]). The 10 guest rooms are each individually furnished (shared and private baths), and there's a field-stone fireplace in the living room. Mackie and Bruce Hefka are the innkeepers. $60–70 per double room; weekend packages, midweek specials; add 15 percent service. No pets. Breakfast and dinner served. No smoking.

The Bradford Inn (938-5309), Main Street, Bradford. A genuine 1890s, three-story village inn, complete with mansard roof and wraparound porch. All rooms have private baths and are simply but nicely furnished with a mix of country furniture and antiques. Innkeepers Tom and Connie Mazol also maintain an attractive public dining room, J. Albert's (named for J. Albert Peaselee, the inn's founder). Rates are reasonable: $59 (with an adjoining bath off the hall) to $99 (for a minisuite with an extra bed in an adjoining room). Special packages available.

On Newfound Lake

The Inn on Newfound Lake (744-9111), Route 3A, Bridgewater 03222. Open year-round. This 1840s, 30-room inn has been thoroughly re-habbed. Outside the focus is on Newfound Lake across the road (there's a 300-foot sandy beach and dock) and inside it's on the dining room. $65–105 per room double occupancy, including continental breakfast; three meals are served; children's rates are available.

In Danbury

The Inn at Danbury (768-3318), Route 104, Danbury 03230. Geared to bicyclists and skiers, great for groups (maximum of 50 people). Fifteen rooms with private baths; ample, comfortable common space and (of all things) an indoor pool. Handy to Ragged Mountain. A variety of bicycle loops—from 5 to 100 miles—have been mapped for guests. Touring and mountain bikes are also sold, rented, and repaired. $79 double with breakfast; winter packages from $99 per person with meals; half price for children under 10.

BED & BREAKFASTS

In the Sunapee Area

✐ **Maple Hill Farm** (526-2248; 1-800-231-8637), 200 Newport Road, New London 03257. Just off I-89, a capacious old farmhouse that once more takes in boarders, the way it did in the nineteenth century. An informal, comfortable place, good for families. One first-floor room with twin beds and private bath is handicapped accessible. There's plenty of acreage and access through meadows to Little Sunapee Lake (there's a canoe). $55–75 double; family suite available, $85. Inquire about weekend packages.

☞ **The Village House** (927-4765), Grist Mill Road, Box 151, Sutton Mills 03221. An 1850s Victorian house with three guest rooms (two baths). Peggy Forand is a quilter herself, and the antique quilts on each bed are carefully chosen; the house throughout is furnished with antiques. You walk out into the village of Sutton Mills, a picturesque old mill village with a town hall, library, and general store. $50 double, $35 single includes a full breakfast. No credit cards.

Haus Edelweiss (763-2100; 1-800-248-0713), Maple Street, PO Box 609, Sunapee 03782. Up a side street in Sunapee Harbor, this is a cheerful house with a wood stove in the living room; five upstairs guest rooms from $30 for a single to $55 for a double with a half bath, including complimentary snacks and breakfast. You can choose from Traditional (bacon, eggs, French toast), Yankee (fish cakes and baked beans with your eggs and muffins), or Bavarian (eggs, cheeses, German hard rolls, German apple pancakes with whipped cream, sausage). The innkeepers are John and Jennifer Dixon. $15 extra per child above age six. No smoking.

In the Highland Lake Area

The English House (735-5987), PO Box 162, Route 4/11 (next to the Proctor Academy campus), Andover 03216. Brits Gillian and Ken Smith are genial, widely traveled hosts who have skillfully restored this shingled, turn-of-the-century house, making the most of its seven spacious guest rooms, now all with private baths. Gillian, a member of the New Hampshire League of Craftsmen in both "wearable art" and jewelry making, has brightened rooms with her quilts and window treatments. Both Gillian and Ken are delighted to turn guests on to some fine swimming, fishing, skiing, and dining options in this little-touristed area. Full English breakfasts and, of course, four o'clock tea are included in $75 per day double, $55 single.

Elsewhere

The Inn on Canaan Street (523-7310), Canaan Street, Canaan 03741. This is the only place to stay on Canaan Street (see *Villages*), and it's a beauty. An early-eighteenth-century house with five guest rooms, all with private bath, one with a canopy bed and working fireplace. Downstairs there are two parlors, one with a wood stove, another with a piano. The breakfast room and a side porch overlook the sweep of lawn and sunsets over Pico and Killington far to the west. The view of Mount Cardigan is out the front door. A path leads through tall pines to the lake and a canoe. $65–95 for two includes afternoon tea as well as breakfast. Dinners ($16–20) are served by reservation to inn guests only.

The Towerhouse Inn Bed & Breakfast (523-7244), One Parker Street, Canaan. Built grandly in 1895, this mansion is one of the few buildings spared (at great effort) by a 1923 fire that leveled the rest of Canaan Village. Rudi and Debbi Widbiller have restored the house with its stained glass windows and wonderful woods—each guest room is named for the wood (each is different) it displays. Rooms are large and nicely furnished; shared bath. Rudi is best known locally for his homemade sausages and wursts, available in the downstairs deli; lunch is served on Sunday, 12–3. $75 per night single or double.

Webster Lake Inn (934-4050), Webster Avenue, Franklin 03235. A 1920s lakeside lodge right on Webster Lake, with a spacious two-story living room, rooms off a second-story balcony (ideal for a group to rent but also good for anyone looking for a reasonably priced lakeside retreat). There are eight rooms; a sandy town beach is within walking distance.

The Victorian Bed and Breakfast (744-6157), 16 Summer Street (5.6 miles from I-93, Exit 23), Bristol 03222. Built solidly and elaborately as the town mill owner's mansion in 1902; now offering unusually spacious, nicely furnished guest rooms, two with working fireplaces. Each of the eight rooms is carefully decorated and named. Our favorites are Spring and Autumn, although Indian Summer is fine, too. A first-floor room is especially designed for elderly and handicapped guests. Four have private baths, and the two loft rooms in the carriage house can each sleep a large family; both have kitchens. Newfound Lake is nearby, as are both Ragged and Tenney mountains. Nancy Truitt charges $65–75 double, $55 single; includes a full breakfast.

MOTELS

Lamplighter Motor Inn (526-6484), 6 Newport Road, New London 03257. Right in New London, a two-story motel with a Tudor facade with some kitchen units, cable TV, phones, friendly staff; close to good restaurants; $55–75 per room (sleeping up to four people), complimentary coffee and doughnuts. Pets permitted.

Burkehaven Motel (763-2788), PO Box 378, Lake Sunapee 03782. Hidden away high on a loop road above Sunapee Harbor. Roomy motel units with mountain views, kitchen units, a tennis court, and attractive swimming pool. Off-season $60–70 double; in-season $69–79.

RENTAL COTTAGES

The New London and the Newfound region chambers of commerce (see *Guidance*) can direct you to local realtors specializing in cottage rentals.

OTHER LODGING

Cardigan Mountain Lodge and Reservation (744-8011) (mailing: RFD, Bristol 03222), Alexandria. The Appalachian Mountain Club, founded in 1876 to blaze hiking trails through the White Mountains, maintains a number of no-frills, outdoors-oriented huts, lodges, and family camps in New Hampshire. This is one of the most interesting, serving three daily meals June to Labor Day; open on weekends for some time before and after, on a caretaker basis the rest of the year. Perched high on the eastern side of Mount Cardigan, it offers access to literally dozens of trails to the top. Many of the lower trails are used by cross-country skiers in winter. Rates are per person, in the $40 range, including three family-style meals; rooms range from doubles to five bunks (bring your own sleeping bag). Platform tent sites and campsites are also available. Summer at Cardigan includes swimming, Sunday barbecues, and canoeing and square dancing. Winter is on a do-it-yourself basis for groups of varying sizes.

☞ **Stone Rest Bed & Breakfast** (744-6066), Fowler River Road, Alexandria 03222. Open daily in summer; between November and May, Monday through Thursday only. Dick and Peg Clarke have created some comfortable guest spaces in their roadside home, just a mile or so down the road from Cardigan Mountain Lodge. An efficiency unit is just $45 for two people, a two-bedroom cottage is $60, and a studio bedroom sleeping four is $50; one person midweek is $25; all rates include breakfast. Use of the hot tub is extra.

WHERE TO EAT

DINING OUT
In the Lake Sunapee Area
Woodbine Cottage (763-2222), Sunapee Harbor. Open May to Columbus Day only—lunch 12–2:30, afternoon tea 3–5, dinner 6–8, Sunday brunch 10–2—but such a landmark deserves top billing. Eleanor and Robert Hill first opened this restaurant in 1928, and Eleanor still works every day to provide the food and atmosphere for which she's famous. The atmosphere is classic tea room: polished wood tables, fresh flowers, real woodbine on the face of the white-clapboard cottage. You can lunch on a cheese and nut sandwich ($2.75) or fresh lobster salad. Afternoon tea is fresh fruit salad or a tea sandwich and cake with your pot of tea. Full dinners are expensive ($20.25 for broiled lamb, sirloin, or tenderloin), but you can have a cheese and olive sandwich at dinnertime, too. Desserts are the specialty of the house: chiffon pies, strawberry shortcake, Venetian cream torte.

New London Inn (526-2791), Main Street, New London. Dinner except Sunday and Monday, breakfast daily, lunch spring through December. Chef Jeffrey Follansbee prides himself on using fresh, local ingredients imaginatively. The dinner menu changes nightly but might feature a terrine of spiced pork, spinach, and mozzarella; a green salad; and broiled breast of chicken stuffed under the skin with (local) goat cheese and basil, served with cabbage and chilis. For lunch you might select an individual strudel with smoked ham, spinach, and Gorgonzola. Dinner is moderately expensive to expensive.

☞ **Millstone Restaurant** (526-4201), Newport Road. Open for lunch and dinner daily. Tom Mills' landmark restaurant, a pleasant atmosphere created by warm colors, watercolors, and plants; a large menu featuring fresh, local ingredients. The same menu all day: sandwiches, pastas like fettuccine Princess (steamed salmon and asparagus on cracked-pepper fettuccine with lemon sauce), great salads, and entrées ranging from New England venison (grilled to order with juniper berry, coriander, and Marsala sauce) to lemon chicken scaloppine. Moderate.

Colonial Farm Inn (526-6121; 1-800-805-8504), Route 11, New London. Dinner by reservation, Wednesday through Sunday in an 1830s house.

The Inn at Sunapee (763-4444), Burkehaven Hill Road, Sunapee. Open for dinner Wednesday through Sunday 6–9:30, by reservation. The country dining room in the nineteenth-century inn overlooks a mountain meadow. You might begin with Chinese spring rolls (the innkeepers have lived in the Far East), then dine on fresh grilled salmon with the sauce of the day or the daily veal special. Moderate.

Seven Hearths (763-5657), Route 11, Sunapee. Dinner Wednesday through Sunday; in summer, Tuesday through Saturday. Guests are encouraged to come 45 minutes before dinner for drinks around the hearth, then settle into one of the elegant candlelit dining rooms for a leisurely dinner. Reservations required. Expensive.

Dexter's Inn and Tennis Club (763-5571), Stagecoach Road, Sunapee. Dinner served from mid-June through October, except Tuesday. The dining room is small and the view is sweeping. The set menu usually offers a choice of fish and meat entrées; specialties include fresh poached or grilled salmon. Moderate.

In the Newfound Area

The Inn on Newfound Lake (744-9111), Route 3A, Bridgewater. Dinner nightly except Monday, Sunday brunch.

The Homestead (744-2022), Route 104, Bristol. Dinner daily, Sunday brunch. A handsome, white, old roadside mansion with a series of dining rooms inside, ranging from traditional to glass to stone-walled. The menu is traditional American and Continental, ranging from pasta to broiled seafood and steak. Moderate.

In the Andover Area

☞ **La Meridiana** (526-2033), Route 11, Wilmot. Many residents consider this the best restaurant in central New Hampshire, and the best value. The menu, like the owner-chef, is northern Italian, and the specialties are tender scaloppine and *bistecca*. Pastas and pastries are outstanding, too, and everything is moderately priced, even the wine list.

Potter Place Inn (735-5141), Route 4/11, Andover. A favorite dining-out place for Proctor Academy faculty and students. Specialties include roast duckling, veal saltimbocca, grilled jumbo shrimp with garlic; fabulous desserts like cream cheese strudel with Chantilly cream. Expensive.

EATING OUT

In the Lake Sunapee Area

Peter Christian's Tavern (526-4042), Main Street, New London. A less pubby, collegiate version of the Hanover landmark, so popular that it's wise to come early or late since there's frequently a line—a consideration if you're planning on a meal before a play (the Barn Playhouse is just down the street). The menu, 11:30 A.M. to closing, stays the same: Victuals, like a cheese-and-meat board (plenty for two), or a hefty sand-

The Craftsman's Fair at Sunapee State Park

wich like Peter's Russian Mistress (open-faced turkey, bacon, Swiss cheese, spinach, tomato, Russian dressing). Dinner specials include mustard chicken *cordon bleu* and hearty beef stew. Inexpensive.

MacKenna's Restaurant (526-9511), New London Shopping Center, New London. Open for breakfast most of the time; lunch 11–3 and dinner 5–7. Every town should be so lucky to have a place like this: clean, friendly, fast, cheap. Homemade soups, great sandwiches on homemade bread (chicken salad was exceptional and just $2.95 with pickles and chips); steak dinners and broiled or fried seafood and chicken (under $8); children's plates.

Four Corners Grille (526-6899), Routes 11 and 114, New London. Same ownership as Millstones. Pleasant atmosphere and a large menu: burgers and sandwiches, ribs, superb soups, pastas, and deep fries ranging from fish and chips to tempura shrimp.

Bradford Junction Restaurant and Bakery (938-2424), Route 114, Bradford. Open 6 A.M.–2:20 P.M. Great road food. Homemade bread, muffins, soups; pot roast for $4.75, baked haddock for $3.95. A counter and cheery dining room, the village gathering place.

Elsewhere

Ryan's Loft at the Whittemore Inn (744-3518), Route 3A (just south of Newfound Lake), Bridgewater. Open for lunch and dinner, Sunday brunch. An informal family place, good for veal Marsala ($10.95) or baked stuffed shrimp ($13.95); wine by the carafe and glass.

Merchant's Family Restaurant, Route 104, Danbury. Closed Tuesday, otherwise 6:30 A.M.–7 P.M.; knotty pine walls, cheerful service, $2.50 for a homemade cup of soup. Daily specials like meatloaf and turkey with potatoes and gravy.

The Foothills Restaurant (456-2140), Main Street, just off I-89, Exits 8 and 9, Warner. Open 6 A.M.–2 P.M. The Brewster family has spiffed up this old restaurant, added lace curtains and daily baked specials like breakfast "platter cakes" and soups made from scratch. Good road food.

Tommy's Anchorage (763-4021). Open spring through fall, Sunday through Thursday 11:30–9, Friday and Saturday 11:30–10. The only lakeside dining spot on Lake Sunapee and good, basic food to boot. Try the root beer.

Baynham's Country Store and Cafe (526-8070), 180 Main Street, New London. Open daily. This is a phenomenon: an English version of a New England country store (you are reminded that this is *New London*) with a classic 1950s soda fountain, tables set for light lunches, and, the specialty of the house, full English teas.

ENTERTAINMENT

THEATER

New London Barn Playhouse (526-6710; 526-4631), Main Street, New London. One of New England's oldest and best summer-stock theaters featuring dramatic, musical, and children's productions. June through August.

MUSIC

Music at King Ridge (526-6575), King Ridge Ski Area, New London. Jazz and classical music series July and August. Concerts are Thursday evenings, and patrons are invited to come spread a blanket and picnic beforehand. Occasional performances in the Colby-Sawyer College Auditorium.

Summer band concerts. Springfield Band concert series held in Sunapee Harbor and Georges Mills on Wednesday evenings. Concerts at New London's Mary D. Haddard Memorial Bandstand on Sargent Common, New London. Call the chamber of commerce for details. (See *Guidance.*) Newport Band concerts every Sunday evening from late June through August. Held in the Opera House in case of rain. Summer music at Mount Sunapee.

SELECTIVE SHOPPING

ANTIQUES

Prospect Hill Antiques (763-9676), Prospect Hill Road, Georges Mills. The selection is immense and the quality outstanding. If you are searching for an armoire or an end table, a desk or stool, this barn—filled with more than 1,000 pieces of furniture and hundreds of collectibles—is worth checking.

Antiquing in the Lake Sunapee–New London Region. A map and guide to nine local antiques dealers is available at local information booths and from the New London Chamber of Commerce (see *Guidance*).

CRAFTS

Nelson Crafts, Antique Collectibles, and Used Books (863-4394), Brook Road, Goshen (Brook Road begins just a mile from the rotary at Sunapee State Park). Open Memorial Day to Labor Day, 10–5 daily, weekends until Columbus Day, then irregularly; call first. "If you stick with one thing you could make a fortune, I figure," Audrey Nelson says, "but it gets boring." Ms. Nelson, an established local photographer, potter, and weaver, is explaining the almost organic evolution of her shop, which now includes a wide array of "collectibles" and 60,000 used books as well as a fine selection of crafts.

Farm Mountain Sheep & Wool Co. (526-WOOL), Route 4A, Wilmot. Open Thursday through Sunday 10–4. Wool comforters, 100 percent wool knitting yarns, spinning fibers, and equipment.

Nancy Lyon Handweaving Studio (526-6754), 102 Shaker Street, New London. The studio is open by chance and appointment. Soft wools and bright, deep colors are the hallmark of the hats, scarves, and a variety of handwoven items produced by this well-known designer and weaver.

SPECIAL SHOPS

Artisan's Workshop (526-4227), PO Box 124, Main Street, New London. A small but full shop displaying jewelry, pottery, prints, paintings, woodenware, glass, cards, books, and much more in the front rooms of the old inn that now houses Peter Christian's Tavern. Frequent summer demonstrations, special exhibits, concerts.

Nunsuch Cheeses (927-4176), Route 114, South Sutton. This 5-acre, licensed dairy welcomes visitors. Former nun Courtney Haase produces justly famous cheese; also goat-milk soap, handmade gift boxes.

Baynham's Country Store (526-8070), 180 Main Street. Open daily. A fascinating English version of a New England country store: country clothing, hand-knit English sweaters, quilts, gourmet foods and kitchenware, AGA cookstoves, nostalgia games—all at prices you might believe wouldn't fly. But they do.

The Crafty Goose, Main Street, New London. Open 10–5. A trove of things handcrafted, from aprons and dolls to furniture, toys, ties, and wind chimes.

Potter Place Gallery (735-5758), Route 4A, Potter Place, Andover. The specialties of the house are etchings, New England landscapes in various media, and sculpture.

FACTORY OUTLETS

Granitewear Inc. (632-7941; 1-800-421-0325), Route 4, Canaan. Tom Mangold designs and manufactures the Granitewear sportswear and

Caboose brand workwear sold on the premises. A great place to bring the family for winter parkas.

The Dorr Mill Store (863-1197), Routes 11/103 between Newport and Sunapee. Open Monday through Saturday 9–5. No longer an outlet for the woolen mill across the street, but a very special place that actually draws bus tours from as far away as Montreal for its line of 100 percent wool used for hooking, braiding, and quilting. Bolts of fabrics, including woolens still made at the mill, but a wider selection; also classic clothing: Woolrich, Pendleton, and others. Specializing in sweaters, woolens.

Mesa International Factory Outlet (526-2127), Elkins Business Loop (off Route 11), Elkins. Hours vary, so call. Some glassware and hand-painted dinnerware is made here, other items are imported. Worth checking.

SPECIAL EVENTS

Note: The following entries represent a fraction of summer happenings in this region; check local listings.

June: Annual **Inn Tour** of the Sunapee Region.

July: **New London Garden Club annual antiques show. Hebron Fair.**

August: **New London Hospital Fair.** Annual **Craftsmen's Fair,** Mount Sunapee State Park. The biggest event of the year by far. The country's oldest and still one of its best crafts fairs: a 9-day gathering of more than 500 juried artisans. Music, an art exhibit, a wide variety of crafts demonstrations, and workshops are included in the admissions ticket, good for two days—the time you need to take in the full range of exhibits, try your own hand at crafting something, and see the featured demonstrations which vary with the theme of the day. **Old Home Day,** Sutton. Annual Lake Sunapee **Antique Boat Show and Parade. Alexandria Fair.**

September: Mount Sunapee **Triathlon.** Danbury **Grange Fair.**

October: Warner **Fall Foliage Festival,** Columbus Day weekend. Major crafts show, food, entertainment.

V. THE UPPER CONNECTICUT RIVER VALLEY

Upper Valley Towns

DARTMOUTH COLLEGE

Baker Library at Dartmouth College

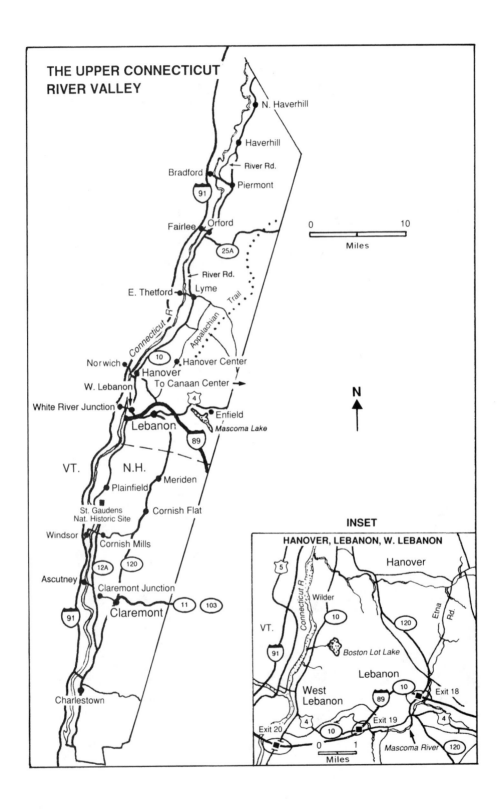

THE UPPER CONNECTICUT
RIVER VALLEY

N. Haverhill

Haverhill

River Rd.

Bradford

91

Piermont

Orford

Fairlee

25A

0   10
Miles

River Rd.

E. Thetford   Lyme

Appalachian Trail

Connecticut R.

Norwich   10   Hanover Center

Hanover

W. Lebanon

To Canaan Center

White River Junction

4

Lebanon

Enfield

Mascoma Lake

89

N

VT.   N.H.

Meriden

Plainfield

St. Gaudens
Nat. Historic Site

Cornish Flat

Windsor

Cornish Mills

12A   120

Ascutney

Claremont Junction

91

11   103

Claremont

Charlestown

INSET

HANOVER, LEBANON, W. LEBANON

5

Hanover

Connecticut R.

Wilder

10

VT.

120

Etna Rd.

91

Boston Lot Lake

Lebanon

10

West
Lebanon

89

Exit 18

Exit 20

4

10

Exit 19

4

Mascoma River   120

0   1
Miles

Upper Valley Towns

The Upper Valley ignores state lines to form one of New England's most beautiful and distinctive regions. Its two dozen towns are scattered along both the Vermont and New Hampshire banks of the Connecticut River for some 20 miles north and south of Dartmouth College.

"Upper Valley" is a name coined in the 1950s by a local daily, *The Valley News,* to define its two-state circulation area. The label has stuck, interestingly enough, to the same group of towns that back in the 1770s tried to form the state of "New Connecticut." The Dartmouth-based, pro–New Connecticut party was thwarted, however, by larger powers (namely New York and New Hampshire) along with the strident Vermont-independence faction—the Green Mountain Boys.

The valley itself prospered in the late eighteenth and early nineteenth centuries, as evidenced by the exquisite Federal-era meetinghouses and mansions still salted throughout this area. The river was the area's only highway in the eighteenth and early nineteenth centuries and was still a popular steamboat route in the years before the Civil War.

Of the dozens of bridges that once linked towns on either side of the river, only 10 survive, but they include the longest covered bridge in the United States (connecting Windsor and Cornish). The Upper Valley phone book, moreover, includes towns on both sides of the river, and Hanover's Dresden School District reaches into Vermont (this was the first bi-state school district in the United States). Several Independence Day parades start in one state and finish across the bridge in the other. The Montshire Museum, founded in Hanover but now in Norwich, combines both states in its very name.

The cultural center of the Upper Valley remains Dartmouth College Green in Hanover. With the nearby medical complex and West Lebanon shopping strip, this area forms the region's hub, handy to the highways radiating, the way rail lines once did, from White River Junction.

North and south of the Hanover area, old river towns drowse and the river roads are well worth finding. On the river itself canoes remain the prime mode of transportation; campsites and inns are spaced along the shore.

GUIDANCE

The Upper Valley Convention and Visitors Bureau (1-800-370-6488). Weekdays 10–4. Advice on local lodging as well as attractions; keeps a log on local vacancies during crunch times like big football game weekends and foliage season.

The Hanover Chamber of Commerce (643-3115), 37 South Main Street, Hanover. Open 9–noon weekdays. The chamber dispenses flyers and brochures year-round and, in conjunction with Dartmouth College, maintains a kiosk on Dartmouth Green during summer months—a source of even more brochures, maps, advice on where to eat, what to see, and the starting point for regularly scheduled tours of the campus.

The Greater Lebanon Chamber of Commerce (448-1203), PO Box 97, on the Mall, Lebanon 03766. Weekdays 9–5. The Upper Valley information line actually rings in this office just off Coburn Park—a source of brochures and advice.

Greater Claremont Chamber of Commerce (543-1296), the Moody Building on Tremont Square, Claremont.

Charlestown Town Office (826-4400), Charlestown 03603.

GETTING THERE

By car: Interstates 91 and 89 intersect in the White River Junction (Vermont)–Lebanon (New Hampshire) area, where they also meet Route 5 north and south on the Vermont side; Route 4, the main east-west highway through central Vermont; and Route 10, the river road on the New Hampshire side.

By bus: White River Junction is a hub for **Greyhound/Vermont Transit** (1-800-321-0707; 802-293-3011) with express service to Boston. This is one of New England's few pleasant bus stations, with clean, friendly dining and snack rooms.

By air: **The Lebanon Regional Airport** (298-8878), West Lebanon, has frequent service to New York and Boston via Business Express (Delta, 1-800-345-3400) and Northwest Airlink (1-800-225-2525); USAir Express (1-800-428-4322) also serves Philadelphia. Rental cars are available from Avis, Hertz, and Alamo.

By train: **AMTRAK** (802-295-7160; 1-800-872-7245) stops in White River Junction en route to and from Washington, New York's Penn Station, and Montreal.

MEDICAL EMERGENCY

Dartmouth-Hitchcock Medical Center (650-5000; 911), off Route 120 between Hanover and Lebanon. Generally considered the best hospital in northern New England.

The Valley Regional Hospital in Claremont (dial 911 in an emergency) also serves the southern towns of the Upper Valley.

VILLAGES

From South to North

Charlestown. Charlestown was a stockaded outpost during the French and Indian Wars (see Fort Number 4 under *Historic Sites*). Its Main Street was laid out in 1763, 200 feet wide and a mile long, with more than five dozen structures that now comprise a National Historic District; 10 buildings predate 1800. Note the 1840s Congregational Church; the former Charlestown Inn (1817), now a commercial building; the Stephen Hassam House (1800); and the Foundation for Biblical Research, housed in a 1770s mansion that's open to the public. "Historic Charlestown Walkabout," a walking guide, is available in most town stores.

Claremont. Traffic from all directions funnels through this city-sized town's Tremont Square with its ornate brick buildings, including the massive Italian Renaissance Revival–style city hall, its recently restored **Opera House** (see *Entertainment*) and the Moody Building, built originally as a hotel in 1892; the mammoth brick **Monadnock Mills** on Water Street (off Broad and Main) on the Sugar River are among the best preserved nineteenth-century small urban mills in New Hampshire; note the 1840s gambrel-roofed brick Sunapee Mill across the river and the small brick overseers' cottages (also 1840s) on Crescent Street. The **Claremont Historical Society** (542-1400) is at 26 Mulberry Street. A walking tour is available from the chamber of commerce (see *Guidance*). You might want to find **West Claremont** (accessible from both Route 12A and Routes 11/103), a vanished village graced by both New Hampshire's oldest Episcopal and Catholic churches. It seems that the Catholic priest who founded Saint Mary's parish in 1824 was the son of the Episcopal rector who built Saint John's across the street. Both buildings are interesting architecturally. The only sign of the congregations that both men taught and served is the West Part Burying Ground adjoining the churches.

Cornish. Best known as the one-time summer home of sculptor Augustus Saint-Gaudens (see *Historic Sites*), Cornish also served as a turn-of-the-century summer home for a number of other prominent artists and writers in his circle. This "Cornish Colony" included actress Ethel Barrymore; artists Charles Dana Gibson, Maxfield Parrish, and George de Forest Brush; and the American novelist Winston Churchill. (A historic marker about 200 yards south of the Plainfield-Cornish line marks his estate, which was used as a summer White House by President Woodrow Wilson in 1914 and 1915.) These fashionable bohemians were attracted by both the beauty of the town's natural setting (with a dramatic downriver view of Mount Ascutney) and of early buildings like vintage 1808 **Trinity Church** (Route 12A), and by the Federal-era farmhouses, really mansions, which they were able to buy cheaply at the time. Their notable contributions include **Aspet**, the home of Augustus Saint-Gaudens; and the **Blow-Me-Down Mill,** Route 12A, just beyond the entrance to Aspet, designed by Stanford White.

Plainfield. A one-street village, Plainfield still clings to the memory of one-time resident Maxfield Parrish. In the 1920s Parrish painted a stage set in the town hall picturing Mount Ascutney and the river in the deep blues for which he is famous. Stop by the vintage 1798 building to see if it's open. You might also want to follow the River Road through town or cut over on Stage Road just north of the village to Meriden, an unusually handsome hilltop village.

Lebanon. As near to the junction of I-91 and I-89 as it can be but still on the New Hampshire (no sales tax) side of the Connecticut River, "West Leb" is the shopping center of the Upper Valley. The strip of malls is a good bet for most basics and the **Powerhouse Mall** north of I-89 offers some pleasant surprises. Positioned between the Connecticut River and Mascoma Lake, with old mills lining the Mascoma River, Lebanon itself—once you find it (east on Route 4)—has a small-town feel, with a vintage 1828 church, handsome homes, and public buildings, including an opera house, grouped around a common (site of summer band concerts); shops and restaurants are found along adjoining (closed to traffic) streets.

Hanover. Hanover is synonymous with Dartmouth College, chartered in 1769 and one of the most prestigious colleges in the country. Dartmouth's student population averages 4,000 undergraduate men and women and 1,000 graduate students. Its handsome buildings frame three sides of an elm-lined green, and the fourth side includes a large inn, an arts center, and an outstanding art museum. The information kiosk on the Green is staffed by knowledgeable Dartmouth alumni during summer months and is the starting point for historical and architectural tours of the campus. **Baker Memorial Library,** a 1920s version of Philadelphia's Independence Hall, dominates the north side of the Green. Visitors are welcome to see a set of murals, *The Epic of American Civilization*, by José Orozco, painted between 1932 and 1934 while he was teaching at Dartmouth. (Some alumni once demanded these be removed or covered because of the Mexican artist's left-wing politics.) In the Treasure Room (near the west stair hall on the main floor), Daniel Webster's copies of the double elephant folio first edition of John Audubon's *Birds of America* are permanently displayed. **Hopkins Center for the Arts** (646-2422) was designed by Wallace Harrison a few years before he designed New York's Lincoln Center (which it resembles). It contains three theaters, a recital hall, and art galleries for permanent and year-round programs of plays, concerts, and films. It's also home base for the Dartmouth Symphony Orchestra. **Dartmouth Row,** a file of striking white Greek Revival buildings on the rise along

Hood Museum of Art and Hopkins Center on the campus of Dartmouth College

the east side of the Green, represents all there was to Dartmouth College until 1845. You might also want to find **Webster Cottage,** maintained as a museum by the Hanover Historical Society, and the vintage 1843 **Shattuck Observatory** (open weekdays 8:30–4:40, also Tuesday and Thursday evening by reservation: 646-2034).

Lyme is known for its splendid **Congregational Church,** completed in 1812, a Federal-style meetinghouse complete with Palladian window, an unusual tower (3 cubical stages and an octagonal dome), and no fewer than 27 numbered horse stalls. The gathering of buildings, including the inn, fine old houses, and general stores, is one of New Hampshire's most stately. Take the **River Road** north by old farms and cemeteries, through an 1880s covered bridge.

Orford is known for its **Ridge Houses,** a center-of-town lineup of seven houses so strikingly handsome that Charles Bulfinch has been (erroneously) credited as their architect. They were built instead by skilled local craftsmen using designs from Connecticut Valley architect Asher Benjamin's do-it-yourself guide to Federal styles, *The Country Builder's Assistant*. These houses testify to the prosperity of this valley in the post–revolutionary war era. Each was built by an Orford resident—with money earned in Orford—between 1773 and 1839. The best-remembered of the residents is Samuel Morey. While all his neighbors were in church one Sunday morning in 1793, Morey gave the country's first little steam-powered paddle wheeler a successful test run on the river. Sam kept tinkering with the boat and in 1797 came up with a sidwheeler, but at this point Robert Fulton, who had encouraged Morey to freely discuss with him and demonstrate the invention, turned around and went into the steamboating business, using a boat clearly patterned after Morey's. It's said that an embittered Morey sank his boat across the river in the Vermont lake that now bears his name. He also heated and lighted his house with gas, and in 1826 he patented a gas-powered internal combustion engine. The **Samuel Morey House** is the oldest of the seven, a centerpiece for the others.

In **Piermont** note the **Polygonal Barn,** built in 1906, a 16-sided barn north of Piermont Village on Route 10.

Haverhill is immense, composed of seven very distinct villages, including classic examples of both Federal-era and railroad villages. Thanks to a fertile floodplain, this is an old and prosperous farming community, and even with agricultural land now less than 9,000 acres, it still boasts more than 20 farms. It has also been the Grafton County seat since 1773. The village of **Haverhill Corner** on Route 10 is a gem. It is a grouping of Federal-era and Greek Revival homes and public buildings around a double, white-fenced common (the site of all-day flea markets on the last Sunday of summer months). Just north of the village (but south of the junction of Routes 10 and 25) a sign points the way, down through a cornfield and along the river, to the site of the Bedell Bridge. Built in 1866, this was one of the largest surviving examples of a two-span covered bridge until it was destroyed by a violent September windstorm in 1979. The site is still worth finding because it's a peaceful riverside spot, ideal for a picnic.

Woodsville. North of North Haverhill you come unexpectedly to a lineup of modern county buildings—the courthouse, a county home, and a jail—and then you are in downtown Woodsville with its ornate 1890s brick Opera Block and three-story, mustard-colored railroad station. The Haverhill-Bath covered bridge, built in 1829 and billed as the oldest covered bridge in New England, is just beyond the railroad underpass (Route 135 north).

TO SEE

Unless otherwise indicated, all telephone numbers are New Hampshire (area code 603).

MUSEUMS

Hood Museum of Art (646-2808), Dartmouth Green. Open Tuesday through Friday 11–5; Saturday and Sunday 9:30–5. Free. Housed in a 1980s building designed by Charles W. Moore, the collection is billed as the country's oldest, begun in 1773 when the colonial governor of

New Hampshire presented Dartmouth President Wheelock with a silver monteith. It now ranges eclectically from Assyrian bas-reliefs (donated by missionary graduates in the 1850s) through Italian masters, American eighteenth-century portraits, and nineteenth-century landscapes to a huge abstract piece by Dartmouth graduate Frank Stella. Treasures include an 1840s polychrome baseball player donated by Abby Aldrich Rockefeller in 1935. A narrow flight of stairs rises dramatically to the high, sky-lit Lathrop Gallery, hung with modern masterpieces such as Picasso's *Guitar on the Table,* gift of Nelson Rockefeller, class of 1930. There are frequently changing exhibits.

The Montshire Museum of Science (802-649-2200), Norwich, VT. The first left after the bridge from Hanover (before the I-91 off-ramp). Open daily 10–5; admission $5 per adult, $3 per child. An offshoot of a fusty old Dartmouth College museum filled with stuffed birds, now a nationally recognized science education center geared to all ages. Few cities have a science museum of this quality, and the superb exhibits, plus trails through 100 wooded acres on the Connecticut River, add up to one of New England's outstanding sights. Don't be put off by the entrance fee, and stop by whether you have children along or not. Do you really understand why night and day occur? The museum answers dozens of such questions. Its avowed goal is to demystify natural phenomena, and it does so in a way that's fun. Exhibits change but usually include an aquarium of northern New England fish, a kinetic energy machine, an elaborate colony of 25,000 leaf-cutter ants, an exhibit on "knot topography," and much more. All exhibits (except the boa constrictor) are hands-on. "Andy's Place," a preschool corner, includes a deep cave complete with a (road kill) bear cub. There's also a playground and a big gift shop; inquire about workshops, guided hikes, special events, and exhibits. The excellent Carnegie Chamber Players perform here frequently.

The American Precision Museum (802-674-5781), South Main Street, Windsor, VT. Open May 30 through November 1, Monday through Friday 9–5; Saturday, Sunday, and holidays 10–4; fee. An important, expanding collection of hand and machine tools assembled in the 1846 Robbins, Kendall & Lawrence Armory, itself a national historic landmark. The firm became world famous in 1851 because of its displays of "the American system" of manufacturing interchangeable parts, especially for what became the renowned Enfield rifle.

HISTORIC SITES

The Saint-Gaudens National Historic Site (675-2175), Route 12A, Cornish. Open 8:30–4:30 daily, late May through October; nominal admission. The sculptor's summer home, Aspet, is furnished as it was when he lived here between 1885 and his death in 1907. Augustus Saint-Gaudens is remembered for such public pieces as the Shaw memorial on Boston Common, the statue of Admiral Farragut in New York's Madison Square, and the equestrian statue of General William T.

Sherman on New York's Fifth Avenue near Central Park. The estate includes a barn/studio, a sculpture court, and an art gallery, set in formal gardens with Mount Ascutney across the river as a backdrop. Saint-Gaudens loved the Ravine Trail, a quarter-mile cart path now marked for visitors, and other walks laid out through the woodlands and wetlands to the Blow-Me-Down Natural Area. Visitors are invited to bring picnics before the Sunday concerts (2 P.M.) in July and August; also to view the changing art exhibits in the art gallery. The site is maintained by the National Park Service.

Old Constitution House (802-674-6628), North Main Street, Windsor, VT. Open daily, mid-May to mid-October. This is Elijah West's tavern (but not in its original location), where delegates gathered July 2, 1777, to adopt Vermont's constitution. It now holds an intriguing collection of antiques, prints, documents, tools and cooking utensils, tableware, toys, and early fabrics.

Fort Number 4 (826-5700), Route 11, 1 mile north of Charlestown. Open Memorial Day to Columbus Day, 10–4 (closed Tuesday, also weekdays during the first two weeks in September). A reconstruction of this stockaded village as it looked in the two decades after 1743. A full 50 miles north of any other town on the Connecticut, it fell once but then withstood repeated Native American attacks. The complex includes the Great Hall, cow barns, and furnished living quarters; there is also an audiovisual program and crafts. Admission fee.

Lower Shaker Village, Route 4A, Enfield. The museum (632-4346) is open June to October 15, Monday through Saturday 10–5 and Sunday noon–5; October 15 to June 1 closing at 4. Admission fee; guided tours extra. The Shaker community, founded in 1793 in this "Chosen Vale" between Mount Assurance and Mascoma Lake, prospered through the nineteenth century, and 13 buildings survive. In 1927 the complex was sold to the Catholic order of La Salette, which added a basilica-shaped chapel. In 1985 the order sold the buildings to developers. The Great Stone Dwelling, said to be the largest Shaker dwelling anywhere, is now a combination restaurant and inn, and surrounding buildings—the former Catholic chapel and school buildings and a developer's new condos—create a hodgepodge effect. The evolving Shaker Museum, housed in the former laundry/dairy building, has varied exhibits, a slide show, and a gift shop. It is the scene of frequent workshops in Shaker crafts: woodworking, chair-taping, natural dyeing, herbal wreath–making. Winter and spring lectures are also offered. The La Salette brothers still maintain a Shrine and Center (632-4301) here; inquire for Mass and devotional schedule. (Also see *Selective Shopping*.)

Webster Cottage (643-2326), North Main Street, Hanover (two blocks north of the Green). Memorial Day to Columbus Day, Wednesday, Saturday, and Sunday 2:30–4:30 and by appointment. Built in 1780 as the home of Abigail Wheelock (daughter of Dartmouth founder Eleazar

Wheelock), it was also the senior-year (1801) residence of Daniel Webster and birthplace in 1822 of Henry Fowle Durant, founder of Wellesley College. Maintained as a museum by the Hanover Historical Society.

COVERED BRIDGES

The Cornish-Windsor covered bridge, Route 12A, is the country's longest covered bridge. It was built in 1866, rebuilt in 1989.

Two bridges, both dating from 1882, span the **Mill Brook**—one in Cornish "City" and the other in Cornish "Mills" between Routes 12A and 120.

FOR FAMILIES

Wilder Dam Visitors' House and Fish Ladder (295-3191), Route 5, Wilder, VT. Open daily 9–5, Memorial Day to Columbus Day; free. Displays about salmon, the fish ladder, and energy. In June and part of July fish, sometimes salmon, can occasionally be seen using the ladders. In winter, when water elsewhere is iced over, a bald eagle often frequents the dam. The best viewing time is early morning.

(Also see the Montshire Museum of Science under *Museums* and Fort Number 4 under *Historic Sites.*)

TO DO

AIR RIDES

Ladco (298-8728), Lebanon Airport. Offers scenic tours of the Upper Valley.

Boland Balloon (802-333-9254), at Post Mills Airport, West Fairlee, VT. Offers year-round morning and sunset balloon rides. On the summer evening we tried it, the balloon hovered above hidden pockets in the hills, and we saw a herd of what looked like brown and white goats that, on closer inspection, proved to be deer (yes, some were white!). After an hour or so we settled down gently in a farmyard and broke out the champagne. Scenic plane rides and flight instruction also offered.

BICYCLING

Given its unusually flat and scenic roads and well-spaced inns, this area is beloved by bicyclists. Search out the river roads (for some reason they're not marked on the official New Hampshire highway map): from Route 12A (just north of the Saint-Gaudens site) on through Plainfield until it rejoins Route 12A; from Route 10 north of Hanover (just north of the Chieftain Motel) through Lyme, rejoining Route 10 in Orford. A classic, 36-mile loop is Hanover to Orford on Route 10 and back on the river road. The loop to Lyme and back is 22 miles. A variety of rides, including some for mountain bikers, are described in the *Hanover Area Recreation Guide* by Carol Selikowitz (see Dartmouth Bookstore under *Selective Shopping*).

BOAT CRUISES

River Queen Pontoon Boat (649-3860). Inquire about cruises from Ledyard Bridge to Wilson's Landing.

CANOEING

With its usually placid water and scenery, the Connecticut River through much of the Upper Valley is ideal for easygoing canoeists. The **Connecticut River Watershed Council** (675-2518), Box 189, Plainfield 03781, with offices on Route 12A in Cornish, publishes *The Complete Boating Guide to the Connecticut River* ($11.95), the bible to the river, essential for nonguided trips. Inquire about educational day and camping trips. "Canoeing on the Connecticut River," a free, detailed pamphlet guide to this particular stretch of the river, is available from the Vermont Division of Recreation and Department of Water Resources Agency of Environmental Conservation, Montpelier, VT 05602.

Most of the outfitters listed below provide their own basic maps.

The Ledyard Canoe Club (646-2753), in Hanover, is billed as the oldest canoe club in America. It's part of Dartmouth but open to the public 9–8 daily in summer, shorter hours in spring and fall. Canoes and kayaks are rented, and instruction is available.

North Star Canoes (542-5802), Route 12A in Cornish. This riverside red barn is well stocked with canoes and free maps; also the source of a reasonably priced shuttle service to the particularly scenic stretch of the Connecticut between Charlestown on the south and Hartland Rapids on the north. Camping is available at Wilgus State Park (802-674-5422) in Windsor.

Inn-to-Inn Tours (802-333-9124), the oldest inn-to-inn canoeing program in New England, is a self-guided, three-day package put together by three inns—two in New Hampshire and one in Vermont.

Vermont Waterways, Inc. (293-7620) offers guided inn-to-inn tours on the Connecticut.

FISHING

You can eat the fish you catch in the Connecticut River—it yields brown and rainbow trout above Orford. There's a boat launch at the Wilder Dam, another just north of Hanover, and another across the river in North Thetford, Vermont.

Lake Mascoma (look for boat launches along Route 4A in Enfield) and Post Pond in Lyme are other popular angling spots.

GOLF

Hanover Country Club (646-2000), Rope Ferry Road, off Route 10, Hanover. Open May to October. Founded in 1899, an 18-hole facility with 4 practice holes, pro shop, PGA instructors.

Carter Golf Club (448-4488), Lebanon. Nine holes, par 36.

Lake Morey Country Club (802-333-4800; 1-800-423-1211). Eighteen holes, site of the Vermont Open for the past 40 years (third Sunday of June).

Windsor Country Club (802-674-6491), Windsor, VT. Nine holes, par 34, no lessons.

Fore-U Driving Range (298-9702), Route 12A, West Lebanon. Buckets of balls to hit off mats or grass.

HANG GLIDING

Morningside Recreation Area (542-4416), Route 12 in Claremont, is the site of events on weekends.

STOCK-CAR RACING

Claremont Speedway (543-3160), Bowker Street, 4 miles east of I-91, Claremont. May to September, racing Saturday 7:30 P.M.

SWIMMING

Storrs Pond Recreation Area (643-2134), off Route 10 north of Hanover (Reservoir Road, then left). Open June through Labor Day, 10–8. Bathhouse with showers and lockers, lifeguards at both the (unheated) Olympic-size pool and 15-acre pond. Fee for nonmembers.

*✐☞***Treasure Island** (802-333-9615), on Lake Fairlee, Thetford, VT. This fabulous town swimming area is on Route 244 (follow Route 113 north of town). Open late June to Labor Day, 10–8 weekends, 12–8 weekdays. Sand beach, picnic tables, playground, tennis. Nominal admission.

Union Village Dam Area (802-649-1606), Thetford, VT. Open from Memorial Day to mid-September; five swimming areas along the Ompompanoosuc River.

CROSS-COUNTRY SKIING

Occum Touring Center (646-2440), Rope Ferry Road (off Route 10 just before the country club), Hanover. Closed Monday. Thirty-five km of trails through Storrs Pond and Oak Hill areas; rentals, lessons, waxing clinics. The center is on the lower level of the Outing Club House.

Ascutney Mountain Resort (802-484-7771; 1-800-243-0011), Route 44, Brownsville, VT. A touring center with instruction, rentals, 32 km of trails.

Lake Morey Inn Resort (802-333-4800; 1-800-423-1211). Turns the golf course into a touring center; rentals, instruction.

DOWNHILL SKIING

✐ **Ascutney Mountain Resort** (802-484-7771; 1-800-243-0011), Route 44, Brownsville, VT. A family-geared, self-contained resort that went bankrupt and was purchased in September 1993 by the Plausteiner family from Lake Placid, New York. Facilities include a 240-room hotel, 25 slope-side condos, a sports center with indoor and outdoor pools, weight and racquetball rooms, a full restaurant, and a base lodge.
Trails: 31.
Lifts: 3 triple chairs, 1 double chair.
Vertical drop: 1,530 feet.
Snowmaking: 60 percent.
Nursery/child care: Six months to six years.
Rates: $34 adult, $22 junior on weekends, $15 weekdays for everyone. Also half-day, multi-day rates.

✐ **Dartmouth Skiway** (795-2143), Lyme Center, an amenity for families as well as the college.
Trails: 16.

Lifts: 1 quad chair, 1 double chair, a beginners' J-bar.
Vertical drop: 900 feet.
Snowmaking: 54 percent.
Rates: $26 adult, $21 junior on weekends, $21 and $16 weekdays.

✐ **Ski Whaleback, Ltd.** (448-1489), Exit 16, I-89, Whaleback Mountain Road, Enfield. A small, family-owned, and family-oriented ski area with full rentals, lodge, night skiing, and public and private lessons every day of the week.
Trails: 16.
Lifts: 1 double chair, 1 platterpull.
Vertical drop: 600 feet.
Snowmaking: 40 percent.
Rates: $21 adult, $17 juniors and seniors on weekends; $16 and $10 weekdays.

ICE SKATING

Occum Pond, next to the country club, Hanover. Kept plowed and planed, lit evenings until 10 unless unsafe for skating; warming hut.

Ascutney Mountain Resort (802-484-7771), Route 44, Brownsville, VT. Lighted skating rink with rental skates.

SLEIGH RIDES

North Star Canoe (542-5802), Route 12A, Cornish. Rides offered along the Connecticut River and up through a hidden valley; hot cider included in price of the ride.

GREEN SPACE

Pine Park, just north of the Dartmouth campus between the Hanover Country Club and the Connecticut River, Hanover. Take North Main Street to Rope Ferry Road and park at the trail sign above the clubhouse. These tall pines along the river are one of the beauty spots of the valley. The 125-year-old trees were saved from the Diamond Match Company in 1900 by a group of local citizens. The walk is 1.5 miles.

Rinker Tract, Route 10, 2.5 miles north of Hanover. This is an 18-acre knoll with a pond, at the bottom of the hill below the Chieftain Motel. The loop trail is marked by blue blazes.

LODGING

HOTELS

The Hanover Inn (643-4300; 1-800-443-7024), Hanover 03755. This is the Ritz of the north country. Like the Boston Ritz it overlooks a cultural common (the Dartmouth Green) and exudes a distinctly tweedy elegance. Guest rooms are each individually and deftly decorated and the junior suites—with canopy beds, eiderdown quilts, armchairs, a silent valet, couch, and vanity—are pamperingly luxurious. A 4-story, 92-

room, neo-Georgian building owned and operated by Dartmouth College, the "inn" traces itself back to 1780 when the college's steward, General Ebenezer Brewster, turned his home into a tavern. Brewster's son parlayed this enterprise into the Dartmouth Hotel, which continued to thrive until 1887 when it burned to the ground. The present building dates in part from this era but has lost its Victorian lines through successive renovations and expansions. It remains, however, the heart of Hanover. In summer the front terrace is crowded with faculty, visitors, and residents enjoying a light lunch or beer. Year-round the lobby, the porch rocking chairs, and the Hayward Room (a comfortable sitting room with claw-foot sofas and flowery armchairs, dignified portraits, and a frequently lit hearth) are popular spots for friends to meet. Roughly half the inn's guests are Dartmouth-related. Both the Ivy Grill and more formal Daniel Webster Room draw patrons from throughout the Upper Valley (see *Dining Out*). Rates are $174 for a standard room, $224 for a junior suite, no charge for children under age 12; senior citizens' discount; honeymoon, ski, golf, and seasonal packages.

✐☞**The Hotel Coolidge** (802-295-3118; 1-800-622-1124), 17 South Main Street, White River Junction, VT. A "find" for the enterprising, economy-minded traveler. Built in 1925 and recently renovated, this 53-room hotel is across from the AMTRAK station, and is one of the last of New England's old railroad hotels. Rooms are brightly papered, furnished in solid old pieces, all with phones and TVs; some adjoining, good for families. Local buses to Hanover and Lebanon stop at the door and rental cars can be arranged. The hotel's informal restaurant, Cashie's, is well-loved locally (see *Eating Out*). Owner and manager David Briggs, a seventh-generation Vermonter, takes his role as innkeeper seriously and will arrange for special needs. $45–55 double.

RESORTS

✐☞**Loch Lyme Lodge and Cottages** (795-2141; 1-800-423-2141), Route 10, RFD 278, Lyme 03768. Main lodge open year-round; cabins, Memorial Day to Labor Day. There are 4 rooms in the inn, 26 brown-shingle cabins (12 with cooking facilities) spread along a wooded hillside overlooking the lake called Post Pond. The big attraction here is a private lakefront beach with a float and fleet of rowboats and canoes; also a windsurfer. Two tennis courts, a baseball field, a basketball court, a volleyball net, and a recreation cabin are there for the using, and babysitting is available for parents who want time off. Lunch and dinner are served and a take-out lunch bar is open for sandwiches and cones. Loch Lyme was founded in 1917 and has been owned and managed by Paul and Judy Barker's family since the 1940s. No credit cards. Pets permitted in cabins. From $24 per person off-season (when there's cross-country skiing on the property and the Dartmouth Skiway is just up the road) to $40 per person per night in summer. Housekeeping cabins are $375–625 per week; cabins without

SHAKER INN

The Shaker Inn at Enfield

kitchens are available on a B&B or MAP ($53 per person) basis; children's
rates range from $7 to $23.

- **Kluge's Sunset Hill Inn** (632-4335), Sunset Hill, Enfield 03748. Seasonal.
  A rambling old family-geared inn with a beach on Mascoma Lake and
  newly renovated housekeeping suites with one, two, and three bedrooms
  as well as B&B rooms. Facilities include swimming and wading pools, a
  play area for younger children, and 300 acres of private woodland and
  meadow; there are also boats for use on the lake. One unit is handicapped
  accessible. $70 double B&B, $65–95 per day for housekeeping suites,
  $350–470 per week. A three-bedroom beach house with fireplace is $525
  July through Labor Day, $425 off-season.
- **Rutledge Inn & Cottages** (802-333-9722), Fairlee, VT 05045. Open May
  through Labor Day on Lake Morey with a private beach, rowboats,
  canoes, sailboats, and an old-fashioned "casino" rec hall. Three bountiful
  meals are served in the cheerful dining room of the central lodge, a
  building that also includes a lounge and library. From $65 per day in the
  lodge to $93 in the best cottages. Less expensive for children, by the week,
  and in May before the dining room opens.

COUNTRY INNS

- **Moose Mountain Lodge** (643-3529), PO Box 272, Moose Mountain
  Highway, Etna 03750. Closed November to December 25 and late
  March through May. Just 7 miles from Dartmouth Green, the feel is
  remote and the view, spectacular. The design is "classic lodge," built from
  stones and logs cleared from these hills, walled in pine. The roomy back

porch (flower-filled in summer) is like a balcony seat above the valley, commanding a view of Vermont mountains from Ascutney to Sugarbush, with Killington off across lower hills, center stage. This is also the view from the sitting room, with its window seats and massive stone fireplace. Upstairs the rooms are small but inviting (with spruce log bedsteads made by Kay Shumway herself) and shared baths, which are immaculate. Kay is justly famed as a cook, one adept at preparing nightly feasts for the groups of hikers (the inn is just off the Appalachian Trail), bikers, and cross-country skiers (there's a long ridge trail) who frequent the place. Kay and Peter Shumway have been innkeepers here since 1975 and still welcome each new guest with enthusiasm and interest. $80 per person MAP, $40 for children 12 and under. No smoking.

The Lyme Inn (795-2222) and **Dowd's Country Inn** (795-4712), on the Common, Lyme 03768. Both inns—one the formal village tavern dating in part from 1809 and the other a 1780s house—are now owned by Mickey and Tami Dowd. Since acquiring the Lyme Inn in 1993, the couple have altered the public spaces: the lobby looks more like a living room and less like a general store and the informal tavern dining area has been enlarged. The 14 antiques-furnished rooms upstairs are $65–95 per couple, breakfast included. Dowd's Country Inn, a couple of doors down the Common, offers 21 guest rooms. The attached barn harbors a large living room, a meeting space, a small dining room, and a row of upstairs rooms overlooking the spacious backyard. Rooms in the old house itself include a cheery breakfast room and a presidential suite, with a sitting room that can comfortably accommodate a family of five. $55–110 per room (depending on room and season) includes breakfast and afternoon tea.

Home Hill Country Inn (675-6165), RR 2, Box 235, Cornish 03745. "Ninety-five percent of my business is dining and five percent is sleeping," admits Roger Nicolas, owner of one of the valley's four-square 1820s river mansions. Rooms are predictable: brass beds, country wallpaper, maybe a handmade quilt. There are also a two-room suite and a three-room cottage by the pool. The setting is beautiful: 25 acres by the river, good for walking and cross-country skiing. But dining is what this place is about (see *Dining Out*). $95–150 per room includes continental breakfast.

The Shaker Inn (632-7800), at Lower Shaker Village, Route 4A, Enfield 03748. This Great Stone Dwelling House, the largest Shaker dwelling ever built, was used as dormitory space for retreats by the La Salette brothers from 1922 until 1985, and 30 rooms ($59–69) are now available as part of the Shaker Inn and Conference Center. At this writing just six rooms have been redone with private baths and Dana Robes Shaker-reproduction furniture, but all are scheduled to be completed in 1994; be sure to reserve a renovated room, because in this case the difference between "before" and "after" is dramatic. Rooms in the

Victorian Mary Keane House include a suite with kitchen and fire-place ($99).

BED & BREAKFASTS

Haverhill Inn (989-5961), Route 10, Haverhill 03765. A classic 1810 Fed-eral-style house with canopied beds, working fireplaces, and river views in its big, square guest rooms (private baths). My favorite is the Blue Room with its graceful old vanity, cane-backed rocking chair, and Victo-rian couch. Downstairs walls are decorated with old Grafton County maps, and comfortable chairs and sofas in the sitting room are within reach of plenty to read. Innkeepers Stephen Campbell and Anne Baird keep local menus and delight in orienting guests to local antiquing, hik-ing, biking, and canoeing. Breakfast is served in front of the mammoth old hearth in the dining room, off a kitchen that's just been splendidly rebuilt. $85 per couple (less for a single) includes a full breakfast.

Animal Track Inn (989-3351), PO Box 91, Haverhill 03765. A beautifully restored nineteenth-century home on Route 25 in East Haverhill. The inn is on the western edge of the White Mountain National Forest and within the 2,000-acre Oliverian Valley Wildlife reserve. Well run, clean, and pleasant, with excellent food and helpful hosts. Guests are encour-aged to hike to a nearby summit (5 miles round-trip); canoe livery and access to the Oliverian River for fishing and swimming also offered. $45–60 per night; a three-room guest house is $275 per weekend, $500 per week.

✎☞**Goddard Mansion** (543-0603; 1-800-736-0603), 25 Hillstead Road, Claremont 03743. A grand, pillared and paneled, turn-of-the-century mansion set on a knoll overlooking Mount Ascutney and tiers of smaller hills. Built in 1905 as a summer home by the president of International Shoe, it has an airy, easy elegance. Debbie Albee, with her late husband Frank, spent two years restoring the house and decorating the eight guest rooms. The living room has a 4½-foot fireplace, a baby grand piano, and a music system, and there's also a comfortable TV room, a splendid library (with a play corner for small children), and an attractive upstairs reading and writing room with a backgammon set on the windowseat below the river view. The nine guest rooms vary from the traditional Bridal Suite, with its canopy bed, to the surreal third-floor Cloud Room; most have river views and private baths. A "natural breakfast" of homemade muffins with preserves made from home-grown fruit, fresh fruit, and whole-grain cereals is served in a formal, Tiffany-lit dining room that has some informal touches—like the completely restored 1939 Wurlitzer jukebox, complete with 78s, and the puzzle always in progress on the sideboard. Despite the grandeur of the house small children are very welcome here (families have the run of the third floor) and babies are free if Debbie (a grandmother herself) gets a hug. Few hosts are as adept at making guests of all ages feel welcome. The rates are $65–95 depending on the room. Smoke free.

The Chase House (675-5391), Route 12A, Cornish 03745. Closed in November. A classic Federal-style mansion, begun around 1775 and moved back from the river in the mid-1840s to make way for the Sullivan County Railroad. Salmon Portland Chase, born here in 1808, is remembered as Lincoln's Secretary of the Treasury, a founder of the Republican Party, namesake of the Chase Manhattan Bank, and the man on the $10,000 bill. The house has been carefully restored, its nine guest rooms exquisitely decorated in period wallpapers and reproduction antiques; fitted with private baths; windows richly draped with swags. Innkeepers Bill and Barbara Lewis have added an unusually attractive function room with genuine old (1810) posts and beams, a fieldstone hearth, and a minstrel loft. Needless to say, this is a popular spot for wedding receptions. You can walk along the riverbank across the road, and there are trails for hiking and skiing. $85–105 includes a full breakfast.

Maple Hedge (826-5237), Box 638, Route 12, Charlestown 03603. Open June through October. Dick and Joan DeBrine have come from California to fulfill Joan's longtime dream of running a New England B&B. This is a beauty, a big, handsome 1790s Main Street house with elegant spaces—five guest rooms with private baths, each decorated around a theme. $75–85 per couple.

Piermont Inn (272-4820), One Old Church Street, Piermont 03779. A 1790s stagecoach stop with six rooms, four in the adjacent carriage house (only the two in the inn are open year-round), all with private baths. The seasonal rooms were closed when we stopped by, but we really liked the two guest rooms we saw in the main house, both carved from the tavern's original ballroom high-ceilinged and spacious, furnished with appropriate antiques. Breakfast and dinner (served Friday and Saturday evening and by prior arrangement). Your hosts are Charlie and Karen Brown, who enjoy tuning guests in to the many ways of exploring this upper (less-touristed) part of the Upper Valley. Rooms in the main house are $60–75, in the Carriage House, $45–55.

☞ **The Stone House Inn** (802-333-9124), North Thetford, VT 05054. Built in 1835 from schist quarried across the river in Lyme, this year-round inn has an unusually comfortable feel. There are a piano and fireplace in the living room and rockers on the wide, screened porch. The six guest rooms share baths; our favorite room is in the back with windows on the river. There are 12 acres in all, stretching flat and green to the river. Innkeepers Art and Diane Sharkey cater to canoeists, but they make all guests feel welcome. $50 double includes breakfast.

Juniper Hill Inn (802-674-5273; 1-800-359-2541), RR 1, Box 79, Windsor, VT 05069. This 28-room, turn-of-the-century mansion, with a view of Mount Ascutney and the valley, was recently renovated by new innkeepers Rob and Susanne Pearl. Adults (and children over 12) can relax by the hearth in the huge main hall, the parlors, and cozy library. One of

Vermont's most romantic getaways, it offers nine guest rooms with fireplaces. Inn guests gather for meals in the formal dining room, newly redecorated in deep burgundy. A choice of four entrées is served by candlelight. The innkeepers encourage guests to canoe (North Star Canoe Livery is just across the covered bridge; see *Canoeing*). $65–100 per room, full breakfast included.

Silver Maple Lodge & Cottages (802-333-4326), RR 1, Box 8, Fairlee, VT 05045. Scott and Sharon Wright offer nine modestly priced, nicely appointed guest rooms in the old farmhouse and five pine-paneled, shaded cabins. The $40–60 per couple rates include continental breakfast; special hot-air balloon, bicycling, canoeing, and walking packages available.

(Also see The Inn on Canaan Street in "The Western Lakes.")

MOTELS

The Chieftain Motor Inn (643-2550), 84 Lyme Road (Route 10 north of Hanover), Hanover 03755. The 22 units are pine-paneled with heat control, air-conditioning, cable color TV, and phones, and a number have views of the river. $62–78 double ($52–68 single) includes a light breakfast.

The Sunset (298-8721), Route 10 in West Lebanon, 2 miles south of Hanover. A tidy, family-run place bordering the Connecticut River; 12 of the 18 units have river views. Rooms are cheery with matching wallpaper and curtains; a help-yourself continental breakfast is included in the $60–75 per couple rates; less November to April.

WHERE TO EAT

DINING OUT

D'Artagnan (795-2137), in the Ambrose Publick House, 7 miles north of Hanover on Route 10 in Lyme. Open for dinner Wednesday through Sunday, lunch Sunday only. Generally considered the best (and most expensive) restaurant in the Upper Valley, and the place we've vowed to celebrate in if this book ever takes off. The setting is a low-beamed, brick-walled room in a reconstructed eighteenth-century tavern near the river, overlooking a brook. The $38 prix fixe, 4-course menu changes nightly but typically includes a choice of 10 appetizers—maybe a salad of pan-roasted Vermont venison with bacon, frisee and watercress in a walnut vinaigrette, followed by roast rack of lamb with a tomatoed rosemary sauce and topped off with white chocolate mousse with almond-hazelnut praline. Needless to say, the wine list is extensive. The French-trained chef-owners are Peter Gaylor and his wife, Rebecca Cunningham. Expensive.

The Daniel Webster Room at the Hanover Inn (643-4300; 1-800-443-7024), on Dartmouth Green, Hanover. This is a large, formal dining room (open daily for all three meals), with windows overlooking the

Green. Executive chef Michael Gray has put it on New England's culinary map. You might begin with braised escargot with wild mushrooms and polenta. Entrées might include a tournedo of salmon with three-potato crust, white Zinfandel and leeks, and roast veal tenderloin with garlic and Gorgonzola flan. Expensive.

Café Buon Gustaio (643-5711), 72 South Main Street, Hanover. Dining nightly from 5:30 to 9:30, café bar from 4:30. An intimate, deep-green dining room with a menu that changes daily. Entrées include serious pastas like lasagna of lobster, spinach, shiitake mushrooms, scallions, and four cheeses in a black-pepper saffron cream and delicacies like braised mahimahi with tomatoes, leeks, garlic, herbs, wine, and shell-fish. You can also dine on a *pizzetta* or a calzone of lobster, tomatoes, leeks, garlic, ricotta, fontina, and aged provolone served with d'Abruzzi red sauce. Wines are a special interest of owner Murray Washburn. Moderate to expensive.

Sweet Tomatoes Trattoria (448-1711), One Court Street, Lebanon. Open for lunch 11:30–2 Monday through Friday and nightly for dinner 5–9:30. A trendy trattoria with a sleek decor and a reasonably priced menu that's the toast of the Valley: plenty of pasta creations like fusilli sautéed with wood-fired roasted chicken, mushrooms, peas, and walnuts in a pecorino Romano carbonara sauce or linguine with sautéed shrimp, crushed black pepper, peas, garlic, parsley, olive oil, and white wine. Other options range from a choice of 16 pizzas baked in a wood-fired oven to nightly specials like grilled fresh Nova Scotia salmon encrusted with cracked black pepper and dill. Moderate.

Home Hill Country Inn (675-6165), River Road, Plainfield. Open for dinner Tuesday through Saturday. A four-square 1820s mansion with a long, formal, blue canopy proclaiming its formal dining status. The series of low-ceilinged dining rooms are dressed in white napery. A prix fixe of $30 for four courses might include a napoleon of fresh salmon with champagne sauce and Peking duck with fresh plum and ginger sauce or Vermont rabbit braised with wine and fresh tarragon. Expensive.

The Lyme Inn (795-2222), on the Common, Lyme. Open for breakfast and dinner nightly. Under new ownership the atmosphere is lighter, less traditional than of yore. Appetizers might include fried mushrooms and buffalo-style wings, and entrées range from Wiener schnitzel to seafood stir fry. Moderate.

The Shaker Inn (632-7800), at Lower Shaker Village, Route 4A, Enfield. Closed for dinner Tuesday, otherwise open daily for breakfast and dinner, Sunday brunch. This is the original Shaker dining hall in the Great Stone Dwelling, and the furnishings are Shaker-style chairs and simple tables; the menu includes Shaker touches. But this is a far cry from the quality of the Creamery at Canterbury Shaker Village (see "The Concord Area"). Its reviews are mixed. A typical dinner menu might include southwest roast chicken lasagna, and tahini- and parsley-crusted salmon. Moderate.

Indian Shutters Restaurant (826-4366), Route 12, North Charlestown. Open for lunch and dinner Tuesday through Saturday; Sunday brunch and dinner. Probably the oldest tavern in the valley, first licensed in 1799. Named for its original inside sliding shutters, both the atmosphere and menu are traditional American. Mixed reviews. Moderate.

La Poule à Dents at Carpenter Street (802-649-2922), Main Street, Norwich, VT. Open for lunch Monday through Friday, for dinner Monday through Saturday. Prix fixe lunch and à la carte dinner menu; after-dinner menu with late-night jazz until midnight. A meal in this 1820s house with a cheerful bar and beamed café might begin with broth of wild mushrooms and include chartreuse of pheasant with braised savoy cabbage and poached figs. Great desserts. Expensive.

EATING OUT
South to North

⌀ **Buster's Restaurant** (542-0200), 170 Charlestown Road (Route 12A), Charlestown. A great family place specializing in seafood (there's an attached fish shop and a lobster tank), BBQ back ribs and chicken; also good for pasta and chicken and veal dishes. Great salad bar. Lobster dinners from $8.95. Popular for breakfast, especially the weekend all-you-can-eat breakfast buffet.

The Claremont Diner, Tremont Square next to the Moody Building, Claremont. A genuine classic railroad-car diner, with blue tile, a counter and booths. A local hangout; specials like homemade beef biscuit and salmon pea wiggle on toast.

Todafrali's (543-3520), Route 103/11 just east of Claremont on the commercial strip. Open for all three meals, a real find for standout deli sandwiches and specials like fresh giant calamari stuffed with basil and mozzarella, marinated tuna on a bed of spinach, and fettuccine with alfredo or pesto sauce. Most regulars stock up on homemade pesto at the deli.

Lui, Lui (298-7070), Powerhouse Mall, West Lebanon. Open daily, Monday through Thursday for lunch and dinner until 9 or 10. The former boiler house for the brick mill complex makes a multi-tiered, attractive setting for this popular, informal Italian restaurant. Pastas, salads, calzones, and specialty pizzas fill the bill of fare.

Good Fortune (448-3888), 45 Hanover Street, Lebanon. Open for lunch and dinner. An outstanding Chinese restaurant specializing in Szechuan and Hunan cuisine, with an excellent sushi bar.

⌀ **West Lebanon fast-food strip.** Route 12A just south of I-89, Exit 20, is lined with representatives of every major fast-food chain in New England—a godsend to families with cars full of kids. Over the years our own carful has come to favor this Burger King, simply for its size and efficiency, but you may prefer McDonald's, Pizza Hut, Wendy's, D'Angelo's, Subway, Del

Pastoral scene along Route 10 near Haverhill

Taco, Shorty's, Kentucky Fried Chicken, or the Weathervane (reasonably priced seafood).

The Ivy Grill at the Hanover Inn (643-3400), on Dartmouth Green, Hanover. An attractive, informal setting for daily lunch and dinner (serving until 10 P.M.); the menu includes pizza and burgers but runs to lobster and crab ravioli.

Lou's (643-3321), 30 South Main Street, Hanover. Open for breakfast weekdays from 6 A.M., Saturday from 7, and Sunday from 8. Lunch Monday through Saturday until 3 P.M.; "Mexican Suppers" Wednesday through Sunday 5–9. Since 1947 this has been a student and local hangout and it's great: a long Formica counter, tables and booths, irresistible peanut-butter cookies at the register—crowded all day, and the Mexican fare is fine.

Peter Christian's Tavern (643-2345), 39 South Main Street, Hanover. Daily from 11:30 A.M.–12:30 A.M. Dark, pubby, and known for good soups and great sandwiches—like turkey *boursin*—at noon; reasonably priced dinner entrées, blackboard specials, a wide selection of ales and beers.

Molly's Balloon (643-2570), 43 Main Street, Hanover. Open daily for lunch and dinner. The greenhouse up front shelters a big, inviting bar that encourages single dining. Youngsters receive helium-filled balloons. The menu is immense and reasonably priced: big salads, enchiladas, elaborate burgers at lunch, pasta to steak at dinner.

Jewel of India (643-2217), 27 Lebanon Street, Hanover. Open for lunch and dinner. A wide range of Indian dishes; Punjabi cooking is the specialty.

Panda House (643-1290), 3 Lebanon Street, Hanover. Good Szechuan, Mandarin, and Cantonese, and some Japanese dishes, plus a sushi bar.

The Village Pancake House and Bakery, Route 10, North Haverhill. Open for lunch except Tuesday; Friday night seafood special. Bishops ice cream. An 1820s house but very simple—good for lunch, home-baked breads, good sandwiches.

Barge Inn Restaurant (747-2551), junction of Routes 10 and 302, Woodsville. Open from 6 A.M. to 10 P.M., across from a lumber mill. A place that's expanded over the years, with basics and specials like linguine and meat sauce and a big salad bar.

Chalet Schaefer (747-2071), Woodsville on Route 10 just south of the Opera Block. A well-established, local German restaurant with a reasonably priced menu featuring hassenpfeffer, sauerbraten, and more.

In Vermont

Windsor Station Restaurant (802-674-2675), Depot Avenue, Windsor, VT. Open daily for lunch and dinner. Windsor's original railroad station is more plush than ever with gleaming woods and brass, velvet, and railroadiana. Lunch can be a burger, but the large dinner menu includes veal Oscar ($13.95), roast duckling with apricot sauce ($13.50), and scallops Mornay ($13.75); a children's menu is offered.

Colatina Exit (802-222-9008), Main Street, Bradford, VT. Open daily for dinner. Casual but candlelit atmosphere (checked tablecloths, pictures of Italy), affordable wines, a great antipasto, homemade pastas, fresh seafood, poultry, and vegetarian dishes. Most entrées under $10.

Cashie's (802-295-3118), Hotel Coolidge, South Main Street, White River Junction, VT. Cheerful pub and restaurant, open daily for all three meals. Entertainment Thursday through Saturday evening. A large well-prepared menu, from taco salads to vegetarian stir fry to prime rib.

ENTERTAINMENT

MUSIC AND THEATER

Hopkins Center (box office: 646-2422), on Dartmouth Green, Hanover. Sponsors some 150 musical and 20 theater productions, plus 200 films per year, all open to the public.

White River Theater Festival (802-296-2505), Briggs Opera House, White River Junction, VT. A wide variety of professional productions.

The Parish Players (802-785-4344), based in the Eclipse Grange Hall, Thetford Hill, VT. Year-round community players.

Lebanon Opera House (448-2498), in Town Hall, Coburn Park. An 800-seat, turn-of-the-century theater hosts frequent concerts, lectures, and summer performances by the North Country Community Players.

Opera North (643-1946), Lebanon Opera House in August and elsewhere in the Upper Valley at other times of the year. Excellent, semiprofessional performances.

Upper Valley Community Band (448-9876). With many teachers among its members, the UVCB sets high standards, performing at the Lebanon Opera House and throughout the Upper Valley.

Claremont Opera House (542-4433), Tremont Square, in the City Hall, Claremont. Recently restored gilded-era theater, the scene of frequent concerts, plays, live performances of all kinds.

FILM

Cinema Six (448-6660), Lebanon. Six first-run films nightly.

Hopkins Center (646-2422). Frequent showings of classic, contemporary, and experimental films in two theaters.

Nugget Theater (643-2769), Hanover. Two current films nightly.

SELECTIVE SHOPPING

ANTIQUES

Pick up a copy of the leaflet map/guide "Antiquing in the North Country," available at most inns and information booths. It lists a dozen dealers between West Lebanon and Haverhill.

William Smith (675-2549) holds antiques auctions at the Plainfield Auction Gallery, Route 12A in Plainfield, year-round.

ART GALLERIES AND CRAFTS CENTERS

AVA Gallery (448-3117), 11 Bank Street (Route 4 just west of Coburn Park), Lebanon. Open Monday through Saturday 11–5. From its Hanover beginnings the Alliance for the Visual Arts has grown to fill a sun-filled former mill building. The Soho-style (and -quality) gallery mounts frequent exhibits of arts and crafts.

BOOKSTORES

Dartmouth Bookstore (in NH: 1-800-462-9009; outside NH: 1-800-624-8800), 33 South Main Street, Hanover. Open Monday through Saturday. One of the largest bookstores in northern New England, in owner Phoebe Storrs Stebbins' family since 1884 and currently managed by her son-in-law, David Cioffi. Supplier of textbooks to the college and its graduate schools; also to local community colleges. The store stocks 130,000 different titles including medical, technical, literary criticism, and history; also general interest titles.

Best Sellers (298-7980), Powerhouse Mall, West Lebanon. Full-service bookstore, mall hours.

Your Idea (448-0123), 160 Mechanic Street, Lebanon, is a unique bookstore featuring how-to and regional titles. Open Monday through Saturday and most Sundays.

Lilac Hedge Bookstore (802-649-2921), Main Street (just past Dan and Whit's general store, also worth a stop), Norwich, VT. Open Thursday through Sunday 10–5, or by appointment or chance. Large stock of not-so-new fiction, art, history, and regional titles; well-arranged.

CRAFTS

Dana Robes—Wood Craftsmen, Inc. (632-5385), Lower Shaker Village, Route 4A, Enfield. Showroom open weekdays 9–5; Sunday 10–5. Meticulously crafted, traditional Shaker-design furniture, each piece signed by the craftsmen who created it. Products, made on the premises, range from cherry oval boxes, trays, and towel racks to custom-designed cupboards, tables, armoires, and beds.

League of New Hampshire Craftsmen (643-5050), 13 Lebanon Street, Hanover. Closed Sunday. Behind Hopkins Center; a wide selection of local and regional crafts pieces.

Vermont State Craft Center (802-674-6729), Windsor House, Route 5, Windsor, VT. Open year-round, Monday through Saturday 9–5; also Sunday, June to January. Housed in a brick, midnineteenth-century hotel, showcasing outstanding work by local craftspeople, most of whom live within an easy drive and welcome visitors.

Emil Nagy (542-2918), 19 Maple Avenue, Claremont. Using machines he designed and built himself, Emil Nagy produces solid-core brass candlesticks of his own design, a popular wedding gift among Upper Valley residents. Visitors are welcome to stop by his shop. Solid brass lamps with handcrafted Tiffany shades are another specialty.

The Mouse Menagerie of Fine Crafts (542-9691), Route 120, Cornish. Admittedly, you have to be into mice, but if you are, they have dozens of stuffed mice in a range of costumes; also mice puppets and dolls.

Heather Hill Farm (543-0137), Route 12A, North Charlestown. Clare Murray designs hooked rugs, made from home-spun yarns and hooked in China. A line of handmade wooden toys is also carried.

FOOD AND DRINK

North Country Smokehouse (543-3016; 1-800-258-4303), Claremont. Follow signs for the airport; it's across the way on a site established by Mike Satzow's grandfather in 1917. Delis throughout the Northeast carry North Country meals: hams, turkey, bacon, smoked goose and Peking duck, sausages, and more. Inquire about the catalog.

Gould's Country Smokehouse (272-5856), Stop & Save Building, Piermont, down by the Connecticut River bridge. Since 1921 ham, bacon, turkey, and chicken are smoked in a local smokehouse; available through a catalog and the retail store, open usual business hours.

Catamount Brewing Company (802-296-2248), 58 South Main Street, White River Junction, VT. Vermont's first brewery in a century. Store hours Monday through Saturday 9–5; seasonal tours.

Beaver Pond Farm (542-7339; 1-800-750-1974), 50 McDonough Road, Claremont. Maple syrup and homemade jams and jellies are available at the farm stand on Route 11 or up at the farmhouse; they will ship anywhere.

Edgewater and Riverview Farms (298-5764), Route 12A, just south of the turn onto River Road in Plainfield. Pick-your-own strawberries and asparagus in the spring, apples and pumpkins in the fall; cider pressing in the fall. Hayrides, greenhouses with bedding plants, a fully stocked farm stand.

SPECIAL SHOPPING CENTERS

Powerhouse Shopping Mall, Route 10, West Lebanon. Open Monday through Friday 10–9; Saturday 10–6; Sunday noon–5. A total of 40 stores is in this unusual complex, which combines an old brick electric powerhouse, a large, new but mill-style, two-story arcade, and several older buildings moved from other places. There is no big anchor store, just a genuine variety of small specialty stores: noteworthy shops include the **Anichini Outlet Store** featuring the Chelsea, Vermont-based company's line of antique and fine linens at substantial savings; **Jackeroos Down Under,** featuring the distinctive coats made in the owner's Australian factory; and a surprising choice of women's clothing stores.

Hanover Park, 40 South Main Street, Hanover. The anchor store here is **Kaleidoscope** (643-4327; 1-800-333-3448), a widely respected source of fine-crafted furniture and furnishings from throughout the world. The complex includes a chocolate shop, jewelry shops, a deli, a florist, and a showroom for Pompanoosuc Mills.

SPECIAL SHOPS

Pompanoosuc Mills (802-785-4851), Route 5, East Thetford, VT. Dartmouth graduate Dwight Sargeant began building furniture in this riverside house, a cottage industry that has evolved into a riverside factory with showrooms throughout New England. Some seconds. Open daily until 6, Sunday 12–5.

Vermont Salvage Exchange (802-295-7616), Railroad Row, White River Junction, VT. Doors, chandeliers, moldings, mantels, old bricks, and other architectural relics.

Dartmouth Co-op, Main Street, Hanover. A large men's department, with sports clothes, and an extensive line of Dartmouthana: T-shirts, sweats, boxes, mugs, cushions. Also a good selection of outdoor sports equipment and footwear.

Mia (643-5398), 37 South Main Street, Hanover. Trendy women's clothing, accessories, and shoes.

Powers Country Store & Family Outfitters (542-7703), Route 120, Cornish. Specializing in sensible, quality country clothing: robes, jeans, mittens, sweaters, boots, jackets.

Fat Hat Factory (802-296-6646), Tucker Mountain, Quechee, VT. Unusual and comfortable women's clothing made on the spot.

The Good Earth (643-4027), 68 South Main Street, Hanover. An environmentally conscious shop featuring only ecological products like cloth diapers, air and water filters, children's science kits.

MAPLE SYRUP

Brokenridge Farm (542-8781), Route 120, Cornish. Sap is gathered with horses on weekends; sugar-on-snow, tours.

Orford has the biggest local concentration of maple-syruping operations, including:

Mount Cube Farm (353-4709), Route 25A. Owned by former New Hampshire Governor Meldrim Thompson. The Sugar House Lodge here serves pancake breakfasts on weekends all winter.

Gerald and Toni Pease (353-9070), Pease's Scenic Highway, off Route 25A. Draft horse with wagon or sleigh.

Sugar House at Indian Pond (272-4950), Indian Pond Road.

Sunday Mountain Maple Products (353-4883), Route 25A. Sugarhouse open year-round, tours.

SPECIAL EVENTS

For details about any of these events, phone the town clerk, listed with information.

Mid-February: **Dartmouth Winter Carnival,** Hanover. Thursday through Sunday. Ice sculptures, sports events, ski jumping.

Early March: **Meriden Wild Game Dinner,** Kimball Union Academy's Miller Student Center. Usually a Saturday: to benefit the Meriden Volunteer Fire Department. Bear, raccoon, and boar are usually on the menu.

Mid-May: **Dartmouth Pow-Wow,** Hanover. A gathering of Native American craftspeople and dancers on the second Saturday of May; sponsored by Native Americans at Dartmouth (646-2110) and the Native American Studies Program (646-3530).

Late May: **Muster Day,** Hanover Center. Memorial Day. Recitation of the Gettysburg Address and Dr. Seuss prayer by children of the third grade on the site of Hanover's prerevolutionary musters.

Mid-June: **Bradford-Thetford Lions Club Fair,** Route 5, 1 mile north of Orford-Fairlee bridge. Carnival rides, ox pulling, demolition derby, fiddlers' contest.

Third weekend in June: **Quechee Balloon Festival and Crafts Fair** (802-295-7900), Quechee, VT. Some 20 hot-air balloons gather, offering rides at dawn and dusk; barbecue, sky diving, crafts, food booths. **Summer Strawberry Festival,** Plainfield Historical Society Clubhouse, Route 12A, Plainfield. **Lyme Summer Suppers and Horse Shed Crafts Festivals,** Lyme Congregational Church horse sheds, Lyme. Begin the last Wednesday in June, then every other week for four Wednesdays. The crafts festivals begin at 1 P.M. and the suppers, also at the church, begin at 6 P.M.

July Fourth: Independence Day **Open Fields Circus,** Thetford, VT. A takeoff on a real circus by the Parish Players. **Fourth of July Celebration,** Plainfield. Community breakfast, foot races, parade, Firemen's Roast Beef Dinner.

Mid-July: **Hanover Street Fest** (643-3115), Hanover. Street bazaar, haywagon rides, entertainment. **Norwich (VT) Fair.** Mix of old-time country fair and honky-tonk carnival. Lobster dinner, parade, ox pulling.

Late July: **Hanover Center Fair,** Hanover. Friday night games, dancing, food; Saturday starts with a children's costume parade, ox pulling, food, games. **Connecticut Valley Fair,** Bradford, VT. Ox and horse pulling, sheep show, midway, demolition derby. **La Salette Fair** (632-4301), at the La Salette Shrine, Route 4A, Enfield. Usually a midway with rides, flea market, crafts booths. **Cracker-Barrel Bazaar,** Newbury. Big old-time fiddlers' contest, antiques show, quilt show, sheep-dog trials, church suppers.

Early August: **Canaan Old Home Day,** Canaan. Dances, parade, booths, suppers. **North Haverhill Fair.** Horse show and pulling, evening live entertainment, midway. **Thetford Hill Fair.** Small but special: a rummage sale, food and plant booths, barbecue.

Mid-August: **The Country Revels,** Lyme. Singing, dancing; bring picnics. **The Shrine Parade and Maple Sugar Bowl,** in the Dartmouth Memorial Stadium, Hanover. Noontime pre-game parade features a dozen Shrine temples. The game pits Vermont and New Hampshire high-school all-stars. **Cornish Fair.** Horse and ox pulling, agricultural exhibits, ham and bean suppers, a Saturday woodsman's field day.

Late August: **Quechee Scottish Festival,** Quechee, VT. Sheep-dog trials, Highland dancing, piping, Highland "games," ladies' rolling-pin toss, more.

Mid-October: **Horse Sheds Crafts Fair,** at the Lyme Congregational Church, Lyme. Saturday of Columbus Day weekend 10–4; also a Fall Festival lunch at the church.

Late November: **Bradford United Church of Christ Wild Game Supper,** Bradford. The Saturday before Thanksgiving this Vermont town nearly doubles its population as hungry visitors pour into the church to feast on 2,800 pounds of buffalo, venison, moose, pheasant, coon, rabbit, wild boar, and bear. But getting in the door isn't easy. Write to Mrs. Raymond Green (802-222-4670), Box 356, Bradford, VT 05033, before the middle of September to request to be put on the mailing list for ticket information.

Early December: **Dickens of a Christmas** (643-3115), Hanover. Begins with Friday evening tree lighting on the green; Charles Dickens himself reads *A Christmas Carol;* Dickensian-style feasting in local restaurants; caroling, street concerts, and dancing; Victorian dress.

Mid-December to Christmas: **Christmas Pageant,** Norwich, VT. Traditional pageant with Mary on a donkey to the Norwich Inn, on to a stable. **Revels North,** in Hopkins Center. Song and dance. **Christmas Illuminations,** at the La Salette Shrine, Route 4A, Enfield.

VI. THE WHITE MOUNTAINS

White Mountain National Forest
The Western Whites
Mount Washington's Valleys

Franconia Notch from Artist's Bluff

ROBERT J. KOZLOW

White Mountain National Forest

The 768,000-acre White Mountain National Forest (WMNF), the largest in the East, was created by the Weeks Act of 1911. Millions of board feet of timber were cut from these mountains in the nineteenth century, and a portion of the Kancamagus Scenic Byway and the Wilderness Trail were the routes of logging railroads, part of an extensive rail system built by the timber companies to harvest the dense stands of mountain trees. The clear-cutting techniques employed by the timber cutters left the steep mountain slopes denuded, leading to massive erosion and downstream flooding. The limbs and branches left behind in the woods quickly dried and fueled huge forest fires that threatened the uncut areas. It was to curtail the clear-cutting, reduce the danger of forest fires, provide for reforestation of the mountains, and prevent erosion and flooding that the forest was created.

A ride across the Kancamagus Scenic Byway provides clear evidence of the success of the forest plan. Despite heavy use by visitors, most of the WMNF is again a wilderness. Although the United States Forest Service continues to harvest timber in this huge woodland, the WMNF is also managed for multiple-use activities: hiking, camping, swimming, fishing, nature study, forest research, and scenic beauty. Protection of watersheds and endangered species of plants, insects, and animals also figures into the operation of this forest. So varied is the forest, from lowland bogs to high alpine mountains, so interesting is its history, from Native Americans to settlers, loggers to scientists, that a whole guide could be written about this wild country.

The WMNF has several self-guided nature trails, is responsible for many miles of backcountry trails, and operates a number of barrier-free day-use facilities and campgrounds. Four congressionally designated wilderness areas within the forest are managed to preserve a wilderness experience. Here no timber cutting is permitted; bicycles and motorized vehicles (snowmobiles or trail bikes) are prohibited; and campsites are limited to 10 people or fewer. In addition to varied WMNF publications, the best guide to the area is the *AMC White Mountain Guide*, the hiker's 600-page handbook of trail details and also some human and natural history information.

GUIDANCE

WMNF headquarters (528-8721), Box 638, 719 Main Street, Laconia 03247. Contact them, especially in the off-season, for details of campgrounds, fishing, hiking, or other activities.

WMNF Saco Ranger Station (447-5448), Kancamagus Highway, just off Route 16, Conway. Open seven days a week, 8–4:30.

WMNF Androscoggin Ranger Station (466-2713), Route 16, Gorham. Open Monday to Friday 7:30–4:30.

WMNF Ammonoosuc Ranger Station (869-2626), Trudeau Road, off Route 302, Box 239, Bethlehem 03574.

WMNF Evans Notch District (207-824-2134), Bridge Street, RFD 2, Box 2270, Bethel, ME 04217. Open Monday to Friday 7:30–4:30.

AMC Pinkham Notch Camp (466-2725), Route 16, Pinkham Notch. (Also see "Mount Washington's Valleys—Mount Washington and Pinkham Notch.")

TO SEE

COVERED BRIDGE

Albany covered bridge, off Route 112 (Kancamagus Scenic Byway), 6 miles west of Conway. Built in 1858 and renovated in 1970, it is 136 feet long.

SCENIC DRIVES/EXCURSIONS

Kancamagus National Scenic Byway (Route 112). The 34.5-mile paved highway is open all year, weather conditions permitting, but there are no motorist services on the road. More than 750,000 vehicles travel this route every year. On the eastern side of the mountains, the road begins on Route 16, just south of Conway Village. One hundred yards from Route 16 is the Saco Ranger Station, a comprehensive information center open daily year-round. Adjacent to the ranger station is a 10-minute interpretive walk. After a few miles, the road closely parallels the winding, rocky Swift River, offering views across the rushing water to South Moat Mountain. There are plenty of places to stop for fishing or picnicking.

Six miles from Route 16, Dugway Road diverges right, through the Albany covered bridge to the **WMNF Covered Bridge Campground**. Near the bridge the **Boulder Loop Nature Trail** (2.5 miles, allow two hours) leaves Dugway Road and ascends rocky ledges, offering views up and down the river valley. An informative leaflet, keyed to numbered stations, is usually found in a box at the trailhead or at the Saco Ranger Station. Across the valley is Mount Chocorua and to its right are Paugus and Passaconaway, named, as was the byway itself, for Native American chiefs who once lived in this region. Dugway Road can be followed east to a junction with the West Side Road, just north of Conway Village. Midway on this route, the road passes the trailhead for

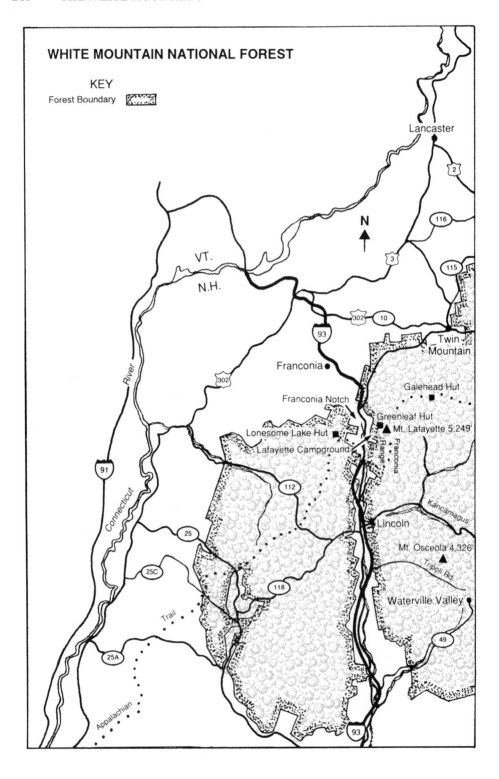

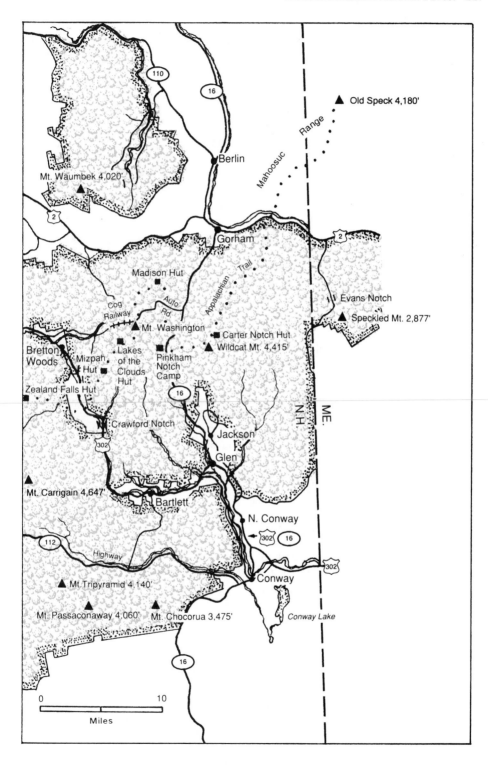

▲ Old Speck 4,180'

110

16

Berlin

Mahoosuc Range

Mt. Waumbek 4,020'
▲

2

Gorham

Madison Hut

Appalachian Trail

Auto Rd.

Evans Notch

Speckled Mt. 2,877'
▲

Cog Railway

▲ Mt. Washington

Carter Notch Hut

Bretton Woods

Mizpah Hut

Lakes of the Clouds Hut

Wildcat Mt. 4,415'
▲

Pinkham Notch Camp

Zealand Falls Hut

16

Crawford Notch

Jackson

302

Glen

N.H.   ME.

Mt. Carrigain 4,647'
▲

Bartlett

N. Conway

112

302   16

Highway

302

▲ Mt. Tripyramid 4,140'

Conway

Mt. Passaconaway 4,060'
▲

▲
Mt. Chocorua 3,475'

Conway Lake

16

0   10

Miles

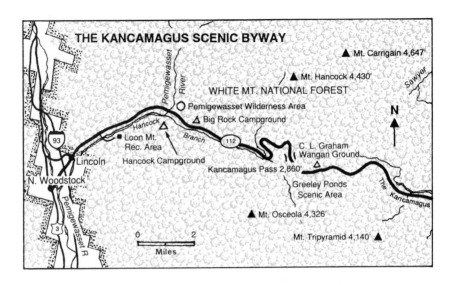

South Moat Mountain (elevation 2,772 feet), one of our favorite hikes. The 2.3-mile trail (two hours) offers magnificent views in all directions from its open, rocky summit. En route, in-season, can be seen lady's slippers and wild blueberries. This trail follows the long ridge to North Moat Mountain, then down to Diana's Baths and the River Road, a total hike of 9.1 miles requiring about six hours.

Opposite the junction of the Kancamagus byway and Dugway Road is the **Blackberry Crossing Campground,** and a half mile west is the **Lower Falls Scenic Area**. Rest rooms, drinking water, and picnic tables. On a summer weekend afternoon you will be amazed at how many people can squeeze onto the rocks at this popular swimming hole. This is not a wilderness experience, but what a treat for people who spend most of their lives in the city!

About 9 miles from Route 16 is the **Rocky Gorge Scenic Area,** an interesting geologic site, where the rushing river has washed its way through the rocks. The footbridge leads to Falls Pond. Barrier-free rest rooms, drinking water, and picnic tables.

About 1.5 miles west is the **Champney Falls Trail** (3.8 miles, 3.5 hours) to Mount Chocorua. The falls are an easy 3-mile round-trip on the lower section of the trail. The falls are named for Benjamin Champney, founder of the White Mountain School of Painting, who worked in this region of the mountains for more than 60 years.

Twelve miles from Route 16, the **Bear Notch Road** (not winter-maintained) diverges right for Bartlett and Route 302. This 9.3-mile gravel road has several impressive overlooks on its northern end.

At the junction with Bear Notch Road, you are entering Albany Intervale, once the township of Passaconaway. Not far beyond the junction is the **Passaconaway Historic Site.** Here the early-nineteenth-

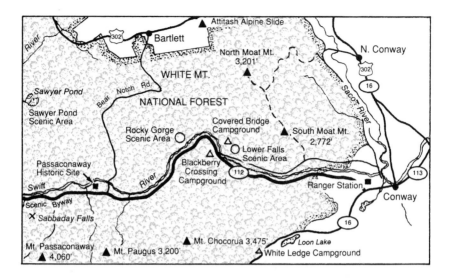

century George House is now an information center, a remnant of the isolated farming and logging community that once prospered here (open daily mid-June to Labor Day, weekends from Memorial Day to Columbus Day). The **Rail 'N' River Trail,** a 0.5-mile interpretive loop from this visitors center, is surprisingly varied.

About 15 miles from Conway is the turnoff for **Sabbaday Falls** (the falls are just a 10-minute hike from the highway). Resist temptation; there is no swimming allowed here.

Next along the highway are the **C. L. Graham Wangan Ground**—a picnic spot (a "wangan" was a logging company store) and picturesque **Lily Pond**. Here the highway begins a long climb to **Kancamagus Pass,** the highest point on this route, where there are scenic lookouts. As you traverse the pass, you leave the valley of the Swift River and cross over to the Pemigewasset River watershed.

West of the pass the highway twists down the mountainside and passes the trailhead for the **Greeley Ponds Scenic Area**. Both ponds are good trout-fishing and picnicking spots. (Hardy hikers can continue from here into Waterville Valley.) Next along the highway is the **Big Rock Campground.**

About 30 miles from Conway on your right is the large parking lot and information center (open on a limited basis year-round, daily mid-June to Labor Day) for the **Pemigewasset Wilderness Area,** one of the largest roadless areas in the eastern United States. Popular in winter with cross-country skiers, this is a prime access point for year-round backcountry hiking. Stop and walk at least as far as the middle of the suspension bridge across the Pemi, frequently a rushing torrent here. The **Wilderness Trail** follows an old logging rail bed along the East Branch of the Pemi; the Black Pond Trail leads to a trout pond.

Both the Wilderness Trail and the highway west to Lincoln follow the bed of J. E. Henry's narrow-gauge East Branch and Lincoln Railroad (see the introduction to "The Western Whites"). Next along the road is the **Hancock Campground,** and then Loon Mountain Ski Area, which is on the left just before the highway ends in the town of Lincoln.

Scenic drives through Crawford, Pinkham, and Evans notches are described in "Mount Washington's Valleys."

TO DO

CAMPING

The WMNF operates 22 campgrounds. Along the Kancamagus Highway (Route 112) there are 6 campgrounds with a total of 267 sites and 1 campground on Route 16 with 28 sites; north of Crawford Notch, just south of Twin Mountain, on Route 302, are 3 campgrounds with 73 sites; and in Evans Notch (Route 113 south of Route 2 east of Shelburne) are 5 campgrounds with 77 sites. Dolly Copp campground in Pinkham Notch has 176 sites, and adjacent to I-93 between Campton and Lincoln are 5 campgrounds with 214 sites. Campers should be self-sufficient since these are not fancy campsites (no electrical, water, or sewer connections, no camp stores, no playgrounds, etc.). Toilets, water, tables, and fireplaces are provided. The sites were designed for tent camping, although trailers and RVs are welcome. Most of the campgrounds are open from mid-May through mid-October, with a few opening earlier and closing later; several are open all winter though the roads are not plowed. The daily fees range from $7–9 per person, and many of these sites are filled every summer weekend on a first-come, first-served basis. However, a toll-free reservation system (1-800-283-2267) operates for some sites in the following campgrounds: White Ledge (Conway); Covered Bridge (Kancamagus); Sugarloaf I and II (Twin Mountain); Basin, Cold River, and Hastings (Evans Notch); Dolly Copp (Pinkham Notch); and Campton, Russell Pond, and Waterville (I-93). The reservation service operates March through September (Monday to Friday 12–9, weekends 12–5) and costs $6 in addition to the camping fee. Reservations may be made 120 days before arrival, but 10 days before arrival is the minimum time.

Backcountry camping is permitted in many areas of the WMNF but generally not within 200 feet of trails, lakes, or streams or within 0.25 mile of roads, most designated campsites or huts, at certain trailheads, or along certain trails. There are also many designated backcountry camping sites, some with shelters, others with tent platforms. The WMNF promotes a carry in–carry out, low impact, no-trace policy for backcountry hikers and campers and suggests (requires in some cases) the use of portable cooking stoves. Restricted-use areas, which help to protect the backcountry from overuse, are located in many parts of the forest. For backcountry information consult the *AMC White Mountain Guide* or contact the WMNF.

FISHING

The WMNF publishes a comprehensive guide to trout fishing in the forest. More than 30 pond sites are listed, plus suggestions for stream fishing. A New Hampshire fishing license is required.

HIKING

The WMNF is crisscrossed with 1,200 miles of hiking trails, some short and quite easy, others longer, and many challenging even to the most experienced backcountry traveler. A long, difficult section of the Appalachian Trail crosses the forest from the southwest to the northeast corner. The weather on the high mountains of the Presidential and Franconia ranges can approach winter conditions in any month of the year so hikers should be well prepared with extra food and proper clothing. Bring your own drinking water since *giardia,* a water-borne intestinal bacteria, is found throughout the mountains. Although trails are well marked, we recommend two guidebooks to make hiking safe and enjoyable. See *50 Hikes in the White Mountains* or *50 Hikes in New Hampshire*, both by Daniel Doan (Backcountry Publications), and the *AMC White Mountain Guide* (Appalachian Mountain Club). *Waterfalls of the White Mountains,* by Bruce and Doreen Bolnick (Backcountry Publications), is a handy guide for 30 walks to 100 waterfalls. Many of the waterfall hikes are easy and perfect for families. The guide also offers interesting bits of human and natural history.

(Also see South Moat Mountain, Champney Falls, Boulder Loop Nature Trail, and other trailheads reached via *Scenic Drives/Excursions*.)

SNOWMOBILING

Large portions of the WMNF are off limits to snowmobiling, trail bikes, or off-road vehicles. For details contact the **Trails Bureau,** New Hampshire Division of Parks and Recreation (271-3254), Box 856, Concord 03301, or the New Hampshire Snowmobile Association (224-8906), Box 38, Concord 03301.

The Western Whites

New England's highest mountains march in a ragged line, heading diagonally northeast across New Hampshire, beginning near the Connecticut River with Mount Moosilauke. We've chosen to divide this spectacular mountain region into "The Western Whites" and "Mount Washington's Valleys," which also includes the eastern peaks of the range.

The heart of the Western Whites is Franconia Notch, a high pass between the granite walls of Cannon Mountain and Mount Lafayette. Here I-93 narrows into the Franconia Notch Parkway, and visitors frequently spend a day viewing the stony profile of Old Man of the Mountain, exploring the Flume, the Pool, and Avalanche Falls, maybe taking the aerial tram to the top of Cannon Mountain, or taking a swim in Echo Lake, ideally hiking at least up to Lonesome Lake.

A footpath from Franconia Notch to the top of Mount Lafayette is said to have been blazed as early as 1825, the year the area's first hotel opened. By the 1880s it was served by a narrow-gauge railroad, and the Profile House, the largest of several hotels here, could accommodate 500 guests. The villages of Franconia and Bethlehem—just north of the Notch—and of North Woodstock—just east of Kinsman Notch as well as south of Franconia Notch—also had their share of elaborate summer hotels.

The area's steep, heavily wooded mountains were even more enticing to loggers than to tourists. While early conservationists fought to preserve the "notches" and "gorges," lumber companies built wilderness railways and employed small armies of men to clear-cut vast tracts. Legendary lumberman James E. Henry transformed the little outpost of Lincoln, with 110 residents in 1890, into a booming logging center of 1,278 by 1910. His J. E. Henry Company owned 115,000 acres of virgin timber along the East Branch of the Pemigewasset River, reducing much of it to pulp.

This Pemigewasset ("Pemi") area became part of the White Mountain National Forest in the mid-1930s. It was still being logged in 1923 when Sherman Adams came to Lincoln to work for the Parker-Young Co., J. E. Henry's successor. Over the next 20 years Adams came to know the valley intimately, and when he returned to Lincoln in the

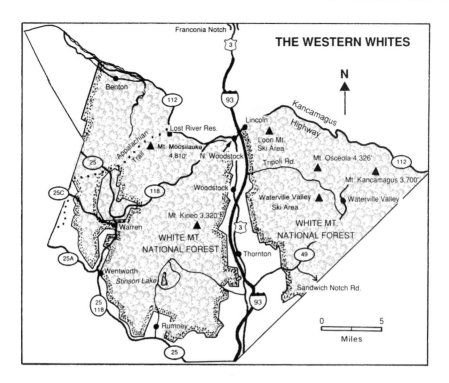

1960s—after having served as New Hampshire's governor and President Eisenhower's chief of staff—Adams opened Loon Mountain Ski Area.

In that same month another public figure—young ex-Olympian skier Tom Corcoran—opened another ski area less than a dozen miles away (as the crow flies) in Waterville Valley. Up in Franconia Notch, state-run Cannon Mountain's aerial tramway and steep slopes had been attracting skiers since 1938, but these newcomers both represented something novel—rather than being just "ski areas," both were "ski resorts," spawning new communities.

Dictated both by the personalities of their founders and the lay of their land, Loon Mountain and Waterville Valley have, however, developed differently.

Conservative Adams saw his business as running a ski area and left condominium development to others. Corcoran, fresh from Aspen, planned a self-contained, Rockies-style resort from the start. Loon's facilities, moreover, lined a narrow shelf of land above the Pemigewasset River on the edge of a mill town, while Waterville was in an isolated valley with two ski hills facing each other across 500 acres just waiting to be filled.

Loon Mountain and Waterville Valley are now New Hampshire's largest, liveliest ski resorts. The abundance of attractive, reasonably

priced, off-season condo lodging is contributing to an interesting phenomenon: after decades as a pass-through place, this area is once more
becoming as popular a summer destination as it was in the 1890s.

Both resort areas cater shamelessly to families, especially in the
summer when organized sports programs and local attractions complement the reasonably priced, family-geared lodging.

The "beaten track" through the Western Whites remains delightfully narrow. The quiet old resort villages of Bethlehem, Franconia,
and Sugar Hill have changed little in many decades, and the
Ammonoosuc Valley has a distinctly hidden-away feel. Farther south,
the Baker River Valley offers another little-traveled, scenic byway
through the mountains.

The full magnificence of the mountains themselves can only be appreciated by climbing (or riding) to their summits, but the beauty of
their high, narrow notches and hidden valleys is accessible to all.

GUIDANCE

Waterville Valley Region Chamber of Commerce (726-3804; 1-
800-237-2307), just off I-93, Exit 28, in Campton. Open daily 9–5.
Serves as a walk-in gateway information center for the Western Whites.

The White Mountains Visitor Center (745-8720; 1-800-237-2307).
Open 8:30–5 daily. A walk-in facility (just off I-93, Exit 32, on the Lincoln–North Woodstock line) with rest rooms, displays, forest service
and commercial brochures, offering information for this entire area.
Also based here, the **Ski 93 Association** (745-8101; 1-800-WE-SKI-
93) is a reservation service for Cannon, Loon, Waterville Valley, and
Bretton Woods ski areas.

Chambers of commerce are also listed under *Guidance* within the
three sections of this chapter, "The Waterville Valley Region," "Lincoln
and North Woodstock" (covering the Loon Mountain area), and
"Franconia and North of the Notches."

THE WATERVILLE VALLEY REGION

Waterville Valley itself is a 10-mile-deep cul-de-sac cut by one of New England's many Mad Rivers and circled by majestic mountains, many of them more than 4,000 feet tall.

Since 1835, the year the village's population peaked, urbanites have been coming here for R&R. By 1868 there were enough people to fill a green-shuttered inn. Less luxurious than most of the White Mountains summer hotels, it appealed to high-minded teachers and ministers who brought their families here to enjoy "sweet Christian living" (no smoking or drinking, lots of hiking). These families, including their children and grandchildren, became devoted to the valley, buying the inn when it came up for sale in 1919, donating all but a few hundred of their 26,000 acres in 1928 to the White Mountain National Forest. These same families founded and filled the ski clubs that kept the inn going in winter, beginning in 1935 when a few trails were etched on Snow's Mountain. And in 1937 the Civilian Conservation Corps (CCC) cut a precipitous mile-and-a-half trail down the southern shoulder of Mount Tecumseh, across the valley from Snow's.

It was to ski the Tecumseh Trail that a Phillips Exeter Academy student named Tom Corcoran first came to Waterville Valley in 1949. Corcoran went on to race with the Dartmouth College ski team, and then the US Olympic ski team, and eventually went to work for the Aspen Corporation, for which he did the feasibility study recommending acquisition of nearby Buttermilk Mountain. By 1965, when Corcoran was ready to buy his own ski mountain, the Waterville Valley Inn was up for sale along with 425 acres—virtually all the town that wasn't in the national forest.

Corcoran's Waterville Valley—complete with four chair lifts, a T-bar, even some snowmaking—opened for Christmas of 1966. The inn burned that first season, but two new ski lodges were ready for the following year—as were some condominiums, then as new to the eastern ski scene as snowmaking.

Something new—a condo hotel here, a new lift or sports center there—has been added to Waterville Valley every year since. It's been a steady, controlled growth all dictated by Corcoran's original plan, which, in just the past few years, has finally clicked into place.

What's made it click is Town Square: three interconnected clapboard buildings 4½ stories high with traditional saltbox lines softened by modern touches like an occasional round window and 100 dormers. A variation on the lines of a massive old White Mountains hotel, this complex does something that no other New England ski-resort building has achieved: it actually heightens the beauty of its setting, a circle of majestic peaks.

JOAN EATON

Famous for skiing, Waterville Valley is also a popular summer destination.

With its shops, restaurants, and frequent special events, Town Square serves as a year-round centerpiece for the resort's 500 or so condominiums, its 5 lodges, and 2 ski areas. It's adjacent to Corcoran's Pond and the covered pavilion, in which summer concerts are performed and which serves as a weather-proofed ice-skating rink in winter. Year-round it's a short walk from the Sports Center.

Future plans call for more lifts on Snow's Mountain, some coming right to Town Square; but at present shuttle buses fill the bill of ferrying skiers from their rooms and condos to ski trails, shops, and restaurants. Some 6,000 guests can bed down in the valley's lodging places, ranging from 1960s-era ski lodges to the Adirondack-style Golden Eagle Lodge with its 7-story towers. Modest, traditional B&Bs can also be found in the nearby villages of Campton and Thornton and along Route 3 south to Plymouth, a former mill town–turned–college town with some interesting restaurants. Note the number of scenic drives in this area.

GUIDANCE
Waterville Valley Central Reservations (236-8371; 1-800-GO-VAL-LEY), Waterville Valley 03215. A walk-in information center in Town Square, a source of information on local activities as well as lodging and services.

Waterville Valley Region Chamber of Commerce (726-3804; 1-800-237-2307), just off I-93, Exit 28, in Campton. Open 9–5 daily. Rest rooms, brochures, phones, a wood stove.

GETTING THERE
By bus: **Concord Trailways** (1-800-852-3317) from Boston's Logan Air-

port stops in Plymouth. Check with lodging to arrange a pickup or cab. *By car:* I-93 to Exit 28, then 10 miles up Route 49.

GETTING AROUND

Buses circulate throughout the resort year-round during the day; also evenings during peak winter and summer seasons.

MEDICAL EMERGENCY

For the local rescue squad call 236-4377. For the Plymouth ambulance service call 524-1545.

TOWNS AND VILLAGES

Plymouth. From I-93 what you see of Plymouth are the high-rise dorms of **Plymouth State College,** a clue to the existence of shops and restaurants catering to the needs of 4,000 students. What you don't see from the highway is the region's appealing old commercial center. Its mills have produced mattresses, gloves, and shoe trees as well as lumber. The long-vanished Pemigewasset House, built by the president of the Boston, Concord, and Montreal Railroad, was favored by Nathaniel Hawthorne, who was living there when he died in 1864. Today the college campus forms the centerpiece for the town, and some good restaurants can be found within walking distance.

Rumney. A picture-perfect village with a classic common, Rumney is in the Baker Valley, just far enough off the beaten path to preserve its tranquility. Note the **Mary Baker Eddy House, Quincy Bog,** the **Town Pound,** and **Stinson Lake,** all described under *Scenic Drives.* Rumney is also a good place to eat and to shop.

Wentworth. Another picturesque white wooden village with a triangular common set above the Baker River.

Warren. A perfectly ordinary white-clapboard village at the base of Mount Moosilauke, Warren has had more than its share of monuments. First there was the massive Morse Museum, built in the 1920s by a Warren native who made a fortune making shoes in Lowell, Massachusetts. It displayed exotica from his travels, also the world's largest private shoe collection. The Morse Museum recently closed (even the mummies were sold off), but the space-rocket booster with "USA" blazoned on its side still towers bizarrely over the common. A local restaurant owner, we're told, brought it back from Huntsville, Alabama, and tried to give it to Derry, New Hampshire (home of astronaut Alan Shepard), which refused to take it. Warren, we understand, remains divided on whether it belongs there or not; the VFW post keeps it painted. There's also a small historical museum and a good eatery at which you can get directions to the Dartmouth Outing Club cabin, from which a former carriage road (to a former summit hotel) is one among a choice of hiking trails to the summit.

TO SEE

COVERED BRIDGES

Blair Bridge. The easiest way to find this is from I-93, Exit 27; at the bottom of the exit ramp, follow Blair Road to the blinking light, then go straight across.

Turkey Jim's Bridge. At I-93, Exit 28, follow Route 49 west. After about 0.5 mile (as you cross over the metal bridge), look for a sign on your right for Branch Brook Campground. You must drive into the campground to see the bridge.

Bump Bridge. At I-93, Exit 28, follow Route 49 east for about 0.5 mile. Turn right at the traffic lights and go over the dam. Turn right again on Route 175 south. After 3 or 4 miles, you come to a sharp left turn; bear to the left and stay straight, down the dirt road. Take the first right and the covered bridge is about 0.5 mile on the left.

FOR FAMILIES

✐ **Polar Caves** (536-1888), Route 25, 4 miles west of Plymouth. Open mid-May through mid-October, 9–5. Discovered by neighborhood children around 1900 and opened as a commercial attraction in 1922, this is an extensive property with a series of caves connected by passageways and walkways with taped commentaries at stations along the way. The name refers to the cold air rising from the first "Ice" cave, where the temperature in August averages 55 degrees. There's much here to learn about minerals and geology, much that's just fun. The complex includes picnic tables and a snack bar. $8.50 for adults; $4 for children ages 6–12; no family rate.

✐ **Curious George House** (236-4093; 236-4803), at the Waterville Valley Resort. Open summer, fall, and winter seasons for infants (from age six weeks) and young children. Both day and evening programs are offered. This house was actually built by Margaret and Hans Rey in the late 1950s and was used as a studio in which to create the internationally loved tales about a monkey named Curious George. It is decorated with authentic Curious George memorabilia.

SCENIC DRIVES

Rumney Loop. The easiest way to begin is from Route 25/3A west of Plymouth. Take Airport Road through the **Smith covered bridge** and go left on Quincy Road. The sign for **Quincy Bog** (786-9465) should be just beyond Quincy State Forest, but if the sign is down, look for stone pillars flanking a small road to the right. One-tenth of a mile down this road look for a left leading to the bog entrance from which to access trails and a viewing deck. This 40-acre peat bog is a place to find frogs in April and May, to see bog plant blooms in May and June, to hunt for salamanders and newts, and to bird-watch. The nature center here is open mid-June to mid-August. En route to the bog you pass the old **Rumney Town Pound,** an unusual natural animal pen formed by gigantic boulders. Continue into Rumney (see *Villages, Eating Out,* and *Selective Shopping*), and then head out Main Street and follow it past the **Mary Baker Eddy House** (786-9943), home of the founder of Christian Science in the early 1860s (open May through October, Tuesday through Saturday 10–5). Continue on along isolated **Stinson Lake,** good fishing (trout, perch, pickerel) year-round. **Stinson Mountain Trail** is marked, beginning with a dirt road, then a left through the woods and a right at the brook, up through spruce and fir to the summit ledges. Great views. Continue east on this road out to West Campton and I-93, Exit 28.

The Baker River Valley. The Baker River charts a natural path from the base of Mount Moosilauke southeast through hilly woodland to the Pemigewasset River. It was known as the Asquamchumauke River until 1712, when a group of soldiers headed by Captain Thomas Baker of Northampton, Massachusetts, defeated a band of local Native Americans on the site that's presently Plymouth. Today Route 25 shadows the river, beginning as a commercial strip west of Plymouth but quickly improving. You pass the **Polar Caves** (see *For Families*), **Rumney** (see *Villages* and *Scenic Drives*), and continue on through **Wentworth** and **Warren** (see *Villages*). To return to Waterville Valley take mountainous Route 118 east to **North Woodstock** (see "Lincoln and North Woodstock"), then I-93 from Exit 32 to Exit 28.

Tripoli Road (closed in winter). A shortcut from Waterville Valley to I-93 North: roughly 10 miles, paved and unpaved, up through Thornton Gap (a high pass between Mount Osceola and Mount Tecumseh) and over a high shoulder of 4,326-foot Mount Osceola. Begin on West Branch Road (a left before the Osceola Library); cross the one-lane bridge and turn right into the national forest. Note the Mount Osceola Trail (see *Hiking*) 3 miles up the road. Continue through the Thornton Gap. Note trailheads for the Mount Tecumseh and East Pond trails.

Sandwich Notch Road (closed in winter). We have fond memories of this steep, roughly 10-mile dirt road from Center Sandwich to Waterville, built 1 rod wide for $300 by the town of Sandwich in the late eighteenth century. When we described it glowingly in the *Boston Globe,* however, we did get a few complaints from readers who attempted it in large, low cars. Be prepared to make way for any vehicle coming from the opposite direction. The road follows the Bearcamp River, and stone walls tell of long-vanished farms. Center Sandwich offers a crafts center, museum, and dining (see "The Lake Winnipesaukee Area").

TO DO

BICYCLING

Mountain Valley Bikes (236-4666), in Town Square, Waterville Valley. Rents mountain bikes, tandem bikes, or bicycle buggies for toddlers. Mountain-bike clinics, special events utilizing cross-country trails and logging roads.

Ski Fanatics (726-4327), Route 49, Campton, just off Exit 28 across from the information center. Mountain-bike rentals and mapped routes, also 10-mile group rides (not for beginners) scheduled twice a week in season.

BOATING

Corcoran's Pond at Waterville Valley Resort (236-4666). Paddleboat, canoe, and Sunfish rentals on 6 acres.

Ski Fanatics (726-4666), Route 49 in Campton, rents "funyaks," billed as "kayaks with training wheels"; guided tours on the Pemigewasset and shuttle service.

CAMPING

Campsites in the White Mountain National Forest can be reserved up to 120 days in advance by phoning 1-800-280-2267. The campgrounds are:

Campton, on Route 49, 2 miles east of I-93, Exit 28, Campton. Open mid-April to mid-October. Fifty-eight sites. Interpretive programs on weekends June through Labor Day. $10 per night; pay shower available.

Russell Pond, off I-93, Exit 31, 3 miles northeast on the Tripoli Road. Eighty-seven sites on a 40-acre pond, good for swimming (no lifeguard) and fishing; Saturday evening interpretive nature programs. Reservations may be made up to 120 days in advance. $10 per night.

Waterville, 8 miles northeast of I-93 on Route 49, Waterville. Twenty-seven sites. $9 per night; half-price in winter.

FISHING

Stream fishing was one of the first lures of visitors to this valley, and the fish are still biting in Russell Pond (Tripoli Road) and all along the Mad River, stocked with trout each spring. Campton Pond (at the lights) is a popular fishing hole.

GOLF

Waterville Valley Resort (236-4805). Nine-hole golf course, rental carts; privileges with 2 local 18-hole courses.

HIKING

Detailed trail maps for short hikes and information about organized hikes can be found in summer months at the information center in Waterville Valley's Town Square. The following trail descriptions are presented as armchair reading.

Cascades Path begins at the base of Snow's Mountain Ski Area and follows a brook for 1.5 miles. Continue along the brook above the cascades for the best view, looking back.

Mount Osceola. A 7-mile, 4½-hour hike beginning on the Tripoli Road (see *Scenic Drives*). The Tripoli Road crests at the 2,300-foot-high Thornton Gap; the Mount Osceola Trail begins some 200 yards beyond. Follow an old tractor road up through many switchbacks and along Breadtray Ridge, then across a brook, up log steps, by another ridge to the summit ledges. This is the highest of the mountains circling Waterville Valley, and the view is spectacular.

Greeley Ponds Trail begins at the end of the old truck road, which is a left off the Livermore Road, just past the clearing known as Depot Camp. The trail crosses a wooden footbridge and follows the course of the river to Greeley Ponds between Mounts Osceola and Kancamagus. It's a gradual grade all the way to the shelter on the upper pond and continues as a gradual ascent to the Kancamagus Highway.

Welch Mountain. Open ledge walking at a surprisingly low elevation overlooking the Mad River Valley. It's a challenging 4-mile round-trip hike but well worth the sweat. According to local hiking guru Steve Smith, the broad sheets of granite offer views and blueberries in abundance. The panorama from the open summit includes Sandwich Mountain, Mount Tripyramid, Mount Tecumseh, and Mount Moosilauke. You can extend the hike into a loop by continuing over the slightly higher **Dickey Mountain** and its fine north viewpoint (the ledges on this hike may be slippery when wet). The trailhead for this loop is on Orris Road, off Upper Mad River Road between Campton and Waterville Valley.

HORSEBACK RIDING

Waterville Valley Resort (236-8311). Guided trail riding during summer months; pony rides for children.

ROLLERBLADING

Rentals available at Waterville Valley's **Town Square;** check at the information center.

SWIMMING

Waterville Valley Resort Sports Center offers an indoor pool. Several lodges also offer indoor pools.

Corcoran's Pond, with a sandy beach, is Waterville Valley Resort's principal summer swimming area.

On Route 49 look for **Smart's Brook Trail**. An easy mile's hike over logging and dirt roads to a swimming hole among the pools of a mountain brook.

TENNIS

Waterville Valley Resort Tennis Center (236-8311). Eighteen clay, outdoor courts, two indoor courts at the Sports Center; clinics, round robins. A junior tennis program for children 18 and under includes private lessons, drill sessions, and round robins.

CROSS-COUNTRY SKIING

Waterville Valley Resort Cross-Country Center (236-4666), in Town Square. Ski school, warming/waxing areas, rentals. More than 100 km through the valley and surrounding national forest; 70 km groomed for diagonal and skating; 35 additional km marked. When all else fails you can count on a 2.5-km loop covered by snowmaking. The trailside Bull Hill Cabin is a source of soups, homemade breads, and sandwiches. The center's location in Town Square has its pros and cons: easy access but too many condos to go by before you get up into the woods. On the other hand, you can drive to the edge of the White Mountain National Forest and ski directly off into the woods. Skating as well as diagonal lessons are offered, also moonlight guided tours, weekly races, and telemark clinics. $11 weekends. Inquire about conditions on the Greeley Ponds Trail.

DOWNHILL SKIING

Waterville Valley (236-8311; snow report 236-4144) is a family-geared resort featuring family-style lodging (including roughly 1,000 kitchens), great children's skiing, and summer programs. A limited-ticket policy ensures lift-line waits of no longer than 15 minutes. It's just a 7½-minute ride to the summit of Mount Tecumseh on the high-speed detachable quad, and the way down is via a choice of long, wide cruising trails like Upper Bobby's Run and Tippecanoe. Mogul lovers will find plenty to please them on True Grit and Ciao, and beginners have their own area served by the Lower Meadows Double Chair.

Trails: 48 on Mount Tecumseh and 5 on Snow Mountain.

Lifts: 1 high-speed detachable quad, 3 triples, 5 doubles, 4 surface.

Vertical drop: 2,020 feet.

Snowmaking: 96 percent.

Facilities: Include the Schwendi Hutte near the top of Mount Tecumseh, Sunnyside-Up Lodge (a mid-mountain oasis with a hearth cafeteria, good soups, and deli sandwiches), the Base Lodge Cafeteria, and the World Cup Bar and Grill.

Ski school: Specializes in clinics for all ages and all abilities, also private lessons for all.

For children: There is a nursery for children from age six weeks. The ski area has one of the country's first and still one of its most outstanding SKIwee programs: SKIwee, ages 3–5; Mountain Cadets, ages 6–8; Mountain Scouts, ages 9–12. Small children have their own hill, with its own lift and terrain garden. Also evening children's programs.

Rates: $39 adult weekend, $65 for two days; $20 junior, $36 for two days; two-day and multi-day rates; ages 70 and over ski free midweek and nonholidays; student and teen rates.

ICE SKATING

A covered hockey-sized ice-skating rink maintained throughout the winter at **Waterville Valley Resort.** Complete with skate rentals, maintenance, and repairs.

SLEIGH RIDES

Throughout the winter, horse-drawn sleigh rides depart afternoons and evenings from **Town Square,** Waterville Valley.

SNOWBOARDING

Snowboarding park on Mount Tecumseh (snowmaking).

FITNESS CENTER

Waterville Valley Sports Center (236-8311). Offers indoor tennis, racquetball, and squash courts, 25-meter indoor and outdoor swimming pools, jogging track, fitness evaluation facilities, Nautilus exercise equipment, aerobics, whirlpools, saunas and steam rooms, tanning booths, massage service, restaurant/lounge, and game room.

LODGING

LODGES
In Waterville Valley 03215
Central reservations numbers are 236-8371 or 1-800-468-2553.

⌖☞**The Golden Eagle** (236-4551). A 1990s version of an 1890s grand hotel: 139 suites, 5½ stories with four 7-story towers. The shingles and fieldstone facing and sloping roofs suggest a classic Adirondack lodge, and the dramatic two-story lobby, with its ornate woodwork, large sash windows, and hearths, underscores that feel. Designed by Cambridge architect Graham Gund (who also designed the Town Square), it's a whimsical combination of old and new. The tower suites have 180-degree views, and even the least expensive units are beautifully executed. Suites include kitchens, sleep four to six. Amenities include an indoor pool, whirlpools, saunas. Rates include access to the Sports Center. From $199–319 per night on winter weekends; $99–209 in low season.

⌖☞**Snowy Owl Inn** (236-2383; 1-800-SNOWY-OWL). An attractive lodge with a central, three-story fieldstone hearth and a surrounding atrium supported by single log posts; there's a cupola you can sit in. A case can be made that this is the most innlike and romantic of the Waterville Valley lodges, but it's also a good place for families, thanks to the lower-level game rooms adjoining a pleasant breakfast room. There are also indoor and outdoor pools. Of the 82 rooms, more than half have a wet bar, fridge, and whirlpool tub, and there are suites with fireplaces. Rates include a breakfast buffet, afternoon wine and cheese, and Sports Center access. From $89 to $159 per night in ski season; $69–119 in low season.

⌖☞**Black Bear Lodge** (236-4501). Less exciting architecturally than the other two lodges but perfectly comfortable, with 107 one- and two-bedroom suites that sleep 4 to 6 people. Each suite has a kitchen, a dining area, a sitting area with queen-size bed and cable TV, and a separate bedroom; indoor/outdoor pool, whirlpool, sauna, and game room and children's cinema on the lower level. Rates include Sports Center access. From $59 in low season to as high as $259 in ski season.

⌖☞**Valley Inn and Conference Center.** (236-8336; 1-800-343-0969). An attractive, 52-room lodge with an indoor/outdoor pool, whirlpool, saunas, exercise room, game room; the only Valley lodge with its own dining room (see *Dining Out*). All rooms have TVs and phones, some have kitchen units, fireplaces, saunas, or whirlpool baths. Rates include après-ski hors d'oeuvres and live entertainment in the lounge. From $79 for a standard room in low ski season to $295 for a suite with a deck, kitchen facilities, fireplace, and whirlpool bath.

BED & BREAKFASTS
In Campton 03223
Note that the village of Campton is just off I-93, 10 miles west of Waterville Valley.

✐☞**The Mountain-Fare Inn** (726-4283), Box 553. An old-style ski lodge run year-round by Susan and Nick Preston, both ski coaches at Waterville Valley. Ten rooms, half with private bath, some dorm-style spaces sleeping up to six, other cozy rooms for two; caters to both family reunions and groups. A large yard, good for cross-country skiing in winter, volleyball and soccer in summer. From $56–70 for a room with private bath includes a full breakfast; MAP rates in winter.

✐☞**Osgood Inn** (726-3543), Box 419. A gracious old home with a comfortable living room and two large upstairs guest rooms sharing a bath. In an adjoining wing, a two-bedroom suite sleeps up to six people and has its own delightful small sitting room and a full kitchen. $50 in the main house, $100 for two-day weekends during ski season; less midweek, off-season, and for more than three days. No charge for small children. All rates include a full country breakfast and tax. Smoke-free.

The Campton Inn (726-4449), Route 175 and Owl Street. A vintage 1835 multi-gabled village house, a long-time inn that's recently been renovated. There's a large living room with a wood stove and piano. Five rooms, one with private bath. $50–60 double includes tax and full breakfast.

Amber Lights Inn (726-4077), RFD 1, Box 828, Route 3, West Thornton 03223. An attractive, vintage 1815 roadside house with five carefully furnished guest rooms. Seven-course breakfasts are served in front of an elegant fireplace. No smoking and no children under seven. From $60 to $75 double; $45–60 with just continental breakfast. Rates include evening hors d'oeuvres and beverage; inquire about murder-mystery weekends.

Elsewhere

Crab Apple Inn (536-4476), RR 4, Box 1955, Route 25, Plymouth 03264. A classic 1835, brick, Federal-style, roadside mansion with four antiques-furnished guest rooms, some with fireplaces, all with private bath. The common rooms are fairly formal and elegant. While the front of the house is shouldered by commercial properties, the grounds are several acres deep, with an English garden and paths leading back into woods. No children. A full breakfast is included in the rates: $75–85.

☞ **The Gateway Inn** (536-3976), RFD 1, Box 256, Plymouth 03264. Sited on Route 3 south of Campton, a wine-red farmhouse filled with antiques that have been in Pam Sinclair's family for generations. There's a ground-floor room with a working fireplace and built-in bookcase; cheerful upstairs bedrooms include one with a brass bed and Pam's great-grandfather's sea chest and a back room brightened by skylights. Baths are shared and guests have access to a fridge, cross-country skis, an exercise bike, and three acres of meadow and pine woods. $40–65 per room.

Wentworth Inn and Art Gallery (764-9923), Ellsworth Hill Road, Wentworth Village 03282. A handsome old country mansion with some elaborate detailing and stained-glass windows, within sound as well as sight of Baker Pond Brook. The seven guest rooms have frilly touches, some with canopy beds. $60–80 double includes a full breakfast; a variety of packages are offered, including dinner.

Hilltop Acres (764-5896), Hilltop Acres, East Side and Buffalo Road, Wentworth 03282. A pleasant old farmhouse with a large pine-paneled rec room with an antique piano, TV, fireplace, and plenty of books; rooms with private baths, $65 per couple; also traditional housekeeping cottages with fireplace and screened porch ($160 per weekend, $425 per week). Pets permitted in the cottages. Rates include breakfast.

CONDOMINIUMS

In Waterville Valley 03215

Village Condominiums (236-8301; 1-800-532-6630) and **Waterville Valley Resort Condo Rentals** (236-4101; 1-800-556-6522) are the 2 primary rental agents for most of the 500 or so condominiums ranged in clusters between the ski slopes and Town Square. Quality is uniformly high, but since these units lack the indoor pools and game rooms enjoyed by lodge guests, it's important to make sure rentals include access to the Waterville Valley Resort Sports Center. The nearer to the Sports Center and to Town Square, the better. It's worth noting that owner occupancy is unusually high at Waterville Valley and the actual number of condo units in the rental pool at prime times can be very low indeed. Rates begin at $89 for a one-bedroom condo in low season; a four-bedroom unit on a ski-season weekend can be more than $350.

WHERE TO EAT

DINING OUT

In Waterville Valley

Valley Inn and Conference Center (236-8336). Candlelight dining, Continental menu, the most elegant dining room in Waterville Valley. We have fond memories of a salmon and apple soup, venison with mushrooms, and an excellent cabernet sauvignon. Moderate to expensive.

The Common Man (236-8885), Town Square. Open daily for lunch and dinner, light bar menu until midnight. Entertainment Thursday through Saturday in July, August, and ski season. Multi-tiered dining space, casual atmosphere. The unabashedly big, American menu is moderately priced.

Brookside Bistro (236-4309), Town Square. Good for breakfast, lunch, dinner. Quite elegant for dinner; you might begin with mussels simmered with tomatoes and fennel in a saffron, garlic, and white-wine sauce, and dine on rack of lamb. Moderately expensive.

In Campton

William Tell (726-3618), Route 49. A long-standing local favorite with tried but true Swiss and German specialties like Wiener schnitzel and "Kalbs Kotelett" (veal loin with fresh mushrooms) prepared by Swiss native Franz Dubach. Moderately expensive.

☞ **Mad River Tavern & Restaurant** (726-4290), Route 49 (just off I-93, Exit 28). Closed Tuesday, otherwise open from lunch through dinner. Serving until 11 P.M. Friday and Saturday. A homey atmosphere with an overstuffed couch, blackboard specials, and a large, varied menu. There's a wide choice of pastas and breads as well as fish. We recommend the veal Oscar, lightly breaded and topped with lobster, asparagus, and béarnaise sauce. Burgers, sandwiches, salads, beer, and wine are also served. Inexpensive to moderate.

In Plymouth

The Backyard (536-1994), 105 Main Street. Open for dinner Wednesday through Sunday 5–9. Back behind and under the Trolley Car Restaurant, this small trattoria features homemade pastas and Italian classics like veal Marsala and chicken parmigiana. The wines are all Italian, too.

✐ **Tree House** (536-4084), 3 South Main Street. Open for lunch and dinner daily. A leafy atmosphere, a bar in one corner, and a big stone fireplace. The menu runs from pastas, burgers, and salads to the schnitzel du jour, steaks (aged and cut on the premises), and Chicken in the Tree (chicken breast stuffed with celery, herbs, and bread crumbs). Children's menu. Inexpensive to moderate.

(Also note The Common Man in Ashland described under *Dining Out* in "The Lakes Region—The Lake Winnipesaukee Area.")

EATING OUT

In Waterville Valley

Jugtown Country Store and Deli (236-8662), the heart of Town Square. Open daily. A grocery store with an extensive deli and some tables; in warm-weather months you just step outside with salads and sandwiches to the tables in the square. Fresh bagels and breads baked daily.

Waterville Valley Coffee Emporium, Town Square. Gourmet coffees, breakfast waffles and omelets, and afternoon tea, gourmet jelly beans.

Alpine Pizza and Ice Cream Shoppe (236-4173). Open daily 7 A.M.–10 P.M. Pizza, subs, ice cream. Also breakfast, burgers, and much more.

✐ **Chile Peppers** (236-4646), in the Sports Center. Cheerful, reasonably priced Mexican fare prepared by Rick and Heather Klaudt (Rick was a member of the team that discovered the vast sunken treasures of Atocha). Try the *especialidad de enchiladas azules* (tortillas of specially ground blue corn layered with shredded beef or chicken, green enchilada sauce, cheese, and topped with sour cream or a fried egg). Don't miss the key lime pie.

In Thornton

Bridge House Inn (726-9853), corner of Route 49 and Hill Road between Campton and Waterville Valley. British-born host Mike Jent is recently retired from more than 20 years on the Bermuda police force. The inn includes a lively pub and a restaurant specializing in delicacies like cottage pie, bangers and mash, and Bermuda fish chowder. Breakfast and lunch are served and dinner runs from vegetarian nut roast and pasta to Oxford John steak (broiled and served in a piquant caper sauce) and

Huntingdon fidget pie (chunks of smoked ham, onions, apples, and cider gravy topped with puff pastry).

In Campton

Spillway Cafe (726-3545), Route 49. Open from 5 A.M. Breakfast features Green Mountain coffees and eggs Spillway and home baking—which extends to the crust for a wide choice of pizzas. Soups, burgers, and Cajun meatloaf are also on the menu. The atmosphere is bright, upbeat, and welcoming.

Sunset Grill (726-3108), corner of Routes 3 and 49. Open daily from 11:30 A.M., Sunday brunch 11:30–3. A funky, friendly roadhouse with good food: a wide selection of pastas and house specials ranging from calves' liver to prime rib; also burgers, chili, and a mean pastrami melt. Sunday brunch is a specialty.

In Plymouth

Jigger Johnson's (536-4FUN). Lots of atmosphere, friendly service, great food. Gourmet burgers and "Wabbit food." Parties a specialty.

Trolley Car Diner and Restaurant (536-4433). A local gathering place for lunch and dinner; genuine 1950s atmosphere.

The Italian Farmhouse (536-4536). Reasonably priced Italian food.

In the Baker River Valley

☞ **Steve's Restaurant** (786-9788), just off Route 25 on Stinson Lake Road, Rumney. Open 6 A.M.–9 P.M. daily, until 9:30 Friday and Saturday; open Sunday for brunch. One of those little family restaurants that's so good it just keeps growing. The menu runs from burgers and Steve's homemade meatloaf to baked scallops and a chicken-and-ribs barbecue.

Glory Jean's Diner (786-2352), Route 25, Rumney, just west of the Polar Caves. A classic chrome diner serving standard diner fare.

Moosilauke View Restaurant, Route 25, Warren Village. Open daily 6 A.M.–7 P.M., Sunday 8–7. A clean, friendly local gathering spot with daily specials like hamburger vegetable soup and hot turkey sandwich.

ENTERTAINMENT

Plymouth Theater (536-1089), Main Street, Plymouth. A 1930s movie palace that's recently been restored; screens a broad assortment of films. (Also see *Special Events* for the New Hampshire Music Festival and the Waterville Valley Music Festival.)

SELECTIVE SHOPPING

ANTIQUES

In Rumney check out **Miller's Antique Market** (786-2243) on Route 25, **Colonial Homestead Antiques** (786-9876) on School Street, **Village Books** (786-9300) on Main Street, and **Antiques Etc.** on Depot Street next to Steve's.

The Wentworth Collection (764-9395), junction of Routes 25 and 25A in Wentworth, features exact re-creations of eighteenth-century American furniture.

Warren New Hampshire Trading Post (764-5376), junction of Routes 25 and 118, is good for antiques and collectibles.

CRAFTS SHOPS

Shanware Pottery (786-9835), Route 25, Rumney. A working studio in a rustic barn; distinctive, functional stoneware pottery and porcelain: mugs, casseroles, chimes, dinnerware, lamps, and distinctive doughnut-shaped wine casks, among many other things.

Calico Cupboard (786-9567), Main Street, Rumney, is a good place for quilts and quilters (fabrics, supplies, and classes).

SPECIAL SHOPS

Jacquith's Greenhouse (536-2283), Main Street, Rumney. This source of flowers, herbs, and perennials, also vegetables in summer, adjoins an exceptional garden, where visitors are welcome; it's one of the most beautiful in the Northeast.

In Waterville Valley Town Square

Daphne's (236-4200). Tom Corcoran's wife Daphne's choice of gifts, cookware, accessories.

Bookmonger and Toad Hall (236-4165). Toys and games for children of all ages, paperbacks, games, CDs, magazines, general titles.

Adornments. Unusual jewelry, all prices.

Three Crowns Boutique specializes in handknit sweaters.

SPECIAL EVENTS

January: **Winter Carnival** at Waterville Valley.

Easter Sunday: **Sunrise service** on Mount Tecumseh.

July Fourth: **Parade and fireworks** at Waterville Valley.

Mid-July through Labor Day: Waterville Valley **Music Festival Concert Series,** in Town Square Concert Pavilion. Every Saturday at 7:30 P.M.

July and August: **New Hampshire Music Festival** (524-1000) at Plymouth State College, with Tuesday evening chamber music concerts; Wednesday evening concerts on the Common; Thursday evening concerts at Silver Hall.

August: **"Ugotta Regatta"** and Chowder Fest on Corcoran's Pond, Waterville Valley. **Plymouth State Fair,** Plymouth.

September: Waterville Valley Labor Day **Italian Festival.**

October: **Octoberfest** at Waterville Valley, Columbus Day weekend.

November: **Ski trails open** mid-month at Waterville Valley; **fireworks and tree lighting** Thanksgiving weekend.

LINCOLN AND NORTH WOODSTOCK

North Woodstock is a sleepy village. Lincoln, a mile east, is one of New Hampshire's liveliest resort towns. Until relatively recently, the opposite was true.

Around the turn of the century, Lincoln boomed into existence as a company town with a company-owned school, store, hotel, hospital, and housing for hundreds of workers, all built by the legendary lumber baron J. E. Henry. And it remained a smoke-belching "mill town" well into the 1970s.

North Woodstock, set against 2 dramatic notches—Kinsman and Franconia—boasted a half-dozen large hotels, among them the Deer Park, accommodating 250 guests.

Today Deer Park is still a familiar name, but only as one of the dozen major condominium complexes that have recently become synonymous with this area. With Loon Mountain as its centerpiece, the Lincoln-Woodstock area now has a bed base (the buzzword for visitors' pillows) of 13,000, more than 8 times what it offered a decade ago.

Loon Mountain was a success from the start, opening in 1966 with a gondola, two chair lifts, an octagonal base lodge, and the then-unheard-of policy of limiting lift-ticket sales. Then in 1973, I-93 reached Lincoln, depositing skiers 3 miles from the lifts. But it wasn't until the early 1980s that the town of Lincoln itself began to boom.

Three things came at that time: all the land owned by the paper mill (see "The Western Whites" introduction), which had closed in 1979, suddenly became available. Loon itself had grown into a substantial ski area, and a real-estate boom was sweeping New Hampshire's lakes and mountains. Positioned just south of Franconia Notch and surrounded by national forest, Lincoln was a developer's dream: relatively cheap land with no zoning.

A heady few years ensued, but now they're over. Zoning has since been imposed, and Lincoln is adjusting to its new status as a major, year-round destination—one that can accommodate as many visitors as any resort in northern New England.

GUIDANCE

Lincoln-Woodstock Chamber of Commerce (745-6621; 1-800-227-4191), Box 358, Lincoln 03251. A helpful, walk-in information center in the small Depot Mall on Main Street; this is also a reservation service for the area.

GETTING THERE

By bus: **Concord Trailways** (228-3300; Greyhound information, 1-800-251-2222) provides daily service to and from Concord, Manchester, and Boston, stopping at the Hobo Railroad, Main Street, Lincoln.

GETTING AROUND

Shuttle service within Lincoln makes coming by bus a viable option, especially during ski season when the Loon Mountain Shuttle serves most inns and condo complexes around town.

The Shuttle Connection (745-3140; 1-800-648-4947) requires 24-hour advance notice but serves Manchester Airport as well as local destinations year-round.

MEDICAL EMERGENCY

Speare Memorial Hospital (536-1120), Hospital Road, Plymouth, or **Littleton Hospital** (444-7731), 107 Cottage Street, Littleton.

TO SEE

Indian Head. Like the Old Man of the Mountain, this craggy profile on Mount Pemigewasset, visible from Route 3, is an old local landmark. Admittedly it needs a chin trim: fir trees have grown up, partially obscuring it. Best seen from the Route 3 parking lot of the Indian Head Resort. The summit is accessible via the Mount Pemigewasset Trail, which starts off the Franconia Notch bike path just north of the Flume Visitors Center (see "Franconia and North of the Notches").

Lost River Reservation (745-8031), Route 112, 7 miles west of North Woodstock. Open mid-May to late October, weather permitting, 9–5:30. This was the first acquisition of the Society for the Protection of New Hampshire Forests, purchased from a local timber company in 1912. The Nature Garden here is said to feature more than 200 varieties of native plants, and the glacial meltwater gorge is spectacular. Boardwalks thread a series of basins and caves, past rock formations with names like Guillotine Rock and Hall of Ships. Now maintained by the White Mountains Attractions, the complex includes a snack bar and gift shop. $6 per adult, $3 for children ages 6–12.

Hobo Railroad (745-2135), Hobo Junction (just east of I-93), Lincoln. Open Memorial Day through Halloween; daily July to Labor Day, otherwise weekends; again weekends Thanksgiving to Christmas. A 15-mile round-trip excursion along the Pemigewasset River in "dining coaches" with velour seats and tables. $7 per adult, $4.50 per child. Optional breakfast, picnic lunch, dinner. Café Lafayette, the deluxe dining car service on the Hobo Railroad, leaves Lincoln at 6:30 P.M. during summer months (see also *Dining Out*).

FOR FAMILIES

Loon Mountain Park offers a "Skyride" to mountaintop hikes and caves, also horseback riding, mountain biking, rollerblading, croquet, archery, and other activities detailed under *To Do*.

Clark's Trading Post (745-8913), Route 3, Lincoln. Open daily July through Labor Day, 10–6; weekends Memorial Day through mid-October. One of the country's oldest theme parks, begun in the 1920s as a dog ranch

(Florence Clark was the first woman to reach the summit of Mount Washington by dogsled). Still owned and managed by the Clark family, known for trained bear shows (July and August); also featuring a haunted house, Avery's old-time garage and the 1890s fire station, a photo parlor, bumper boats, and Merlin's Mystical Mansion. $7 adults, $5 children ages 6–11; $1 ages 3–5.

White Mountain Motorsports Park (745-6727), Route 3, Woodstock. A 0.25-mile asphalt track, races every weekend, Memorial Day through Columbus Day.

The Whale's Tale Waterpark (745-8810), Route 3, Lincoln. Open late June to Labor Day daily, weekends from Memorial Day. Wave pool, speed and curvy slides, wading pool for small children, tube rentals. Rates are figured by height: 47 inches and up, $14 all day; 37–46 inches, $12; reduced rates after 1 P.M. and 3 P.M.; children under 36 inches tall and adults over age 65, free.

SCENIC DRIVES

The Kancamagus National Scenic Byway. Open year-round, this is the 34.5-mile stretch of Route 112 east from Lincoln to Conway (Route 16) through the White Mountain National Forest. Officially recognized as one of the most scenic highways in the country, it climbs to 2,855 feet in elevation at the Kancamagus Pass, the ridge line dividing two watersheds. (Streams run downhill west to the Pemigewasset and east into the Saco.) This is also the point considered the heart of the White Mountains, which, we're told, stretch for a radius of 35 miles in all directions. The highway was completed in 1959, after 25 years in the building. It offers four scenic overlooks, four picnic sites, a half dozen campgrounds (see *Camping*), several scenic areas, and access to myriad hiking trails ranging from the 0.5-mile Rail 'n' River Trail to multi-day treks into the Pemigewasset Wilderness.

Before setting out from Lincoln, you might want to stop at the **White Mountains Visitor Center** (see *Guidance* under "The Western Whites"), where you can pick up a map and guide to the highway and detailed sheets on specific trails and campgrounds. July fourth through Labor Day, forest service visitor information specialists are also here on weekends to steer would-be campers to vacant sites and hikers to appropriate trails.

A detailed description of the highway is offered under *To See* in "White Mountain National Forest."

For detailed descriptions of longer hikes from the "Kanc," consult the *AMC White Mountain Guide;* descriptions of individual trails are available from the White Mountains Visitors Center and the Saco Ranger Station.

Tripoli Road. Pronounced "triple eye," this shortcut from I-93 (Exit 31) Woodstock to Waterville Valley accesses a number of hiking trails and campsites. It is also a fine foliage-season loop, returning to Woodstock via Routes 49 and 175. (See "The Western Whites—The Waterville Valley Region.")

Kinsman Notch. Route 112 west from North Woodstock is less traveled but as beautiful as the Kancamagus, climbing quickly into Kinsman Notch, past Lost River (see *To See*) and Beaver Pond (see *Green Space*), crossing the Appalachian Trail. You can continue on by the Wildwood Campground to Mount Moosilauke (see *Hiking*) or cut up Route 116 to Easton, Sugar Hill, and Franconia, and back down through Franconia Notch. Another option is to take the dirt "North-South" road off Route 116 beyond Kinsman Notch, through the national forest to Long Pond where there is a boat launch and, we're told, good fishing; also picnic sites. You can return to Route 116 or continue on to Route 25.

Route 118 west from North Woodstock climbs steeply through the national forest, then down into the Baker River Valley. You may want to stop at the Polar Caves in Plymouth (see *For Families* in "The Western Whites—The Waterville Valley Region") and cut back up I-93; or take Route 25 to Haverhill with its handsome old village center (just south of the junction of Routes 25 and 10), returning via Routes 116 and 112 through Kinsman Notch.

TO DO

AERIAL RIDE

Loon Mountain Gondola Ride (745-8111). Ride to the summit, where there's an observation tower, a summit cafeteria, summit cave walk, hiking trails. $8 per adult, $3 per child ages 6–12.

(Also see *Green Space* in "Franconia and North of the Notches" for Cannon Mountain's aerial tramway.)

BICYCLING

Loon Mountain Bike Center (745-8111), Lincoln. Open Memorial Day to late October. Mountain-bike rentals, guided group tours, 35 km of cross-country trails along the Pemigewasset River; bikes may be hooked to the gondola and ridden down selected trails.

The Franconia Notch Bike Path is a favorite loop (12 miles round-trip). Buses shuttle bicyclists to Echo Lake for a guided tour (slightly downhill the whole way) back. $35 includes the shuttle and bike rental.

CAMPING

The campgrounds along the Kancamagus Highway are among the most popular in the White Mountain National Forest and are accessible only on a first-come, first-served basis.

Covered Bridge Campground (1-800-283-CAMP) takes reservations.

Pemigewasset Region (536-1310): **Hancock** (4 miles east of Lincoln) is open year-round with 56 sites, $8 per day; and **Big Rock** (6 miles east of Lincoln) is open year-round with 23 sites.

Saco Region (447-5448): **Passaconaway** has 33 sites, $8 per day; **Jigger**

Johnson has 75 sites, $8 per day; **Covered Bridge** has 49 sites, $8 per day; and **Blackberry Crossing** has 26 sites.

Ammonoosuc Region (869-2626): **Wildwood** is open mid-April through early December. Offers 26 campsites, good fishing.

(See "The Waterville Valley Region" and "Franconia and North of the Notches" in "The Western Whites" for more White Mountain National Forest campsites.)

FISHING

The free "Freshwater Fishing Guide" is available at local information centers. Fishermen frequent the East Branch of the Pemi, Russell Pond, and many mountain streams.

HIKING

Mount Moosilauke. The Benton Trail ascends the northwest flank of Mount Moosilauke at a steady, moderate grade. The trail begins in a parking area off the Tunnel Brook Road; take Route 112 west from North Woodstock about 10 miles, and drive 3 miles south on Tunnel Brook Road. Other trails, the most popular being the George Brook Trail, begin at the Dartmouth Outing Club cabin. The 4,802-foot summit offers one of the most extensive views in New Hampshire. Our favorite description is credited to clergyman and author Dr. Washington Gladden: "I give my preference to Moosilauke over every mountain whose top I have climbed. The view from Washington is vast, but vague; the view from Lafayette is notable, but it shows little of the sweet restfulness of the Connecticut Valley; on Moosilauke we get all forms of grandeur and all types of beauty."

Greeley Ponds. This easy trail is 4.5 miles round-trip, beginning on the Kancamagus Highway, 9 miles east of Lincoln. As local hiking guru Steve Smith describes it: the trail climbs gradually to the high point of Mad River Notch, then dips down to Upper Greeley Pond, a deep tarn hemmed in by the cliff-studded slopes of Mount Osceola's East Peak and Mount Kancamagus. A half mile farther you reach the south shore of boggy Lower Greeley Pond, where you can look north into the cleft of the notch.

(Also see *Scenic Drives* in "The Western Whites—The Waterville Valley Region," and "—Franconia and North of the Notches" for other brief trail descriptions.) Detailed descriptions of all these hikes are found in *50 Hikes in the White Mountains* by Daniel Doan (Backcountry Publications) and in the *AMC White Mountain Guide*.

HORSEBACK RIDING

Loon Mountain (745-8111). July and August. Trail rides offered; "walking" rides are $26; rides for more experienced riders by arrangement. Also pony rides.

GOLF

Jack O'Lantern Country Club (745-3636), Route 3, Woodstock. Eighteen-hole, par-70 course, instruction, rental clubs, golf carts, and pull carts.

MINIATURE GOLF

White Mountain Miniature Golf (745-2777), Route 3, Lincoln. Open mid-June to Labor Day, daily 1–10; weekends and midweek evenings during shoulder seasons. Grass-carpeted, 18-hole course.

Hobo Hills Adventure Golf (745-2125), Main Street, Lincoln. Open daily June to Labor Day, weekends in spring and fall. Eighteen holes with hills and water.

ROLLERBLADING

Loon Mountain offers a Rollerblade Arena with lessons and rentals.

SWIMMING

The Mountain Club Fitness Center at Loon Mountain (745-8111), Route 112, Lincoln. Open 7 A.M.–10 P.M. daily. Indoor lap pool, outdoor pool in summer.

Swimming holes. "The Lady's Bathtub," in the Pemi, Lincoln. Maybe 15 feet deep, fringed with a little sand, accessible through the parking lot at Riverfront Condos. In North Woodstock the **Cascades** is a favorite dunking spot in the Pemi right behind Main Street. Other spots on the Pemi can be found along Route 175 in Woodstock. One is just across from the Tripoli Road, I-93 interchange.

(Also see the Whale's Tale Waterpark under *For Families*.)

TENNIS

Indian Head Resort (745-8000). Outdoor tennis courts.

Mountain Club. Loon Mountain also offers outdoor courts.

CROSS-COUNTRY SKIING

Loon Mountain (745-8111). Thirty-five km of trails, some winding partway up the mountain, others following the riverbed. Rentals, instruction, special events. Trail fee $8.

Lincoln Woods Trail. Off the Kancamagus, a large parking lot on the left is your clue to a major ungroomed cross-country system maintained by the forest service. The visitors center here is maintained on a limited basis in winter.

DOWNHILL SKIING

Loon Mountain (745-8111), 2 miles from I-93, Exit 32, Lincoln. With its long cruising trails and easy access, Loon attracts more skiers per year than any other New Hampshire ski area. It is a nicely designed mountain, with dozens of intermediate trails streaking its face and a choice of steeply pitched trails, served by their own high-altitude East Basin chair lift, on North Peak. Beginners have the Little Sister chair and slope to themselves, then graduate to a choice of equally isolated (from hot-rod skiers) runs in the West Basin. The only hitch is that the main base area and West Basin are separated by a long, string bean–shaped parking lot. The lay of the land dictates the strung-out shape of Loon's base facilities that line a narrow shelf along the Pemigewasset River, which in turn has cut this steep Upper Pemi Valley.

The one big hitch to skiing Loon is securing a lift ticket. Since 1966

View from Loon Mountain Ski Area

DOROTHY I. CROSSLEY

its limited-ticket policy has ensured that lift lines are kept to 15 minutes or under, but this means that tickets are occasionally unavailable. Tickets are available in advance through local inns and condos, by ordering on a "Loon Reservation Card" ($35), through Ticket Master. Next-day tickets may also be purchased daily at the ticket window from noon Friday, Saturday, and during vacations.

Obviously the demand for Loon to expand is large, but the corporation's long-standing plans to double its ski terrain (with an eventual build-out on some 900 acres of national forest on adjacent South Mountain) have been stymied by federal Environmental Protection Agency review boards. At this writing a scaled-down expansion has been approved and skier capacity should be increased from 6,000 to 10,000 skiers per day any year now.

Trails: 41, with 25 percent easiest, 55 percent more difficult, 20 percent most difficult (22 miles total).

Lifts: 9, including a fast 4-passenger gondola, 2 triple chairs, 5 double chairs, and 1 surface.

Vertical drop: 2,100 feet.

Snowmaking: 85 percent of total top-to-bottom terrain.

Facilities: Include two base lodges, three lounges, two rental shops, summit cafeteria, and mid-mountain lodge (Camp 3) at the base of North Peak. Slopeside lodging at the 234-room Mountain Club includes condo units, indoor pool, game rooms, and restaurants; ice skating, cross-country skiing.

Ski school: 170 full- and part-time instructors, modified ATM system, freestyle, mountain challenge, and NASTAR.

For children: Loon Mountain Nursery for ages 6 weeks to 6 years; Honeybears SKIwee (ages 3–5), Bear Cubs SKIwee (ages 6–8), Mountain Explorers (ages 9–12).

Rates: $39 adult, $27 junior weekends; $34 adult, $28 for ages 13–21, and $23 for ages 6–12 on weekdays; also half-day and multi-day rates.

ICE SKATING

Loon Mountain (745-8111) maintains a lighted rink near the main base lodge.

Millfront Marketplace (745-6261) maintains a lighted rink behind the complex.

SLEIGH RIDES

Sleigh Rides (745-6261; 745-8766) depart regularly from the front of the Millfront Marketplace. (Also see "The Western Whites—Franconia and North of the Notches.")

SNOWMOBILING

Trail maps available locally detail the extensive local system.

GREEN SPACE

Beaver Pond, Route 112 west from North Woodstock in Kinsman Notch, beyond Lost River. A beautiful pond with a rock promontory for picnicking or sunning and a view of Mount Blue.

For Franconia Notch, see "The Western Whites—Franconia and North of the Notches."

(Also see *Hiking* in this chapter and the detailed description of the Kancamagus Scenic Byway under *Scenic Drives* in "White Mountain National Forest.")

LODGING

RESORTS

All resorts listed are in Lincoln 03251.

✐ **The Marriott Mountain Club on Loon** (745-8111; 1-800-229-STAY). With 234 rooms, this is one of New England's largest, most elaborate slopeside hotels. Bellmen hover and the front desk is always covered. The two-tiered lobby has a hearth and a concierge. Cars are parked in the garage on arrival and needn't budge until departure. Guests can wake up to a room-service breakfast and ski in at noon to pop a frozen pizza in the microwave, drop by the sauna and pool, play some racquetball before dinner. The skating rink and cross-country trails are also within walking distance. In summer a full program of activities is also available. Babysitters are available, and older children keep busy enough with video games and table tennis in the game room, then a movie on the VCR in their "unit," to free parents to dine in Rachel's, the hotel dining room. In winter from $109 for a standard, double room, $139 for a "studio" with kitchen, and $169 for a Mountain Club suite sleeping six; less in summer; packages available.

☞✐**The Mill House Inn** (745-6261; 1-800-654-6183), Route 112. A 96-room hotel built from scratch but connected (a luxury in winter) to the Millfront Marketplace (see *Selective Shopping*), a complex that incorporates 3 of the old paper-mill buildings. It is connected to the ski area in winter by Loon's shuttle. Amenities include indoor and outdoor pools, saunas, Jacuzzis, and exercise room. Some suites have kitchen facilities but most are simply spacious one- or two-room, nicely designed spaces with phones and color cable TVs. Downstairs public spaces include a library with fireplace and ample comfortable corners. Doubles are $75–95 in summer and fall, $70–85 during ski season when family suites (with a separate room with bunks for children, sleeping up to six) are $80–95; suites sleeping six are $90–140. Five-day summer vacation packages start at $602 for a family of four, including selected daily meals and other perks. Many packages.

Rivergreen Condominiums at The Mill (754-2450; 1-800-654-6183), PO Box 1056, Route 112. A separate building, unattached to the Mill House Inn or the marketplace but part of the same complex. In summer and fall kitchen units $90 (sleeping two people), $125 (sleeping four), $140 (sleeping six), $150–175 (sleeping eight); more on weekends; weekly and package rates available.

☞✐**Lodge at Lincoln Station** (745-3441; 1-800-654-6188), midway between town and mountain, with studios, one-bedroom, and loft suites overlooking the river (be sure to request one) and a central "Great Room" with a hearth, also indoor and outdoor pools, a Jacuzzi, saunas, game room, and tennis courts. A standard studio is $70–85 and a one-bedroom suite with kitchenette sleeping four is $100–135.

✐ **The Village of Loon Mountain** (745-3401; 1-800-258-8932). Of the 650 units here, 200 are in the rental pool. Positioned directly across the road from Loon Mountain, this development is nicely designed to blend into the hillside. Amenities include 2 indoor pools, 12 outdoor tennis courts (2 are flooded to form a skating rink in winter), a kids' game room with arcade, and table tennis. $47.50–72.50 per person per night with a two-night minimum in winter.

RESORT MOTELS

Indian Head Resort (745-8000; 1-800-343-8000), Lincoln 03251. First opened in the 1920s, gradually evolving to its present 90 motel rooms, 50 cabins (with fireplaces). Indoor and outdoor heated pools, tennis courts, game room, coffee shop, and dining room. $31–41 per person in ski season.

Woodward's Motor Inn (745-8141), Route 3, Lincoln 03251. Closed between foliage and ski season and in spring. An 80-room complex that has grown gradually over the past 39 years, carefully managed by the Woodward family. Amenities include indoor and outdoor pools and an indoor racquetball court. In summer there are also lawn games. The Colonial Dining Room serves breakfast daily, and dinner is served nightly in the Open Hearth Dining Room; there's also a lounge. $31–41 per person; MAP rates, packages, off-season prices.

Jack O'Lantern Resort (745-3636), North Woodstock 03262. Closed between foliage and ski season, again in spring. Another landmark local motel that has evolved into a resort with 25 motel rooms, 50 one- to three-room cottages and condominiums. Amenities include a pool, tennis, Jacuzzi, 18-hole golf course. $36–81 per person in winter without meals; MAP in summer.

INN

The Woodstock Inn (745-3951), PO Box 18, Main Street (Route 3), North Woodstock 03262. Known for both its formal dining (on the glassed-in front porch) and informal dining (in Woodstock Station out back; see *Where to Eat*), but there are also 19 antiques-furnished rooms, 6 in the main house (sharing 3 hall bathrooms), 11 across the street in "Riverside" (each with private bath and access to a porch overlooking the river), and 2 in the Deahman House. This isn't your ordinary country inn. There is no real common area for guests, the rooms seem impersonal, and we really don't think that a two-person Jacuzzi right next to a canopy bed is particularly classy (the Ellsworth Room features a king-size canopy bed, Jacuzzi, fireplace, and fridge). $22.50–67.50 per person; breakfast included in winter.

BED & BREAKFASTS

The Birches (745-6603), Route 175, Box 59, North Woodstock 03262. Former schoolteacher Ruth Ballmer offers her guests a sense of what it's like to live in an unusually spacious, sun-filled house on the banks of the Pemigewasset. But you must like dogs—Ms. Ballmer breeds large, well-behaved Bernese mountain dogs. Request the tower room. Rates for the three rooms range from $60 to $70 most of the year, $70 during ski season; 10 percent discount for 3 nights.

Wilderness Inn (745-3890), Route 3 and Courtney Road, North Woodstock 03262. This is a bungalow-style house in the village of North Woodstock, with a comfortable living room and five upstairs guest rooms, one downstairs, and a cottage that's the real gem in the place. Within earshot of the Lost River, the cottage has a sleigh bed, a TV, and deck. Breakfasts are exceptional here (see *Eating Out*) and included in the $40–85 per room rate.

MOTELS

☞ **Franconia Notch Motel** (745-2229), Route 3, Lincoln 03251. The nicest kind of family-run motel: 6 two-room cottages (summer only) and 12 standard motel units, backing on the Pemigewasset River where picnic tables and grills are in place. Franconia Notch State Park is a half mile up the road. Each unit is different; most have twin beds. Board games and morning coffee are available. One small single with a view of the river is

$15–33 per person in season, less in shoulder seasons.

OTHER LODGING

☞ **The Ledges Hostel** (745-8433), Route 3, Woodstock 03293. A cheery and companionable lodging place for hikers to find ample information about local trails as well as a comfortable bunk, kitchen privileges, canoe rentals; bikers and skiers also welcome. Very reasonably priced.

WHERE TO EAT

DINING OUT

The Woodstock Inn (745-3951), Main Street (Route 3), North Woodstock. Open nightly and for Sunday brunch. The Clement Room, a glassed-in porch set crisply with white linen tablecloths and fine china, is the setting for the finest dining in the Lincoln-Woodstock area. The menu includes frogs' legs Provençal followed by a wide choice of entrées like rack of lamb, beef Wellington, salmon with asparagus and sun-dried tomatoes and dill poached in heavy cream, and a half dozen versions of veal. Moderate to expensive.

Café Lafayette (745-2135; 745-3500), on the Hobo Railroad, Hobo Junction, Lincoln. The typical set menu on this two-hour excursion run in a vintage 1924 Pullman railroad car begins with caviar or pâté, proceeds through sorbet to a choice of chicken, salmon, or beef bourguignonne. Moderately expensive.

Rachel's (745-8111) in the Mountain Club at Loon Mountain. Open daily for all three meals. Named for Mrs. Sherman Adams and decorated with her paintings. Standard crowd pleasers like poached halibut in Swiss chard, salmon with lobster mousse in pastry, and chicken with cheddar and apple glaze. Moderately expensive at dinner.

☞ **The Tavern at the Mill** (745-3603), Millfront Marketplace, Route 112, Lincoln. Family restaurant prices but a pleasant, brick-walled, dimly lighted, multi-tiered place in a part of the original mill; a night club–lounge that's the liveliest place in town on ski weekends. The vast menu ranges from pasta to blackened prime rib to fresh poached salmon to chicken teriyaki to fajita falmeado (huge, gloppy, and delicious) to lemon-pepper chicken salad. Moderate.

Gordi's Fish and Steak House (745-6635), Route 112, Lincoln. The decor is glitzy Victorian mixed with photos of ski heros past and present (the owners include two past members of Olympic ski teams). The specialties are lobster (note the tank), seafood, and beef. You can also make a meal of the salad bar. Moderate.

The Common Man (745-3463), at the corner of Pollard Road and Main Street, Lincoln. Open nightly except Thanksgiving and Christmas. The winning formula here is a limited menu stressing simplicity and fresh ingredients: broiled and grilled swordfish, freshly made pastas, spare ribs, steaks, chicken Kiev. Moderate.

EATING OUT

☞✐**Woodstock Station** (745-3951), at the Woodstock Inn, Main Street (Route 3), North Woodstock. This railroad station was built in the late 1800s in Lincoln and continued to serve visitors—including skiers bound for Cannon Mountain—into the 1930s and 1940s. In 1984 it was sawed in half and moved to its present location; the old freight room is now the bar and the passenger waiting room is the lower dining room. This large, eclectically furnished space, recently expanded, is one of the liveliest dining spaces in the North Country, and the menu is immense: everything from frogs' legs to Peking ravioli to quesadilla and nachos and burritos (lots of Mexican) to a wide choice of original sandwiches to pastas to baked scrod to ribs and burgers. The children's menu includes a $2 hot dog. Beverages fill four more pages of the menu and include a wide variety of imported beers.

☞✐**Truants Taverne** (745-2239), Main Street, North Woodstock. Open daily 11:30 A.M.–10 P.M. ("or so"). Hung over the river in a back-behind kind of space, part of an old millyard. Polished pine tables and a large menu that's fun to read: for lunch choose from the Class Bully, the Salutatorian, the Class Clown, the Elementary Burger, or maybe the Exchange Student (a flour tortilla stuffed with spicy beef, cheese, and sour cream, etc.). At dinner the Dean's List includes veal Marsala but you can also scrape by with that old Exchange Student or Elementary Burger. A good place.

☞ **Jasmann's Cafe, Bakery, and Country Store** (745-2626) in the Millfront Marketplace, Lincoln. Recently promoted to roomier and more prominent digs in the mall, this is a place with an obvious sense of someone (Jody Mann) hard at work, caring about what she produces here: everything from homemade bread (50 cents per slice) and pumpkin pancakes to homemade soups. Turkey BLTs (it really works) and—the most expensive thing on the menu—crab-salad plate ($6.75). Twenty gourmet coffees are offered.

Govoni's Italian Restaurant (745-8042), Lost River Road, Route 112 west of North Woodstock. Open nightly from Memorial Day to Labor Day. Northern Italian specialties served in a traditional New Hampshire house overlooking Agassiz Basin. Moderate.

✐ **Cookouts on the Summit.** Mid-June through Labor Day, Wednesday through Sunday 4–6:30. Cookout price includes the "Skyride" gondola ride to the Loon Mountain summit as well as the meal: a choice of BBQ chicken, hamburgers, and hot dogs.

Chieng Gardens (745-8612), Lincoln Square, Main Street, Lincoln. A better-than-average Chinese restaurant with a large, reasonably priced menu and the best view (upstairs, facing the mountains) of any restaurant in Lincoln.

Elvio's Pizzeria (745-8817), 117 Main Street, Lincoln. "Best pizza north of the Bronx." The best pizza in town; subs and basic Italian dinners to go, too.

For Breakfast

The Woodstock Inn (745-3951), Main Street (Route 3), North Woodstock. A wide range of waffles, omelets, and other memorable breakfast fare—like homemade red-flannel hash, poached egg, and home fries.

Wilderness Inn and Cafe (745-3890), Route 3 and Courtney Road, North Woodstock. Freshly ground coffee, homemade muffins, selected hot crêpes, omelets.

New England Yogurt Company (745-6782), Millfront Marketplace, Lincoln. The claim is for 1,152 flavors. The yogurt and ice cream are made on the premises and the combinations are endless: carrot cake, applesauce, mocha banana . . .

ENTERTAINMENT

North Country Center for the Arts (745-2141), The Mill at Loon Mountain. Late June through mid-October. Musicals, comedy, classics, children's theater, Wednesday at 11 A.M. and 1:30 P.M. Machine Room #1 of the old Franconia Paper Mill is now a 250-seat theater, and plans call for converting the former Finishing Room into a 475-seat theater.

Lincoln Cinemas 4 (745-6238), Lincoln Center North, Main Street, Lincoln. Four screens.

Summer band concerts. Regularly on the common in North Woodstock.

Loon Mountain Lecture Series (745-8111). Saturday evening during the summer. The North Country Chamber Players also perform regularly at the Governor's Lodge during summer months.

SELECTIVE SHOPPING

Pinestead Quilts (745-8640), 99 Main Street, Lincoln. An unusual selection of locally made quilts, machine-pieced but hand-tied, traditional designs. From $65 for quilted wraps to $650 for king-size quilts.

Lahout's Country Clothing and Ski Shop, Inc., Main Street, Lincoln. Open daily. A branch of the Littleton store opened in 1922 and was billed as "the oldest continually operated ski shop in New England." Operated by the three sons of the original Lahout and dedicated to "beating anyone's price," this is unquestionably one of *the* places in the North Country to shop for ski gear, sturdy footwear, long johns, etc., etc.

Rodgers Ski Outlet, Main Street, Lincoln. Open daily 7 A.M.–9 P.M. "Lawho?" the competition may well ask if you mention Lahout's. Over 1,500 pairs of skis in stock at any time; tune-ups, rentals, repairs are the specialties. Billed as "Northern New England's largest volume ski shop."

The North Face, Main Street, Lincoln. This Berkeley, California–based company claims to be the largest manufacturer of its kind of sports equipment—tents, skiwear, backpacks, and the like—in the world.

While its products are available in all major sports stores, this is its only outlet in the Northeast: a large space filled with sportswear, skiwear, sleeping bags, and technical outerwear at savings of 20 to 50 percent.

Cartoon World (1-800-698-3671), Millfront Marketplace, Lincoln. Original cartoon art—animated cartoons, comic strips, and books—are displayed and sold.

Fadden's General Store, Main Street, North Woodstock. Open daily. One of the few genuine old-time general stores left in New England (now run by the third generation of Faddens), filled with genuine relics of storekeeping past; also an amazing assortment of current stock.

Antiques, Crafts, and Collectibles (745-8111), at Loon Mountain. Open daily late May through October. More than 50 dealers exhibiting furniture and furnishings, stained glass, pottery, crafts, and more.

Deke's Sport House, Route 112, Lincoln. Ski, bike, and tennis sales; rentals; fishing, hiking, and camping equipment.

Dick's Dugout, Main Street, North Woodstock. A baseball card–collector's oasis.

Millfront Marketplace, Route 12, Lincoln. Twenty shops and restaurants in a complex incorporating three turn-of-the-century mill buildings. The complex includes:

The Country Carriage. "Country" gifts, reproduction furniture, tinware, collectible dolls.

Innisfree Bookshop (745-6107). The only full-service bookstore in the region, specializing in New England titles, White Mountain guides and trail maps, ski titles, field guides, and children's books.

SPECIAL EVENTS

January 15: **Independence Day Weekend,** at Loon Mountain, "celebrating Loon's independence from nature."

Mid-winter: **Snowfest,** Lincoln-Woodstock. A full week of festivities.

February: **Snowmobile Easter Seal ride.**

March: **Spring Fling** at Loon Mountain.

June: Annual **Fiddlers Contest,** sponsored by Lincoln-Woodstock Lions Club.

July: **Fourth of July Celebration,** Lincoln-Woodstock. **Arts and Crafts Fair** at Loon Mountain.

September: **Lumberjack Festival,** Labor Day weekend, at Loon Mountain. **New Hampshire Highland Games,** Loon Mountain.

September-October: **Royal Lipizzan Stallions** performing at the Millfront Marketplace, Lincoln.

October: **Fall Foliage Festival** at Loon Mountain.

November-December: **Holiday Celebrations** at the Millfront Marketplace, Lincoln.

FRANCONIA AND NORTH OF THE NOTCHES

Wrapped in forest and dominated by granite White Mountain peaks, the Franconia-Bethlehem area seems to be the distilled essence of northern New Hampshire. Northwest of this high, wooded country, the landscape changes suddenly, flattening around Littleton, the shopping town for this region. For views of both the Green Mountains and the White Mountains, follow this Ammonoosuc Valley south to Lisbon and Bath, then back up to Sugar Hill and Franconia on memorable back roads.

The town of Franconia alone packs into its 65 square miles more splendid scenic vistas and unusual natural attractions than many states or provinces can boast. Curiously, while annual visitors to Franconia Notch are said to outnumber New Hampshire residents, relatively few stray into the delightful neighboring valley, which seems happily trapped in a 1950s time warp.

Franconia and its small satellite towns of Sugar Hill and Easton have been catering to visitors of one sort or another for more than 150 years. Travelers were first attracted to Franconia Notch by its convenience as a north-south route through the mountains; but they were invariably impressed by the scenery, and their tales of natural wonders like the granite profile of the Old Man of the Mountain circulated widely.

Sight-seers and health seekers began trickling into the notch after the War of Independence, and a few inns and taverns catered to them along with more conventional travelers. Then in the midnineteenth century the railroad arrived, inaugurating a grand resort era. Such literary notables as Nathaniel Hawthorne, Washington Irving, John Greenleaf Whittier, and Henry Wadsworth Longfellow were all Franconia summer visitors whose enthusiastic accounts of the region fanned its fame. Hawthorne even wrote a story about the Old Man, "The Great Stone Face."

One of the most celebrated hotels in America in its day, and a symbol of the White Mountains' golden age, was the 400-room Profile House, which stood in the heart of Franconia Notch. Besides elegant service in a rustic setting, the hotel offered its guests a superb view of the Old Man. An institution for 70 years, Profile House burned down in 1923, just as the automobile began permanently altering America's vacation habits and the grand-hotel era was ending. The hotel site is now part of Franconia Notch State Park.

Grand hotels also appeared in Bethlehem, known for its pollen-free air. It became headquarters for the National Hay Fever Relief Association, which was founded here in the 1920s, and at one time Bethlehem had 34 hotels, some large and luxurious indeed, and a 2-mile-long boardwalk for their guests to stroll along.

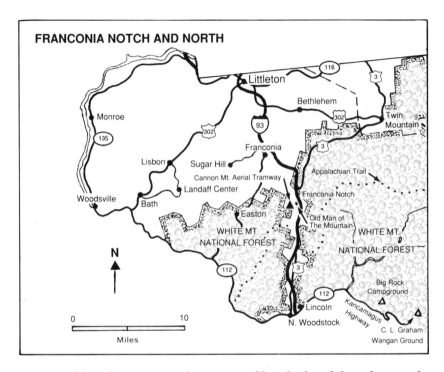

FRANCONIA NOTCH AND NORTH

Although many once-famous grand hotels closed their doors in the 1920s and 1930s, a few lasted until the 1950s, when railroad service to the White Mountains ended and a resort way of life ended with it. A few traces of Bethlehem's glory days remain, such as the impressive fieldstone and shingle clubhouse of the Maplewood Golf Course (formerly The Casino), an outbuilding of the very grand but long-vanished Maplewood Hotel.

Summer residents and hotel guests, outraged at what unrestricted logging was doing to their beloved mountain scenery, founded the still-active Society for the Protection of New Hampshire Forests. The efforts of this pioneering conservation organization eventually led to the creation in 1911 of the 768,000-acre White Mountain National Forest, the first national forest in the country.

When the summer resort scene began to fade in the White Mountains, a winter one commenced, thriving as Americans discovered skiing. The Franconia area can claim a number of skiing firsts. Among them: the nation's first ski school (which opened at Pecketts-on-Sugar Hill in 1929) and this country's first aerial tramway (constructed in 1938), which ran to the summit of state-owned Cannon Mountain. Cannon also hosted America's first racing trail in the 1920s and its first World Cup race in the 1960s.

In 1945 a flamboyant Austrian aristocrat, Baron Hugo Von Pantz, founded Mittersill, a Tyrolean-style resort adjacent to Cannon. The baron's resort attracted high-society types from New York and Boston, and, for a time, Franconia was the New England equivalent of Aspen or St. Moritz. Cannon remains a popular ski area, and its expansion plans include reopening the (now dormant) Mittersill ski slopes.

Times change. The current winter hot spot is south of the notch (see "The Western Whites—Lincoln and North Woodstock"), and the socialites have gone the way of the old hotels. An unusual number of craftsmen have settled in—graduates of Franconia College, a liberal institution of the 1960s that was housed in the (since demolished) old Forest Hill Hotel but that died with the 1970s. Some of New Hampshire's most pleasant inns and bed & breakfasts are scattered throughout the folds of the valleys and gentler hills north and west of Franconia Notch.

GUIDANCE

Franconia-Easton-Sugar Hill Chamber of Commerce (823-5661), Box D, Main Street, Franconia 03580. Downtown information booth is open through foliage season; another is open at the Cannon Mountain tramway base station through ski season.

Bethlehem Chamber of Commerce (444-9921), PO Box 748, Bethlehem 03547. Seasonal information booth on Route 302 near the intersection of I-93.

Littleton Area Chamber of Commerce (444-6561), 141 Main Street, Box 105, Littleton 03561. Seasonal information booth located in front of the office.

Lisbon Chamber of Commerce (838-6397), Lisbon 03585.

Twin Mountain Chamber of Commerce (846-5407; reservations 1-800-245-TWIN), Box 194, Twin Mountain 03595, produces a brochure and operates a summer information center at the junction of Routes 3 and 302.

WMNF Ammonoosuc Ranger Station (869-2626), Trudeau Road, off Route 302, Box 239, Bethlehem 03574. Open Monday through Friday 7–4:30.

GETTING THERE

By bus: **Concord Trailways** (228-3300; 1-800-852-3317) has daily service from Boston, Manchester, Concord, Lincoln, and Littleton.

By car: From north or south, take I-93 to Franconia Notch Parkway (Route 3). Route 116 west leads to Franconia and the adjacent towns of Sugar Hill and Easton. Route 302 east leads into Bethlehem from the north, Route 142 east from the south.

MEDICAL EMERGENCY

Littleton Hospital (444-7731), 107 Cottage Street, Littleton.

Franconia Life Squad (823-8123). Franconia-Easton rescue service.

Bethlehem Volunteer Ambulance (869-2232).

VILLAGES

Bath. The village of Bath itself is known for its vintage 1832 covered bridge and for its 1804 Old Brick Store, billed as the country's oldest general store. Upper Bath Village, a few miles north on Route 302, is a striking cluster of Federal-era brick homes set against surrounding fields.

Landaff Center. Set well back into the hills east of Route 302, this is one of New Hampshire's most photographed old hill towns. The town hall commands a superb view. The latest population count is 286. You can't help wondering what it would be if Dartmouth College had been sited here the way Governor John Wentworth suggested in 1770.

Sugar Hill. Once part of Lisbon, whose center was some 10 miles away, the folks of this village petitioned the legislature to become a separate town. Set high on a ridge with views to the Franconia and the Presidential ranges, this cluster of homes, inns, and churches is one of the state's prettiest communities.

TO SEE

Mount Washington Cog Railway. See "Mount Washington's Valleys—Crawford Notch and Bretton Woods."

(Also see *Green Space*.)

MUSEUMS AND HISTORIC SITES

The Robert Frost Place (823-8038), Ridge Road, off Route 116, Franconia. Former home of the noted poet, now a town-run museum and center for poetry and the arts. Displays of rare editions of Frost's books, photos, and memorabilia and a slide presentation about Frost's life and work in Franconia. A nature trail behind the house is signposted with quotations from appropriate Frost poems. In summer there are frequent poetry readings and workshops. Open weekends spring and fall; daily except Tuesday in July and August. Admission $3 adults, $2 seniors, $1.25 children.

New England Ski Museum (823-7177). Adjacent to the tramway base station at Franconia Notch State Park, the privately operated museum tells the story of New England skiing with exhibits of skis, clothing, and equipment dating from the nineteenth century to the present, along with vintage still photos and film. Open daily except Wednesday, May 27 through October 16 and December 15 through March 31. Admission $2 adults; $1 children ages 12–18.

Sugar Hill Historical Museum (823-8142), Main Street (Route 117), Sugar Hill. Interesting, small local museum with changing exhibits about aspects of the town from its pioneer settlement in 1780 until the present. Open July to mid-October, Thursday, Saturday, and Sunday afternoons. Admission $1.

Littleton Historical Society, One Union Street (lower level of the 1894 town office building), Littleton. In summer open every Wednesday and Saturday 1:30–4:30. A large collection of local items includes stereoscopic slides (unique photographs published by the famous Kilburn Brothers of Littleton).

Crossroads of America (869-3919), corner of Trudeau Road and Route 302, Bethlehem. Open June through foliage season 9–6; closed Monday. A must-stop for rail fans: the world's largest ³⁄₁₆-scale model railroad on public exhibit. Tours offered every hour. Admission fee.

SCENIC DRIVES

I-93, the parkway through Franconia Notch, is perhaps too obvious since it is a destination for many visitors to New Hampshire. It is one of the state's most scenic corridors, so take your time to enjoy the views and the many roadside natural attractions.

Route 117 from Franconia Village steeply uphill to Sugar Hill (take the short Sunset Hill Road for breathtaking mountain views), then continue down to Lisbon on Route 302/10, turn north beside the Ammonoosuc River to Littleton, or turn south through Lisbon Village to Bath, with its old country store and covered bridge.

Route 116 follows the valley between Franconia and Easton. Old farms and mountain scenery.

TO DO

AIR RIDES

North Country Flying Service (823-8881), Route 116, Franconia. Open daily late May through October. Glider rides and scenic biplane rides. Flights from $10.

Twin Mountain Airport (846-5505), 300 yards off Route 302, Twin Mountain. Year-round, weather permitting, Joe O'Brien offers sight-seeing flights over Mount Washington and the surrounding area.

BICYCLING

An 8-mile-long bicycle path, used in winter as a cross-country ski trail, traverses Franconia Notch.

GOLF

Bethlehem Golf Course (869-5745), Main Street (Route 302), Bethlehem. Eighteen holes.

Maplewood Golf Course (869-3335), Main Street (Route 302), Bethlehem. Eighteen holes.

Sunset Hill Golf Course (823-5522), Sugar Hill. Nine holes.

Profile Club (823-9568), Franconia. Nine holes.

HIKING

Hiking information is available at the Franconia-Easton-Sugar Hill Chamber of Commerce and the Bethlehem Chamber of Commerce information booths; the Franconia Notch State Park Visitors Center by the

The Franconia Ridge Trail

entrance to the Flume; the park's Lafayette Campground; Cannon Mountain; and the national forest's Ammonoosuc Ranger Station (see entries under *Guidance* and *Green Space*). Franconia Notch offers some of the most rewarding short hikes in the White Mountains. They include:

Artist's Bluff and Bald Mountain. From Route 18 in Franconia Notch State Park, 0.5 mile north of its junction with Route 3. The parking lot is across from Cannon Mountain's Peabody Ski Slopes. Favored by nineteenth-century guests at the notch's former hotels, Bald Mountain is an easy ascent with sweeping views. First you follow an old carriage road to a saddle between two summits, then branch left to Bald Mountain, right to Artist's Bluff. You should investigate both. The round-trip is 1 or 1.8 miles.

Basin-Cascades Trail (3 miles). Start at the Basin, marked from Route 3 in Franconia Notch State Park, and ascend along Cascade Brook leading to the Cascade Brook Trail.

Lonesome Lake Trail. From Lafayette Place on Route 3 in Franconia Notch, an old bridle path leads to an 80-acre lake that sits at an elevation of 2,734 feet and is warm enough in summer for swimming. The Appalachian Mountain Club's Lonesome Lake Hut offers overnight lodging and a variety of family-geared programs. Contact the AMC Pinkham Notch Camp (466-2727).

Mount Lafayette via the Old Bridle Path. This is a full day's hike, and you should pick up a detailed map before attempting it. After 2.5 miles you reach the AMC Greenleaf Hut (for lodging phone 466-2727); the summit—with magnificent views—is another 1.1 miles. If the weather

ROBERT J. KOZLOW

is good and your energy high, continue along the Franconia Ridge Trail south over Mount Lincoln to Little Haystack. This narrow, rocky route is spectacular, but there are steep drops on both sides of the trail. At Little Haystack turn right (west) on the Falling Waters Trail. This trail passes more waterfalls in 2.8 miles than any other trail in the mountains; it ends back at Lafayette Place.

HORSEBACK RIDING

Franconia Inn (823-5542), Route 116, Franconia.

Mittersill Riding Stable (823-5511), Mittersill Resort, Route 18, Franconia.

CROSS-COUNTRY SKIING

White Mountain National Forest. Detailed maps of all these trails are available from the Franconia-Easton-Sugar Hill Chamber of Commerce, at Cannon Mountain, and from the Ammonoosuc Ranger Station (see *Guidance* and *Downhill Skiing*).

Lafayette Trails, Route 3, Franconia Notch. The Notchway Trail is the old Route 3 road bed, accessed from Route 141 just east of I-93, Exit 36. It's identified by a metal sign with a skier symbol. The trail is 2.1 miles, and side loops include the short Bog Trail, the more difficult Scarface Trail (1.2 miles), and the Bickford Trail (0.3 mile).

The Pemi Trail, Franconia Notch. Just over 6 miles long, this trail extends from Profile Lake to the Flume parking lot and is open to cross-country skiers, snowshoers, and hikers. It can also be accessed from the Echo Lake, tramway, and Flume parking areas. Pick up a map at the information booth at the Cannon Mountain base lodge in Franconia Notch.

Beaver Brook Cross Country Trails begin at the Beaver Brook Wayside on Route 3 between Twin Mountain and Franconia Notch. The Beaver Loop is 2.3 km, Badger is a more difficult 3.1 km, and Moose Watch is classified as "most difficult," a total of 8.6 km with some spectacular views. These trails are ungroomed and not regularly patrolled, so be sure not to ski alone.

Zealand Valley Trails. See *Cross-Country Skiing* in "Mount Washington's Valleys—Crawford Notch and Bretton Woods."

Franconia Inn (823-5542; 1-800-473-5299), Easton Road, maintains 29 miles of trails, and an additional 15 miles meander across this 1,100-foot-high valley. Rentals and lessons available.

Sunset Hill House Touring Center (823-5522; 1-800-SUN-HILL), Sunset Hill Road, Sugar Hill. Sixty km of groomed trails from this hilltop inn. Ski shop.

DOWNHILL SKIING

Cannon Mountain (823-5563), Route 3, Franconia. One of New Hampshire's oldest ski mountains, state-owned Cannon has a whopping 2,146-foot vertical drop. Its aerial tram (the country's first, in the 1930s) was replaced in the 1980s, and snowmaking has since been substantially increased to cover 85 percent of the 28 trails. Lifts include two quad chairs, a triple, and two doubles as well as the tram. While its image remains "The Mountain That'll Burn Your Boots Off!," in reality many trails have recently been softened—broadened and smoothed as well as carpeted with snowmaking. In addition to runs in Franconia Notch itself, more than a dozen intermediate and beginner runs meander down the mountain's gentler northern face to the Peabody Slopes base area. The only trails still "au naturel" are Taft Slalom (a remnant of that 1920s racing trail) and the Hardscrabbles—both of which command their own following.

SNOWMOBILING

In Franconia Notch the bike path serves in winter as a corridor connector for the 100-mile network of snowmobile trails in this area. Twin Mountain is a popular snowmobiling center. Some winter weekends are as busy as those in the summer. Many motels and lodges have trails right from the door that connect to a large trail network. For maps and other information write **Twin Mountain Snowmobile Club,** Box 179, Twin Mountain 03595; the **Trails Bureau** (271-3254), New Hampshire Division of Parks and Recreation, Box 856, Concord 03301; or the **New Hampshire Snowmobile Association** (224-8906), Box 38, Concord 03301. (Also see "Mount Washington's Valleys—Crawford Notch and Bretton Woods.")

GREEN SPACE

Franconia Notch State Park (823-5563). This 6,440-acre park runs between the Franconia and Kinsmen mountain ranges and contains many of the White Mountains' most notable natural sights. As it passes through the 8 miles of the notch, I-93 is scaled down to the Franconia Notch Parkway (Route 3), built (after a 25-year controversy) to funnel traffic through with minimum scenic and environmental impact. The principal sights of the notch are all within the park and easily accessible from the parkway.

The **State Park Visitors Center** by the entrance to the Flume provides information and shows interpretive films of the area. It also has a snack bar, rest rooms, and a souvenir shop. A $10 combination ticket is available—good for a round-trip tramway ride and admission to both the Flume and Echo Lake beach.

The Flume. An 800-foot-long, deep and narrow gorge—no more than 20 feet wide but up to 90 feet high—through which Flume Brook flows. A system of staircases and boardwalks takes visitors through the Flume to Ridge Path, which leads to Liberty Cascade and on to Sentinel Pine covered bridge that overlooks a clear mountain pool. The Wildwood Path loops past giant boulders brought down by the glaciers and returns to the Flume entrance. Admission charge is $5.50.

GEORGE A. SYLVESTER

The Flume at Franconia Notch State Park

Echo Lake. A 28-acre lake at an elevation of 1,931 feet, the mirrorlike surface of which perfectly reflects Mount Lafayette and Cannon Mountain. There are picnic tables, a swimming beach, a boat-launching area, and 10 sites for RV hookups. Admission is $2 per adult weekdays, $2.50 weekends.

Cannon Mountain. One of New Hampshire's most popular ski areas and the site of America's first aerial tramway. The present tramway, which replaced the 1938 original in 1980, carries 80 passengers to the summit of the 4,180-foot-high mountain, where there is an observation tower and the panoramic Rim Trail. Besides operating during ski season, the tram runs from late May through Columbus Day, when autumn colors are usually at or near peak. A round-trip tram ticket is $7. (Also see *Downhill Skiing.*)

The Old Man of the Mountain. The famous 40-foot-high rock formation—the state's official symbol—resembles the profile of a craggy-featured male. (The pioneers who discovered the profile in 1805 thought it looked like Thomas Jefferson.) The great stone face juts out from a sheer cliff above Profile Lake, and the best view and photograph is from the lakeshore.

The Basin. A deep glacial pothole or natural pool almost 30 feet in diameter created over eons by the churning action of water rushing down from the nearby waterfall.

The Rocks (444-6228), Route 302, RFD 1, Bethlehem 03574. Owned by the Society for the Protection of New Hampshire Forests (SPNHF), this estate with its huge barns is the northern headquarters for the state's largest and most active conservation organization. The estate's 1,200 acres are managed as a tree farm by the SPNHF; a large area is reserved as a Christmas-tree plantation. Trees are sold during the annual Christmas tree celebration held in December. There are various conservation and family programs (see *Special Events*) held through the year, plus a self-guided nature trail and cross-country skiing.

Bretzfelder Park (444-6228; 869-2683), Prospect Street, Bethlehem. Owned by the SPNHF, this 77-acre site is managed as a community park, with various summer programs plus picnic tables, fishing, and a nature trail.

LODGING

RESORT

Mittersill (823-5511), Franconia Notch 03580. A 500-acre, Tyrolean-style resort developed just after World War II. Plans call for a new lift to connect Mittersill's state-owned slopes with the Cannon trail system. There is a dining room and lounge in the central Alpine Lodge and riding stables on the grounds. Accommodations include hotel rooms, efficiency units, one- and two-bedroom suites, and free-standing chalets. All units except the hotel rooms have fully equipped kitchens and are furnished with linens, towels, and TV. Room rates start at $45, efficiencies $60, suites $75, and chalets $180.

INNS

Lovett's Inn (823-7761; 1-800-356-3802), by Lafayette Brook, Route 118, Franconia 03580. A venerable inn, parts of which date to the eighteenth century, Lovett's has a fine view of Cannon Mountain and an established reputation for food and wine (see *Dining Out*). Built in 1784, the inn today has 6 rooms with fieldstone fireplaces and exposed 200-year-old hand-hewn beams, plus 20 fireplaced rooms in cottages. All rooms, with kings, queens, and doubles, are mostly furnished with antiques. There is a pool and outdoor spa, and the place is close to Cannon Mountain. MAP $90–138 for two, depending on weekdays or weekend.

Franconia Inn (823-5542; 1-800-473-5299), Route 116, Franconia 03580. Founded just after the Civil War, the 34-room Franconia Inn was rebuilt after a fire in 1934; its decor and ambience remain those of about a half-century ago. It is a pleasant period piece that appeals to active people who like genteel, old-fashioned surroundings. Available activities include horseback riding, tennis, cross-country skiing, sleigh rides, and gliding. Amenities include a paneled library and a heated pool. Wheelchair ramp and accessible rooms on the first floor. Rates are from $58 to $108 per couple depending on season and accommodations. Also a variety of MAP, B&B, and multi-night plans available.

The Ammonoosuc Inn (838-6118), Bishop Road, Lisbon 03585. Open year-round. A nineteenth-century farmhouse positioned on a knoll above the Ammonoosuc River. In the 1920s its fields were smoothed into golf links, and in recent years an outdoor pool and clay tennis court have been added. In winter Cannon Mountain is just a 15-minute drive and Bretton Woods, 30 minutes. The inn has cross-country trails on its own 136 acres. Innkeepers Steven and Laura Bromley have renovated the nine rooms (each with private bath) and turned the old carriage house into attractive condominiums ranging in size from one to three bedrooms. Cobblers, the inn's restaurant, is popular locally (see *Dining Out*). Common space includes two spacious parlor rooms, a lounge with a full bar, and a big wraparound porch. Rates are $49–79 per room, $90–200 for condominiums. Rates include a continental breakfast; MAP rates also available.

Ledgeland Inn and Cottages (823-5341), RR 1, Box 94, Sugar Hill 03585. Built as a rustic private home, and managed by the Whipple family for nearly 50 years, the inn itself has 9 rooms and is open from late June until mid-October. The 14 cottage units are open year-round and have fireplaces, kitchens, and fine views of the Franconia range. Daily rates start at $60 for double inn rooms; $74 for cottages.

The Hilltop Inn (823-5695), Main Street, Sugar Hill 03585. Owners Meri and Mike Hern welcome guests to this 1895 Victorian inn in the middle of sleepy Sugar Hill. Amenities include private baths for all six rooms, period antiques, English flannel sheets, sunsets from the deck, and very large breakfasts. Children over four and well-behaved pets welcome. Rates per couple from $60 to $110 depending on the season. Dinners by reservation only served Wednesday through Saturday from June to October, and Friday through Saturday from end of December through March (see *Dining Out*).

Sunset Hill House (823-5522; 1-800-SUNHILL), Sunset Hill Road, Sugar

Hill 03585. Open all year. Built in 1880 as the annex for a large hotel, this 23-room inn with its own 7-room annex has been completely renovated and remodeled by its new owners, the Coyle family. High on a ridge, the view from the five dining rooms and many of the guest rooms stretches from the Franconia range to the Presidential range, perhaps the most striking panorama in the mountains. All guest rooms are freshly decorated with comforters and coordinated fabrics, antique and reproduction furniture, and private baths. Beds are kings, queens, and doubles. There are three parlors and a small bar, and a golf course across the street. B&B $70–90, MAP $110–160. Dinner by reservation only to the public (see *Dining Out*).

Sugar Hill Inn (823-5621; 1-800-548-4748), Route 117, Franconia 03580. A gracious, restored colonial-era farmhouse with 10 rooms in the main house and 4 in adjacent cottages. Nonsmoking. Afternoon tea and full breakfast. Barbara and Jim Quinn, innkeepers. Rates $92–124 per couple. Dinner also available (see *Dining Out*).

Horse & Hound Inn (823-5501; 1-800-450-5501), Wells Road, Franconia 03580. Built in the 1830s as a farmhouse, the 10-room Horse and Hounds was converted to an inn just after World War II by an enthusiastic horseman who was master of a hunt, hence the name. Lots of pine paneling and fireplaces; the dining room specializes in Continental cuisine (see *Dining Out*). Rates for a double room are from $60 with full breakfast, $100 with full dinner and breakfast.

The Beal House Inn (444-2661), 247 West Main Street, Littleton 03561. Open year-round. Another New Hampshire classic recently expanded to offer dining, this inn has 14 rooms, all furnished with antiques (most of which are for sale), and all rooms but 2 have private baths. The rooms vary in size; the smaller ones are cozy and comfortable. Beds range from twins to kings, and some have canopies. A common room with plenty of books and a game room. Hot tea is available any time and complimentary drinks and refreshments are served in the afternoon and evening. Continental breakfast includes Belgian waffles cooked by your Belgian host. Rates for two are $50–75, depending on season and accommodations. French cuisine served Wednesday through Saturday in two intimate dining rooms (see *Dining Out*). Catherine and Jean-Marie (John) Fisher-Motheu, innkeepers.

Thayer's Inn (444-6469; 1-800-634-8179), 136 Main Street, Littleton 03561. Open year-round. Listed on the National Register of Historic Places, this in-town hotel has been welcoming White Mountain travelers since it was built in 1843. Most of the 40 rooms have private baths, TV, and telephones. Each room is individually furnished so guests are invited to select their own room on arrival. The two-bedroom suites are great for families. Coffee shop, restaurant, and lounge on the premises. Don and Carolyn Lambert, innkeepers. EP $30–40, two-bedroom suites $70 for up to four people.

Wayside Inn (869-3364; 1-800-448-9557), Route 302 at Pierce Bridge, Bethlehem 03574. A historic eighteenth-century inn building with an attached modern motel. The inn's Riverview Restaurant is one of the area's best (see *Dining Out*). Room rates from $42; suites start at $65.

BED & BREAKFASTS

Bungay Jar (823-7775), PO Box 15, Easton Valley Road, Franconia 03580. An enlarged eighteenth-century barn, moved to a wooded riverside and mountain-view site, that owners Kate Kerivan and Lee Strimbeck have filled with an eclectic antiques collection. Amenities include king-size suites, skylights, a sauna, huge old-fashioned tubs (one belonged to Benny Goodman), a two-story common room, afternoon tea, and a full country breakfast. Rates are from $60 per couple.

Blanche's B&B (823-7061), Box 75, Easton Valley Road, Franconia 03580. A homey last-century farmhouse, with five guest rooms (one queen, the rest doubles) sharing two baths. Owners Brenda Shannon and John Vail got turned on to B&Bs in England. Antique furnishings are accented by Brenda's artistic talents. She works with decorative wall coverings such as stenciling and wall glazing and also does hand-painted floorcloths (canvas rugs), which are for sale in her studio. No smoking. Full breakfast served. $60–65 per couple.

Foxglove, A Country Inn (823-8840), Route 117, Sugar Hill 03585. Open all year. This newly renovated, designer-decorated, turn-of-the-century country home has been turned into a cozy B&B. The grounds are beautiful, with extensive gardens, fruit trees, a small pond, hammocks, and outside terrace. Six rooms have private baths, with colorful wallpapers and linens. Two of the rooms form a small suite complete with kitchen and sitting room. A sun room overlooks the backyard and a common room has a fireplace and lots of books. The full gourmet breakfast is cooked to order. Using the innkeepers' extensive collections of china, crystal, and linens, place settings are changed daily. $85–95 per couple.

The Homestead (823-5564), on Route 117, Sugar Hill 03585. This family-run inn traces its history back to Sugar Hill's first settlers, some seven generations ago. The main building of this 20-room place is a former farmhouse, which has been an inn since 1880. Rooms are filled with family antiques and heirlooms; the dining room is decorated with hand-painted plates depicting local scenes and events. Free cross-country skiing and downhill skiing packages available. Full three-course country breakfast. Rates from $70 per couple.

Adair (444-2600), Old Littleton Road at the junction of I-93 and Route 302, Box 359, Bethlehem 03574. Open all year except late March to early June. This deluxe Georgian colonial was built in 1927 as a wedding gift and has only recently become an elegant country inn. Located at the end of a winding driveway on some 200 acres, it has extensive landscaping and a tennis court. Eight luxurious guest rooms have private baths, king or queen beds, and are furnished with antiques or reproductions. There are comfortable dining and living rooms with fire-places, a cozy library, a sun porch, and a tap room with games, TV, and VCR. Guests are served afternoon tea, bar setups are provided, and a full breakfast is served. Patricia and Hardy Banfield, innkeepers. $125–175.

Maplewood Inn (869-5869), Main Street, Bethlehem 03574. Six rooms, four with bath. No smoking, pets, or children under 12. Two-day mini-mum. Rates are $65–80 per couple.

The Mulburn Inn (869-3389), Main Street, Bethlehem 03574. Two sisters and their husbands run this spacious mansion that has been converted into a seven-room B&B. All rooms have private baths with kings, queens, doubles, or twin beds. Large wraparound porches and spacious grounds. Full country breakfast. Bob and Cheryl Burns, Moe and Linda Mulkigian, innkeepers. Rates from $55 to $80.

Northern Zermatt Inn and Motel (846-5533; 1-800-535-3214), Route 3, Twin Mountain 03595. Open May to October. Seventeen rooms (each of eight rooms in the inn has a queen or a double bed, each of seven rooms in the motel has two doubles, and there are two cottage suites), all with private baths, TV, and air-conditioning. Three motel rooms have kitchens. Swimming pool, picnic area, and lawn games. Country break-fast bar. Joe and Sheila Terra, innkeepers. Rates from $38 to $78.

MOTELS

The Red Coach Inn (1-800-COACH-93), PO Box 729, Franconia 03580. The 60-room Red Coach Inn is the newest and largest hostelry in the area. Amenities include a heated indoor swimming pool, sauna, and Jacuzzi. There is also a gift shop, beauty shop, fitness room, and a full-service restaurant. Rates for a couple $52.50–85.

Gale River (823-5655; 1-800-255-7989), Route 18, Franconia 03580. The motel building has 10 rooms, and there are 4 cottages with 1 to 5 bed-rooms, rentable by the week. Amenities include in-room coffeemakers, refrigerators, TV, and telephones, plus heated pool, whirlpool, and hot tub. Rates for a double from $55. Cottages, which sleep 6 to 12, start at $95 with a 5-day minimum; weekly rates begin at $450.

Raynor's Motor Lodge (823-9586; 1-800-634-8187), at junction of Routes 18 and 142, Franconia 03580. Thirty rooms, about half air-conditioned. Heated pool, coffee shop, and bar. Doubles from $36.

✑ **Stonybrook Motor Lodge** (823-8192; 1-800-722-3552), Route 18, Franconia 03580. Two heated pools. Doubles from $51, June to mid-October. Kids free.

Twin Mountain has many motels. Among them are **Carlson's Lodge** (846-5501), **Paquette's Motel and Restaurant** (846-5562), and **Profile Deluxe Motel** (846-5522).

LODGE

✑ **Pinestead Farm Lodge** (823-8121), Route 116, Franconia 03580. Pinestead has been taking in guests since 1899 but is still a working farm run by the

Sherburn family. The locally renowned Pinestead quilts are made on the premises. The nine rooms are in clusters of three with shared baths and fully equipped kitchens. The three-room units can be rented by families or groups. There is a children's play yard, tennis court, and other lawn games, plus easy access to fishing, hiking, downhill and cross-country skiing. Room rate for a couple from $30.

CONDOMINIUM

Village at Maplewood (869-2111; 1-800-873-2111), Main Street (Route 302), Maplewood 03574. Twenty condo townhouse units are available for daily or weekly rental. Rates from $100 a night.

CAMPS

Several **Appalachian Mountain Club High Huts** (466-2727), Box 298, Gorham 03581, are located in this area. Nearest to Route 302 off Zealand Road is the **Zealand Hut** (2.8-mile hike); adjacent to I-93 in Franconia Notch are **Lonesome Lake** on the west side of the highway and **Greenleaf Hut** (2.5-mile hike) on the east. Lonesome Lake is the nearest AMC hut to a road, just 1.7 miles and a mild one-hour walk (our five-year-old daughter made it with ease); there is swimming and fishing in the lake. On the trail between Greenleaf and Zealand is **Galehead**. You must hike to the huts and supply your clothes and towels; they provide meals, bunks, and blankets. Some AMC programs involve guided hikes to the huts. Contact the AMC for rates and other information, and see the *AMC White Mountain Guide* for trail routes.

CAMPGROUNDS

WMNF campgrounds are located along Route 302, east of Twin Mountain. Sugarloaf I and II have 62 sites, and Zealand has 11 sites. The Sugarloaf sites are part of the **toll-free reservation system**, 1-800-283-2267. (See *Campgrounds* under "Mount Washington's Valleys—Mount Washington and Pinkham Notch.")

Lafayette Campground (823-5563), a popular state park facility just off the parkway in the heart of Franconia Notch, has 97 wooded tent sites available on a first-come, first-served basis. A central lodge has showers and a small store with hiking and camping supplies. Site fees are $8–17.

Echo Lake in Franconia Notch also has 10 sites for RV hookups.

Local private campgrounds include **Fransted Campground** (823-5675), Route 18, Franconia, with 65 wooded tent sites and 26 trailer sites; and **Apple Hill Campground** (869-2238), Route 142 north, Bethlehem, with 45 tent sites, 20 trailer hookups, a store, and a bathhouse.

WHERE TO EAT

DINING OUT

Franconia Inn (823-5542), Easton Road, Franconia. Dinner nightly 6–9. Long considered the local restaurant for elegant dining and special occasions, the Franconia Inn's handsome candlelit dining rooms offer black-tie service and a mountain view. Cocktails are served in the cozy, paneled Rathskeller Lounge. The à la carte menu features American and Continental cuisine and changes frequently. Typical entrées are saltimbocca, filet mignon with smoked veal breast, shrimp primavera, and veal medallions au champagne. Expensive.

Lovett's by Lafayette Brook (823-7761), Profile Road, Franconia. Dinner nightly 6–8. This old inn is well known for its fine food and wine. Drinks are served in an intimate lounge, with a marble bar from a Newport, Rhode Island, mansion, and the notable four-course menu is served in three connecting open-beamed dining rooms. Soups are frequently unusual and may include cold bisque of fresh watercress, black bean soup with Demarara rum, and wild blueberry soup. Entrées might include chicken with apples and Calvados, curried lamb with grape chutney, baked duck, and sautéed Norwegian salmon or poached Colorado trout. Reservations only. Moderate to expensive.

The Hilltop Inn (823-5695), Main Street, Sugar Hill. Dinners by reservation only served Wednesday through Saturday from June to October, and Friday through Saturday from the end of December through March. The menu changes weekly, and the six entrées might include Delmonico steak, fillet of salmon, roast pork, tuna fillet, breast of chicken, or pasta. Moderate.

Sunset Hill House (823-5522; 1-800-SUNHILL), Sunset Hill Road, Sugar Hill. Dining by reservation only, 5:30–9:30. Candlelight dining in five dining rooms, with a fireplace, in this recently renovated old inn. The menu changes seasonally and may include roast leg of lamb, pepper-stuffed beef tenderloin, rainbow trout with hash brown cakes and walnut sauce, or cassoulet with white beans, confit of duck and sausage. Distinctive appetizers, soups, salads, and desserts. Moderate.

Sugar Hill Inn (823-5621; 1-800-548-4748), Route 117, Franconia. Dinner, by reservation only, served nightly during foliage season; two sittings, at 6 and 8. Thursday through Monday the rest of the year, 6 and 8. The four-course dinners range from tenderloin of pork with red currant sauce to stuffed chicken with wild rice, and fish of the day to French-cut rack of lamb with herb and rosemary crumbs. $25.

The Beal House Inn (444-2661), 247 West Main Street, Littleton. Open year-round. Authentic French cuisine served Wednesday through Saturday in two intimate dining rooms. The menu, which changes every two weeks, includes steaks, seafood, lamb (noisettes of lamb served with red currant sauce topped with toasted pine nuts), and duck or chicken. Appetizers and rich desserts to match the entrées. The wine list offers 300 varieties and throughout the year there are special wine-tasting dinners. Moderate.

Tim-bir Alley (444-6142), 28 Main Street, Littleton. Dinner Wednesday to Sunday 5:30–9:30; Sunday brunch 9–1. Cash or check only, no reservations. Fine dining has come to the North Country with this seven-table gourmet restaurant, serving an eclectic menu that changes weekly and features six nightly entrées and homemade desserts. Entrées might include salmon with Brie and walnut cream; scaloppine with date and pecan sauce; or mixed grill with lamb, veal, and beef, each one enhanced separately with herbs and sauces. Each entrée is beautifully presented, making the dining experience as exciting for the eye as it is for the palate. Moderate.

Cobblers (838-6118), Bishop Road, Lisbon. Open for dinner nightly except Monday in winter. The pleasant dining room in the Ammonoosuc Inn offers entrées like chicken Pommery (chicken pieces with peppers and onions sautéed in a Pommery mustard sauce, served over linguine) for $12.95, or shrimp and scallops jambalaya for $13.95. It's a large menu.

Horse & Hound Inn (823-5501), off Route 18, Franconia. Open nightly except Tuesday, 6–9. The dining room of this small, traditional inn is paneled and warm; drinks are served in the cozy, book-lined combination library and lounge. The nightly menu includes beef, chicken, veal, and seafood dishes, prepared with a French flair. Prices moderate to expensive.

The Riverview Restaurant (869-3364; 1-800-448-9557), Route 302 at Pierce Bridge, Bethlehem. Open nightly, except Monday, spring through fall, Thursday through Sunday in winter, 6–9. The dining room of the Wayside Inn, the Riverview has long been regarded as the town's toniest restaurant. The inn's Pierce Lounge is also a popular drinking spot. The European-born owners, Victor and Kathe Hoffmann, emphasize Continental cuisine. Swiss specialties are served every Friday night, but fondue is always available in ski season. Prime rib tops the menu on Saturday.

EATING OUT

☞ **Polly's Pancake Parlor** (823-5575), Route 117, Sugar Hill. Housed in an 1830s former carriage house with a grand mountain view, Polly's is a local institution with a menu that includes cob-smoked bacon and just about every kind of pancake known, from blueberry to walnut. Nice atmosphere. Reasonable prices.

Franconia Village House Restaurant (823-5405), Main Street, Franconia. Open for breakfast, lunch, dinner year-round. Good family-style American fare: soups, chili, bulky sandwiches, and pastas (made fresh daily).

Dutch Treat Restaurant (823-8851), Main Street, Franconia Village. A local standby. The dining room features Italian entrées and the adjoining Sports Lounge serves homemade pizza and screens sports events and classic movies on its giant TV screen.

Lloyd Hills (869-2141), Main Street, Bethlehem. Pleasant, informal, pub-style restaurant. Moderate.

Rosa Flamingo's (869-3111), Main Street, Bethlehem. Cheery and infor-

ROBERT J. KOZLOW

Polly's Pancake Parlor in Sugar Hill

mal, serving a variety of Italian dishes. Moderate.

Cannonball Café and Deli (823-7478), Main Street, Franconia Village. Sandwiches, salads, and specialty dishes to eat in or take out. Unusual sandwiches include Brie, apple, and walnut on French bread. The menu also features offbeat international dishes such as "Himalayan Hen," a Cornish game hen marinated in fresh garlic, ginger, coriander, and other exotic spices.

The Clamshell (444-6445), Dells Road, Littleton. Monday to Saturday 11:30–4; Monday to Thursday 5–9, Friday and Saturday until 10; Sun-

day brunch 11–2. Just off Exit 42 of I-93, this is a popular seafood restaurant serving lobster, steaks, and prime rib; also sandwiches and a
salad bar.

SELECTIVE SHOPPING

Franconia Marketplace, Main Street, Franconia. Selling only products
made in Franconia, this complex in the heart of town houses the **Grate-
ful Bread Quality Bakery** (823-5228), which makes whole-grain and
organic breads; **Cannonball Café and Deli** (823-7478), serving fresh
sandwiches, salads, and international dishes; **Gale River Outlet,** with
more than 100 styles of cotton clothes and sleepwear; and **Tiffany
Workshop** (823-5539), featuring crystal jewelry, candles, and air-
brushed shirts.

Sugar Hill Sampler, Route 117, Sugar Hill. A 1780s barn with a folksy
pioneer museum and a large selection of candies, cheese, crafts, and
antiques.

Harmons Cheese and Country Store (823-8000), Route 117, Sugar Hill.
The specialty is well-aged cheddar, but the store also stocks maple sugar
products and gourmet items.

Bungay Jar (823-7775), Route 116, Easton. An eclectic collection of antiques in an eighteenth-century barn; also a B&B (see *Bed & Breakfasts*).

Abigail's Antiques (869-5550), Bethlehem Flower Farm, Main Street
(Route 302), Bethlehem. Antiques and reproductions. Also on Main
Street are a number of seasonal antiques shops.

Littleton Stamp and Coin Company (444-5386), 253 Union Street,
Littleton. A local business with a national reputation for selling and
buying stamps and coins.

The Village Bookstore (444-5263), Main Street, Littleton. Open daily.
The largest and most complete bookstore (and one of the state's best)
north of the mountains.

SPECIAL EVENTS

February: **Forest Festival** (444-6228), the Rocks Estate, Route 302,
Bethlehem. A mid-February day in the woods with logging demonstrations plus snowshoeing and cross-country skiing. **Frostbite Follies.** A
week-long series of events around Franconia, including sleigh rides, ski
movies, broom hockey, ski races, community suppers.

April: **Maple Season Tours** (444-6228), the Rocks Estate, Route 302,
Bethlehem. Early April weekend features a workshop about maple
trees; also learn about gathering sap and boiling it down to make maple
syrup.

June: **Wildflower Festival** (444-6228), the Rocks Estate, Route 302,

Bethlehem. Guided walks, workshops, demonstrations, and a children's walk on a Sunday in early June. **Open for the Season Celebration,** Bethlehem. Old-fashioned festival that includes golf tournament, crafts fair, and ball. Last weekend of the month. **Old Man in the Mountains USA and Canada Rugby Matches,** Cannon Mountain House Field, Route 116, Franconia.

July: **North Country Chamber Players,** Sugar Hill. Classical concerts Friday at 8 P.M. in the Sugar Hill Meeting House. **Hayseed Blue Grass Festival,** Dow Strip, Franconia. Bluegrass and fiddle music played outside. **Day Lily Festival,** Bethlehem.

August: **Horse Show,** Mittersill Resort, Franconia.

September: **Franconia Scramble,** Franconia. A 6.2-mile footrace over Franconia roads. **New England Boiled Dinner,** the town house, Franconia. Corned beef and all the fixings. **Annual Antique Show and Sale,** Sugar Hill Meeting House. Selected dealers of antiques and collectibles.

October: **Quilt Festival,** Franconia. **Durrell Methodist Church Bazaar,** Franconia, Saturday of Columbus Day weekend. **Crafts Fair,** Elementary School, Bethlehem, Sunday of Columbus Day weekend. **The Halloween Tradition** (444-6228), the Rocks Estate, Route 302, Bethlehem. Ghosts and goblins haunt the estate in a program co-sponsored by local Boy and Girl Scouts; also apple bobbing, pumpkin carving, and ghost stories told around the fire.

December: **Oh! Christmas Tree** (444-6228), the Rocks Estate, Route 302, Bethlehem. Weekends in early December. Celebrate Christmas with wreath making, ornament making, and a hay-wagon tour of the Christmas-tree plantation. Pick your own tree to cut. Tree sales daily in December.

Mount Washington's Valleys

The first recorded "tourist" in the White Mountains was Darby Field, who walked into the so-called "crystal-hills" in 1642 and climbed the highest peak—probably the first person ever to climb the mountain, since Native Americans considered it the home of the Great Spirit, a holy place to be feared and avoided by mortals. Some 350 years have passed since Field's first visit, and now approximately 250,000 people a year walk and ride to the summit of Mount Washington, the highest point in the Northeast and the focal point of the valleys east, south, and west of the mountain.

Despite Field's early visit, it was to be more than 150 years before tourism had an impact on this region. The industry began in the early 1800s when small inns served only a few visitors among the commercial travelers, men who hauled goods and supplies by wagon from the sea-coast to the villages south of the mountains and through Crawford Notch to the settlements beyond. The roads were rough and the accommodations worse, so those early travelers had to be adventurous by nature. Many of them sought out Mount Washington, attracted by sci-entific reports from geologists and botanists. The Crawford family, for whom the notch is named, might be called the first developers of tour-ism in the mountains. Abel Crawford and his sons, Tom and Ethan Allen, aware that increasing numbers of people were coming to the mountains for pleasure, built inns in the notch, constructed bridle paths into the mountains, led guided hikes (sometimes carrying guests over portions of trails), and advertised their services in Boston newspapers.

Because it was on the major route to the mountains, which fol-lowed the Saco River through Crawford Notch, the village of Conway began catering to visitors. A sleepy farming community, Conway had five inns by 1825, becoming the hotel center of the region. Tourists reached the mountains by stage and private coaches, but it was the ex-tension of railroads into the region that opened up the mountains to vast numbers of visitors and created the basis for the hospitality we enjoy today. By 1876, for example, when the West was still wild and settlers and Native Americans were at war, formally dressed ladies and gentlemen from the eastern cities could ride by train to luxurious hotels in the mountains, transfer to the Cog Railway to ride up Mount Wash-

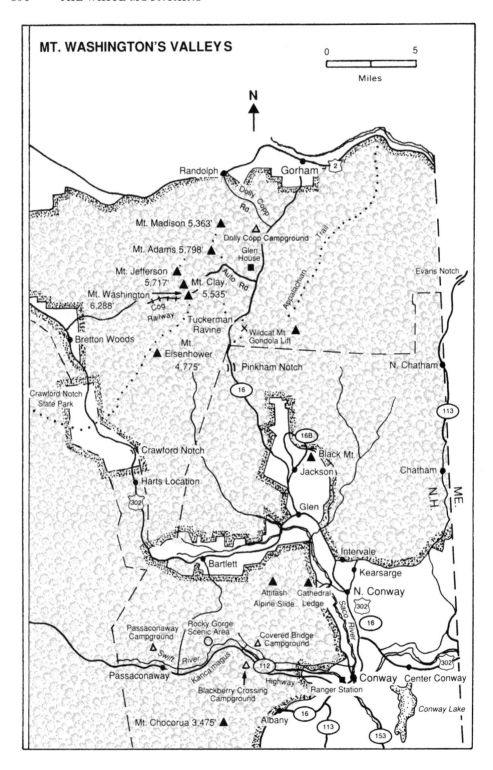

MT. WASHINGTON'S VALLEYS

0 — 5
Miles

N

Randolph · Gorham · 2

Dolly Copp Rd.

Mt. Madison 5,363' ▲ △ Dolly Copp Campground

Mt. Adams 5,798' ▲ Glen House ■

Mt. Jefferson ▲ Auto Rd.
5,717' ▲ Mt. Clay 5,535'

Mt. Washington ▲
6,288' Cog Railway

Tuckerman Ravine

× Wildcat Mt. ▲
Gondola Lift

Bretton Woods · Mt. Eisenhower 4,775' ▲

Appalachian Trail

Evans Notch

Pinkham Notch

16

N. Chatham

Crawford Notch State Park

16B

Black Mt. ▲

113

Crawford Notch · Jackson

Harts Location ● Chatham

302 Glen

N.H. ME.

Intervale
Kearsarge
Bartlett ▲ Attitash Alpine Slide ▲ Cathedral Ledge N. Conway

Saco River 302

16

Passaconaway Campground △

Rocky Gorge Scenic Area ○

Covered Bridge Campground △

Swift River Kancamagus 112 Highway

302

Conway · Center Conway

Passaconaway

Blackberry Crossing Campground Ranger Station

Conway Lake

Mt. Chocorua 3,475' ▲ Albany

16

113 153

ington, spend a night in a summit hotel, then travel by carriage down the eastern side of the mountain to connect with a stage for a trip back to the railroad line. The three-day journey cost $17. The golden age of White Mountains hotels was under way, and the region had more beds for overnight visitors than at any time since, except for the past few years when development has again boomed. Years ago it was a prosperous summer business, and many guests came with trunks for vacations of a month or more.

The work of well-known artists and writers spread the fame of the White Mountains, and religious leaders set up tents and preached to crowds daily. Trenchermen, industrialists of the day, clad in suits and bulging at the waist, sat down to three huge daily meals and rocked away their days on wide verandas before the high mountain peaks. Several hotels accommodated 500 or more guests, and hotel owners bought farms to raise their own produce; generated their own lights and power; built ponds, hiking trails, golf courses, and tennis courts; and maintained post offices.

Fires and automobiles changed the business after a few decades. Many large hotels regrettably burned and were not replaced, and the auto provided mobility. It was no longer necessary to stay at one resort for a month; and, although the rates seem low by today's prices, many visitors couldn't afford to stay at the fancy hotels. The budgets of the middle-class travelers led to the development of cabin colonies and eventually motels. Those hotels that didn't burn were eventually closed and torn down, and none of the major hotels of the Victorian era in the White Mountains remains today, except for the Mount Washington Hotel, which was built in 1912.

A few hardy folks used to enjoy the mountains in the winter, especially for snowshoeing, skating, or sleigh rides. Clubs and other groups came by train for winter weekends, often staying with farmers or in small inns since the large hotels were closed. It was great sport for a few but nothing on which to build an industry. In the 1920s New Englanders "discovered" skiing, a way of life and a sport enjoyed in Europe for centuries. Later, in 1938, businessman Harvey Gibson built the famous Mount Cranmore Skimobile and a year later brought Austrian ski instructor Hannes Schneider to North Conway. Soon the region had another season for tourists, and since then the mountains have never been the same. There are now six downhill ski areas and two cross-country areas within 20 miles of North Conway.

Not to be overlooked in the development of tourism is the impact of folks who appreciate the outdoors and the mountains themselves. During the nineteenth century most of the mountains were owned by logging companies, which clear-cut their way up one ridge and down another. While unsightly, the clear-cut areas were also subject to frequent forest fires, and rains and melting snows on the denuded mountainsides eroded the slopes and caused flooding downriver. Organizations such as the Appalachian Mountain Club (AMC), formed in 1877, and the Society for the Protection of New Hampshire Forests, formed in 1903, led the way to the protection of mountains as natural areas; and they continue to work for these purposes. The Weeks Act of 1911 established the White Mountain National Forest as the largest national forest in the East. While the AMC hardly invented hiking, many of its early members were instrumental in constructing trails in the White Mountains; today it not only maintains trails but sponsors group hikes and seminars, publishes guidebooks, and operates a series of high mountain huts open to the public.

Today North Conway is the region's liveliest resort town. A summer haven for nearly 200 years and one of the country's first ski destinations, it's now a major shopping center—with more than 200 shops and factory outlets. And it represents the White Mountains' largest concentration of inns, motels, and restaurants.

The Mount Washington Valley—as North Conway and surrounding villages are generally known—is a particularly appealing winter destination. Its four ski areas—Mount Cranmore, Attitash, Black Mountain, and Wildcat—are each very different and all honor interchangeable tickets. With more than 200 km of cross-country trails between North Conway and Jackson, this is also one of the top places to ski-tour in the East.

The village of Jackson, by contrast, is strictly zoned and far quieter. Here the winter accent is on cross-country skiing, and while there are plenty of inns and a few restaurants, nightlife tends to consist of reading by the fire, relaxing in a hot tub, or skiing under a full moon.

Pinkham Notch, just up Route 16 from Jackson, is the most dramatic pass in the mountains and is less developed than Franconia Notch. There is plenty to do here, especially for those who are able to do some walking. The most popular Mount Washington trail begins at the Appalachian Mountain Club's Pinkham Notch Camp, a center for year-round hiking since the 1920s.

Between Jackson and North Conway is Bartlett. The Route 16 end of Bartlett, the area called Glen, and nearby Attitash Ski Area, with motels, commercial attractions, and restaurants, seems more like North Conway; yet Bartlett Village is quiet and unchanged by recent development.

North of Bartlett is Crawford Notch, the least developed and among the most magnificent of New Hampshire's high mountain passes. Above this notch, at the western base of New England's highest mountain, the vast white, red-roofed Mount Washington Hotel still stands, a reminder of the other huge summer hotels—the Crawford House, Fabyan's, the Mount Pleasant House, and Twin Mountain—which have vanished with the railroad that used to bring guests. The Mount Washington Hotel's own future is bright now that it has new North Country ownership. In winter the Bretton Woods Resort offers one of New Hampshire's most attractive and least crowded ski areas and one of its most extensive and dependable cross-country trail networks. Year-round the resort offers a choice of restaurants and condominiums, an inn, and a motor lodge. In summer Bretton Woods offers golf, horse-back riding, and the Mount Washington Cog Railway, which has been chugging up the western flank of the mountain since 1869 (see *To See* in "Mount Washington's Valleys—Crawford Notch and Bretton Woods").

Bretton Woods is technically a village in the town of Carroll, for which the commercial center is Twin Mountain, a crossroads village at the junction of Routes 3 and 302. Its motels cater to hikers, skiers, and snowmobilers.

Because there are so many places to stay and dine and things to do in the Mount Washington Valley, this chapter has been broken into several sections: North Conway and Vicinity, Jackson and Bartlett, Mount Washington and Pinkham Notch, Crawford Notch and Bretton Woods, and Evans Notch. (For Twin Mountain, see "The Western Whites—Franconia and North of the Notches"; for Gorham and Jefferson, see "The North Country—Along Route 2.")

GUIDANCE

Mount Washington Valley Chamber of Commerce (356-3171; 1-800-367-3364), Box 2300, North Conway 03860. Free vacation guide, visitor information, and central reservation service. By calling the toll-free number, you can get information and make reservations at 90 lodging properties including condos, resorts, inns, bed & breakfasts, and motels.

State of New Hampshire Information Center, Route 16, Intervale, just north of North Conway. Rest rooms and telephones. Open all year.

Country Inns of the White Mountains (356-9460; outside NH 1-800-562-1300), Box 2025, North Conway 03860. Twenty-two inns (in Tamworth, Eaton, Snowville, Conway, North Conway, Intervale, Bartlett, Jackson, plus Ashland and Campton) are part of this service. Your call is answered in one of the inns, and you can make a reservation with that inn, receive information about the other inns, or have your call transferred to one of the other inns in the group.

(See *Guidance* within each section of this chapter for other chambers of commerce.)

GETTING THERE

By car: Route 16 threads through the valley, bringing visitors north from Boston and places south to Conway, Glen, Jackson, and Pinkham Notch and connecting with Route 2 in Gorham. Route 302, from Portland, joins Route 16 south of North Conway, then at Glen branches west through Bartlett and Crawford Notch to Bretton Woods and connects with Route 3 at Twin Mountain.

By bus: **Concord Trailways** (1-800-852-3317), provides scheduled service from Boston's Logan Airport to central and northern New Hampshire via Manchester, Concord, and Meredith. Mount Washington Valley stops, via Meredith, Centre Harbor, Moultonborough, West Ossipee, and Chocorua, include Conway, North Conway (disembark only), Jackson, Glen, and Pinkham Notch. Daily service varies.

NORTH CONWAY AND VICINITY

The town of Conway is composed of the villages of Conway, Intervale, and North, East, Center, and South Conway. It is North Conway, however, that dominates the community and this region. Long a summer tourist spot, it was placed on the winter map when Mount Cranmore opened in the 1930s, but even that development is overshadowed by the commercial growth of the 1980s. North Conway was once a village roughly bounded by the Victorian railroad station and Cranmore. One could walk to almost anywhere, from inns and restaurants to skiing to shopping.

As late as the 1930s, the strip along Route 16 south of town was a dirt road; but it was the only area left for development, and business began to establish itself there. With no zoning, commercial enterprises began to line the strip, slowly at first; then in the 1980s the factory outlet craze took over and North Conway became one of the major shopping destinations in New England. This development has worsened an already serious traffic situation on Route 16. With one exception, it is the only north-south way through the town, and on summer weekends and most holidays, the traffic is likely to be stop-and-go for several miles north and south of North Conway Village, especially in the afternoons. Visitors can always plan nonweekend travel to avoid the problem. Since the stores are open all year, it also makes sense to shop here off-season when sales are common, traffic is lighter, and accommodations are easy to get.

Shopping aside, North Conway is a bustling village with plenty of inns, resorts, and restaurants. Many of these places have nightly entertainment. Downhill skiing is as near as Cranmore, and the newly organized Mount Washington Valley Ski Touring Association has trails that connect many of the inns listed below. Hiking trails are abundant, offering both challenging hikes and short, easy ones. There is always the Saco River for swimming and canoeing. North Conway is what you make of it.

GUIDANCE

Conway Village Chamber of Commerce (447-2639), Conway 03818. A summer information booth is on Route 16, located south of town adjacent to the railroad tracks.

Mount Washington Valley Visitors Bureau (356-3171; 1-800-367-

3364), Box 2300, North Conway 03860. Free vacation guide, visitor information, and central reservation service. A year-round visitors center is located on Main Street opposite the railroad station.

GETTING AROUND

Taxi service (356-5577; 374-2453).

MEDICAL EMERGENCY

Memorial Hospital (356-5461), Route 16, north of North Conway Village. As you might imagine, this facility has great experience in treating skiing injuries!

Ambulance (356-6911, North Conway; 447-5522, Conway).

VILLAGE

Eaton. A rural village with an idyllic setting beside Crystal Lake. Several of the region's best inns are located here, but the bustle of North Conway is only 15 minutes' drive north on Route 153. Check out the **Eaton Center Village Store** (groceries and small coffee shop) for local information.

TO SEE

Conway Scenic Railroad (356-5251), Box 1947, North Conway 03860. Open daily from the second weekend in June through the fourth Saturday in October, weekends in May and early June. Also runs on Thanksgiving weekend; Santa Claus specials on December weekends until Christmas. Usually four trips daily, except sunset runs Tuesday through Saturday in July and August. Ride behind the steam engine for an 11-mile, 1-hour round trip between North Conway's 1874 railroad station and Conway Village. Lunch and dinner are now served in a refurbished steel dining car (see *Dining Out*). There are also exhibits such as a diesel engine, the large turntable, and an old depot; gift shop. Adults $7.50, ages 4–12 $5.00, under 4 free.

MUSEUMS

Mount Washington Observatory Resource Center (356-8345), Route 16, North Conway. Open all year. The public outreach center for the world-famous summit observatory, this facility is a museum, library, and gift shop devoted to Mount Washington history and science specifically and the White Mountains in general. Winter overnight educational trips to Mount Washington's summit via snow tractor are coordinated through this office. Observatory memberships are also available, and include an active volunteer program. (See under "Mount Washington's Valleys—Mount Washington and Pinkham Notch.")

HISTORICAL SOCIETIES

Conway Historical Society (447-5551), the Eastman-Lord House, 100 Main Street, Conway. Open Tuesday 5–7, Wednesday 2–4 and 6–8. This

historic house contains local memorabilia plus special exhibits including items related to White Mountain artist Benjamin Champney, a Victorian parlor, and a 1940s kitchen.

COVERED BRIDGES

Saco River covered bridge, on Washington Street (turn north at the
Route 16 lights), Conway Village. Just rebuilt, this 240-foot 2-span
bridge is the one you see from the modern Route 16 bridge just north
of Conway Village.

Swift River Bridge, West Side Road (turn north at the Route 16 lights),
Conway Village. No longer used for traffic, this 144-foot 1869 bridge
has been restored (after being threatened with demolition) by the town
and a citizens' group.

FOR FAMILIES

Fun Factory Amusement Park (356-6541), Route 16, North Conway.
Open daily and evenings May through October, water slide Memorial
Day to Labor Day, arcade open all year. A minipark with miniature golf,
water slides, an arcade, and a snack bar.

Pirate's Cove Adventure Golf (356-8807), Route 16, North Conway. Open
May to mid-October. Eighteen-hole miniature golf with plenty of chal-
lenges for young and old.

Hartmann Model Railroad and Toy Museum (356-9922), Norcross
Place, North Conway. Open July through Christmas holidays. Extensive
model train layout. Hobby shop.

Outdoor Explorations in Mt. Washington Valley, by Ned Beecher (Tin
Mountain Conservation Center), is a marvelous handbook for adults
and children providing information about the natural environment of
this entire region.

SCENIC DRIVES

West Side Road, running north from the Conway Village traffic lights to
River Road in North Conway, is not only a scenic road that passes two
covered bridges, working farms, and mountain views, it is also the best
and only way to avoid much of the Route 16 traffic snarl between
Conway and North Conway. About a mile north of Conway, Still Road
turns left, eventually joins Dugway Road in the White Mountain National Forest, and connects with the Kancamagus Scenic Byway at
Blackberry Crossing. At the intersection with River Road, turn west
past Echo Lake State Park, Cathedral Ledge, Diana's Baths, and
Humphrey's Ledge, and travel along the Saco River to join Route 302
west of Glen.

East Conway and Chatham. Off the main roads, both of these towns are
great for an afternoon's ride. East Conway, with its many dairy farms,
recalls Conway's farming past. Chatham, nearly completely surrounded
by the national forest, has a small population and is the south gateway
to Evans Notch. Near Redstone on Route 302 between Center and
North Conway, turn north for East Conway. Eventually this road joins

ERIC M. SANFORD/STATE OF NEW HAMPSHIRE

Cathedral Ledge, a mecca for rock climbers, west of North Conway

(elevation 3,268 feet) is just north of North Conway, and this hike has been popular since the turn of the century. At Intervale, north of North Conway Village, Hurricane Mountain Road diverges east. Follow this road for 1.5 miles to the trailhead. From the summit fire tower there are views across the Saco River Valley to the Moat Range and north to Mount Washington and the Presidential Range. (Also see *Green Space.*)

HORSE-DRAWN RIDES

Horse n' Around (356-6033). In the summer, horse-drawn excursions and wagon rides to Echo Lake and Diana's Baths from Schoeller Park, North Conway; winter sleigh rides from Mount Cranmore and the White Mountain Hotel, Hale's Location.

Mount Cranmore (356-5543) has sleigh rides all year. Also **Nestlenook Farm** (383-0845), Jackson.

Madison Carriage House Buggy and Sleigh Rides (367-4605), Route 113, Madison 03849. An added feature of the B&B is buggy and sleigh rides. In any season, with advance notice, Earl Baxter harnesses up the Belgian horses for trips for couples or groups on the farm's 70 wooded acres. $9 adults.

ROCK CLIMBING

Here is one sport that is definitely for the well-equipped and well-trained

Route 113, just above Fryeburg, Maine, and meanders thr
Chatham. The road is not winter-maintained through Evans
it is a smoothly graded road used in other seasons. Hurricane
Road, paved but not winter-maintained, turns east from Inter
North Conway and steeply winds and twists across a mountai
connect with Route 113 in Chatham.

Route 153, also beginning at the Conway Village lights (turn sou
other country ride through Eaton, Madison, Freedom, Effing
Wakefield. (See "The Lakes Region—The Lake Winnipesauke

TO DO

CANOEING

The Saco is a popular canoeing river. Many people like to put i
River Road (turn west at the traffic lights at the north edge
Conway Village) crosses the river, then paddle about 8 mile
stream to the Conway Village covered bridge. In the summer
is wide and slow, except for light rapids between the Swift Ri
ered bridge and the Conway (second) covered bridge. Take c
the second bridge at Davis Park.

Saco Bound (447-2177), Box 119, Route 302, Center Conway 0381;
als, sales, instruction, canoe camping, and guided trips. They al
a seasonal office on Main Street, North Conway. (Also see *Can*
"The North Country—Berlin and Route 16 North.")

Rentals also available at **Canoe King** (356-5280) and **Northboun**
3820), North Conway; **Saco River Canoe and Kayak** (207-935-
Fryeburg, Maine; **Down East Rafting Company** (447-3002),
Conway.

FISHING

Brook and brown trout, lake trout, bass, and salmon are the target f
anglers in this area. Try your luck in the Saco or Swift rivers, Cc
Lake, Crystal Lake, and at a number of ponds in the White Mou
National Forest. Fishing licenses are required.

North Country Angler (356-6000), Route 16, north of North Conwa
lage. Specialists in trout and Atlantic salmon fishing, they sell e
ment and clothes and offer local fishing information. There is a
small wildlife art gallery, a professional fly-tying school, and multi
fly-fishing instruction programs in combination with Nereledge In

GOLF

North Conway Country Club (356-9391, pro shop), in the center of
village, North Conway. Eighteen holes.

The White Mountain Hotel and Country Club (356-2140 for tee tim
on the West Side Road, Hale's Location. A new nine-hole course.

HIKING

Mount Kearsarge North Trail (3.1 miles, 2.75 hours). Mount Kearsa individual. Cathedral Ledge is famous for its many challenging routes, and from the base you can observe climbers inching up cracks and crevasses. For those who would like to join the climbers, **Eastern Mountain Sports Climbing School** (356-5433), **International Mountain Equipment Climbing School** (356-7064; 447-6700), or **Mountain Guides Alliance** (356-5287) offer instruction and guided climbs. **Cranmore Mountain Recreation Center** (356-6301) has an artificial, indoor climbing wall and offers instruction programs.

CROSS-COUNTRY SKIING

Mount Washington Valley Ski Touring Foundation (356-9304; outside NH 1-800-282-5220; ski info 356-9920), Route 16A, Intervale 03845. Formerly the Intervale Nordic Center, this nonprofit operation features 60 km of groomed trails, rentals, lessons, wax clinics, instruction, lighted night-skiing, and a large backcountry loop for the experienced skier. A 30-km loop connects a number of inns with Mount Cranmore, and you can set up an inn-to-inn ski package. Weekday, weekend, and season rates.

DOWNHILL SKIING

✐ **Mount Cranmore** (356-5543; lodging package information outside NH 1-800-543-9206; ski info 1-800-SUN-N-SKI), Kearsarge Road, North Conway 03860. The granddaddy of New England ski areas and still a favorite for its in-town location, moderate slopes, night skiing, and extensive snowmaking. The 28 trails and 4 open slopes are served by a triple chair lift and 4 double chair lifts, with 100 percent snowmaking. A family area with kids' programs plus trailside condos, ski school and rentals, a sports center, and a variety of ski and lodging packages. (Also see Attitash and Black Mountain under "Mount Washington's Valleys—Jackson and Bartlett" and Wildcat under "Mount Washington and Pinkham Notch.")

✐ **King Pine Ski Area** (367-8896; 1-800-367-8897 for NE, except NH), Route 153, East Madison 03849. Operated by the Hoyt family and part of the Purity Spring Resort complex (see *Inns*), this is a fine family ski area with snowmaking, night skiing, ski school, equipment rentals, triple and double chair lifts, and two J-bar lifts.

GREEN SPACE

Echo Lake State Park, off River Road, 2 miles west of Route 16 in North Conway. Open weekends beginning Memorial Day, then daily late June to Labor Day. A swimming beach with picnic tables and bathhouse plus dramatic views across the lake to White Horse (can you see the horse?) Ledge and Cathedral Ledge. Drive the mile-long road to the top of **Cathedral Ledge State Park** for broad views across the valley of the Saco. Rock climbers ascend these steep ledges, and they can be seen from the road as they pick their way along the cracks and crevasses.

Rare peregrine falcons nest on the ledges and sometimes can be seen soaring on the updrafts.

Whitaker Woods, Kearsarge Road, North Conway. A wild area with trails for walking or winter cross-country skiing.

Davis Park, Washington Street, Conway. A great swimming beach with picnic tables next to the Saco River covered bridge, plus tennis and basketball courts.

Diana's Baths, River Road, 2.2 miles west of North Conway. Watch for a dirt road on the left and park beside the road. A short walk to the stream. No swimming since this is a public water supply. Lucy Brook has eroded and sculpted the rocks in this beautiful place. Moat Mountain Trail (4.2 miles, 3.5 hours) leads to the summit of North Moat Mountain (elevation 3,201 feet).

Madison Boulder Natural Area, on a side road off Route 113, Madison. Open all year, although access is limited to walking in the winter. During the ice age, this massive chunk of rock was plucked off a mountaintop and carried along by a glacier until it reached this spot. Some 3 stories high and more than 80 feet long, it is one of the largest glacial erratics in the world and has been designated a national natural landmark. No facilities and no fees.

LODGING

North Conway has a large number of motels, most of which are located along Route 16, south and north of the village.

INNS

Purity Spring Resort (367-8896; 1-800-367-8897), Route 153, East Madison 03849. Open year-round. In the good old days, summer visitors often came to the country for long stays, perhaps a week or more. Automobiles brought motels and the one-night stop, but Purity Spring evokes past travel patterns. Most of its warm-weather guests stay for a week. Many are families, vacationers who enjoy the varied activities that range from swimming, canoeing, boating, water skiing, and fishing in pristine Purity Lake to tennis, volleyball, myriad other outdoor games, and arts and crafts. The inn's van delivers guests to a trailhead for a guided hike, to a river for a canoe trip, or to Tamworth for a performance of the Barnstormers summer theater. There are also trails covering part of the resort's 1,400 acres. Everything, including a nursery, is included in the rates, except for theater tickets and tennis lessons. Some guests leave their autos in the parking lot all week long, and others simply take public transportation to Conway or Portland, Maine, to be met (by reservation and extra fee) by a car from the resort. Operated since the late 1800s by the Hoyt family, the third generation is now in charge. The fourth generation can be seen scampering around the grounds, helping out the resort's operation. Accommodations are quite varied, furnished country-style, and all rooms have either two twins, two doubles, one double, or a queen-size bed. Most rooms have a full bath, some have half-baths, and others share baths. There are some 70 rooms in 10 separate buildings, some of which are remodeled farmhouses and barns. Several buildings with five to eight rooms are suitable for groups. Three deluxe rooms with balconies are now open in a new building that includes an indoor pool, hot tub, and a fitness center. The summer season runs from late May through mid-October. Rates vary from AP to MAP depending on the time of the season. The dining room is open to the public in the summer season but serves guests-only in the winter. There are also breakfast and dinner cookouts weekly in the summer. Except for groups, the dining room is closed from late October until the end of December when the ski season begins, then closed in April and most of May (B&B available during these times). There is a variety of winter packages in connection with the King Pine Ski Area (see *Downhill Skiing*). $80 MAP to $142 AP.

Rockhouse Mountain Farm Inn (447-2880), off Route 153, Eaton Center 03832. Open mid-June through October. In an earlier time, farmers often took in summer boarders, usually city folks who just wanted to relax in the country, walk open fields, take a canoe trip, and enjoy ample New England cooking. That experience has been possible here since 1946 thanks to the Edge family. With 450 acres of fields and forests to roam and a variety of farm animals (peacocks, llamas, horses, steers, cows, ducks, geese, hens, pigs, etc.), plus a private beach and boats on Crystal Lake, this is a great family spot. Guests often help with haying or feeding the animals or gathering fresh vegetables from the garden for the evening meal. There are 18 rooms, 7 with private baths; the rest share 1 bath for 2 rooms. Breakfast and dinner are served daily, and the children are served at an early first course. The single-entrée meals are typical country cooking with roasts, scalloped potatoes, homemade breads and cakes, and plenty of farm-picked vegetables, which vary over the course of the summer. Fresh eggs, milk, and cream come from their own animals. There are weekly steak roasts, riverside picnics, and chicken barbecues. Most guests are families who stay for a week (Saturday to Saturday), especially in July and August. $96–112; reduced rates for children who stay in parents' room, depending on age.

The Inn at Crystal Lake (447-2120; 1-800-343-7336), Route 153, Eaton Center 03832. Open all year. This large Greek Revival building, with wide porches and balconies offering views over Crystal Lake, began as an inn soon after it was built in 1884 and was once a private school. Walter and Jacqueline Spink have remodeled the old place into a distinctive Victorian-era furnished inn. All 11 rooms have double, queen, or canopy beds and private baths. There is a library-den and a parlor for guests, and a lounge where smoking is permitted. Guests may use Crystal Lake for swimming. Walter is a teaching geologist by profession, who apprenticed at a country inn and at a French restaurant before buying this business. He prepares European cuisine for guests and the public by reservation. Rates vary and include lodging only, B&B, or MAP. Multiple-day discounts also offered. $84–96 per couple B&B; $124–140 per couple MAP.

Snowvillage Inn (447-2818; 1-800-447-4345), Snowville 03849. Open May 1 through March 31. In a "suburb" of Eaton just off Route 153, this inn is located 1,000 feet up Foss Mountain, a hillside setting that offers a panoramic view of Mount Washington across broad lawns and flower gardens. One of New Hampshire's classic inns, it was built in 1912 as a summer home and has been operated since 1987 by Peter, Trudy, and Frank Cutrone. There are 18 rooms—each named for an author and all furnished with antiques—with private baths, in 3 buildings: the main inn, a remodeled barn, and the new Chimneyhouse, which has fireplaced guest rooms. Each building has guest living rooms with books and games, and the main inn has a huge stone fireplace and a spacious porch. The inn has a 14-km groomed cross-country course. Trudy cooks single-entrée gourmet meals, ranging from chicken Madeira to gingered lamb. Vegetarian meals are available on request. Meals are served to the public by reservation ($25 per person). Guests are offered B&B or MAP. There are some package plans and a special cooking school conducted in the off-season by Stephen Raichlen. $38–68 per person B&B; $58–88 per person MAP.

The Darby Field Inn and Restaurant (447-2181; outside NH 1-800-426-4147), Bald Hill Road, Conway 03818. Open all year. Another New Hampshire classic. Operated by Marc and Maria Donaldson since 1979, the place is named for that intrepid first climber of Mount Washington, whose summit and other high peaks can be seen from the inn. The secluded hilltop location only adds to the charm of this place, surrounded by woods and landscaped grounds, including a large vegetable garden. All but 2 of the 17 antiques-furnished rooms have private baths, and the beds range from kings to doubles to twins. There is a two-room suite and a large room with a queen-size bed and air-conditioning. All the rooms are lovely, but those on one side have the broad mountain views. The common room is spacious and cozy, with a fireplace and lots of books. Adjacent is the lounge with a wood stove and hanging plants. Guests may use the swimming pool or the cross-country ski trails. Dinner served nightly (see *Dining Out*). B&B $60–110, MAP $110–$180, depending on the season and accommodations. Three- and five-day package plans available.

Cranmore Inn (356-5502; outside NH 1-800-562-5502), Kearsarge Street, Box 1349, North Conway 03860. Open all year. A traditional village inn, opened 130 years ago, this is the oldest continuously operating inn in the valley. It has 18 rooms including 2 two-room suites. Fourteen rooms have private baths; beds are mostly queens and some rooms have two beds. Country decor with matching bedspreads and curtains, stenciled wallpaper, and antique bed frames. Seasonal drinks are served in the afternoons; the common room is cozy, with a fireplace and a piano; and there is a separate TV room. This inn has a pool and lawn games, and guests have membership privileges at nearby Mount Cranmore Recreation Center. A big plus is the inn's location, just a block from North Conway's main street. Full breakfast served; dinner (choice of three entrées, price varies) available in ski season. No smoking in guest rooms. Chris and Ginny Kanzler, innkeepers. $39–84, depending on the season and accommodations. Children under 4 free, over 4 $1 per year to age 12.

Cranmore Mountain Lodge (356-2044; 356-3596), Kearsarge Road, Box 1194, North Conway 03860. Open all year. Everyone is welcome here, but families and active folks especially will enjoy the facilities. This seems appropriate since Babe Ruth's daughter once owned the place; and, if it's not taken, you can ask for the Babe's old room (#2, with his original furniture). The main inn has 11 rooms (many of which are suitable for families of 4 or more) and a 2-room suite, all with private baths. Next door is the barn with four loft rooms, all with antiques, private baths, air-conditioning, and TVs. A new addition is the "owner's digs" town house, a two-story unit with full kitchen, dining room, living room, cable TV, and a deck/patio. It has a master bedroom, two full baths, and crib, and can sleep up to nine. A dorm sleeps 40 in 2 bunkrooms, popular with groups of bicyclists, hikers, skiers, and church members. This area includes its own recreation room with fireplace. Outside is a swimming pool; tennis, volleyball, and basketball courts; farm animals; a pond, which doubles as a winter (lighted) skating rink; a mountain stream; plus an outdoor Jacuzzi hot tub. Try the toboggan run, cross-country skiing from the door, or downhill skiing nearby at Mount Cranmore. Cross-country and downhill rentals to guests. Innkeepers Dennis and Judy Helfand moved here from Alaska, and they brought enthusiasm from the last frontier with them. Full breakfast year-round, single-entrée dinners during ski season. Spring, summer, and fall: B&B $69–102; the suite and the town house are higher. Winter: MAP $89–109; dorm rooms $29 pp. Inquire about mid-week packages and group rates for the dorm.

The New England Inn and Resort (356-5541; outside NH 1-800-826-3466), Route 16A, Box 428, Intervale 03845. Open all year. This is a large family-owned country complex. It offers a variety of accommodations, all with private baths; beds are queens or doubles; and some have two doubles. The main inn, built in 1809, has 11 rooms plus the dining room, tavern, and 3 fireplaced living rooms. There are 10 cottage suites with king-size beds or 2 doubles, phones, and fireplaces; 3 private cottages with queen-size brass beds, phones, and fireplaces; and 14 more rooms in the Hampshire House, which has a large meeting room suitable for a conference. Rooms are well furnished in a country style, some with four-poster canopy beds. There are tennis courts, a swimming pool, a wading pool for children, and cross-country skiing from the door. The inn's dining room, open to the public, features candlelight and a roaring fireplace (see *Dining Out*). Intervale Tavern serves a country-style lighter fare. Robert and Martha Munson, innkeepers. MAP for two, $114–192, depending on the season and accommodations. Various package plans available.

The 1785 Inn (356-9025; outside NH 1-800-421-1785), Route 16 (mailing: Box 1785, North Conway 03860), Intervale. Open all year. Perhaps the most scenic vista in all the White Mountains is the view across the Saco River intervale to Mount Washington. This inn, part of which was built in 1785, is one of the oldest buildings in the valley and sits on a knoll overlooking the intervale, where the dining room and guest rooms benefit from the panorama. The inn's 17 rooms, 12 with private baths, have king-size and double beds. Rooms are comfortably country-furnished, and some have two beds. The dining room, considered one of the best restaurants in the valley, serves Continental cuisine nightly (see *Dining Out*). Check out the extensive wine list and the desserts. There is a swimming pool and many trails for walking in the summer or cross-country skiing in the winter. Part of the Mount Washington Valley Ski Touring Foundation circuit, the inn serves lunch during the cross-country season. Becky and Charlie Mallar, innkeepers. $60–115, depending on the season and accommodations.

Scottish Lion Inn and Restaurant (356-6381), Route 16, North Conway 03860. Open all year. Scottish decor is the accent here, with bright tartan rugs to accent the seven country guest rooms, all with private baths and air-conditioning. Five rooms have double beds; the other two have twins. New owners have spruced up the rooms. A full Scottish-style breakfast (to guests), lunch, and dinner are served daily (see *Dining Out*). A no-smoking inn. Michael and Janet Procopio, innkeepers. $65–75.

Stonehurst Manor (356-3113; 1-800-525-9100), Route 16, Box 1937, North Conway 03860. Open all year. This three-story inn, accented with stonework, fine oak woodwork, and gables, is located on a 33-acre site off Route 16. The 24 large rooms (all but 2 with private baths) have TVs and are well furnished, many with antiques. Beds are queens and doubles, and some rooms have two beds. Fourteen of the rooms are in the manor, and 10 are in an attached motel section. Townhouse accommodations are also available. There are tennis courts, an outdoor swimming pool, and guided walking and hiking vacation packages. Dinners nightly, with a Continental menu (see *Dining Out*). $96–156 for two MAP. A variety of special weekend and holiday MAP plans available.

Riverside Country Inn (356-9060), Route 16A, Intervale 03845. Open all year, dinner served Friday and Saturday evening. Built in 1906 by the innkeeper's grandfather, this large Victorian home has been tastefully decorated and furnished with antiques, art, and plenty of books. Seven rooms, three with private baths; beds are doubles and twins. Two third-

Ice skating in North Conway

floor rooms could be a cozy suite. Located beside a rushing mountain stream, the inn offers cross-country skiing from the door. Full breakfast. Geoff and Anne Cotter, innkeepers. $45–95, gourmet dinners plus unusual appetizers and rich desserts (see *Dining Out*).

The White Mountain Hotel and Resort (356-7100; 1-800-533-6301), West Side Road at Hale's Location, Box 1828, North Conway 03860. This impressive new 80-room hotel is located about 1 mile off the West Side Road at the base of White Horse Ledge. Amenities include a lounge, nine-hole golf course, year-round outdoor heated pool and Jacuzzi, sauna, fitness center, and tennis courts. After all this activity, relax in a luxurious room or one of the 11 suites, all with air-conditioning, TV, and telephones. The dining room, open to the public, serves three meals daily (see *Dining Out*). B&B $78–130 per couple, depending on season and accommodations; MAP, midweek, golf, and other special plans available.

BED & BREAKFASTS

The Lavender Flower Inn (447-3794; 1-800-729-0106), Main Street, Center Conway 03813. This remodeled farmhouse, located in the quiet village of Center Conway, is just minutes from five ski areas and North Conway shopping. It has eight antiques-furnished rooms, four with private baths, and two baths for the other four. The beds, some four-posters and canopied, are queens and doubles. Two rooms are suites with extra beds for the whole family. Wraparound porches, wicker chairs, and a piano in the fireplaced common room make this a restful spot in any season. No smoking. Full breakfast. $45–92.

Mountain Valley Manner (447-3988), West Side Road, Box 1649, Conway 03818. Open all year. In Conway Village, this inn is just across the street from the Swift River covered bridge and only a short walk to swimming and tennis at Davis Park. Furnished with Victorian antiques, the inn has four cozy guest rooms, all with air-conditioning and private baths. Beds are king, queen, and double. One room is a suite with a king-size waterbed. Ask about their antiques shop. A no-smoking inn. Full breakfast. Bob, Lynn, and Amy Lein, innkeepers. $45–78, depending on season and accommodations.

B&B Beside the River (447-6468), Washington Street, Conway 03818. Just a couple of rooms in this 80-year-old remodeled country house situated right on the Saco River beside the Conway covered bridge. Walk to river swimming or public tennis courts. The rooms have queen beds and share two baths. Ralph Cowdrey, innkeeper. $45–55.

Madison Carriage House B&B (367-4605), Route 113, Madison 03849. Located in Madison Village, off Route 153 (turn west just north of Purity Spring), or turn east on 113 from Route 16 in Chocorua Village. Open all year. Sally Perrow has five rooms with TVs and shared baths in her family farmhouse. She serves a full country breakfast. $55.

The Buttonwood Inn (356-2625; out of NH 1-800-258-2625), Mount Surprise Road, Box 817, North Conway 03860. Open all year. One-entrée dinners are served on Saturday night in the winter. This genteel inn has nine guest rooms (three with private baths, six share three baths). Beds range from queens to doubles with some twin beds, and many furnishings are antiques. Two common rooms, one downstairs with a fireplace, wet bar, and games to play. An outdoor swimming pool for summer fun or cross-country skiing from the door in winter. Not far from Mount Cranmore or Route 16, the inn is tucked away on a quiet country road— just the right place to relax. Full breakfast. Ann and Hugh Begley, innkeepers. $23–48 per person, depending on the season and accommodations. Special multi-day packages also available.

By The Brook Inn (356-2874), Kearsarge Street (Box 303), Kearsarge 03847. Open year-round. Three cousins, Kathy, Mary, and Margaret, operate this new four-room inn near Mount Cranmore. One room has a queen-size bed, the rest are doubles; one shared bath for each set of two rooms. Two rooms open to a second-floor screened porch. Comforters on the beds and Margaret's bright abstract paintings on the walls. Full breakfast served in the fireplaced kitchen or the summer porch. A common room has a TV with VCR and movies, plus a refrigerator and microwave oven. $50–90, depending on the season.

Cabernet Inn (356-4704; 1-800-866-4704), 3552 White Mountain Highway (Box 38, Intervale 03845), North Conway. Begin with an 1840 house, raise it 13 feet, totally renovate and update with every modern facility, and you have this striking new inn just south of the Intervale. The nine rooms, all with queen beds, AC, and private baths, are colorfully decorated, mostly with antiques. One room, with a private entrance, is totally handicapped accessible right down to the roll-in shower. A two-room suite is also available. Enjoy the vintage decor, sauna, player piano, books, games, TV, 10-foot fireplace, or the patio barbecue. The inn is on a 65-km cross-country trail. Full breakfast. Bruce and Vickie Pantti, innkeepers. $70–110.

Nereledge Inn (356-2831), River Road, North Conway 03860. Open all year. Nine rooms, three with private baths, one with a half bath. Two comfortable sitting rooms, one with a wood stove. This inn appeals to active people, and many of their guests are hikers, rock climbers, and cross-country skiers. Walk to the village or to Saco River swimming. They serve dinners to groups by reservation, and their English-style pub (with dart board) is BYOB. With North Country Angler, the inn hosts a fly-fishing program. A no-smoking inn. Full breakfast. Valerie and Dave Halpin, innkeepers. $59–85, higher during holiday weeks and foliage season, children $1 per year to age 12.

The 1787 Center Chimney B&B (356-6788), River Road, Box 1229, North Conway 03860. Four comfortable rooms, all with shared baths. Rooms have king, double, or two or three twin beds. One large room has a TV and balcony. Farley Whitley, innkeeper. $44–55 per room with continental breakfast (fresh fruit and muffins, coffee and tea).

Victorian Harvest Inn (356-3548; out of NH 1-800-642-0749), Locust Lane, Box 1763, North Conway 03860. Open all year. Situated on a quiet side street south of the village, this inn has mountain views from each of its six well-furnished rooms. Four rooms have private baths, two rooms have king beds, three have queens, and one has a double bed. Radios and books in rooms; swimming pool; common rooms with TV, games, and wood fire. Full breakfast. A no-smoking inn. Bob and Linda Dahlberg, innkeepers. $55–100.

Sunny Side Inn (356-6239; 1-800-600-6239), Seavey Street, North Conway 03860. Open all year. Nine rooms, all with private baths and AC. Two rooms have kings, one a queen, and the rest doubles. Several rooms also have a twin, perfect for children, who are welcome here. Walking distance to North Conway Village shopping, near Mount Cranmore. Fireplace in the common room. Full breakfast. Newly remodeled by Peter and Diane Watson, hosts. $50–100, depending on the season and accommodations; children age four and up $16.

The Forest Inn (356-9772; 1-800-448-3534), Route 16A, Box 37, Intervale 03854. Open all year for B&B; MAP in ski season and for some special weekends. This antiques-furnished inn celebrated its 100th anniversary in 1990. Its 11 rooms, 10 with private baths, include a special 2-room stone cottage with a fireplace, and four 2-room suites. Beds are doubles and twins. Afternoon tea is served, and rooms have complimentary wine and sherry. The Victorian-furnished common rooms have a fireplace and wood stove. Swim in their pool or cross-country ski from the door.

Full breakfast. Ken and Rae Wyman, innkeepers. $50–98 depending on the season and accommodations. Special multi-day package plans available, including inn-to-inn bicycling.

Wildflowers Guest House (356-2224), Route 16, Box 802, Intervale 03845. Open May through October. Six large rooms, two with private baths; beds are doubles and twins, some rooms with both. Designed as the summer home of a famed Victorian Boston architect, this delightful place is enhanced by period antiques, bright wildflower wallpaper, and the original Douglas fir moldings and doors, plus an exquisite front-porch flower garden. Flowers, fresh and pictured, are everywhere. Innkeepers Eileen Davies and Dean Franke serve a continental breakfast. $50–92 depending on the season and accommodations.

Mountain Vale Inn (356-9880), Route 16A, Box 482, Intervale 03845. Open all year. Three large rooms—two with double beds, one with twins—and shared baths. Swimming pool; pool table; common room with TV, VCR, and fireplace. Many furnishings collected during the innkeepers' travels to exotic countries. Full breakfast. Helen and Rusty Cook, innkeepers. $50–65, depending on the season, plus package plans.

WHERE TO EAT

DINING OUT

Bellini's (356-7000), Seavey Street, North Conway. Open daily at 5. The Marcello family has more than 50 years' experience in the Italian food business, and they use all of their talents in this colorful restaurant. The pasta is imported, but everything else is freshly prepared. All the well-known southern and northern Italian specialties are offered here, including chicken, veal, and vegetarian entrées, with homemade soups and salads, and cannolis and other rich desserts. Prices inexpensive to moderate.

✎ **Conway Scenic Railroad** (356-5251), Box 1947, North Conway 03860. Lunch (noon and 2, daily), tea (4 P.M. daily), and dinner are served in the refurbished, steel-exterior, oak-interior, 47-seat dining car *Chocorua*. Food is prepared in the on-board kitchen. Dinner served Friday and Saturday from early June to July 4, and second week of September to mid-October; Tuesday through Saturday from early July to first week in September. The luncheon menu features four entrées: usually turkey club, salad plate, stuffed chicken breast, or ham and cheese croissant. $18 includes the train ride and tax; children's menu available. Afternoon tea includes a variety of pastries and finger foods and beverage, $13. For dinner, served at 6:30, the dining car is transformed into a deluxe restaurant with white linens and china. Along with a choice of appetizers and dessert, dinner selections range from Shaker pot roast and roast turkey to fish of the day and vegetarian entrée, $29.95 includes a half-hour longer ride. Reservations recommended for dinner. BYOB, but the railroad expects to have a liquor license soon.

The 1785 Inn (356-9025), Route 16 at the Intervale (mailing: Box 1785, North Conway 03860). Nightly, 5–9 or 10; lunch during the cross-country season. A recent newspaper poll awarded this inn first place for best restaurant, wine list, and dessert. They list more appetizers (14, priced from $5.85 to $9.85) than many restaurants have entrées. Filet mignon, duck-liver pâté, crab imperial, smoked salmon, or Caesar salad for two (made at your table) could make a delightful meal by themselves. But then you would miss such entrées as veal and shrimp in a rum cream sauce with artichoke hearts, sherried rabbit, raspberry duckling, rack of lamb, scallops in a cream sauce with garlic and leeks, or tournedos Bordelaise (pan-broiled tenderloin with a Burgundy sauce). The fine dining is enhanced by a wine list of some 200 titles, a roaring fireplace, and a comfortable colonial atmosphere. Moderate to expensive.

Scottish Lion Inn and Restaurant (356-6381), Route 16, North Conway 03860. Lunch Monday to Saturday 11:30–2; Sunday brunch 10:30–2; dinner 5:30–9. A longtime favorite with valley visitors, this dining room has Scottish decor and menu offerings to match. Finnan haddie, Edinburgh broil (prime rib), Highland game pie (beef, hare, pheasant, venison, and goose), or beef Wellington are enough to make Scots of us all. The lunch and dinner menus also have a variety of traditional chicken, fish, and beef offerings. Relax before or after dinner in the Black Watch pub. Moderate.

Stonehurst Manor (356-3113), Route 16, Box 1937, North Conway 03860. Dining nightly 6–10; reservations required. Victorian splendor with tuxedoed waiters in an English-style country house complete with exquisite woodwork and leaded stained-glass windows. The cuisine is classic Continental to match the decor. Beef Wellington, veal Oscar, salmon steak, and paella for two (must be ordered in advance) are among the house specialties. Watch as they make your pizza in a wood-fired, stone oven ($8.95–12.95). Appetizers lean to seafood with oysters, salmon, and shrimp plus escargot, lobster spring rolls, and Caesar salad. There is a fine selection of domestic and imported wines, rich desserts, and espresso. Prices range from moderate to $45 (for rack of lamb for two).

The New England Inn (356-5541; 1-800-826-3466), Route 16A, Box 428, Intervale 03845. This inn's candlelit dining room serves a country-style menu. The house specialty is Shaker cranberry pot roast; other entrées include seafood imperial, swordfish, turkey, pork chops, and other New England favorites. Moderate.

Riverside Country Inn (356-9060), Route 16A, Intervale 03845. Dinner served Friday and Saturday evening 6–9. Cozy European-style gourmet dining in a country setting. The menu is limited and changes weekly, since Anne Cotter cooks to match seasonal specialties and the freshest available ingredients. The menu always offers three appetizers (such as shrimp with Thai dipping sauce), three or four desserts, and, with entrées, a choice of two salads, two vegetables, and two starches. Chicken, beef, fish, and veal are always offered. A recent menu included hot-and-sour chicken, sirloin tips with horseradish sauce, veal à la creme, and salmon fillet dressed with dill. Finish with lemon cake with blueberries, strawberries, and oranges, or chocolate ginger mousse! Prices moderate.

The Darby Field Inn and Restaurant (447-2181; outside NH 1-800-426-4147), Bald Hill Road, Conway 03818. Dinner served nightly 6–9; reservations recommended, especially on weekends. Candlelight dining is a pleasure with appetizers such as country pâté and baked stuffed mushroom caps, followed by lamb chops, veal saltimbocca, roast duckling (a house specialty with Grand Marnier orange sauce), or chicken marquis (breast of chicken sautéed with garlic, mushrooms, tomatoes, scallions, white wine, and lemon juice). The fish dish changes daily and there are three to four nightly specials. A favorite dessert is Darby cream pie. Moderate to expensive.

The White Mountain Hotel and Resort (356-7100; 1-800-533-6301), West Side Road at Hale's Location, Box 1828, North Conway 03860. Lunch 11:30–2 daily except Sunday and dinner served every day in a large dining room with views across the valley to Mount Cranmore. The dinner menu ranges from roast duckling and shrimp to lobster thermidor and coquilles Saint-Jacques. Varied appetizers, salads, and desserts. Moderate.

EATING OUT

☞ **Horsefeathers** (356-2687), Main Street, North Conway. Open daily 11:30–11:30. Comfortable and affordable dining in the middle of the village marks this longtime favorite. Soups, salads, sandwiches, pastas, and nightly specials ($3.50–12.50).

✎ **Carriage Inn Restaurant** (356-2336), Route 16, north of North Conway Village. Open all year 5–9, until 10 on weekends in summer and fall. A large, reasonably priced ($11.95–15.95) family restaurant featuring steaks, seafood, and veal. They also have an extensive children's menu.

Peking Restaurant (356-6976), Route 16, North Conway. Open all year, daily from 11:30. Called the best Chinese restaurant in Carroll County, this place has all of your favorites to eat in or take out, including Polynesian dishes and hot and spicy Peking and Szechuan ($8.95–13.45).

Mario's (356-9712), Route 16, south of North Conway Village. Open all year 11–9. A longtime favorite family Italian restaurant. Italian sandwiches, fried chicken, seafood marinara, spaghetti, lasagna and ravioli, baked tortellini, and more.

✎ **The Homestead** (356-5900), Route 16, south of North Conway Village. Open all year 4:30–10. Traditional New England fare served in a restored 1793 homestead. Susan's mother's fish chowder, broiled brook trout, baked shrimp, rack of lamb, broiled scallops, and seafood Newburg are featured ($12.95–19.50) along with rich desserts such as Indian pudding and hot cherry crisp with ice cream. Fresh baked treats from the Homestead kitchen. For children under 12, half portions at half prices. No smoking.

A Step Above Bakeshop and Cafe (356-2091), Main Street, North Conway Village. Open daily 8–3, Sunday 8–1. Breakfast and lunch ($3–5.25) featuring creatively prepared eggs such as frittatas, an Italian version of the omelet with lightly sautéed ingredients (broccoli, tomato, pepper, potatoes, and onions), eggs added, and baked in the oven.

ENTERTAINMENT

Arts Jubilee (356-9393), offers summer musical performances, weekly afternoon children's programs, and fall art show.

Mount Washington Valley Theatre Company (356-5776), Eastern Slope Playhouse, Main Street, North Conway.

SELECTIVE SHOPPING

From the traffic lights on Route 16 in Conway Village north through North Conway, this is a shopper's heaven. This has always been a good shopping destination, but now there are more than 200 specialty shops and outlet centers. A longtime favorite is **Yield House,** at the south end of the Route 16 strip, offering reproduction finished and unfinished furniture and kits. In North Conway Village are two original **Carroll Reed** shops (clothing and ski rentals); **Eastern Mountain Sports** (outdoor clothing and equipment), located in the Eastern Slope Inn; and the **Joe Jones Shop** (more clothing and ski rentals). Newly opened in North Conway Village is **Annalee Dolls.**

  The **factory outlet** boom hit in the 1980s, and most of the leading manufacturers have opened stores along Route 16, especially south of North Conway Village. Everything from clothing and luggage to shoes and boots to tools, dishes, and jewelry can be found in one shop or another. Most of the outlet stores are open daily 9–6. Everyone has favorite shops; we like the **L.L. Bean Factory Store** (clothing and outdoor equipment, the first Bean store outside of its home base in Freeport, Maine), the **White Birch Booksellers** (a wonderful New England and travel bookstore, where most of the guidebooks we mention are available), **J. G. Hook** (clothing), **Timberland** (shoes and boots), and **Brookstone** (every kind of tool imaginable, some needed and others just intriguing). You might like **Ralph Lauren** or **Dansk, Bugle Boy** (jeans), **Danskin,** or **Arrow Shirts**.

ART GALLERIES AND ANTIQUES SHOPS

There are many art galleries and antiques shops in the region, most open daily in the summer and by appointment the rest of the year. Check with the chamber of commerce information center for listing brochures.

ARTS AND CRAFTS AND SPECIAL SHOPS

League of New Hampshire Craftsmen (356-2441), North Conway Village. Quality handmade crafts including pottery, jewelry, clothing, and furnishings. Open all year.

Handcrafters Barn, Route 16, North Conway. Open all year. A collection of 35 stalls where artists from throughout New England display their handmade items including pottery, quilts, jewelry, clothing, wooden items, and paintings.

Peter Limmer and Sons (356-5378), Route 16A, Box 88, Intervale 03845. Closed Sunday. If anything is a craft item, it is a pair of handmade mountain boots, fabricated by the third generation of the Limmer family. The boots are expensive ($245 per pair), and you may wait a year or more to have a pair custom-made to fit your feet; but our pair, purchased 25 years ago, is on its third set of soles and, after hundreds of miles of mountain trails, is still in great shape. "Limmers" have gone from Mount Washington to Mount Everest, and many hikers wouldn't enter the woods without a pair. You'll also find street and golf shoes.

SPECIAL EVENTS

We have primarily listed annual events but not specific dates since the exact dates change each year. Contact any of the places listed under *Guidance* for more details about these and many other one-time events held throughout the year. Cranmore Recreation Center is often the host for professional tennis tournaments, and world-class skiing races are often held at valley ski areas.

Late June: **Conway Village Festival,** Conway.

July through Labor Day: **Mount Washington Valley Band** plays free concerts on Tuesday at 7:30 at the Conway Recreation Center, Main Street, Conway Village, and Sunday at 6:30 at the gazebo in North Conway Village.

July Fourth: **Carnival,** North Conway. Fireworks and parade.

Early September: **World Mud Bowl,** North Conway. Some people enjoy this annual football game, played in knee-deep mud. At least local charities benefit from the proceeds.

Late September: Annual **Arts Jubilee,** North Conway.

First week in October: **Fryeburg Fair,** Fryeburg, Maine. This is a large agricultural fair, with horse and cattle pulling, livestock exhibits and judging, midway, and pari-mutuel harness racing. Just across the border from Mount Washington Valley, this annual fair attracts a huge crowd in the middle of foliage season.

JACKSON AND BARTLETT

From its covered bridge and rushing river flowing through the middle of town to its 1847 white community church, Jackson is one of New Hampshire's special villages. It has been hosting guests for more than a century, yet it has little of the glitz found farther south. Careful zoning and a strong community spirit have resulted in a tourist atmosphere that is relaxing and comfortable for guests as well as for residents. As a group, its inns and restaurants are as nice as can be found anywhere, and they are especially pleasant in the quieter, nonwinter seasons.

The town is perhaps best known now for cross-country skiing, a sport promoted by the Jackson Ski Touring Foundation, a nonprofit organization founded in 1972 when the sport was in its infancy in America. The foundation maintains the 154-km trail system, rated by *Esquire* magazine as one of the top four areas in the world. On winter weekends the town bustles with skiers who bring enough business to keep the inns and restaurants busy and make last-minute reservations difficult, except for midweek. The ski center is right in the middle of the village and so are golf and tennis. In summer one could also hike the local trails or climb among many mountains near the village or just up the road in Pinkham Notch. Jackson also has several art galleries and a few antiques shops to keep the shopper happy, and there is always North Conway just a few minutes away.

Meanwhile Bartlett appears as two villages—one the residential center stretched along Route 302, the other a commercial center located between Attitash Ski Area and the junction of Routes 302 and 16. The town of Harts Location, primarily a strip of land situated between Bartlett and Crawford Notch, has a small population and a couple of commercial establishments; it is surrounded by the White Mountain National Forest. Its few voters can meet in a private home to hold town meetings. Crawford Notch is described in a separate section of this chapter.

GUIDANCE

Jackson Resort Association (383-9356; outside NH 1-800-866-3334), Box 304, Jackson Village 03846. Information and a reservation system.
Mount Washington Valley Visitors Bureau (356-3171; 1-800-367-3364), Box 2300, North Conway 03860. Free vacation guide and visitor information.
State of New Hampshire Information Center, Route 16, Intervale, just north of North Conway. Rest rooms and telephones. Open all year.

TO SEE

FOR FAMILIES

⌁ **Heritage New Hampshire** (383-9776), Route 16, Box 1776, Glen 03838. Open Memorial Day to mid-June and Labor Day to mid-October, 10–5; mid-June to Labor Day, 9–6. Heritage New Hampshire evokes the history of this state as you travel from England on a seventeenth-century vessel, visit with important individuals from the past such as Daniel Webster, and enter the twentieth century on a train ride through Crawford Notch. Designed around an 1,800-foot walkway, which is handicapped accessible, this attraction is a 300-year review of New Hampshire history through photographs, dioramas, rides, and talking mannikins. Created long before the more technologically advanced but essentially similar attractions at Epcot, this is, nevertheless, a fine introduction to the state's past. Allow two hours. Adults $7, ages 4–12 $4.50, under age 4 free.

⌁ **Story Land** (383-4293), Route 16, Box 1776, Glen 03838. Open Father's Day to Labor Day 9–6; weekends from Labor Day through Columbus Day 10–5. Created more than 35 years ago and regularly expanded, Story Land is a leading family theme park, organized around well-known fairy tales and children's stories. Fifteen rides range from a pirate ship, railroad, and antique autos to an African safari, voyage to the moon, and Dr. Geyser's remarkable raft ride. Cinderella, the Old Woman Who Lived in a Shoe, the Three Little Pigs, and Billy Goats Gruff are all here along with Heidi of the Alps, farm animals to pet and feed, and dozens of other favorites. There is a restaurant, gift shop, and free parking. Ages four through adult $12, which covers all rides. Operated, along with Heritage New Hampshire next door, by the Morrill family.

⌁ **Attitash Alpine Slide and Waterslides** (374-2368), Route 302, Bartlett 03812. Open weekends 10–5, late May to mid-June and Labor Day to early October; open daily 10–6, late June through Labor Day. Great fun for the kids and adults too. The Alpine Slide includes a ride to the top of the mountain on the ski lift, then a slide down a curving, bowed .75-mile chute on a self-controlled sled. Then cool off in the Aquaboggin water slide. Fees: Alpine Slide, adults $5, ages 6–12 $4.50; 2 rides all ages $8; all day includes unlimited Alpine Slide and 1-hour Waterslide, all ages, $14; Waterslide, ages 6 through adult, ½-hour, $5. Under age 4 and over 70 ride free.

SCENIC DRIVES

When you are in the middle of the mountains, most any road is a scenic drive. The **Five-Mile Circuit** drive begins in Jackson Village. Follow Route 16B at the schoolhouse, up the hill, and, eventually, past farms and views across the valley to Whitney's; then turn left for a couple of miles to Carter Notch Road, where you turn left again, past the Eagle Mountain House and Jackson Falls, before reaching the village. For another variation of this drive, turn right at Whitney's, and right again at Black Mountain on **Dundee Road,** which changes to gravel now and again as it passes abandoned farms and mountain scenery en route to Intervale at Route 16A. Turn right and pick up Thorn Hill Road to return to Jackson.

TO DO

GOLF

Wentworth Resort Golf Club (383-9641), Jackson Village. Eighteen holes, with pro shop, club and cart rentals, full lunch available. Call for tee times.

Eagle Mountain House (363-9111), Carter Notch Road, Jackson. Nine holes, full hotel facilities.

HIKING

The Jackson Resort Association publishes a small folder describing short walks in and around the village. *Note:* While some cross-country trails are suitable for hiking, many of them are on private land and not open to the public except for the ski season.

Eagle Mountain Path (1 mile; 50 minutes). Begins behind the Eagle Mountain House.

Black Mountain Ski Trail (1.7 miles; 1.6 hours). Begins on Carter Notch Road, 3.7 miles from the village. Leads to a cabin and a knob that offers a fine view of Mount Washington.

North Doublehead, via the Doublehead Ski Trail. Begins on Dundee Road, 2.9 miles from the village. Follows an old ski trail to the WMNF Doublehead cabin on the wooded summit. A path leads to a good view east, and by using the Old Path and the New Path, one can make a round-trip hike from Dundee Road over both North and South Doublehead and back to the road. To North Doublehead, 1.8 miles and 1.6 hours; a round-trip to both summits is about 4.3 miles and four hours.

Rocky Branch Trail makes a loop from Jericho Road off Route 302 in Glen to Route 16 north of Dana Place. We suggest walking the Jericho Road end (turn off 302 in Glen and follow the road about 4.3 miles to the trailhead), which follows the brook for a couple of miles to a shelter. Allow two hours to make the round-trip on a smooth trail. The Rocky Branch is one of the better trout-fishing brooks, and in the spring it is prime wildflower country (look but don't pick!).

SWIMMING

There is nothing like an old swimming hole, and there are several here. The best is probably at Jackson Falls in Jackson Village. Here the mountain-cool Wildcat River tumbles over rocky outcrops just above the village. There are several pools and picnic spots along the falls. Another favorite spot is on the Rocky Branch Brook, just off Route 302 in Glen. Driving west, watch for Jericho Road on the right and follow it to the Rocky Branch trailhead. Walk about 50 yards along the river back toward Route 302 for the swimming place.

CROSS-COUNTRY SKIING

Jackson Ski Touring Foundation (383-9355), Box 216, Jackson Village 03846. This nonprofit organization promotes the sport of cross-country skiing and maintains some 154 km of groomed trails in and around the village. The trails range from easy to difficult so be sure to consult the map before heading off for a ski. On the trail system one can ski from inn to inn for lunch or après-ski activities. Foundation members get free instruction on technique and waxing, invitations to such special club events as a gourmet ski tour, ladies' tours, and the end-of-the-season barbecue, plus unlimited use of the trails. Every winter weekend there are events such as citizens' races and workshops. Trail fees/memberships pay for trail maintenance and such improvements as the Northeast's newest covered bridge, built to provide easier access to the Ellis River Trail, a 10-km route from the village north to Dana Place Inn, where lunch is served and there is a warming hut. All trail users must be daily or seasonal members of the foundation.

Jack Frost Ski Shop (383-9657), Jackson Village 03846. Cross-country rentals and instruction; also alpine and telemark rentals. Rent a pulk (sled) and pull the baby on the trail.

Nestlenook Farm (383-9443), Dinsmore Road, Jackson Village. Open daily in season. Rentals and instructions plus a groomed trail network that connects to the Jackson system (additional charge for the Jackson trails).

DOWNHILL SKIING

Attitash Ski Area (374-2368; outside NH 1-800-223-7669), Route 302, Bartlett 03812. A family area, Attitash has 27 trails ranging from beginner to intermediate to expert, all on a 1,700-foot vertical drop, served by 2 triple and 4 double chair lifts. A new trail, opened in 1990, claims to be the longest, steepest lift-serviced trail east of the Rockies. The area makes 8–10 feet of snow per year on most of its trails, ensuring good conditions throughout the season. Individual and group lessons are offered, plus rentals. Package plans include skiing, lessons, and lodging at motels, condos, resorts, or country inns.

Black Mountain (383-4490; lodging 1-800-252-5622), Route 16B, Jackson 03846. Another of the historic New Hampshire ski areas, dating from the 1930s when Bill Whitney made a tow with shovel handles. There are some 20 trails served with a T-bar and a double and triple lift, with 95 percent snowmaking. Country views enhance the fun of this quiet, family area. Dining and lodging at the base in Whitney's Inn plus ski school, rentals, and a connection to Jackson's 154 km of cross-country trails.

ICE SKATING

A town-maintained ice-skating rink is located in the center of the village across from the grammar school, and Nestlenook Farm has skating for a fee or free to guests.

SLEIGH RIDES

Nestlenook Farm (383-9443), Dinsmore Road, Jackson Village. Daily except Wednesday. Sleigh rides last 25 minutes and take you through the woods beside the Ellis River in a 25-person rustic sleigh or a smaller Austrian-built model. Oil lamps light the trails at night. Wheels are added for summer rides.

Horse Logic (383-9876), Jackson Village. Open seasonally for horse-drawn sleigh rides and hayrides around the village.

LODGING

Glen, Bartlett, and Jackson have a number of motels situated along Routes 302 and 16.

RESORTS

Eagle Mountain Resort (383-9111; 1-800-777-1700), Carter Notch Road, Jackson 03846. Open all year. Not many of the old Victorian White Mountain hotels remain; but this is one of them, completely renovated and now managed by Colony Hotels/Resorts. All 94 rooms, including several suites, have private baths, phones, and cable TV. Most rooms have double beds and are furnished in a country style, not in typical hotel fashion. There are a nine-hole golf course, lighted tennis courts, health club, and heated pool. Winter guests can schuss right out on a large cross-country trail network. Unwind in the Eagle Landing Lounge, where lunch is served in-season. Breakfast, Sunday brunch, and dinner are served in Highfields, the hotel dining room. The dinner menu is quite varied, featuring seafood, trout, beef, chicken, and veal. Jed Smith, manager. $55–155 per room depending on season and accommodations; also a variety of package plans, especially in ski season.

Wentworth Resort Hotel (383-9700; 1-800-637-0013), Jackson Village 03846. Another old-timer, built in the 1880s and once known as Wentworth Hall, the core of this hotel has been renovated and modernized; the rest of the hotel was razed. Its 62 rooms are identically furnished, with king, queen, and twin beds; private baths; wall-to-wall carpeting; and cable TV. The hotel has an outdoor pool, or guests can walk to the river for a dip in the cool mountain water of the Wildcat River. From the hotel's location right in the middle of the village, guests can walk to skiing, golf, tennis, or lunch. Breakfast and dinner are served in the hotel dining room, which is also open to the public (see *Dining Out*). Dinner entrées range from quail, roast duckling, and rack of lamb to Atlantic salmon, grilled shrimp in red pepper sauce, and scallops sautéed with leeks in a cream sauce. Fritz Koeppel, innkeeper. $49–99, depending on season and day of the week; MAP add $25.

INNS

The Bernerhof (383-4414; 1-800-548-8007), Route 302, Box 240, Glen 03838. Open all year. Breakfast for house guests, lunch and dinner to the public. Another New Hampshire classic inn and one of the premier restaurants in the region as well as a cooking school. The inn has nine rooms with private baths. Four large new rooms and two suites (with spas) in a recent addition are beautifully decorated, each with a Jacuzzi, air-conditioning, TV, and a brass king or queen bed. Oak paneling accents the lounge (named for the Zumsteins, the longtime former owners) and adjacent dining room where lunch is served. Dining is European with six veal entrées as specialties (see *Dining Out*). Ted and Sharon Wroblewski, owners. B&B $69–139; MAP $109–189; a complimentary champagne breakfast in bed is served to guests on the third morning of their stay.

Christmas Farm Inn (383-4313; outside NH 1-800-HI-ELVES), Route 16B, Jackson 03846. Open all year. Celebrate Christmas here all year in rooms named for Santa's reindeer while relaxing in the Mistletoe Lounge or dining in the holiday-decorated dining room. Since purchasing the old place in 1976, the Zeliff family has transformed the property into one of the state's more imaginative inns. The main inn, a portion of which was built 200 years ago, has 10 regular rooms, all with private baths and king, queen, double, or twin beds. Five deluxe rooms also have Jacuzzis. Adjacent buildings include the Saltbox House, with nine new rooms; the Barn, with four deluxe suites; and the two-bedroom Log Cabin and Sugar House, each with a sun deck, fireplace, refrigerator, and telephone. All rooms have clock radios and are furnished country style with a Christmas accent. Spacious gardens surround the outdoor pool; and, for winter visitors, a cross-country trail passes right by the inn, connecting it with a large trail network. Longtime innkeepers Bill and Sydna Zeliff might not be so much in evidence now that he has been elected to Congress, but son Will remains as host and the inn's chef (see *Dining Out*). B&B $58–108, MAP $98–148 per couple, plus a variety of package plans.

The Notchland Inn (374-6131; 1-800-866-6131), Route 302, Harts Location (Bartlett 03812). Open all year. Located near the site of Abel Crawford's early White Mountain Hotel, once called the Inn Unique (this place is still unique). Situated on a mountainside and surrounded by wilderness, it was built of granite in 1852 by Samuel Bemis, a Boston dentist and pioneering photographer. Maps and photographs feature local history. There are 11 rooms (including 4 two-room suites), each with private bath and a working fireplace. Beds are king-, queen-, and twin-size. Two cozy sitting rooms also have fireplaces, and for summer guests a sun room with wicker furniture overlooks the swimming pool. The inn grooms cross-country ski trails for guests only, and there is ice skating on their pond, snowshoeing, rock and ice climbing, and many nearby hiking trails. Innkeepers John and Pat Bernandin raise llamas and miniature horses and also maintain a refuge for rare and endangered species, primarily wool-producing animals. Their Belgian horses pull carriages and sleighs. A professional chef, Pat prepares five-course, three-entrée dinners, generally for guests but also to the public by reservation and when space permits (see *Dining Out*). MAP (two-night minimum, reservations usually required for weekends) $87 per person per night high-season weekends; $52 per person low-season weekdays.

Inn at Thorn Hill (383-4242/6448; 1-800-289-8990), Thorn Hill Road, Jackson Village 03846. Open all year. Another of New Hampshire's classic inns, this 1895 mansion was designed by famed architect Stanford White, and it has been furnished to reflect its Victorian heritage. It has 19 rooms, all with private baths. The 10 Victorian rooms in the main building vary in size, but most beds are queens; a few have canopies. There are six rooms in the Carriage House plus three cottages. The main inn has several common areas, including a pub with a fireplace, the dining room, a Victorian sitting room with TV, plus a drawing room with a view down the valley to the village and across the hills to Mount Washington. Catering to artists, the inn offers special three- and five-day art workshops. Dining nightly 6–9 (see *Dining Out*). Swim in the inn pool, relax in the outdoor hot tub, or cross-country ski from the door. The village is just a short walk down the hill. No smoking. Jim and Ibby Cooper, innkeepers. MAP $130–212, depending on season and accommodations; plus various package plans. For B&B, deduct $15 per person.

✍ **Whitneys' Inn** (383-3916; 1-800-677-5737), Route 16B, Jackson 03846. With Black Mountain (one of the state's oldest ski areas) in the backyard, this old inn is a popular destination for winter vacationers; but its country location is a relaxing spot in other seasons as well. The inn's 30 rooms offer a variety of accommodations from regular rooms to deluxe rooms with private sitting areas, plus eight family suites in a separate building (where children under 12 stay and eat free from May through August), two cottages with fireplaces, and the four-room Brookside Cottage, also with fireplaces. All the rooms are bright and colorful with private baths and king, queen, or double beds. Rooms in the deluxe section overlook the ski slopes. The lounge and dining room have fireplaces, and there is also a separate common room for guests. The remodeled barn, used for lunch during ski season, has recreation rooms for teens and younger children; there are lawn games, a mountain pond for swimming, tennis and volleyball courts, plus outdoor skating in winter. The dinner menu (see *Dining Out*), changes seasonally. Kevin Martin, innkeeper. MAP $120–175, but various package plans are available.

✍ **Wildcat Inn and Tavern** (383-4245), Jackson Village 03846. Open all year. If you would like to be in the middle of everything, try this longtime favorite. Walk to cross-country skiing, shopping, golf, or tennis; plus their tavern offers folk music on weekends. There are 12 rooms, 10 with private baths. The rooms are cozy, with country furniture and some antiques, and most of them can be arranged as suites for families. There is also a large TV and game room and a separate living room with a fireplace, plus the tavern. Three country gourmet meals are served daily in one of the area's most popular restaurants (see *Dining Out*). B&B $70–90; MAP $130–140; plus theater, tennis, and golf package plans.

BED & BREAKFASTS

The Blake House (383-9057), Route 16, Jackson 03846. Open all year. Sara Blake Maynard's father built a portion of this place as a ski cabin in the 1930s, but more recently it has been expanded and now offers five rooms with two shared baths. One room has a king-size bed, one a double with a separate screened porch; others have twins. The guests' living room has cozy chairs, TV, VCR, books, games, and a fireplace, while the dining room features a huge window overlooking the forest and the rushing Ellis River, which nearly surrounds the wooded property. Located north of town and surrounded by white birches, this is a quiet, woodsy place. Breakfast is an expanded continental offering with fresh fruit and breads, hot and cold cereals, and hard- or soft-boiled eggs. Sara and Jeff Maynard, innkeepers. $50–80.

The Country Inn at Bartlett (374-2353), Route 302, Box 327, Bartlett 02812. Open all year. Just west of Bartlett Village, this place has 6 inn rooms with shared baths and 11 cottage rooms, each with private bath and TV. Three rooms have fireplaces, as does the living room, and there is an outside hot tub. The inn appeals to hikers, skiers, and lovers of the outdoors—folks with whom innkeeper Mark Dindorf worked when he was an AMC employee. Mark is eager to share his knowledge of backcountry hiking, white-water canoeing, and telemark skiing. B&B $28–48 per person, children under 12 free.

Ellis River House (383-9339; outside NH 1-800-233-8309), Route 16, Box 656, Jackson 03846. Open all year. Situated just off the main road, backed up to its namesake river, this renovated turn-of-the-century farmhouse offers cozy, comfortable accommodations. Eighteen antiques-furnished rooms, 15 with private baths, 3 with shared baths. Three rooms are family suites. Eight rooms have fireplaces, one has a two-person Jacuzzi, and most rooms are also air-conditioned. In a two-room cottage for four people, there is a sitting room with TV, private bath, and a second-floor room with a queen. A recent addition is a heated outdoor swimming pool, and there is a Jacuzzi in a bright atrium overlooking the river. You can swim or fish in the river, play volleyball, or cross-country ski from the door. Hot toddies are served in the afternoon. The dining room is one of several sitting areas and has easy chairs, a wood stove, and a grand piano. The full breakfast includes fresh eggs and sausage and bacon from the inn's farm animals. A full-course dinner is also available to guests only by request ($24.50 per person), and it features a choice of entrées and vegetables from the inn garden. Barry and Barbara Lubao. B&B $55–195, depending on the season and accommodations, plus package plans; children under 12 free.

The Inn at Jackson (383-4321; 1-800-289-8600), Jackson Village 03846. Open all year. This old summer mansion overlooks the village from its hillside lot. There are nine large, well-furnished rooms, all with private baths; most beds are queens; three rooms have fireplaces. There is a second-floor common room, a hot tub–Jacuzzi, and a panoramic view of the village and the mountains from the breakfast sun porch. Cross-country ski from the door or walk to lunch or dinner. Full breakfast. Lori Tradewell, innkeeper. B&B $56–105, children free April through August.

Jackson House (383-4226), Route 16, Jackson 03846. Open all year. Peter and Laraine Hill have spent several years transforming this c. 1868 country home into a comfortable inn. They have 14 rooms, 9 with private baths, each with a double, queen, or a double and a twin. Several rooms are new with bright comforters, handmade items, and custom-built Shaker beds. Swing in the hammock or jump into the hot tub in the solarium. Full breakfast. B&B $50–90.

Nestlenook Farm (383-9443), Dinsmore Road, Jackson Village 03846. Open all year. Elaborately furnished and decorated, this renovated Victorian (one of Jackson's original houses) is a romantic inn for couples only. Painted peach and green, the inn is part of a million-dollar development with extensive gardens, a gazebo, a pond, and a location beside the Ellis River. Each of the seven guest rooms has a private bath with a Jacuzzi. Some rooms have working fireplaces or parlor stoves. Rooms have queen-size beds, many with canopies, and separate sitting rooms. The rooms are named for local artists (some famous ones from the nineteenth century), and many feature an original painting as part of the decor. Guests may enjoy complimentary sleigh rides and skating, and they have free use of the inn's cross-country rentals, instruction, and trails, which connect to the extensive Jackson trail network. You can also pet the inn's herd of reindeer. A no-smoking inn. B&B $125–250.

Paisley and Parsley (383-0859), Route 16B, Box 572, Jackson 03846. Open most of the year. Bea and Chuck Stone have turned their contemporary home into a cozy, three-room B&B. One downstairs room (with a king-size bed and Jacuzzi) has a private entrance. Upstairs are two rooms, each with its own sitting room—one with two doubles, the other with a canopy bed. All have private baths, telephone, cable TV, and are furnished with antiques. Don't miss the beautiful rock gardens and the spectacular view of Mount Washington. No smoking. Full gourmet breakfast. $55–115, depending on season and accommodations.

The Village House (383-6666), Box 359, Jackson Village 03846. Open all year. This old cozy inn is right in the village, where you can walk to tennis, cross-country skiing, golf, lunch, or dinner. Ten rooms, all but two with private baths, furnished country style with braided rugs on the floors. They have an outdoor swimming pool, and the common room has a fireplace, TV, and games. Continental breakfast in summer, full breakfast in winter. Robin Crocker, innkeeper. $40–100.

WHERE TO EAT

DINING OUT

Wildcat Inn and Tavern (383-4245), Jackson Village. Open all year. Three country gourmet meals are served daily in one of the area's most popular restaurants. Dinner ranges from lasagna and baked scallops to lobster fettuccine, roast lamb, tavern steak, and scampi. Marty and Pam Sweeney are the longtime innkeepers. He is the dinner chef while she bakes and serves lunch (consider lobster Benedict or one of many unusual sandwiches). Moderate.

Christmas Farm Inn (383-4313; outside NH 1-800-HI-ELVES), Route 16B, Jackson. Open all year. Dinner served 5–9, Saturday until 10. Celebrate Christmas here all year while relaxing in the Mistletoe Lounge or dining in the holiday-decorated dining room. Baked salmon, shrimp scampi, chicken Kiev, lamb kabob, steak, pasta, and vegetarian dishes highlight the menu, along with fresh-made desserts and such appetizers as "a warm slice of duck with diced vegetables and fresh greens." Moderate.

Inn at Thorn Hill (383-4242/6448; 1-800-289-8990), Thorn Hill Road, Jackson Village. Open all year. Dining nightly 6–9. The menu changes quarterly but includes six appetizers, nine entrées, and six desserts. Specialties include New England shellfish fricassee in phyllo nest and smoked fillet of beef with curry butter. Four-course meal, $28, reservations required.

Whitneys' Inn (383-3916; 1-800-677-5737), Route 16B, Jackson. Best known for its location at the base of Black Mountain, this old inn also has a fine restaurant serving dinner nightly. The menu changes seasonally but might include baked haddock, roast duckling with cranberry-pear glaze, veal, or chicken *picatta*. Special dinner requests available with advance notice; most entrées can be prepared plain, broiled, or baked. Moderate.

Wentworth Resort Hotel (383-9700; 1-800-637-0013), Jackson Village. Dinner served 6–9, reservations recommended. Dinner entrées range from quail, roast duckling, and rack of lamb to Atlantic salmon, grilled shrimp in red pepper sauce, and scallops sautéed with leeks in a cream sauce. Moderate to expensive.

The Thompson House (393-9341), Jackson Village. Daily 11:30–10, open year-round. Owner-chef Larry Baima prepares a host of distinctive and imaginative combination sandwiches, soups, salads, and dinner entrées in a 1790 farmhouse. Try something Italian, oriental, or traditional

American, from pastas to chicken, veal, and seafood; it's all made fresh daily, to order, and can be prepared to suit dietary needs. A few lunch choices: a Reuben with turkey, sauerkraut, cheddar cheese, and Russian dressing; knockwurst marinated in beer and grilled with tomatoes, Swiss cheese, and spicy mustard sauce; or cheese tortellini with sun-dried tomato and basil vinaigrette, served atop fresh greens with artichoke hearts, prosciutto, tomatoes, and lots more. Dinner choices range from seafood Francesca and pork *picatta,* to oriental stir fry with chicken and shrimp, or chicken San Remo, a specialty of white chicken sautéed with eggplant, sweet peppers, onions, and sun-dried tomatoes in a garlic herb wine sauce, garnished with prosciutto. Sandwiches starting at $2.50, entrées starting at $11.25. Full bar plus sangria, hot buttered rum, and spiced cider. Patio dining in the summer and a roaring wood stove in the winter makes this place popular with locals, too.

The Bernerhof (383-4414; 1-800-548-8007), Route 302, Box 240, Glen. Open all year, lunch served noon–3, dinner 6–9. Another New Hampshire classic inn and one of the premier restaurants in the region as well as a cooking school. Dining is European with six veal entrées as specialties. Try Wiener schnitzel or schnitzel *cordon bleu.* Cheese and beef fondues for two and roast duckling are other highlights, but if you fancy something else, just give the chef 48 hours' notice and he will prepare it especially for you. Cooking flexibility is easy here, since Richard Spencer and Scott Willard direct A Taste of the Mountains Cooking School. Three- and 5-day, hands-on classes are conducted in spring, winter, and fall; a special 15-week Wednesday class is taught from January through April by a variety of New England chefs. Ted and Sharon Wroblewski, owners. Daily lunch specials, dinner starting at $12.50. Cooking school: three days, $375–425 per person; five days, $950–1,050 per person. Cooking-school prices include five-course gourmet lunches and dinners with suitable wines and lodging.

I Cugini (374-1977), Route 302, Bartlett. Open 4:30–9, weekends until 10. Cousins (*cugini*) Michael DiLuca and Anthony DiStefano operate this Italian restaurant, featuring many old recipes passed down from family members. Several veal dishes are featured along with a seafood marinara with shrimp, calamari, scallops, and clams, simmered in a spicy marinara sauce and served over linguine. The lounge, open until midnight, serves lighter fare, such as pizza and calzones. Prices inexpensive to moderate.

The Red Parka Pub (383-4344), Route 302, Glen. Open daily 4–10. A favorite with the locals and for après ski, this is a traditional ski tavern, with skis dating back to the 1930s adorning the walls and ceilings. Outside dining on the patio. Famous for steak and prime rib, the Red Parka Pub also features baked seafood, barbecued spare ribs and pork, shrimp, and varied chicken dishes. An extensive salad bar rounds out the meal; special kids' menu. Prices inexpensive to moderate.

PETER E. RANDALL.

The Appalachian Mountain Club's Pinkham Notch Camp

The Notchland Inn (374-6131; 1-800-866-6131), Route 302, Harts Location (Bartlett). Open all year. Located near the site of Abel Crawford's early White Mountain Hotel, once called the Inn Unique (this place is still unique). A professional chef, Pat Bernandin prepares five-course, three-entrée dinners, generally for guests but also to the public by reservation and when space permits. A typical menu might include beef Wellington; baked haddock; pan-fried veal with vegetables, shrimp, and onion in a cream-and-cheese Czarina sauce; or Cajun-style chicken; plus homemade soups, appetizers, and rich desserts. Call for reservations and prices.

EATING OUT

Stanley's Restaurant (383-6529), Route 16, Glen. Tom and Helen have been serving their breakfast menu all day (plus fried foods and sandwiches for lunch) since 1949.

Glen Junction (383-9660), Route 302, Glen. Open for breakfast, lunch, and dinner. Take-out sandwiches, deli, and home-style cooking in a family atmosphere. Kids (and adults) are fascinated with the two large-scale model trains that circle the dining rooms on tracks near the ceiling.

SPECIAL EVENTS

AMC Pinkham Notch Camp (466-2725) organizes and hosts weekend activities and workshops throughout the year.

Cross-country Skiing, Jackson Village. Throughout the ski season weekend citizens' races are held, and often special international events use the Jackson trails.

May: **Queen Victoria Festival and Clambake,** Jackson Village. A weekend festival for Canadian and American visitors alike.

Late May: **Quacktillion and Wildquack River Festival,** Jackson Village. A weekend of dancing, then cheer on one of 2,000 rubber duckies as they race down the river. Rent your own for $5.

Early June: **Jackson Covered Bridge 10 km,** Jackson Village. One of the most demanding 10-km road races in New England. **Wildflower Guided Tour and Barbecue,** Jackson Village. See more than 400 wildflowers and ferns, and classic eighteenth- and nineteenth-century gardens plus a chicken barbecue.

July Fourth: **Family in the Park,** Jackson Village. An old-fashioned Fourth of July celebration.

Mid-July: **Jackson Jazz Festival,** Black Mountain Ski Area.

Mid-August: **Attitash Equine Festival** (374-2372), Attitash Ski Area, Bartlett. World-class riders and horses compete for $100,000 in prizes at a weekend of show jumping, plus an international food fair and a country fair exposition.

MOUNT WASHINGTON AND PINKHAM NOTCH

Rising 6,288 feet above sea level, Mount Washington is the highest peak in the Northeast and one of the most popular scenic attractions in the state. It offers varied recreational opportunities for the most hardy to the most sedentary visitor. P. T. Barnum called the mountain and its attractions the Second Greatest Show on Earth. Since the days of Darby Field's first climb in 1642, the mountain has been the source of recreation, adventure, scientific research, and not a few tragedies. Annually some 250,000 people of all ages visit the summit, the location of Mount Washington State Park, the Mount Washington Observatory, and the transmitter facilities for a television station and several radio stations. There are three ways to reach the summit, each described in more detail below: hiking; the Mount Washington Auto Road; and the Mount Washington Cog Railway.

Perhaps the most impressive aspect of the mountain is its weather. Mount Washington Observatory records prove that the mountain has the worst combination of wind, cold, and ice of any regularly inhabited place on earth. It can, and often does, snow every month of the year, although summer snowstorms are somewhat rare and the snow usually melts quickly. Winds over 100 mph are common, although not usual in the summer when the July breeze averages 25 mph and the temperature averages about 49 degrees. February is the coldest month, averaging 5.6 degrees; and January is the windiest, averaging 35 mph. Hurricane force winds (over 75 mph) occur more than 100 days annually, and the highest recorded wind velocity, 231 mph, blew over the mountain in April 1934. The highest recorded temperature is just above 70 degrees while the low approaches –50 degrees. In addition, it is foggy more than 300 days per year, although this condition can appear and dissipate rapidly over the course of a day. Visitors should be patient if the summit is in the clouds—it might, and often does, clear suddenly. At other times, the valley is cloudy and the summit is open. When the weather is clear, the view extends some 130 miles to New York, Canada, Maine, and the Atlantic Ocean. However you reach the summit, take along an extra jacket or sweater since it is always cooler there than at the base of the mountain.

Because of the elevation and the weather conditions, Mount Washington's vegetation is also unusual. Squatty, spreading evergreens, called krummholz, are seen as one approaches tree line and are actually balsam fir and black spruce, which grow as tall as normal trees lower on the mountain. The trees grow as krummholz as a defense against the harsh weather conditions, especially the wind. Many tiny, flowering alpine plants found here are more common to Labrador, while some other species are unique to this mountain alone. Mid-June is the prime season for flower viewing; and while the best approach is by hiking, the flowers also grow along the Auto Road. The study of these plants brought scientists to the mountains in the early nineteenth century, and many of the mountain's features are named for these individuals. The AMC offers annual guided walks to the best viewing areas and also publishes *Mountain Flowers of New England,* the best flower handbook available. Another AMC book is *At Timberline: A Nature Guide to the Mountains of the Northeast.*

GUIDANCE

WMNF Androscoggin Ranger Station (466-2713), Route 16, Gorham. Open Monday to Friday 7:30–4:30.

AMC Pinkham Notch Camp (466-2725 for weather, trail, or general information; 466-2727 for overnight or workshop reservations; 617-523-0636 for membership details), Route 16, Box 298, Gorham 03518. Opened in 1920 and expanded several times since, this is the North Country headquarters for an organization of some 37,000 members. The main office is at 5 Joy Street, Boston, and chapters serve members from the mid-Atlantic states to New England. Members receive discounts on hikes, books, workshops, accommodations, and meals; but everyone is welcome to use the facilities and participate in their programs.

The club offers a variety of special weekend programs throughout the year, ranging from hiking, skiing, snowshoeing, woods crafts, and canoeing to bird study, photography, art, and writing. The AMC publishes annual and monthly publications and a variety of books and operates eight full-service, high-mountain huts, to which you must walk on trails ranging from 1.7 miles to more than 4 miles in length. Write to the address above for a brochure describing the huts and fees. A recent innovation is a shuttle-bus system for hikers, which provides service between popular trailheads in Pinkham, Crawford, and Franconia notches. The organization, especially its North Country headquarters, trail maintenance crew, and hut crews, is staffed primarily with young men and women who love the outdoors and who are hired for their energy and willingness and ability to relate to the public. They are a source of information and advice for the novice and more experienced hiker alike. These staffers cook all meals, maintain trails, guide hikes, teach workshops, and, when needed, participate in all manner of mountain rescue missions. This facility includes the full-service Joe Dodge Center (see *Camps*); the Trading Post, which sells snacks, books, postcards, and some equipment and has rest rooms with showers; and administrative offices. The AMC, with its trained staff and large membership, is one of New England's strongest conservation voices, urging careful use of and protection for the mountains.

Mount Washington: A Guide and Short History, by Peter E. Randall (The Countryman Press), is a paperback guide to the mountain with photographs and a unique fold-out panorama guide to the surrounding mountains.

GETTING THERE

Daily **Concord-Trailways bus service** (1-800-852-3317) to Pinkham Notch Camp from Boston's Logan Airport.

TO SEE

Mount Washington State Park, on the summit of the mountain. Open daily, Memorial Day through Columbus Day. Although most of Mount Washington is part of the White Mountain National Forest, there are several other owners. One is the state of New Hampshire, which operates the Sherman Adams Summit Building, named for the former governor who was the chief of staff for President Eisenhower. This contemporary, two-story curved building sits into the northeast side of the mountain, offering a sweeping view across the peaks of the Presidential Range. Park facilities include a gift shop, snack bar, post office, rest rooms (all handicapped accessible), and a hiker pack room. The mountain and its summit have a fascinating history, too detailed to be explained here, but the old Tip Top House, originally built as a summit hotel in 1853, has been restored and is open daily as a reminder of the past. Free. Other summit buildings include the transmitter and generator facilities of Channel 8, WMTW-TV, which provides transmitter service for radio stations and relays for state and federal government agencies.

Mount Washington Museum, on the summit. Open daily when the building is open. Located one flight below the main building, the museum is operated by the Mount Washington Observatory and offers historical exhibits and a wealth of scientific information on the meteorology, geology, botany, and biology of the mountain. A small gift shop helps support the activities of the observatory. Fee charged.

Mount Washington Observatory (356-8345), on the summit, Gorham 03518. Closed to the public, but members may tour the facility. (See *Museums* in "Mount Washington's Valleys—North Conway and Vicinity" for details of winter overnights on the summit.) This private, nonprofit, membership institution occupies a section of the Sherman Adams Summit Building and is staffed all year by rotating crews of two to three people who change each week. Weather observations are taken every three hours, providing a lengthy record of data that extends back to the 1930s when the institution was formed. The staff endured the highest wind ever recorded on Earth, 231 mph, in April 1934. The original building was the old Stage Office, a replica of which is on the summit. Various on-going research projects study the effects of icing, aspects of atmospheric physics, and related subjects. The observatory has conducted research for a variety of commercial, institutional, and governmental organizations. Facilities include crew quarters, a weather-instrument room, a radio room, a photography darkroom, and a library. The observatory publishes a quarterly bulletin. The staffers provide live morning weather reports on several area radio stations, including WMWV 93.5 FM in Conway. Write for membership information.

Mount Washington Cog Railway (846-5404, advance reservations recommended), off Route 302, Bretton Woods 03589. (See *To See* in "Mount Washington's Valleys—Crawford Notch and Bretton Woods.")

SCENIC DRIVES

Mount Washington Auto (Carriage) Road (466-2222; 466-3988), Route 16, Pinkham Notch, Box 278, Gorham 03518. Open daily, weather permitting, mid-May to mid-October, from 7:30 A.M. to 6 P.M. most of the summer, with shorter hours earlier and later in the season. Opened in 1861, originally for mountain stagecoaches or carriages, this 8-mile auto graded road climbs steadily without steep pitches, but with an average grade of 12 percent, from the Glen to the summit. Although the road is narrow in spots and skirts some steep slopes, it has a remarkable safety record and annually carries some 100,000 visitors. En route, there are many places to pull off and enjoy the view, and it is crossed by several hiking trails. At various times the road is used for annual foot and bicycle races (each record is about 1 hour) and, once again, for auto races. While it's a long way compared to hiking trails, some people prefer to walk its smooth grade to the summit. The route is the year-round supply line for the summit facilities and is followed by tractor-treaded snowcats in the winter. You may drive your own passenger car to the summit or take a 1.5-hour guided tour in one of the chauffeur-driven vans, called stages, to keep alive a historical tradition. At the base is a gift shop and snack bar. Passenger-car rates: $11 for car and driver, $3 each additional passenger. Guided tour: $15 for adults, $10 for children.

Mount Washington from the ski slopes of Wildcat Mountain

Pinkham Notch Scenic Area, Route 16, between Jackson and Gorham. This 5,600-acre section of the White Mountain National Forest covers the eastern side of Mount Washington and includes several spectacular ravines and other natural features and a most important human re-source, the Appalachian Mountain Club Pinkham Notch Visitors Cen-ter (see *Camps*). Tuckerman Ravine is famous for spring skiing and hiking, while adjacent Huntington Ravine is a challenge to winter ice climbers. The Great Gulf Wilderness is a larger glacial valley sur-rounded by the state's highest peaks.

Approaching from the Jackson end of the notch, Route 16 begins a long, gradual ascent, passing the beginnings of several hiking trails and a few pullouts adjacent to the Ellis River. Watch the ridge of the moun-tains on the west side, and gradually the huge Glen Boulder becomes silhouetted against the sky. This glacial erratic was dragged to this seem-ingly precarious spot eons ago by an ice-age glacier. Situated at an el-evation of about 2,500 feet, the boulder is a steep 1.5-mile, 2-hour hike from the highway, a short but steep climb to tree line. At the top of the notch, the mountainside drops steeply to the east and allows a pan-oramic view south down the Ellis River Valley toward Conway and Mount Chocorua. Across this valley rises the long ridge of Wildcat Mountain. Just ahead is a parking lot for Glen Ellis Falls, one of the picturesque highlights of the notch. To see the falls, cross under the highway by the short tunnel, then walk .2 mile down a short trail to the base of the falls.

North along Route 16, as the highway skirts under the side of Mount Washington, are the AMC Pinkham Notch Camp, an informa-tion center with rest rooms and snacks for sale, then Wildcat Mountain

Ski Area (with summer and fall mountain gondola rides), and the Mount Washington Auto Road at the Glen. Here is one of the most magnificent views in all the mountains. At left can be seen the summit of Mount Washington, although it doesn't appear to be the highest spot around. Rising clockwise above the Great Gulf, another glacial valley, are Mounts Clay, Jefferson, Adams (the state's second highest peak), and Madison. Route 16 continues north to Gorham, passing en route WMNF Dolly Copp campground and the entrance to Pinkham B (Dolly Copp) Road, which connects to Route 2 at Randolph. Just north of Pinkham Notch, several hiking trails head east into the Carter Range. One, the Nineteen Mile Brook Trail (3.8 miles, 2.5 hours) leads to the AMC Carter Notch Hut, another full-service facility. It is also open on a self-service, caretaker basis in the winter.

TO DO

HIKING

Mount Washington is crisscrossed with trails, but there are two popular routes. The **Tuckerman Ravine Trail** (4.1 miles, 4.5 hours) begins at the AMC Pinkham Notch Camp on Route 16. It is nearly a graded path most of the first 2.5 miles where it approaches the ravine; then it climbs steeply up the ravine's headwall and reaches the summit cone for the final ascent to the top. The ravine has open-sided shelters for up to 86 people, and each person has to carry up everything needed for an overnight stay. (Register at the AMC Pinkham Notch Camp, no reservations.) This is the trail used by spring skiers, and it can be walked to the ravine by anyone in reasonably good condition. The beginning of this trail is an easy 0.5-mile walk on a graded path to the pretty Crystal Cascade.

On the west side of Mount Washington is the **Ammonoosuc Ravine Trail** (in combination with Crawford Path; 3.86 miles, 4.5 hours). It begins at the Cog Railway Base Station, located off Route 302 north of Crawford Notch. About 2.5 miles from the start is the AMC Lakes of the Clouds Hut, a full-service facility, serving two meals daily and complete with bunk rooms and blankets. (Make reservations with the AMC, 466-2727.) Near this hut are the best areas to view the alpine flowers. Here also is a junction with popular **Crawford Path,** the oldest continuously maintained hiking trail in the country, built in 1819 by the Crawford family. This trail is 8.2 miles long and requires six hours to reach the summit of Mount Washington. It begins just above Crawford Notch, and at about 2.5 miles is the AMC Mizpah Spring Hut, another of the full-service facilities. In the vicinity of the AMC Pinkham Notch Camp are many short hiking trails or paths suitable for family groups. Ask for suggestions and directions at the camp.

A few words of caution about hiking on Mount Washington and the Presidential Range. Most of these trails lead above tree line and should be attempted only by properly equipped hikers. Winter weather conditions can occur above tree line any month of the year. Annually some 50,000 hikers safely reach the summit, many in the winter, but hiking is a self-reliant activity, so even fair-weather summer hikers are warned to climb well prepared with extra clothing and food in addition to maps and a compass. Most of the trails to the summits are 4–5 miles in length and require four to five hours to reach the top. Although these trails are not exceptionally long, there is an elevation gain of some 4,000 feet, a distance that becomes painfully evident to those who are not in reasonably good physical condition. Western hikers, used to the higher Rockies, soon appreciate the ruggedness and the elevation change when climbing this mountain. About 100 people have died on the slopes of the mountain, some from falls while hiking, rock or ice climbing, or skiing; but others have died in the summer when they were caught unprepared by rapidly changing weather conditions. Since the weather can be most severe above tree line, cautious hikers will assess the weather conditions when reaching that point on a climb. The AMC (466-2725) provides daily weather information. Also call 466-5252 for recorded weather information.

Since AMC staffers often volunteer for mountain rescues, they are careful to give considered advice to beginning and more experienced hikers. The *AMC White Mountain Guide* has the most comprehensive trail information available for hikers, but also see Daniel Doan's *50 Hikes in the White Mountains.*

CROSS-COUNTRY SKIING

AMC Pinkham Notch Camp. There are a number of trails in the notch near the AMC headquarters, although they are not groomed and would be considered backcountry trails. One expert trail, part of the Jackson system, goes down the back side of Wildcat.

DOWNHILL SKIING

Wildcat Mountain (466-3326, lodging 1-800-255-6439), Route 16, Pinkham Notch, Jackson 03846. One of the East's biggest ski mountains, Wildcat was first used in the 1930s when skiers had to climb to the top of the ski run. Now it has some 30-plus trails with 97 percent snowmaking and a 2,100-foot vertical drop; its 6 lifts can handle 8,500 skiers per hour, the largest capacity in the valley. The gondola goes to the top of the 4,000-foot mountain, which is just across the valley from towering Mount Washington, offering the best view for skiers in the East. This high-mountain location, which makes Wildcat colder than some lower-elevation areas, also provides a season from mid-November to April. Although considered a world-class area with challenging expert runs, Wildcat's easier Polecat Trail offers a 2.75-mile run from the top of the hill. Telemark, cross-country, and downhill rentals; ski school; and snack bars at the base and summit. Wildcat's gondola is also open for passengers in the off-season. The two-person cars make a half-hour round-trip to the summit. The cars stop at stationary platforms, making boarding and exiting easy for all ages. At the summit are picnic tables, a snack bar, and hiking trails plus that great view across the valley to Mount Washington. The gondola is open weekends Memorial Day to late June, then daily until early October.

Tuckerman Ravine (call Appalachian Mountain Club, 466-2725), off Route 16, Pinkham Notch. Spring skiing has become an annual rite for many skiers, and there is nowhere better than the steep slopes of Tuckerman Ravine. There are no lifts, so you have to walk more than 3 miles to reach the headwall of this cirque, a little valley carved out of the eastern side of Mount Washington by glaciers during the ice age. Winds blow snow from the mountain into the ravine, where it settles to a depth of 75 feet or more. When snow has melted from traditional ski slopes, it still remains in the ravine; skiers by the thousands walk the trail from the AMC Pinkham Notch Camp to reach the slopes. Skiing begins in early April, and we have seen some diehards in June skiing the small patches of snow remaining in the ravine.

Early in the season when there is plenty of snow, the steep John Sherburne Ski Trail provides a brisk run from the ravine back to Pinkham Notch Camp. Spring sun warms the air, and many people ski in short-sleeved shirts and shorts, risking sunburn and bruises if they fall. Skiing here is for experts, since a fall on the 35- to 55-degree slopes means a long, dangerous slide to the bottom of the ravine. A volunteer ski patrol is on duty, and WMNF rangers patrol the ravine to watch for avalanches. The 3-sided Hermit Lake shelters offer sleeping-bag accommodations for 86 hardy backpackers, who must carry everything up to the site for overnight stays. Winter-use only (November to March) tent platforms are also available in the ravine. Register for shelters or tent platforms through the AMC Pinkham Notch Camp (466-2727, no reservations; first-come, first-served only).

LODGING

See "Mount Washington's Valleys—Crawford Notch and Bretton Woods," "The Western Whites—Franconia and North of the Notches," and "The North Country—Along Route 2" for additional listings of lodging at Twin Mountain, Gorham, and Jefferson.

CAMPS

Appalachian Mountain Club Pinkham Notch Visitors Center (466-2727), Route 16, Pinkham Notch, Box 298, Gorham 03581. This is a full-service facility offering two meals a day, bunk beds, and shared baths. Bunk rooms for 2, 3, and 4 people accommodate 106 guests in the **Joe Dodge Center.** It appeals mostly to outdoorspeople (hikers, skiers, and such), but it is clean, comfortable, and inexpensive, with a library and a huge fireplace in the living room and another in the main lodge dining

Skiers ascending Tuckerman Ravine

area. Families are encouraged. Meals are served family style, and no one goes hungry here since the one-entrée offerings are generous. Saturday night dinner is followed by a free lecture. Open to AMC members and the general public. Reservations strongly recommended. B&D (dinner) $44 per person; MAP $57 per person; members save $7 per night. (Also see Pinkham Notch Scenic Area under *Scenic Drives.*)

Appalachian Mountain Club High Huts (466-2727), Pinkham Notch, Box 298, Gorham 03581. The AMC maintains eight full-service mountain huts (only reached by walking) in the White Mountain National Forest. You supply your sheets and towels; they provide meals, bunks, and blankets. Reservations strongly recommended. Some AMC programs involve guided hikes to the huts. Contact the AMC for rates and other information and see the *AMC White Mountain Guide* for trail routes.

CAMPGROUNDS

WMNF Dolly Copp Campground (466-3984, July through Labor Day), Route 16, Pinkham Notch, Gorham 03581. Open mid-May through mid-October. Some of the 176 sites are available through a **toll-free reservation system** (1-800-283-2267). The reservation service operates March through September (Monday to Friday 12–9, weekends 12–5) and costs $6 in addition to the camping fee. Reservations may be made 120 days before arrival, but 10 days before arrival is the minimum time.

SPECIAL EVENTS

AMC Pinkham Notch Camp (466-2725) organizes and hosts weekend activities and workshops throughout the year.

Late June: **Mount Washington Auto Road Footrace and Auto Hill Climb,** Mount Washington Auto Road, Pinkham Notch. On consecutive weekends, first runners, then autos race from the Glen to the summit over the steep winding course. For footrace details call 863-2537; for auto-race details 466-3988.

Mid-September: **Mount Washington Bike Race** (466-3988), Mount Washington Auto Road, Pinkham Notch. This event attracts some of the top United States racers.

CRAWFORD NOTCH AND BRETTON WOODS

Crawford is the least developed of New Hampshire's mountain passes, although historically it has been important since the eighteenth century when settlers followed today's Route 302 from Conway north to establish towns above the mountains. The notch was "discovered" by white men in 1770, but undoubtedly it was the location of an earlier Native American trail. It was in this narrow notch, flanked by steep mountains, that the Crawford family began taking in travelers, and thus created the tourist industry that dominates the White Mountains today. At the turn of the century some of the region's largest and best hotels were located just above the notch; now only the Mount Washington Hotel remains.

Although Crawford Notch itself has few attractions, there are many sights to see, including fine waterfalls and one of the best views in all the mountains.

"Look at me gentlemen . . . for I am the poor fool who built all this!" coal baron Joseph Stickney is reported to have exclaimed on the July day in 1902 when the Mount Washington first opened. It's noted that he "laughed heartily at his own folly." By and large the 194-room hotel has been lucky. Although Stickney died in 1903, it remained in his family until World War II and was then lavishly refurbished by the United States government for the 1944 Bretton Woods Monetary Conference, which set the gold standard and created both the World Bank and the International Monetary Fund. In ensuing decades it's had its ups and downs. Perhaps the best White Mountains news in recent years was the 1991 purchase of the hotel and adjacent properties by a group of North Country businesspeople who have made a long-term commitment to returning the hotel to its former status as the showplace of the mountains.

GUIDANCE

Twin Mountain Chamber of Commerce (846-5407; 1-800-245-TWIN), Box 194, Twin Mountain 03595, produces a brochure and operates a summer information center at the junction of Routes 2 and 302.

TO SEE

Mount Washington Cog Railway (advance reservations recommended: 846-5404, ext. 6; 1-800-922-8825, ext. 6), off Route 302, Bretton Woods 03589. Open weekends in May, daily until early November. Opened in 1869, this is the world's first mountain-climbing cog railway, and it remains one of the few places where you can observe steam locomotives at work. At one time regular trains followed a spur line to the Base Station, where passengers boarded the cog railway directly for the summit. So unique and ambitious was the plan to build the railroad that its promoter, Sylvester Marsh, was told he might as well "build a railway to the moon." The eight little engines, each made for this purpose by this railroad company, have boilers positioned at an angle because of the steep grade up the mountain. On the three-hour round-trip, which permits a visit at the summit, each engine pushes a single car up, then backs down in front of the car to provide braking. Unique cogwheels fit into slots between the rails to provide traction and braking. The average grade along the 3.25-mile track is 25 percent, but at Jacob's Ladder trestle it rises to 37.5 percent. Several switches permit ascending and descending trains to pass en route. The Base Station, a short drive on a paved road from Route 302, includes a new visitors center and museum, a restaurant, a gift shop, a B&B, and an RV park. Adults $32, children 6–12 $22.

TO DO

GOLF

Bretton Woods Golf Course (278-1000), Route 302, Bretton Woods (at the Mount Washington Hotel). Offers a total of 27 holes with the Presidential Range as a backdrop.

HIKING

Many hiking trails cross and parallel the notch. One is the Appalachian Trail—follow it north to Maine or south to Georgia. Consult the *AMC White Mountain Guide* for details of the many trails. Below are some less ambitious alternatives.

Arethusa Falls Trail is a 1.3-mile, one-hour, easy-to-moderate walk to New Hampshire's most impressive and highest waterfall, at its best in the spring and early summer when water is high. The well-marked trail begins on the east side of Route 302 near the southern entrance to the park. Silver Cascade, also a pretty waterfall, can be seen from your vehicle at the top of the notch, where there is a parking lot and a scenic outlook.

Mount Willard Trail begins at the AMC Crawford Notch Information Center, a year-round facility with rest rooms located in a restored railroad station just above the top of the notch. It is a 1.4-mile, one-hour walk, most of which is easy, along a former carriage road. It leads to rocky ledges with a panoramic view down through Crawford Notch. The railroad station once served the old Crawford House, one of the earliest of the old hotels. It was closed in the 1970s and finally burned.

Saco Lake Trail (.4 mile, 15 minutes) is across the street from the information center. Saco Lake is the source of the river that flows through Crawford Notch, and behind it is Elephant Head, a rocky ridge shaped like a pachyderm.

Crawford Path, from Route 302 (opposite the Crawford House site) to Mount Washington, is the oldest hiking trail in the country, built in 1819 by the Crawford family and used as a bridle path in the 1870s. Mount Washington is a long 8.2-mile, six-hour walk. The AMC Mizpah Spring Hut (466-2727 for reservations) is a 2.5-mile, two-hour walk over the well-worn trail.

Ammonoosuc Ravine Trail (See *Hiking* in "Mount Washington's Valleys—Mount Washington and Pinkham Notch.")

HORSEBACK RIDING

Mount Washington Hotel (278-1000), Route 302, Bretton Woods. The Mount Washington Hotel's impressive stables offer unusually scenic trail rides, pitched to riders with at least some experience.

CROSS-COUNTRY SKIING

Bretton Woods Touring Center (278-5181) at the Mount Washington Hotel, across Route 302 from the ski area. A shuttle service operates back and forth. The 86-km network is considered one of the best in New England, and it's groomed for both touring and skating techniques. There are 39 trails, all mapped and marked, divided into 3 linked trail systems. One trail leads down from the summit of the alpine area.

Backcountry skiing is popular in the Zealand Valley, off Route 302 between Bretton Woods and Twin Mountain. Well-equipped and -prepared skiers can schuss from Route 302 some 2.5 miles into the AMC Zealand Hut (466-2727), which is open all winter on a caretaker basis. Bring your own sleeping bag and food; use their cabin and cooking facilities.

DOWNHILL SKIING

Bretton Woods Ski Area (278-5000), Route 302, Bretton Woods. While it's not the most challenging ski area in New Hampshire, this is certainly one of the most enjoyable, and its 26 predominantly intermediate trails command magnificent views of the Mount Washington Range. The vertical drop is 1,500 feet, and the longest run is 2 miles. Snowmaking covers 98 percent of the terrain, and the 5 lifts include 2 double chairs, a triple chair, and a detachable quad. Night skiing is offered every weekend, and the multi-tiered base lodge is unusually attractive.

SNOWMOBILING

Large portions of the WMNF are off-limits to snowmobiling, trail bikes, and off-road vehicles, but there are marked trails in Crawford Notch. A popular ride is along Mount Clinton Road (begins opposite the Crawford House site on Route 302) to the Base Station Road and over the Jefferson Notch Road to Jefferson. (See *Scenic Drives* in "The North Country—Along Route 2.") For details contact the **Trails Bureau,** New Hampshire Division of Parks and Recreation (271-3254), Box 856, Concord 03301, or the New Hampshire Snowmobile Association (224-8906), Box 38, Concord 03301.

GREEN SPACE

Crawford Notch State Park. This large state park is located in the middle of the White Mountain National Forest, some 12 miles north of Bartlett. The park headquarters is located at the Willey House Memorial, the site of an unusual mountain tragedy. In August 1826 a terrible rainstorm blew through the notch, frightening the Willey family, who operated a small inn. Hearing an avalanche sliding down the steep side of the mountain, the family and two employees ran from the inn only to be swallowed up in the debris as the avalanche split above the inn, leaving it intact. Seven people died; the avalanche scar can still be seen on the mountain. This park was established in 1911 when the state purchased the virgin spruce forest to save it from loggers' axes. Today there is a seasonal gift shop (selling New Hampshire–made craft items), a waterfowl pond, and a self-guided nature trail. Several major hiking trails begin within the park's borders.

Eisenhower Memorial Wayside Park is on Route 302, 2 miles above Crawford Notch. This small park is a tribute to the former president in whose honor one of the nearby mountains in the Presidential Range was named. A short walk leads to a magnificent view of Mounts Eisenhower, Monroe, Washington, Jefferson, Adams, and Madison. The tracks of the Mount Washington Cog Railway can be seen ascending the side of Washington, and sometimes a bit of smoke can be seen as one of the little engines puffs up the steep track.

LODGING

Additional lodging is available at Twin Mountain (see "The Western Whites—Franconia and North of the Notches").

RESORTS

Lodging at the **Mount Washington Hotel and Resort** in Bretton Woods, which includes the **Bretton Arms Inn, Bretton Woods Motor Inn,** and **Bretton Woods Townhouses,** is accessed by phoning 278-1000 or 1-800-258-0330. Special packages, such as golf or romance weekends, theme weekends, and seasonal specials are offered throughout the year. The mailing address is Bretton Woods 03575.

✐ **The Mount Washington Hotel,** Route 302, Bretton Woods. Open May to November. Everything about this hotel mirrors the scale of its majestic surroundings. The 194-room hotel rises like a white cruise ship from a surrounding sea of green woods, dwarfed only by its backdrop: New England's highest mountains. Its approach is up a mile-long drive; the veranda is vast, the lobby high and columned, the dining room grand, the menu immense. The new owners are making a special effort to open the hotel to the public, so several-times-daily tours of this large complex are offered, and the public is welcome to attend various lectures on White Mountain human and natural history. Families are especially welcome here, with a number of two-room suites joined by a common bath being most popular. King of the Mountains Kids Kamp offers daily and evening programs for children ages 5–12, including hikes, visits with the golf pro and the chef, crafts, outings to local attractions, and various sports. Other amenities include the granite-walled Cave lounge with nightly live entertainment; a beauty salon; gift, clothing, flower, and ice-cream shops; indoor and outdoor pools; 12 tennis courts; horseback riding; movies; guided hikes; and a 27-hole golf course. A health and fitness center, open all year, is adjacent to the hotel. MAP (dine at any of the resort's four dining rooms), $165–485 per couple. (See the introduction to this section for more about the hotel's history.)

The Bretton Arms, Bretton Woods. A former annex of the Mount Washington Hotel, built in 1896, this is a small, restored, attractive inn with 34 rooms, facilities for a small conference, a lounge with weekend entertainment, and intimate dining. EP $80–155 per night.

Bretton Woods Motor Inn. The 50 rooms are all motel style, large and pleasant with 2 double beds and TV. Amenities include an indoor pool, a spa pool and sauna, and comfortable common rooms with fireplaces. Its restaurant, Darby's, serves breakfast as well as dinner. EP $60–95 per night; $225 for five nights.

The Townhouses at Bretton Woods. A variety of one- to five-bedroom condominiums complete with full kitchens and fireplaced living room; includes access to the health and fitness center and the resort shuttle. $80–335 per night.

BED & BREAKFAST

Mount Washington Cog Railway B&B Chalet (summer 846-2256; year-round 846-5404), off Route 302, Bretton Woods 03595. Open all year, but call for details about lodging in the winter. Located at the Base Station of the Cog Railway, this chalet has five rooms, some with private baths. Various bed combinations allow some rooms to sleep four to six people. Surrounded by the national forest, with great views, this is a unique place to stay.

CAMP

Zealand Hut, an **Appalachian Mountain Club High Hut** (466-2727;

Box 298, Gorham 03581), located off Route 302 at Zealand Road. You must hike 2.8 miles to the hut and supply your clothes and towels; they provide meals, bunks, and blankets. Reservations required. Some AMC programs involve guided hikes to the huts. Contact the AMC for rates and other information, and see the *AMC White Mountain Guide* for trail routes.

CAMPGROUNDS

Camping is prohibited along the roadside in Crawford Notch State Park, but there are two campgrounds. **Dry River Campground,** Route 302, Crawford Notch. A state-owned facility, open mid-May through mid-October, with 30 tent sites. No reservations. **Crawford Notch General Store and Campground** (374-2779), Route 302 (south of Crawford Notch), Harts Location. The store sells gas, groceries, and hiking and camping supplies and is open all year; the campground, with wooded sites, tables, fireplaces, and hot showers, is open May through October.

WMNF Campgrounds, just south of Twin Mountain on Route 302, are 3 campgrounds with 73 sites. A **toll-free reservation system** (1-800-283-2267) operates for Sugarloaf I and II. (See *Campgrounds* in "Mount Washington's Valleys—Mount Washington and Pinkham Notch.")

HOSTEL

Appalachian Mountain Club Shapleigh Hostel (466-2727), Route 302, north of Crawford Notch. Located in one of the remaining outbuildings of the old Crawford House, the hostel is open year-round on a caretaker basis with accommodations for 20 people, plus 8 people each in 2 cabins, which are heated with wood stoves. There is a self-service kitchen with cookware and utensils; bring a sleeping bag and food.

EVANS NOTCH

Evans Notch is one of the lesser known of the White Mountain passes. Route 113 through the notch (not winter-maintained) connects Hastings, Maine (on Route 2 west of Shelburne, New Hampshire), with Chatham, New Hampshire, on the south. The best views in this notch are seen traveling from north to south. There are four campgrounds (see *Campgrounds*) in the notch, many hiking trails, and good fishing along the Wild River.

GUIDANCE

WMNF Androscoggin Ranger Station (466-2713), Route 16, Gorham. Open Monday to Friday 7:30–4:30.

WMNF Evans Notch District (207-824-2134), Bridge Street, RFD 2, Box 2270, Bethel, ME 04217. Open Monday to Friday 7:30–4:30.

LODGING

CAMPGROUNDS

WMNF Campgrounds, Evans Notch. Seventy-seven wooded sites. Four of the campgrounds are open all year; and three—Hastings, Cold River, and Basin—are part of the **toll-free reservation system** (1-800-283-2267) . (See *Campgrounds* in "Mount Washington's Valleys—Mount Washington and Pinkham Notch.")

VII. THE NORTH COUNTRY

Along Route 2
Berlin and Route 16 North
Littleton, Whitefield, Lancaster, Groveton, and Stark
Colebrook, Pittsburg, and Vicinity

45th PARALLEL

As you stand at this point on the 45th parallel you are half way between the Equator and the North Pole.

JON-PIERRE LASSEIGNE

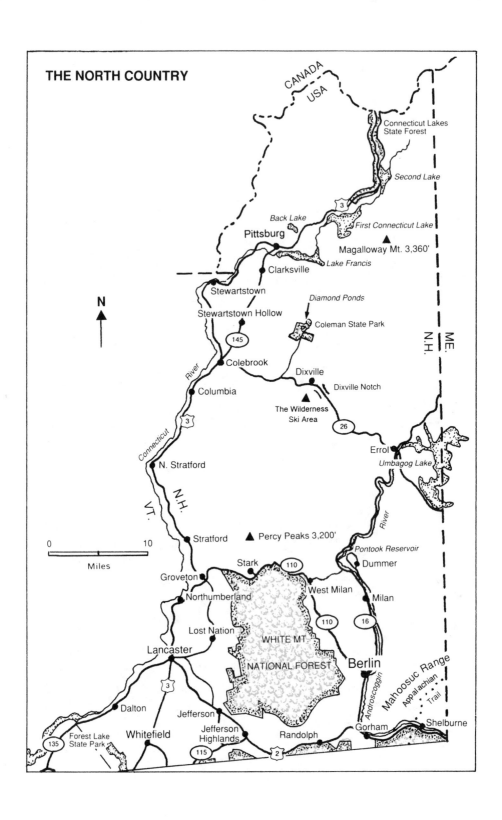

THE NORTH COUNTRY

Introduction

The vast region north of the White Mountains, an area larger than Rhode Island, is New Hampshire's remaining frontier. Route 2, which connects Gorham in the east and Lancaster in the west, is considered the southern boundary of the North Country. Route 16, from Gorham to Errol; Route 26, from Errol to Colebrook; and Route 3, from Lancaster north through Colebrook to Pittsburg are the main, and sometimes the only, roads for travelers. The broad forests, fast-running rivers, and rugged mountains are cut by only a few roads, and many of the towns are small and scattered. Although most of the privately owned woodlands have been cut more than once to feed the voracious paper mills, the overall impression is one of wilderness. Trees are harvested as a cash crop, but cutting is usually back from the highways and only the sight of huge, heavily loaded logging trucks gives evidence of how much wood is cut annually. The paper and timber-management companies, who own most of this forested country, allow recreational use of their property for hunting, fishing, hiking, and snowmobiling while managing the woods for a continuous yield.

This system has worked well for decades, but there are signs that changes are coming. Huge sections of land were sold to developers in 1988; even though the state of New Hampshire, various conservation groups, and the federal government were able to buy some environmentally critical acreage, other parcels may be used for vacation homes or other types of developments.

Economically, this is the poorest section of the state. While New Hampshire is the fastest-growing state in the Northeast, the North Country is losing population as many young people are forced to seek employment elsewhere. Working in the woods and in the paper mills are important occupations; but with woodlands being sold for development, and the changing status of three large paper mills, residents are naturally concerned about the future. Land sold for development is lost for outdoor recreation, yet when acreage is acquired by the state or federal governments, these small towns lose badly needed tax revenues.

Tourism is becoming more important to the economy. Hunting and fishing are leisure-time activities for residents and visitors alike. Trapping remains a winter occupation for a few people, and others make a living as hunting and fishing guides.

All of the North Country is part of Coos County (to sound like a native pronounce it as "Co-oss"). Although the Kilkenny District of the White Mountain National Forest occupies a large section of the North Country, campers are reminded that most of the North Country is private property, and open fires and camping are not permitted except at campgrounds.

Travelers in the North Country are reminded that lodging and dining establishments are few and far between, especially on Route 16 north of Berlin. This is great country for taking along a picnic to enjoy as you fish, canoe, or just relax in New Hampshire's northern wilds.

Moose are becoming more common in New Hampshire, especially in the North Country. While fun to observe, these large animals are oblivious to moving vehicles. The state has recorded nearly 200 collisions between moose and autos and trucks. A common bumper sticker reading "Brake for Moose" means just that. Be extremely wary when driving near moose along a roadside, especially near dusk when vision is difficult and the moose are active.

GETTING THERE

With only limited bus service, no taxis, and no scheduled air service, a private vehicle is the best way to travel in the North Country.

By car: Routes 16, 302, or I-93 to Route 3 from the south; Route 2 from Maine or Vermont; Route 257 from Montreal; and Route 147 from Quebec City.

By bus: **Concord Trailways** (1-800-639-3317) provides scheduled service from Boston's Logan Airport and Atlantic Avenue (adjacent to Boston's South Station, an AMTRAK stop) to central and northern New Hampshire via Manchester and Meredith. Western North Country stops include Plymouth, Franconia, and Littleton. Eastern North Country stops, via Meredith and West Ossipee and Chocorua, include Conway, North Conway (disembark only), Jackson, Glen, Pinkham Notch, Gorham, and Berlin. Daily service varies.

By air: There is no scheduled air service anywhere near the North Country. Fly to commercial airports in Portsmouth (Pease), Lebanon, or Manchester, New Hampshire; Portland, Maine; or Boston, Massachusetts, and get rental cars at the airports. Several private airports are listed in the following chapters (see *Airplane Rides*), but there are no taxis. Some inns and lodges arrange for pickup on request.

MEDICAL EMERGENCY

See *Medical Emergency* in each chapter for hospitals, or call the State Police (1-800-852-3411).

Along Route 2

Gorham has been catering to tourists since 1851, when the newly built Atlantic and St. Lawrence Railroad (now the Canadian National) began to bring thousands of tourists from southern and central New England via Portland to the White Mountains. Today it is a prime crossroads where east-west Route 2 intersects north-south Route 16. Strung out along the Androscoggin River, Shelburne is famous for its stand of white birches that straddles Route 2 a few miles east of Gorham. Large in land area, small in population, the two towns of Randolph and Jefferson stretch out along Route 2 bordering the northern peaks of the Presidential Range of the White Mountains. Randolph is a center for White Mountain hiking, while Jefferson has long been a popular resort community.

GUIDANCE

Northern White Mountains Chamber of Commerce (752-6060; 1-800-992-7480), 164 Main Street, Box 298, Berlin 03570.

Town of Gorham Information Center (466-3103), Main Street, Gorham. Open weekends Memorial Day through June, then daily from July to Columbus Day weekend.

Gorham Resort Bureau (466-2520).

A seasonal **New Hampshire Information Center,** with rest rooms and picnic tables, is located on Route 2, Shelburne.

White Mountain National Forest, Androscoggin Ranger Station (466-2713), Route 16, Gorham. Open Monday through Friday 7:30–4:30.

MEDICAL EMERGENCY

Androscoggin Valley Hospital (752-2200), 59 Page Hill Road, Berlin. Ambulance: 752-1020.

TO SEE

HISTORIC MUSEUM

Gorham Historical Society, Railroad Street, Gorham. The Railroad Station Museum contains displays on local history and especially railroading, tourism, and logging.

FOR FAMILIES

⚲ **Moose Tours** (466-3103), Gorham Information Center, Main Street, Gorham. From June through foliage season, nightly moose-viewing van tours are offered. Adults $7. Call for reservations; 2¼-hour tours leave about dusk from the information center.

⚲ **Six Gun City** (586-4592), Route 2, Jefferson. Open daily 9–6, Father's Day to Labor Day; weekends until Columbus Day. Cowboy skits and frontier shows are combined with 35 western town buildings; a 100-piece, horse-drawn vehicle museum; miniature burros and horses, and other animals; 11 rides; and 2 water slides. Food and gift shops. Admission includes unlimited rides and shows. Age four to adult $8, age three and under free with an adult.

⚲ **Santa's Village** (586-4445), Route 2, Jefferson. Open daily 9:30–7, Father's Day to Labor Day; weekends 9:30–5 until Columbus Day. Santa and his elves, along with the reindeer, make this Christmas in the summer for children and adults. Ride the Yule Log Flume, the railroad, Ferris wheel, or roller coaster; watch the trained macaw show; see the new animated Twelve Days of Christmas kiosk; and, of course, sit on Santa's lap. Food and gift shops. Admission includes unlimited rides and shows. Age four to adult $10, age three and under with an adult free as Santa's guest.

SCENIC DRIVES

Pinkham B Road (formerly Dolly Copp Road) is a mostly unpaved wilderness road running from Dolly Copp Campground on Route 16, past the base of Mount Madison to Route 2. Several hiking trails begin on this road. Not winter-maintained.

Jefferson Notch Road is a historic route beside the western edge of the Presidential Range. Not winter-maintained, this winding gravel road reaches the highest elevation point of any public through-road in New Hampshire at Jefferson Notch (3,008 feet). Drive with care, because snow and mud leave late in the spring and ice returns early in the fall; it is best used in the summer. The Caps Ridge Trail, at the 7-mile point on Jefferson Notch, offers the shortest route to any of the Presidential Range peaks: 2.5 miles to Mount Jefferson. From the north, Jefferson Notch Road leaves Valley Road (which connects Routes 2 and 115) in Jefferson and runs south to the Cog Railway Base Station Road. At that intersection, paved Mount Clinton Road continues on to the Crawford House site on Route 302.

Shelburne's North Road is a winding country byway with great views of the Presidential Range across the Androscoggin River.

TO DO

AIRPLANE RIDES

Screaming Eagle Aviation (466-3431; 356-5809), Gorham Airport, Routes 16 and 2, Gorham. Airplane rides over the White Mountains in a vintage 1941 Fairchild 24, a classic luxury design of the 1930s. The windows roll down for picture taking. Rates begin at $20 per person for three passengers.

GOLF

Androscoggin Valley Country Club (466-9468; pro shop 466-2641), Route 2, Gorham. Eighteen holes, bar and food service.

The Waumbeck Country Club (586-7777), Route 2, Jefferson. The 18-hole course, overlooked by the Presidential Range, is about all that remains from one of the largest nineteenth-century resort hotels. Food and beverages, also tennis.

HIKING

White Mountain Adventures (466-2363), Route 2, Shelburne 03581, is a guide service for hiking, backpacking, and snowshoeing in the White Mountains. All food and group equipment is provided for day hikes or two- to three-day overnight trips. Trips are organized to suit hikers' abilities. All participants receive detailed lists of needed personal gear. Rates vary for type and length of trip.

White Mountain Llamas (586-4598), Route 115, Jefferson Meadows 03583. Something new for the hiker is a trek with these unusual animals hauling the gear and your experienced guides pointing out the flora and fauna and preparing a mountainside gourmet lunch. One- to four-day treks with accommodations at **Stag Hollow Inn and Llama Keep** (see *Bed & Breakfasts*) and two meals daily is $150–500 per couple; without accommodations, $55 per person.

Presidential Range Hiking. For any White Mountain hiking consult the *AMC White Mountain Guide* for details about trailheads, routes, distances, hiking time estimates, and special information. (Also see *50 Hikes in the White Mountains* or *50 More Hikes in New Hampshire*, both by Daniel Doan, Backcountry Publications.) A map is vital here since there are myriad trails interconnecting on the north side of the rugged Presidential Range peaks. There are three parking areas on Route 2 and another on Pinkham B (Dolly Copp) Road, connecting Routes 2 and 16, which are at the most popular trailheads for climbing the northern peaks of Madison, Adams, and Jefferson. Most of these trails lead above tree line and should be attempted only by properly equipped hikers. Winter weather conditions can occur above tree line any month of the year. Most of the trails to the summits are 4–5 miles in length and require four to five hours to reach the top. The lower portions of the trails pass through wooded areas along streams and are suitable for short walks.

High on the side of **Mount Adams,** the **Randolph Mountain Club** (Randolph 03570) maintains two cabins and two shelters for hikers. Overnight fees of $1–2.50 per person are charged. The cabins have cooking utensils and gas stoves in July and August, but hikers must supply their own food and bedding.

The **Appalachian Mountain Club** (reservations 466-2727) has operated **Madison Hut** since 1888, a full-service, summer-only facility at tree line on Mount Madison (see full listing for the High Huts under *Camps* in "Mount Washington's Valleys—Mount Washington and Pinkham Notch").

A less-rigorous hike to **Pine Mountain** offers fine views of the Presidential Range. Off Pinkham B (Dolly Copp) Road (2.4 miles from Route 2 or 1.9 miles from Route 16), a private road that is open to public foot-traffic only leads to the summit and connects to a loop trail. Estimated hiking time is two hours for a 3.4-mile round trip.

Pinkham Notch; AMC Pinkham Notch Camp, headquarters for Mount Washington hiking; **Wildcat Ski Area;** and the **Mount Washington Carriage Road** are just south of Gorham on Route 16. (See "Mount Washington's Valleys" for details.)

North of Route 2 in Jefferson, **Waumbek** and **Starr King** mountains are popular hikes. The climb is 3.8 miles and requires just over three hours to the top.

LODGING

INN

Philbrook Farm Inn (466-3831), North Road, Shelburne 03581. Open May 1 to October 31 and December 26 to March 31. This unique inn has been operated by five generations of the Philbrook family since it began in 1861. A treasure of White Mountain historical artifacts, the inn retains its old-time character; a visitor from 100 years ago probably would still feel right at home even though there have been changes and additions over the years. Situated in a quiet spot a mile and a half from Route 2, the place has been popular with artists and writers who enjoy the solitude and with hikers who can wander the inn's 1,000 acres that back up to the national forest. Swim in the barnyard pool, rock on the porch or beside a huge fireplace in the living room with its historical treasures, or play a variety of indoor and outdoor games. There is snowshoeing or cross-country skiing from the door. The country-style accommodations vary. The large main inn has 19 rooms—some have private baths, others share baths. There are twin-, double-, and king-size beds. Five summer-only out-buildings offer more private accommodations with from one to five bedrooms, fireplaces, living rooms, porches, and kitchens—just right for a family or small groups. MAP rates include a full breakfast and single-entrée New England dinner. The inn can accommodate those with special diets with advance notice. Most of the vegetables come from the inn's or its neighbor's gardens. Fresh breads and pastries are cooked daily in a huge commercial-size wood stove. Rates are $100–130 MAP for two, full American plan available to weekly guests; housekeeping cottages for up to eight persons are $450 a week.

BED & BREAKFASTS

The Gorham House (466-2271), 55 Main Street, Box 267, Gorham 03581. This 1891 Queen Anne–style Victorian B&B has four rooms with shared baths. Rooms have double beds or a double and a twin. Innkeepers: Ronnie, Maggie, and Sam. Rates are $55 for two people.

The Jefferson Inn (586-7998; 1-800-729-7908), Route 2 (at the junction with Route 115A), Jefferson 03583. Open year-round, except parts of November and April. This fine, old (built in 1896) inn has 13 rooms, all with private baths. There are three family suites plus a large family room with a kitchenette. Many rooms have themes such as New England or Shaker motifs. A trail for nearby Waumbek and Starr King mountains leaves from the inn, and just across the street is a wonderful old stone swimming pool with a beach for children. Afternoon tea with homemade baked goods is served at 4:30 P.M. Rates are $44–80, breakfast is an additional $4.

Applebrook B&B (586-7713; 1-800-545-6504), Route 115A, Box 178, Jefferson 03583. Open year-round. A rambling old Victorian building, this inn has 12 rooms—3 with private baths; the others share 4 baths. There's a hot tub and cross-country/walking trails nearby. The two large dorm rooms with three and seven beds each are great for groups. A full breakfast is included and dinner is available to groups by advance reservation. Innkeeper Martin Kelley charges $45–60 per couple, dorm rooms $20 per person.

Stag Hollow Inn and Llama Keep (586-4598), Route 115, Jefferson Meadow 03583. Three rooms, one with two double beds, share a large bath. Large living room with fireplace, cross-country skiing from the back door, a nearby natural swimming hole in the Israel River, plus 13 llamas (see White Mountain Llamas under *Hiking*). Innkeeper Joanna Fryon charges $55–65 per couple, breakfast $5 additional.

MOTELS

Motels line Gorham's Main Street, two of which are open year-round: **Royalty Inn** (466-3312) and **Gorham Motor Inn** (466-3381).

Town and Country Motor Inn (466-3315), Route 2, Shelburne 03581. Open year-round. Situated in the midst of the famous birches, this 160-room resort includes a restaurant (see *Where to Eat*), health club, indoor pool, whirlpool, and steam bath. Rooms have air-conditioning, phones, and color cable TV. Rates are $52–72 for two.

Evergreen Motel (586-4449), Route 2 (Box 33), Jefferson. Open mid-May through Columbus Day weekend. Eighteen units, air-conditioning, TV, swimming pool, coffee shop, and across the street from Santa's Village. Rates are $34–48 for two.

Lantern Motor Inn (586-7151), Route 2 (Box 97), Jefferson. Open mid-May through October. Thirty units, air-conditioning, TV, pool, and playground. Rates are $38–48 for two.

CAMPING

Moose Brook State Park, Route 2, Gorham. Open daily June to Labor

Day, on weekends from mid-May. This small park has a large outdoor pool (known for its cold water), a small beach, and 42 tent sites. No reservations. Camping and day-use fees charged.

(Also see "Mount Washington's Valleys—Crawford Notch and Bretton Woods.")

WHERE TO EAT

Yokohama Restaurant (466-2501), Main Street, Gorham. Serves lunch and dinner; closed Monday. A longtime, popular American–Oriental eatery. Moderately priced.

Via Sorrento (466-2520), Main Street, Gorham. Closed Sunday. Serves lunch and dinner. An Italian restaurant where everything is homemade. Moderately priced.

Town and Country Motor Inn (466-3315), Route 2, Shelburne. The restaurant has a diverse menu for breakfast and dinner and Sunday dinner. Lounge with entertainment. Moderately priced.

SPECIAL EVENTS

First weekend in June: **Moose Mania Weekend** (752-6060; 1-800-992-7480). A variety of events in Gorham and Berlin celebrate New Hampshire's largest wild animal.

Berlin and Route 16 North

Called "the city that trees built," Berlin is the industrial center of the North Country. While the heavy aroma often emitted from the paper mills offends the nostrils of visitors, natives call it the smell of money since the mills are the chief employers in the region. Actually, millions of dollars have been spent in recent years to clean up the water pollution in the Androscoggin River. There's a strong French Canadian influence here because many residents are descended from Quebec immigrants who came to work in the woods and in the mills. French remains a second, and sometimes the primary, language of many people. Though not considered a tourist destination, Berlin is the largest community in the North Country and a service center for a wide area.

Milan, Dummer, and Errol are small towns north of Berlin along Route 16 that are known for outdoor opportunities—especially on the Androscoggin River, which flows through the communities.

Not so much a town as it is a place (since its tiny population is mostly connected with the Balsams Resort), Dixville gets a moment of fame every four years when all of its 30 voters stay up past midnight to cast the first early votes in the presidential election. The most northerly of New Hampshire's notches, Dixville is worth the ride just for the views of this narrow pass and the picturesque Balsams as you drive through the steep, rugged mountains.

GUIDANCE

Northern White Mountains Chamber of Commerce (752-6060; 1-800-992-7480), 164 Main Street, Box 298, Berlin 03570.

MEDICAL EMERGENCY

Androscoggin Valley Hospital (752-2200), 59 Page Hill Road, Berlin. Ambulance: 752-1020.

TO SEE

View the **James River Corporation's paper mills** along the Androscoggin River from Cascade to Berlin—once the largest complex of its type in the world—still producing a variety of paper products.

Holy Resurrection Church, 20 Petrograd Street, Berlin. An unusual Eastern Orthodox church, complete with onion domes, built by Russian immigrants in 1915.

Berlin Public Library (752-5210), Main Street, Berlin, has a collection of Native American stone implements, some dating back 7,000 years.

TO DO

AIRPLANE RIDES

Mountain Rain (482-3323), Errol Airport, Errol 03579. David Heasley operates the airport, offers sight-seeing rides and charters; also flies canoeists, kayakers, and fishermen into backcountry areas.

CANOEING

Androscoggin River paddlers are advised to check with the *AMC River Guide* or *Canoe Camping Vermont and New Hampshire Rivers* (Backcountry Publications).

Northern Waters in Errol Village has rentals, instruction, guided trips, or other canoeing information. They offer raft float trips every Wednesday in July and August from their location beside the river, and they also coordinate flat-water kayak trips on the Magalloway River and Lake Umbagog. For information or reservations, contact **Saco Bound** (447-2177), Box 119, Route 302, Center Conway 03813.

FISHING

The **Androscoggin** is a popular trout stream. New Hampshire fishing licenses, required for adults, are sold at many stores throughout the region. Another recommended fishing spot is **South Pond Recreation Area,** located off Route 110 in West Milan. It also has a picnic and swimming area.

GOLF

Panorama Golf Course (255-4961), part of the Balsams Resort, Dixville Notch. This 18-hole, par-72 course, rolling over beautiful mountain slopes, was designed by Donald Ross in 1912. Adjacent is an executive par-3 course. Pro shop, lessons, and cart rentals; tee times are required.

HIKING

There are plenty of hiking opportunities in the area north of Route 2, but trails are not well marked and some are obliterated as a result of logging operations. Consult the *AMC White Mountain Guide* or *Walks & Rambles in the Upper Connecticut River Valley* (Backcountry Publications), or ask locally for trail details.

Mahoosuc Range. Stretching from Shelburne northeast to Grafton Notch in Maine, this rugged range offers some of the most difficult hiking on the Appalachian Trail (the mountains are not high, but the trails steeply ascend and descend the peaks). Many of the peaks as well as rocky Mahoosuc Notch, where the ice stays in crevasses year-round, are most easily reached by Success Pond Road, a smooth logging road on the north side of the mountains. In the middle of Berlin, turn east at the traffic lights across the river, through the log yard of the paper company, then travel up to 14 miles along the road to get to the various

GEORGE A. SYLVESTER

Fishing on the Androscoggin River

trailheads. Watch for logging trucks on this road. (See the *AMC White Mountain Guide* for hiking details.)

CROSS-COUNTRY SKIING

The Balsams Resort (1-800-255-0600; in NH 1-800-255-0800), Route 26, Dixville Notch 03576. This 100-km network (73 km tracked) is one of New England's best-kept secrets. Elevations range from 1,820 feet at Lake Gloriette in front of the hotel to 2,686 at the summit of Keyser Mountain. The majority of the 35 trails are generally skiable even when far more famous White Mountain touring centers are brown or icy. Most trails are double-tracked and packed for skating, but a few remain narrow and ungroomed like our favorite, Canal Trail, a 2-km corridor between tall balsams, following the turn-of-the-century canal that still channels water from Mud Pond (where there's a warming hut) to the hotel. Rentals, lessons. $7 trail fee.

DOWNHILL SKIING

The Balsams/Wilderness (1-800-255-0600; in NH 1-800-255-0800), Route 26, Dixville Notch 03576. The most remote ski area in New Hampshire, with abundant natural snow, rare lift lines, and a country-club rather than commercial–ski area feel. Geared to guests at the resort.
Trails: 13.
Lifts: 4 (1 double chair, 2 T-bars, 1 surface).
Vertical drop: 1,000 feet
Services: Ski school, rentals, restaurant, child care.
Rates: Free to inn guests, otherwise $23 per adult on weekends, $18 weekdays; $15 per junior weekends, $13 weekdays.

SNOWMOBILING

The North Country is the state's most popular snowmobiling area. On hundreds of miles of woods roads and some specially maintained trails, the snowmobile enthusiast can travel to Quebec, Vermont, and Maine. Some winter weekends are as busy as those in the summer. Many motels and lodges, especially in Colebrook and Pittsburg, have trails right from the door that connect with a lengthy trail network. For maps and other information, write **Northern White Mountains Chamber of Commerce** (752-6060; 1-800-992-7480), 164 Main Street, Box 298, Berlin 03570; **North Country Chamber of Commerce** (237-8939), Box 1, Colebrook 03576; the **Trails Bureau** (271-3254), New Hampshire Division of Parks and Recreation, Box 856, Concord 03301; or the **New Hampshire Snowmobile Association** (224-8906), Box 38, Concord 03301.

GREEN SPACE

Nansen Wayside Park, Route 16, 4 miles north of Berlin. The state-owned ski jump is across the street from this small park beside the Androscoggin River. Several picnic sites and a boat-launching ramp.

The **Androscoggin River** is one of New Hampshire's natural treasures. It enters the state from Maine at Wentworth Location, just north of the village of Errol, and flows south through Dummer and Milan to Berlin, where, unfortunately, it picks up wastes from the paper mills before turning sharply west and flowing back into Maine. In recent years millions of dollars have been spent on treatment plants in Berlin, and the river is now much cleaner than it has been for decades. North of Berlin, the river is one of the state's most popular canoeing and fishing waters. There is plenty of history here as well. The river was used to float logs down to the mills. Just above the Berlin city center are large pilings in the river, once used to anchor booms which kept the logs moving swiftly to the mills. The most beautiful stretch of the river is the **Thirteen-Mile Woods Scenic Area,** just south of Errol, where the road and river curve along side by side through a wild area. At about the midpoint is the riverside **Androscoggin Wayside Park,** situated on a bluff overlooking the river, with picnic tables. No fee.

Lake Umbagog National Wildlife Refuge (482-3415), Route 16 (5.5 miles north of Errol village), Errol. This largely undeveloped lake, one of the finest wild areas in northern New England, has been designated as a national wildlife refuge. Under discussion for many years, the refuge became a reality when state, federal, and private agencies worked together with private landowners to set aside a large area for conservation purposes. Here live the only known nesting New Hampshire bald eagles, sharing the skies with ospreys, loons, and varied waterfowl. Moose amble the shorelines, and the fishing is great. The northern end of the lake is most interesting, especially in the extensive freshwater marshes where the Androscoggin and Magalloway rivers meet. Inexpensive, primitive campsites make this an ideal destination for family or group canoeing. Boats and canoes may be launched north of Errol on Route 16 and south of Errol on Route 26 at Umbagog Lake Campground, where arrangements can be made to rent the campsites (see *Campgrounds*). Tours are available on request to the refuge manager.

Dixville Notch State Park, Route 26, Dixville Notch. There are two roadside picnic areas and pretty waterfalls here. For the hardy, there is a steep, 30-minute, 0.3-mile climb up the south side of the notch to Table Rock, which offers a panoramic view of the Balsams and Lake Gloriette.

LODGING

RESORT

✐ **The Balsams Resort** (1-800-255-0600; in NH 1-800-255-0800), Route 26, Dixville Notch 03576. Open mid-May to mid-October and mid-December through March. A four-star, grand resort, this is New Hampshire's (and arguably New England's) finest hotel. Dating back to 1866, this rambling, French provincial–style, castlelike hostelry, on the shore of Lake Gloriette and overlooked by the jagged spires of Dixville Notch, appears like a piece of the Alps in America. With more staff members than guests (up to 400 for 215 rooms) and 15,000 acres, mostly of wilderness, the Balsams is an American-plan destination resort. Guests spend their days playing golf, hiking, and swimming in summer, and skiing downhill on the hotel's own 12-trail ski hill, or cross-country on 70 km of high-elevation, dependably snow-covered trails in winter. One way or another they steep themselves in the magnificence of these mountains.

In the evening gentlemen don jackets and ladies dress. Even the children—of whom there are always a number—seem to sense what's expected of them in this opulent world of intricately carved teak, ginger jars, potted palms, and endless carpeting. Youngsters find their way (via an ornate vintage 1917 Otis elevator) to the library with its tiers of books and piles of puzzles. Some never make it to the pool tables, TV, or game rooms. For adults there is evening music in "The Cave," off the lobby, but that's just the prelude.

Dinner is the big event of the day. At 6 P.M. promptly, the leaded glass doors of the dining room slide open and guests begin strolling in to eye samples of each dish on the menu—appetizers through desserts—all exhibited on a specially designed two-tiered table topped by a silver candelabra. Dishes on view might include smoked mussels with marinated lentils and basil emulsion; sautéed veal *forestière* with Marsala and herbed tomato sauce; diced red bliss potato with bacon, mushrooms, and asparagus spears; and pecan whiskey pie. The evening's entrée "for the junior gourmet" is also displayed.

Most guests come for a week, beginning with Sunday, the night

The Balsams Grand Resort Hotel in Dixville Notch

that Steve Barba, president of the Balsams Corporation, welcomes guests with a talk about the evolution of the hotel, from the 25-room Dix House, opened in 1866, to an 1890s resort with a man-made lake and 9-hole golf course, to the present combination of buildings—the rambling white-clapboard, green-shuttered Dixville House and the 6-story stucco Hampshire House, New Hampshire's first steel-frame and masonry multi-story structure when it opened in 1918.

What Barba doesn't explain is why the Balsams remains New England's only truly grand, multi-season resort hotel. The truth is that it's been luckier in its ownership than dozens of similar so-called grand hotels that have since vanished from northern New England. Between 1875 and 1944 it had only four dedicated and colorful owners and in 1954, when it hit the skids, the old place really lucked out. Neil Tillitson, a descendant of Dixville Notch homesteaders, bought the resort and its (then) 5,000 acres for a couple hundred thousand dollars. His first move was to install a rubber factory in the former garage. (It now produces millions of medical exam gloves weekly.) An inventor and an inventive businessman, Tillitson has conferred total responsibility for the property on four longtime employees (including the chef and head of maintenance).

Over the last few years most guest rooms have been totally renovated, from plumbing and windows to flower-patterned wallpaper, and their number has been reduced as rooms have been merged to create sitting areas and new bathrooms. Closets remain deep and large, and the windows are still curtained in organdy, the better to let in the amazing view.

In contrast to most large hotels, guest and conference seasons are strictly segregated. Rates are on a per-person, per-diem basis and vary with the day and room. In winter they range from $80 to $142 per person per night, double occupancy, plus tax and service, all meals included. Inquire about special ski and summer week and children's rates.

BED & BREAKFAST

Stark Village Inn (636-2644), just across the covered bridge off Route 110, west of Milan or east of Groveton (mailing: RFD 1, Box 389, Groveton 03582). (See *Bed & Breakfast* in "Littleton, Whitefield, Lancaster, Groveton, and Stark.")

OTHER LODGING

Except for the Balsams Resort, there is not much in the way of lodging in this section of New Hampshire. The **Errol Motel** (482-3256), Route 26, Errol, is open year-round and has three housekeeping units. Snowmobile trails from the motel connect with all local trails. Rates are $43 per couple.

CAMPGROUNDS

Milan Hill State Park, Route 110B (off Route 16), Milan. A small park with 24 primitive camping sites, picnic tables, and a playground. A fire tower atop the 1,737-foot-high hill offers sweeping views of the North Country and into Canada. Camping and day-use fees charged.

13-Mile Woods Campgrounds (482-3373), Box 34, Errol 03579. Open mid-May through hunting season, depending on the weather. Ed "Moose" Damp operates the 50-site Mollidgewock Campground, located about 4 miles south of Errol Village, in the 13-Mile Woods Scenic Area. He also has a few other campsites along the river. These are somewhat primitive sites with picnic tables, fireplaces, water, and outhouses, but they are beside the river and perfect for fishing and canoeing. $6 per adult per night.

Umbagog Lake Campground and Cottages (482-7795), Route 26, PO Box 181, Errol 03579. Open late May to mid-September. Umbagog is a 14-mile-long lake that straddles the New Hampshire–Maine border, mostly in wilderness. Around the lake and on some of its small islands are 25 primitive camping sites that are reached by your own canoe or boat (rentals available). Campers must bring tents and food; there are picnic tables and fireplaces. Here you can see moose, eagles, ospreys, and a variety of waterfowl. Fall asleep to the sounds of loons calling in the night. At the base camp, just south of Errol on Route 26, there is also a family campground, with a camp store for supplies and some housekeeping cabins.

WHERE TO EAT

DINING OUT
See the Balsams Resort under *Resort*.

EATING OUT

The Northland Dairy Bar and Restaurant (752-6210), Route 16, Berlin. Located just north of the city and popular with canoeists and hikers, the eatery features fresh seafood, sandwiches, and their own fresh-made ice cream and pastries.

Errol Restaurant (482-3852), Errol Village. Open daily at 5 A.M. year-round. Country menu, seafood to steaks; breakfast, lunch, and dinner. Home of the mooseburger.

SPECIAL EVENTS

First weekend in June: **Moose Mania Weekend** (752-6060; 1-800-992-7480). A variety of events in Gorham and Berlin celebrates New Hampshire's largest wild animal.

Littleton, Whitefield, Lancaster, Groveton, and Stark

Lancaster is the Coos County seat and the place to visit for people searching deeds or probate records. It is the local shopping center for a wide area. A hilly community midway between Littleton and Lancaster, with a perfect village square surrounded by shops, homes, and churches, Whitefield looks like everyone's all-American town. Groveton is the business center of the town of Northumberland. Coming upon the town from the south, one is greeted with a perfect tableau combining North Country history and the region's prime industry. Before the large James River Company paper mill is Groveton covered bridge and beside it an old logging engine, dating to the days when logging railroads spread over the North Country and the White Mountains. Rising high in the background are the distinctive Percy Peaks, reminders, perhaps, that the future of the North Country lies in its wilderness. Tiny Stark village, on Routes 110 and 110A/110B between Groveton and Milan–Berlin, is best known for a picturesque covered bridge and Union church, both built in the 1850s, just beside the highway. During World War II, German prisoners of war were brought to a prison camp here to work in the woods.

GUIDANCE

Lancaster Chamber of Commerce (788-2578), Main Street, Lancaster 03584. Summer-only information booth.

Whitefield Chamber of Commerce (837-2609), Whitefield. Information booth on the square.

MEDICAL EMERGENCY

Weeks Memorial Hospital (788-4911), Middle Street, Lancaster 03584.

Littleton Regional Hospital (444-7731), 107 Cottage Street, Littleton 03561.

Covered bridge in Stark

TO SEE

COVERED BRIDGES

The **Lancaster, New Hampshire–Lunenburg, Vermont** covered bridge crosses the Connecticut River 5 miles southwest of Lancaster off Route 135. The **Mechanic Street** bridge is east of Routes 2/3 in the village of Lancaster. The **Groveton** bridge is just south of the James River Company paper mills. The **Stark** bridge is just off Route 110, west of Milan or east of Groveton.

HISTORIC HOMES

Weeks State Historic Site, Route 3, 2 miles south of Lancaster. Open daily late June to Labor Day and weekends in September, weather permitting. Situated atop Mount Prospect, this was the summer home of Lancaster native John Sinclair Weeks, a Massachusetts congressman responsible for the bill that established the White Mountain National Forest and all national forests in the eastern United States. By the turn of the nineteenth century, logging companies were clear-cutting the northern forests, destroying wildlife habitat and the forest wilderness. Without trees on the steep mountain slopes to hold back rainwater, soil erosion was increasing and downriver flooding threatened communities every spring. Weeks' love of the wilderness led him to file the legislation that passed in 1911 and resulted in the 768,000-acre White Mountain National Forest of New Hampshire and Maine. The house and a nearby observation tower offer broad views of the Presidential Range. Fee charged.

Wilder-Holton House (788-3004), 226 Main Street, Lancaster 03584. The first two-story house built in Coos County (1780), this is the museum of the Lancaster Historical Society. Open by appointment.

SCENIC DRIVES

North Road (Route 116) connects Lancaster with Jefferson and offers country views of the mountains, especially Mount Cabot and the Kilkenny Wilderness Area east of Lancaster. Just south of Lancaster, **Lost Nation Road** departs from North Road and runs north to Groveton. According to one tradition, this area was named by a traveling preacher, who, when he could get only one person to attend church, likened the local folks to the lost tribes of Israel. **Route 110 and Routes 110A/110B** from Groveton to Milan and Berlin are picturesque in any season, but also try the secondary road that runs parallel to Route 110, north of the Upper Ammonoosuc River, from Groveton Village, through Percy and Stark, to rejoin Route 110 just west of the 110/110A intersection.

TO DO

AIRPLANE RIDES

White Mountain Regional Airport (837-5505), off Routes 3, 115, or 116, Whitefield. Sight-seeing rides.

GOLF

Mountain View House Country Club (837-3885), Whitefield. Nine-hole course operated by the Spalding Inn (see *Resort*). This golf course served the Mountain View House, still standing but now closed. On a clear day the summit of Mount Washington seems but a long 2-iron shot away.

HIKING

The best hiking area is the Kilkenny District of the White Mountain National Forest, although the trails are not as well marked as in the mountains farther south. One popular climb is **Mount Cabot** (4 miles; three hours), east of Lancaster. The **Percy Peaks** (2 miles; two hours), north of Stark, offer views across the North Country and are not likely to be crowded with other hikers. Check the *AMC White Mountain Guide* for directions to Cabot and the Percy Peaks.

GREEN SPACE

Forest Lake State Beach, Dalton, on a side road off Route 115 between Littleton and Whitefield. Open weekends from Memorial Day, daily late June through Labor Day. One of the original state parks dating from 1935, this 50-acre site has a 200-foot-long swimming beach, a bathhouse, and picnic sites. Handicapped accessible. Fee charged.

Nash Stream (788-4157) is a 40,000-acre undeveloped, state-owned wilderness located in the towns of Odell, Stratford, Columbia, and Stark. It is open to day use for hunting, fishing, hiking, cross-country skiing, or snowmobiling. There is a seasonal, maintained gravel road off Route 110 (4 miles west of Groveton, turn north off Emerson Road).

LODGING

RESORT

The Spalding Inn (837-2572; 1-800-368-8439), Mountain View Road, Whitefield 03598. Open Memorial Day through October. Since 1926 this family-owned inn has been one of the state's finest resorts, offering a relaxed country location, personal service, and a host of amenities. The inn is famous for its lawn bowling, and it has often hosted the United States singles and doubles championships. There is also tennis, golf (nine-hole and par-three), a swimming pool, and organized activities if desired. Nearby is a popular summer theater. The inn and adjacent lodge have 42 rooms, with twin, double, and queen-size beds, all with private baths and phones. Six separate cottages (pets permitted) have a total of 16 rooms, and some of these have fireplaces and kitchenettes. Breakfast and dinner served daily, dinner-only to the public (see *Dining Out*). Diane Cockrell and Michael Finder, innkeepers. B&B $117–145; MAP $147–175. EP is also available.

INN

Maxwell House B&B Inn (837-9717; 1-800-776-9719), Parker Road, Whitefield 03589. Open all year. Situated about 1 mile off Route 116 in a quiet country spot. Five rooms share four baths. A two-room suite has a fold-out sofa, full kitchen, private bath, and a balcony. The rooms are bright, with comforters on antique queens, doubles, or twins. Guests can walk or cross-country ski the inn's 32 acres, work out free at Bretton Woods sports center, or relax in the common room with its TV and VCR. Winslow and Lisa Maxwell, innkeepers. Afternoon tea and complimentary cordials are served, and dinner by reservation (see *Dining Out*). B&B $60–85, three-night package includes two dinners, $249.

BED & BREAKFAST

Stark Village Inn (636-2644), just across the covered bridge off Route 110, west of Milan or east of Groveton (mailing: RFD 1, Box 389, Groveton 03582). Open year-round. The Upper Ammonoosuc River ripples between this inn and a picturesque church and under the covered bridge. It is a classic location in which to spend the night or a few days. Nearby is trout fishing, hiking, bicycling, cross-country skiing, skating on the river, or snowmobiling. The old restored farmhouse, furnished with antiques and comfortable furniture, has three rooms—two with double beds and all with private baths. A full breakfast is cooked on the wood stove. The Spaulding family, innkeepers. Rates are $45 for two; single room is $30.

WHERE TO EAT

DINING OUT

The Spalding Inn (837-2572), Mountain View Road, Whitefield. Open Memorial Day through October. The menu changes daily, and the five-course dinner usually offers beef, chicken, and seafood, all cooked in a Continental style. Dinner $25.

Maxwell House B&B Inn (837-9717; 1-800-776-9719), Parker Road, Whitefield 03589. Dinner served by reservation in the new candlelit dining room. The five-course meal is fixed at $25. Entrées include chicken Française, steak au poivre verte, and grilled lake trout. Soups, appetizers, and desserts are homemade. Imported wines and beers served.

EATING OUT

Barbara's (837-3161), Route 3, north of Whitefield Village. Open daily 6 A.M. to 9 P.M. A varied menu from sandwiches to full dinners. Inexpensive.

ENTERTAINMENT

Weathervane Theatre (837-9322), Route 3, Whitefield. Open July and August. A repertory theater in an old barn (since 1966) featuring old favorites, especially musicals.

SPECIAL EVENTS

Late June: **Old Time Fiddlers' Contest** (636-1325), Whitcomb Field, Stark. Bring a picnic lunch, blanket or lawn chairs and enjoy the music of dozens of fiddlers. Food available. Admission fee.

Labor Day weekend: **Lancaster Fair** (837-2770) is a real old-fashioned country fair, highlighted by nonbetting harness racing. A large midway, food, and thrill rides plus 4-H animal judging competition, Grange exhibits, displays of vegetables and handicrafts, and oxen and horse pulling. Admission fee, children under 12 free.

Colebrook, Pittsburg, and Vicinity

Bustling, friendly little Colebrook on the Connecticut River is a service oasis for people traveling north from Berlin over Routes 16 and 26, north from Lancaster on Route 3, or south from Canada and Pittsburg. It is a recreational center, especially for hunting, fishing, and winter snowmobiling; and it is the shopping center for a number of small towns including Pittsburg, Columbia, Stewartstown, Dixville Notch, Errol, and adjacent Vermont communities.

New Hampshire's largest (190,000 acres) and most northerly community, Pittsburg retains a frontier atmosphere appreciated by anyone who enjoys the outdoors. Many residents work in the woods and spend their spare hours hunting and fishing, often displaying a spirit of independence that goes back to 1832 when portions of this town became an independent nation called the Indian Stream Republic. The name comes from a tributary of the Connecticut River, but the nation evolved when local settlers, disgruntled by boundary squabbling between Canada and the United States, solved the problem by seceding from both countries. They created their own stamps, coins, and government, but their independence lasted only a few years before the Treaty of Washington in 1842 made the republic part of New Hampshire.

Pittsburg is where the foliage begins to change first in the fall, snow arrives early, and it gets down to 30 below zero in the winter. It is closer to Montreal than it is to Boston, and a four-wheel-drive vehicle is the favorite family car. Route 3 is the main road through Pittsburg, and it connects with Canada at the north end of the town. Although Pittsburg is mostly wooded wilderness, no overnight camping or open fires are permitted except at campgrounds.

GUIDANCE

North Country Chamber of Commerce (237-8939), Box 1, Colebrook 03576. Serves Colebrook, Pittsburg, and surrounding towns. Open summer through early fall, and sometimes winter weekends, the information center is located south of town on Route 3.

New Hampshire Information Center, Route 3, north of Colebrook. Open daily from Memorial Day to Columbus Day, with rest rooms and picnic tables.

Connecticut Lakes Tourist Association (538-9900), Box 38, Pittsburg 03592.

The folks at **Trading Post General Store** (538-6533), in the middle of Pittsburg, can probably answer most local questions, and there is a small **information booth** also in the center of town.

GETTING AROUND

Crossing the border. The United States Customs and Immigration Service maintains a point of entry station in Pittsburg on Route 3 at the International Border (819-656-2261). Hours: April 2 to June 15, 8–8; June 16 to Labor Day, 8–midnight; the day after Labor Day to November 30, 8–8; December 1 to April 1, 8–4. The border may be crossed from Canada to the United States when the station is closed, but federal law requires individuals to proceed directly without stopping to the Beecher Falls, Vermont, station (customs 802-266-3336; immigration 802-266-3320) to report in. Follow Route 3 to West Stewartstown and across the Connecticut River to Vermont Route 114 to Beecher Falls. Failure to report directly may result in a seizure of the vehicle and heavy fines for individuals.

MEDICAL EMERGENCY

Upper Connecticut Valley Hospital (237-4971), Corliss Lane (off Route 145), Colebrook. This little, well-equipped hospital is the health care center for a large area of northern New Hampshire, Quebec, Vermont, and Maine. At least one doctor has a private plane and makes house calls by air.

TO SEE

Pittsburg Historical Society, Pittsburg. The society maintains a museum in the town hall. Open July 4 and Saturday in July and August.

Shrine of Our Lady of Grace (237-5511), Route 3, Colebrook. Open Sunday, May through October, for a guided tour and a short ceremony beginning at 1 P.M.; groups are welcome by appointment, individuals anytime. A shrine and outdoor monuments of sculpture depict the Way of the Cross. Maintained by the Oblates of Mary Immaculate.

COVERED BRIDGES

Columbia Bridge crosses the Connecticut River just south of Colebrook in Columbia Village. Pittsburg has three covered bridges: The **Pittsburg-Clarksville bridge,** 91 feet long, is off Route 3, 0.25 mile west of Pittsburg Village; **Happy Corner bridge,** 86 feet long, is south of Route 3, 6 miles northeast of the village; **River Road bridge,** 57 feet long and one of the state's smallest covered bridges, is south of Route 3, 5.5 miles northeast of the village.

SCENIC DRIVES

Route 26, from Colebrook through Dixville Notch to Errol and down Route 16 to Milan is one of the prettiest drives in the state. Just east of

Colebrook, Fish Hatchery Road departs Route 26 north for the Diamond Ponds and Coleman State Park. The road is paved most of the way, but several gravel side roads wind over and around the hills of East Colebrook, and one continues on to Stewartstown Hollow on Route 145, which connects Colebrook and Pittsburg. This is one of the most picturesque and least-known parts of the state. Red-barned dairy farms are impressive, dotting the hillsides and views. **Beaver Brook Falls,** just north of Colebrook on Route 145, is popular with photographers.

Route 3, north from Pittsburg Village, is 22.5 miles to the border. The evergreen forest stretches as far as you can see, broken only by the several lakes and streams. Drive to the border station, perched high on a hill, if only to see the views north into Canada and south over the North Country.

Route 145 from Pittsburg south to Colebrook is best driven from north to south, especially for the sweeping view from Ben Young Hill. En route to and from Pittsburg, you will cross the 45th parallel, halfway between the North Pole and the equator.

TO DO

CANOEING

The **Connecticut River** is popular for fishing and canoeing, although its rather placid flow makes paddling it less challenging than the Androscoggin. The upper Connecticut watershed, including Hall and Indian Streams, forms the border between New Hampshire and Quebec, and, farther south, it is the border between New Hampshire and Vermont. Actually, the boundary between the two states is the low-water mark on the Vermont shore, so the river is in New Hampshire until it crosses into Massachusetts. This river also has a long history of log drives and was infamous for destructive flooding before many dams, most of which were built as hydroelectric power sources, tamed it. Most canoeists start at the Vermont end of the Canaan–West Stewartstown Bridge off Route 3. The only difficult rapids (class 2) in this area are below Columbia. They run for about 7.5 miles and cannot be navigated when the water is low. Paddlers are advised to check with the *AMC River Guide* or *Canoe Camping Vermont and New Hampshire Rivers* (Backcountry Publications). No canoe rentals available in this section of the river, but see "Berlin and Route 16 North" (*Canoeing*) or "Upper Valley Towns" (*Canoeing*).

FISHING

Fishing is the prime warm-weather attraction in Pittsburg, and operators of most of the 14 or so lodges, motels, and campgrounds depend on seekers of trout and salmon for their livelihoods. The several Connecticut lakes; Lake Francis; Back Lake; Hall, Indian, and Perry streams; and the Connecticut River provide miles of shoreline and

Farmland near Stewartstown

hundreds of acres of world-class fishing, more than enough fishing waters to satisfy the most ardent angler. Many of the older lodges have guests who have returned annually for decades, and likely some of these folks still find new places to wet a line each year. The trout season runs from the fourth Saturday in April through October 15, but the best fishing months are May, June, and early fall. Most of the lodges provide guides, sell licenses, sell or rent tackle, rent boats, and will give fishing information.

Grant's Fly Shack (237-8137), RR 1, Box 142, Colebrook 03576. Open mid-May to October. Although Grant Woodbury no longer has a retail shop, he does guide up to two people at a time in boats (for fly-fishing only) on the Connecticut and Androscoggin rivers. Full-day or afternoon/evening trips. By reservation only; rates vary.

Yankee Sportsman (237-8867), Route 1, Box 357, Colebrook. Open on Lake Winnipesaukee from ice-out until May 20, then on Lake Francis and the First and Second Connecticut lakes until September 30; also Connecticut River trips from spring through October 15. Registered guides Bud Pierce and Jackie Cass have a fully equipped 22-foot commercial lobster boat, with a trailer, for up to four passengers for four- and eight-hour (including dinner) trips. A small boat is used for Connecticut River fishing. By reservation, rates vary.

GOLF

Colebrook Country Club (237-5566), on Route 26, east of Colebrook Village. A 9-hole, par-36 course.

The Panorama Golf Course (255-4961), at the Balsams Resort, Dixville Notch (see *Lodging* in "Berlin and Route 16 North").

HIKING

Overlooking Colebrook from the Vermont side of the river is **Monadnock Mountain,** which rises steeply and offers a nice view from the summit fire tower. The trail begins in a driveway off Route 102 near the bridge between Colebrook and Lemington, Vermont. You may have to inquire at a residence to find the exact location of the trail.

Walks & Rambles in the Upper Connecticut River Valley (Backcountry Publications) lists a number of hikes in this area, including **Mount Magalloway** (4.5 miles, 3.5 hours), at 3,300 feet the highest peak in the North Country.

MOUNTAIN BIKING

There are miles and miles of woodland roads just right for mountain biking in this section of New Hampshire. Roads are unmarked for the most part, but inquire at Ramblewood Cabins (538-6948) or The Glen (538-6500) for route assistance (see *Lodging*).

CROSS-COUNTRY SKIING

Ramblewood Cabins and Campground (538-6948), Route 3, Box 52 Pittsburg. Twenty-five km of groomed trails beside the First Connecticut Lake. Winter camping welcome.

SNOWMOBILING

More than 125 miles of groomed trails connect all areas of the North Country and even provide access to Maine, Vermont, Quebec, and southern New Hampshire. From the Pittsburg lodges and Colebrook motels, the snowmobiler can head off after breakfast and have lunch in Maine or Canada, then return to the lodge for dinner. For maps and other information, write the **North Country Chamber of Commerce** (237-8939), Box 1, Colebrook 03576; the **Trails Bureau** (271-3254), **New Hampshire Division of Parks and Recreation,** Box 856, Concord 03301; or the **New Hampshire Snowmobile Association** (224-8906), Box 38, Concord 03301.

GREEN SPACE

Throughout this section of the North Country, and especially in Pittsburg, moose are quite common and are often seen wandering along beside Route 3. *Note:* Moose are oblivious to autos, trucks, and trains; proceed slowly if you see a moose heading for the road.

The **Connecticut Lakes** are great for bird-watching.

Coleman State Park is in Stewartstown, but it is most easily reached from Route 26 east of Colebrook. Open May to mid-October. There are 30 tent-camping sites, a recreation building, and picnic tables. Fishing is good in the Diamond Ponds and surrounding streams. No reservations. Fee charged.

Lake Francis State Park, off Route 3 on River Road, 7 miles north of Pittsburg Village. Open from mid-May through Columbus Day. This small park beside the 2,000-acre, man-made lake has 40 primitive camp-sites, a boat-launching ramp, and a picnic area. A popular camping site for anglers and canoeists. No reservations. Fee charged.

Connecticut Lakes State Forest is a wooded corridor on both sides of Route 3 from the north end of the First Connecticut Lake to the Cana-dian border. Most of the rest of the wilderness is owned by large timber companies. In 1990 the Champion International Corporation gave the Nature Conservancy a 78-acre parcel of land that includes the tiny Fourth Connecticut Lake, the source of the longest river in New En-gland. To see this small woodland lake, park and sign in at the Customs Station on Route 3, then follow a steep, rough 0.5-mile trail (which is on the border) to the lake. Deer Mountain Campground, 20 miles north of Pittsburg village (open May through October), has 20 primitive campsites with fireplaces, wood, and spring water. No reservations. Fee charged.

LODGING

RESORT
See the Balsams Resort in "Berlin and Route 16 North."

INN
The Glen (538-6500; winter 508-475-0559; 1-800-445-GLEN), First Con-necticut Lake, Pittsburg 03592. Open early May to October. For half a century this former private estate has been catering to hunters, fisher-men, and vacationers. Betty Falton has been here for more than 30 of those years, operating a cozy, comfortable lodge situated on 180 acres on the shore of the First Connecticut Lake. For the nonsport, the place offers excellent birding and moose-watching, mountain biking, or ca-noeing. Curl up by the stone fireplace, and if you do go fishing, the staff will serve your catch. The main lodge, where three home-cooked meals are served daily, offers rooms with twins and doubles with private baths, and there are several log cabins with one or more bedrooms and porches overlooking New Hampshire's North Country wilderness. Boats and motors for rent. AP $60–72 per person, discounts for seven days or more.

BED & BREAKFASTS
Monadnock B&B (237-8216), corner of Monadnock and Bridge streets, Colebrook 03576. Open year-round. Built in 1916 in the bungalow ar-chitectural style, this B&B retains its exquisite natural woodwork. Its eclectic furnishings were gathered by Barbara and Wendell Woodard during their many travels when he was in the armed services. There are three main guest rooms—one with a double and two single beds, the others with double beds. There is a crib and a small room with a sink and coffeemaker. All share a single bath. A basement section has four bedrooms (two singles, one with a double bed, one with twins), an open

area with a TV and table tennis, and a living room. Bicyclists are especially welcome here. A full breakfast is served. $43.20 double; $32.40 single.

Room with a View (237-5106; 1-800-499-1506), Forbes Road, Colebrook 03576. Open all year. Recently built as a B&B, this large house sits high on a hill overlooking the Mohawk River Valley and Dixville Notch. Its quiet country location requires that you get the directions. There are seven rooms, two with private baths; five rooms share two baths. With handmade quilts and antiques, it's a comfortable, relaxing spot to spend a few nights. No smoking. Full breakfast cooked to order. Outdoors are yard games and access to hundreds of miles of snowmobile trails. Miles of dirt roads are great for mountain biking as well. Charles and Sonja Sheldon, innkeepers. $60–65 for two, $15 for additional person in room.

MOTELS

There are several Colebrook motels including the **Northern Comfort** (237-4440); the **Colebrook Country Club and Motel** (237-5566), which also has a dining room and a lounge; and the **Colebrook House** (237-5521), a small village hotel with motel section, lounge, and dining room.

SPORTING LODGES

Most of the lodges are open for deer, moose, and game-bird hunting seasons and cater to snowmobilers in the winter.

Tall Timber Lodge (538-6651; 1-800-835-6343), Back Lake, off Route 3, Pittsburg 03592. Open year-round. Founded in 1946 by the legendary guide Vernon Hawes and his wife Pearl, and now operated by the Caron family, this is one of New England's most popular sporting lodges. Many guests have returned for the same week annually for decades; and while some families come just to relax in the wilderness and swim at the nearby beach, the business here is fishing, hunting, and snowmobiling. The lodge maintains 28 rental boats and motors, some on Back Lake and others on local ponds. Guides are also available, and fishing tackle is sold. Accommodations are comfortable. The lodge has 8 rooms sharing 3 baths, and there are 2 two-bedroom cabins and 12 other housekeeping units on the lake, plus 3 units just across the street. There are dorm rooms, and some separate units sleep 8 to 10 people. Home-cooked meals are served in the knotty-pine dining room overlooking the lake, and box lunches are available on request. Most guests stay for a week or longer; since many return annually, leading to a strong repeat business, make reservations as far in advance as possible. MAP, one to three nights, $35–42 per person per night; housekeeping cabins begin at $25 per person.

Other popular Pittsburg sporting lodges include **Powder Horn Lodge and Cabins** (538-6300), **Wander Inn** (538-6535), **Timberland Lodge and Cabins** (538-6613; 1-800-545-6613), **Spruce Cone Cabins** (538-6361; 1-800-538-6361), **Ramblewood Cabins and Campground**

(538-6948), and **Partridge Cabins** (538-6380). Reservations are suggested, especially in prime hunting and fishing seasons.

WHERE TO EAT

DINING OUT

Sutton Place (237-8842), 152 Main Street, Colebrook. Open daily year-round 5:30–9; closed Sunday in the winter. Here's fine, intimate dining in the front rooms of a Queen Anne–style house. Chicken *cordon bleu* to steak au poivre, with seafood, a few Italian specialties, and a light menu with smaller portions for the diet-conscious. Reservations suggested, especially on weekends. Moderately priced.

See the Balsams Resort in "Berlin and Route 16 North."

EATING OUT

Howard's Restaurant (237-4025), Main Street, Colebrook. Open daily 5 A.M.–8 P.M.; Sunday at 6 A.M., Friday night until 9 P.M. A full-service restaurant with a large menu, daily specials, and homemade pies and puddings. A longtime favorite with the locals.

Wilderness Restaurant (237-8779), Main Street, Colebrook. Open 4 A.M.–9 P.M. daily. All homemade cooking; lounge and entertainment on weekends.

Also try the **Colebrook Country Club** (237-5566), Route 26, east of Colebrook Village, and the **Colebrook House** (237-5521), Main Street, Colebrook Village.

SPECIAL EVENTS

North Country visitors should be self-sufficient, since, unlike other areas of the state, there are few activities designed to entertain them. Exceptions are:

Late January: **North Country Sled Dog Races** (237-8939). A 100-mile race begins Friday morning in Rangeley, Maine, and finishes in East Colebrook on Saturday; a 70-mile race begins Saturday morning at Murphy Dam in Pittsburg and finishes in Errol.

February: **Pittsburg-Colebrook Winter Carnival,** Kiwanis Club. Activities and events daily during the week of February school vacation.

June: **Blessing of the Motorcycles** (237-5511), Shrine of our Lady of Grace, Colebrook. Held the weekend after Father's Day.

Late June: **Family Fly-Fishing Weekend,** Coleman State Park (271-3254), Stewartstown.

July Fourth: **Fourth of July Celebration,** Kiwanis Club, Colebrook. Parade, barbecue, and mud volleyball tourney.

Third Sunday of August: Annual **Pittsburg Guide's Show** (538-6984), on Back Lake, Pittsburg. The area's working guides show off their skills in log rolling, canoe and kayak competition, and fly casting. Admission.

General Index

Lodging Index

Books from The Countryman Press

Other Explorer's Guides

The Hudson Valley and Catskill Mountains: An Explorer's Guide
by Joanne Michaels and Mary-Margaret Barile, $15.00
Vermont: An Explorer's Guide, Sixth Edition
by Christina Tree and Peter S. Jennison, $17.00
Maine: An Explorer's Guide, Sixth Edition
by Christina Tree and Mimi Steadman, $17.00

A selection of our books about New England

Full Duty: Vermonters in the Civil War
by Howard Coffin, $30.00
Camp and Trail Cooking Techniques (Kyvar cover)
by Jim Capossela, $20.00
Ponds & Lakes of the White Mountains
by Steven D. Smith, $16.00
Waterfalls of the White Mountains
by Bruce and Doreen Bolnick, $15.00
Family Resorts of the Northeast
by Nancy Pappas Metcalf, $12.95
Fifty Hikes in the White Mountains, Fourth Edition
by Daniel Doan, $13.00
30 Bicycle Tours in New Hampshire, Third Edition
by Adolphe Bernotas and Tom and Susan Heavey, $11.00
25 Mountain Bike Tours in Vermont
by William J. Busha, $11.00
The New England Herb Gardener
by Patricia Turcotte, $15.00
New England's Special Places, Revised Edition
by Michael A. Schuman, $13.00
Perennials for the Backyard Gardener
by Patricia Turcotte, $18.00
Canoe Camping Vermont and New Hampshire Rivers
by Roioli Schweiker, $9.00
Walks and Rambles in the Upper Connecticut River Valley
by Mary L. Kibling, $10.00

We offer a variety of fiction and nonfiction, and outdoor recreation guides. Our books are available in bookstores and specialty stores, or may be ordered directly from the publisher. Shipping and handling costs are $2.50 for one book, 50¢ for each additional book. To order, or for a complete catalog, please write to The Countryman Press, Inc., Dept. APC, PO Box 175, Woodstock, VT 05091, or call toll-free 1-800-245-4151. Prices and availability are subject to change.